AMERICAN SECRET PROJECTS 1

AMERICAN SECRET PROJECTS

1

Fighters, Bombers and Attack Aircraft, 1937 to 1945

TONY BUTTLER AND ALAN GRIFFITH

www.crecy.co.uk

Crécy Publishing Ltd

www.crecy.co.uk

American Secret Projects
Fighters, Bombers and Attack Aircraft, 1937 to 1945
Tony Buttler AMRAeS and Alan Griffith

This book is dedicated to the design and industrial genius of the American aviation industry, which first conceived and then built an amazing panoply of aircraft to oppose the Axis Powers during the Second World War.

First published in 2015 by Crécy Publishing

A CIP record for this book is available from the British Library

Printed in Bulgaria by Multiprint

ISBN 9781906537487

Crécy Publishing Ltd
1a Ringway Trading Estate, Shadowmoss Rd
Manchester M22 5LH
Tel (0044) 161 499 0024
www.crecy.co.uk

FRONT COVER AND TITLE PAGE artwork by Daniel Uhr

REAR COVER
TOP: The XP-56 with a higher vertical tailfin.
Gerald Balzer
MIDDLE The original manufacturer's model of the L-133-2.
John Aldaz
BOTTOM A view of the Curtiss XP-55 lightweight
flying model. *Gerald Balzer*

Contents

Introduction

This volume is the third in a series of titles covering the development of American military aircraft, and it is part of a wider series of 'Secret Project's books now owned by Crécy Publishing. The two earlier American volumes covered fighter and bomber development in the post-war period, but this work looks at an earlier era – the run-up to, and duration of, the Second World War. Together these three volumes trace the evolution of US military aircraft design from the late 1930s right through to the late 1970s.

As with the other volumes, this book has drawn on original source material to explain just how each design came about, looking at changing military requirements as well as advances in technological capability. It looks at the tortuous development paths that were to lead to some of the world's greatest warplanes, as well as many of the competing designs that were discarded along the way. More than anything, it reveals the heroic efforts of the aircraft industry to keep up with the demands of a nation at war. Once again extensive use has been made of the US National Archives at College Park and of the manufacturers' own archives. However, there is no doubt that the records of a good number of the projects produced during this period are now probably lost forever. And such is the paucity of information for some that have been uncovered that it is difficult to establish just where certain designs fit in the overall picture; there are undoubtedly many important gaps. Nevertheless, it is believed that this volume – which includes extensive material never published before – offers by far the most extensive coverage of US Second World War proposals for fighter and bomber designs ever produced.

As with the previous volumes, this title is intended for an international readership. For consistency with the other Secret Projects titles, British spellings ('programme' rather than 'program') and terms ('tailplane' rather than 'stabilizor') have generally been used throughout. The exception is when quoting original documents. All data figures are given in both imperial and metric units (with gallons referring to US gallons).

It has been a great pleasure and a privilege for us to have the opportunity to research the efforts of an industry under huge pressure in a time of war, to see the remarkable ingenuity displayed by its engineers and designers, and to bring the whole picture together in a book. By far the greater part of the research (including very long periods camped in Washington) was undertaken by Alan Griffith, who also has laboured long on redrawing many three-views. Most are done with the assistance of original factory drawings together with photographs of mock-ups. Given such input, Tony Buttler's task of writing the text was relatively straightforward. It has been hugely enjoyable for the two of us to work together while on opposite sides of the Atlantic. We hope the reader enjoys the results of these labours as much as we have in gathering the material together and putting it into publishable form.

Tony Buttler, Worcestershire, England
Alan Griffith, Iowa, USA
February 2014

Acknowledgements

As ever, great and sincere thanks must go to the following for their help in researching this book. We apologise if we have left anyone out.

John Aldaz; Stéphane Beaumort (Moderator, Secret Projects forum); Dana Bell; Tony Chong; Peter Clukey (Lockheed Martin); Ryan Crierie; Larry Feliu, Lynn McDonald and Bob Tallman (Northrop Grumman History Center); René Francillon; Hassan Hesham; Dennis R. Jenkins; Craig Kaston; Jim Keeshen; Scott Lowther; Mike Lombardi (Boeing Historical Archives); Kim McCutcheon (Aircraft Engine Historical Society, AEHS); Jay Miller; Justo Miranda; Dave Ostrowski; Alain Pelletier; Allyson Vought, and the staff of the National Air and Space Museum.

Extra special thanks must go to the following for any number of reasons.

Dick Atkins and Bill Spidle (Vought Archive drawings); Gerald H. Balzer (drawings and photos, especially Northrop); Bob Bradley and Alan Renga (San Diego Aerospace Museum); David Giordano, Dave Miller and the staff of the US National Archives at College Park; Dan Hagedorn (Museum of Flight, Seattle); Mark Nankivil (Greater St Louis Air & Space Museum) and Stan Piet (Glenn L. Martin Aviation Museum (GLMMAM) drawings).

We must make specific mention of George Cox, who helped with the narrative, and Tommy H. Thomason, who undertook a great deal of the Navy aircraft research on our behalf at NARA II and supplied many photos.

Glossary

AAC	Army Air Corps
AAF	Army Air Force
AFB	Air Force Base
AFFTC	Air Force Flight Test Center
Anhedral	Downward slope of wing from root to tip
Angle of attack	Angle at which the wing is inclined relative to the airflow
Angle of incidence	Angle between the chord line of the wing and the fore and aft datum line of the fuselage
Aspect ratio	Ratio of wingspan to mean chord, calculated by dividing the square of the span by the wing area
ASW	Anti-submarine warfare
Brig	Brigadier
BuAer	Bureau of Aeronautics (US Navy). Organisation responsible for the development and procurement of Navy aircraft between 1921 and 1960
BuWep	Bureau of Naval Weapons. Organisation responsible for the development and acquisition of aircraft for the Navy between 1960 through to 1966
Chord	Distance between the centres of curvature of the wing leading and trailing edges when measured parallel to the longitudinal axis
CofG	Centre of gravity
Col	Colonel
CP	Circular Proposal
Critical altitude	Maximum attitude at which in standard atmosphere it is possible for a piston engine to maintain a specified power rating
Dihedral	Upward slope of the wing from root to tip
FY	Fiscal year (financial year)
Gen	General
Gross weight	Usually signifies the maximum weight with internal fuel together with all weapons aboard, but not external drop tanks
mg	Machine gun
NACA	National Advisory Committee for Aeronautics (became NASA in 1958)
NAF	Naval Aircraft Factory
NASA	National Aeronautics and Space Administration
NASM	National Air and Space Museum
nm	Nautical mile
ONR	Office of Naval Research (in Washington)
P&W	Pratt & Whitney
RFP	Request for Proposals

s.l	Sea level
t/c	Thickness/chord ratio
USAAC	United States Army Air Corps
USAAF	United States Army Air Force
USAF	United States Air Force
USN	United States Navy
VBT	Navy bomber-torpedo, carrier-based
VF	Navy fighter, carrier-based
VPB	Navy patrol bomber
VSB	Navy scout-bomber, carrier-based
VTB	Navy torpedo-bomber, carrier-based
VTSB	Navy torpedo-scout-bomber, carrier-based

Chapter One
USAAF Single-Engine Fighters

ABOVE Early examples of the P-47N 5 Thunderbolt.

Three aircraft provided the backbone of the fighter activities of the US Army Air Corps (USAAC) during the Second World War: the Republic P-47 Thunderbolt, the North American P-51 Mustang and the Lockheed P-38 Lightning. Each had its different strengths and each can be counted amongst the most successful fighter aircraft of all time. The background to the development of the first two, which took very different routes, is covered in this chapter, while the third, having twin engines, takes its place in the subsequent chapter. However, the story of the development of Second World War fighter design needs to be started a little earlier. Back in 1937 the two most important new pursuit programmes for the Army Air Corps were the Bell P-39 and Curtiss P-40, and they need to be covered to enable the later developments to be put in perspective.

Before doing so, it is worth clarifying some basic points regarding the use of terms and categorisation:

1. Until 1948 most if not all Army Air Corps fighters and interceptors were actually described as 'pursuit' aeroplanes and given a P-designation; only with the establishment of a separate US Air Force was the term 'fighter' introduced. However, the latter term will be used liberally throughout this book.

2. American radial piston engines all had an R-prefix to their designation number. Liquid-cooled in-line engines had a V-prefix, but in fact the only indigenous V-12 liquid-cooled engine to be developed in America and to see front-line service in fighter aircraft during the Second World War was the Allison V-1710, which had been run for the first time in 1930. The fitting of the British Rolls-Royce Merlin in the North American P-51 saw that engine given the designation

V-1650 and it was manufactured in the US by the Packard Company. Experimental engines received an 'X' prefix as well, while the Continental 1430 is referred to in different documents with an 'I' prefix or a 'V'. Whatever the original document says has been reproduced here.

3. Although this first chapter looks at single-engine fighters, the twin-engine Fairchild Model 85 is also included since it slots into a section covering a specific type of engine.

Bell P-39 Airacuda

At the start of the Second World War the Bell P-39 was one of the Army Air Corps's principal fighter aircraft, and it was an aeroplane with some highly innovative features. There were two in particular, one of which was to install the engine behind the pilot in the centre fuselage and use a long shaft to drive a propeller in the nose. The other was to use a tricycle undercarriage, something that in time would become increasingly common in aircraft design. Specification X-609 of March 1937 had requested a single-engine high-altitude pursuit interceptor, and Bell's submissions were the Models 3 and 4. The unusual Model 3 had its V-1710 liquid-cooled engine mounted over the wing near the centre of gravity, with the cockpit set well back along the fuselage. The smaller Model 4 looked more conventional with the cockpit further forward to improve pilot vision, but it now had the engine behind. Both used a three-blade propeller – that of the Model 3 was 12ft 0in (3.66m) in diameter, and the Model 4 10ft 0in (3.05m) – and rocket motors were available, certainly for the Model 3, to provide boost and give a rate of climb at sea level of 7,275ft/min (2,217m/min).

Little is known about the other competitors, but it is understood that Curtiss, North American, Northrop and Sikorsky were all invited to bid against X-609, and later on Seversky joined the competition with a design called AP-9. The streamlined Model 3 was highly rated except for its poor forward vision, and it was the Model 4 that won the competition for Bell. The new fighter

was named Airacobra and the prototype XP-39 made its first flight on 6 April 1938. It was subsequently produced in great numbers, but proved more successful in a close support 'fighter-bomber' role than in air-to-air Combat. The P-39 was the Army Air Corps's first 'modern' fighter for this period.

BELOW Bell Model 3 (3.37).
Alan Griffith copyright

Bell Model 3 data	
Span	unknown
Length	29ft 8in (9.04m)
Wing area	299sq ft (27.81sq m)
Powerplant	one Allison V-1710-E2
Armament	one 25mm cannon and two 0.50in (12.70mm) machine guns or four 0.50in (12.70mm)
Maximum speed	400mph (644km/h)

Model 4 data	
Span	35ft 0in (10.67m)
Length	28ft 7.5in (8.72m)
Wing area	c200sq ft (18.60sq m)
Gross weight	5,550lb (2,517kg)
Powerplant	one Allison V-1710-E2
Armament	one 25mm or one 37mm cannon, two 0.50in (12.70mm) machine guns
Maximum speed	'approaching' 400mph (644km/h)
Sea level rate of climb	7,275ft/min (2,217m/min)

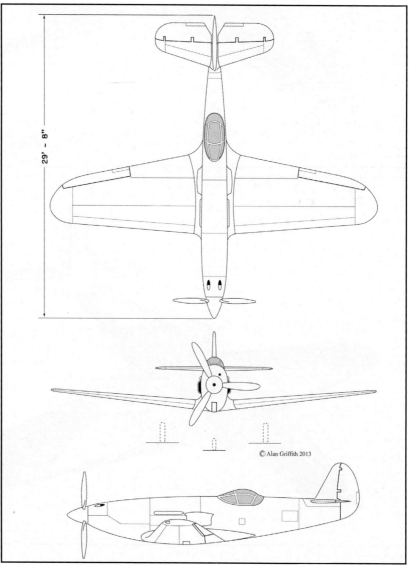

29' – 8"

© Alan Griffith 2013

ABOVE Internal detail for the Bell Model 3.
David Stern

LEFT Internal detail for the Bell Model 4.
David Stern

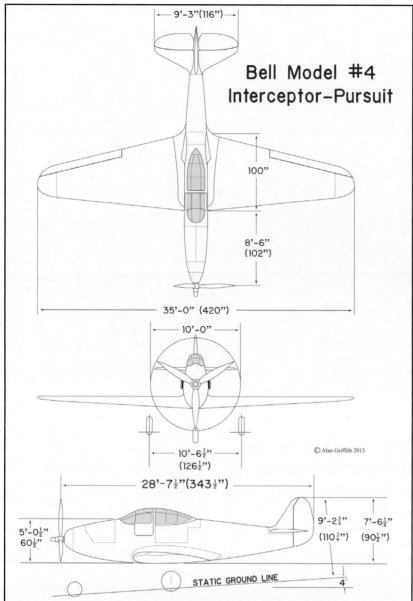

9'-3"(116")

Bell Model #4
Interceptor-Pursuit

100"

8'-6"
(102")

35'-0" (420")

10'-0"

© Alan Griffith 2013

10'-6½"
(126½")

28'-7½"(343½")

5'-0½"
60½"

9'-2¾"   7'-6½"
(110¾")   (90½")

STATIC GROUND LINE

4'

LEFT Bell Model 4 (3.37).
Alan Griffith copyright

Bell XP-39 data

Span	35ft 10in (10.92m) (production 34ft 0in/10.36m)
Length	28ft 8in (8.74m)
Wing area	200sq ft (18.60sq m) (production 213sq ft/19.81sq m)
Gross (loaded) weight	5,550lb (2,517kg)
Powerplant	one 1,150hp (858kW) Allison V-1710-17
Armament	(P-39C) one 37mm cannon, two 0.50in (12.70mm) and two 0.30in (7.62mm) machine guns
Maximum speed	390mph (628km/h) at 20,000ft (6,096m)
Service ceiling	32,000ft (9,754m)
Range	390 miles (628km)

LEFT The clean lines of a pre-series Bell YP-39 are shown beautifully by this image. *David Stern*

ABOVE Serial AH925 was a Curtiss Tomahawk Mk IIA supplied to the RAF.

Curtiss P-40 Warhawk

The prototype XP-40 prototype was converted from a Curtiss P-36 airframe with an Allison V-1710 rather than the latter's radial, and made its first flight on 14 October 1938. During 1939 it was evaluated at Wright Field and was selected for procurement almost immediately. The first deliveries were made in May 1940 and the type went on to become the second important American fighter type of the early war years. Although never quite on a par with many other current types, in some theatres the P-40 was the best fighter available at the time. Certain versions had a Packard Merlin installed and, although all American examples were named Warhawk, in RAF service it was also known as the Tomahawk and the Kittyhawk.

New Requirements – the P-47 Thunderbolt

The Republic P-47 Thunderbolt was the outcome of a series of projects from Seversky and Republic: the P-35 of 1935, the experimental private venture XP-41 first flown in March 1939, the P-43 Lancer of 1940, and the P-44. A subsequent design competition conducted by the Army Air Corps and held in 1939 would help to bring the P-47 to the fore, but many of its competitors were also flown at least in prototype form, so also need to be mentioned. This 1939 competition was the result of Army Circular Proposal 39-770 (previously CP 39-13) and Specification XC-616, and the designs assessed apparently included the P-39C version of the Bell Airacobra above (which for a period was to be designated P-45), Curtiss's P-40D Warhawk variant, the Seversky/Republic P-44, the Curtiss

XP-40 data

XP-40 data	
Span	37ft 3.5in (11.37m)
Length	31ft 8.75in (9.67m)
Wing area	236sq ft (21.95sq m)
Gross weight	6,280lb (2,849kg)
Powerplant	one 1,150hp (858kW) Allison V-1710-19
Armament	two 0.50in (12.70mm) machine guns (production aircraft had more), 120lb (54kg) bombs
Maximum speed	327mph (526km/h) at 12,000ft (3,658m)
Service ceiling	31,000ft (9,449m)
Range	460 miles (740km)

XP-46, the Seversky/Republic AP-10 project, which became the XP-47, the Douglas XP-48, and the Bellanca Models 17-110 and 20-115. Only the two Bellanca offerings, the P-44 and the XP-48, did not fly (although none of the submissions were flying when the competition took place). The prime objective behind XC-616 was to procure a lightweight fighter, but it was subsequently replaced by Specification XC-619.

Seversky/Republic P-43 Lancer and XP-44 Rocket

ABOVE The private-venture Seversky XP-41. *Alan Griffith*

Seversky's AP-4 project was built as the XP-41 and took part in a 1939 fly-off competition with the Bell XP-39 and Curtiss XP-40 (and the Lockheed XP-38 in Chapter Two). As a result it won an order for thirteen YF-43 pre-production airframes powered by a 1,300hp (969kW) Pratt & Whitney (P&W) R-1830-55 engine, and the first of these flew in March 1940. By the time the first production deliveries arrived in September 1940, however, the type had fallen behind the capability of the fighters likely to be offered by a potential enemy and consequently no further large contracts were placed.

The improved XP-44 was then offered by Republic, which introduced a more powerful P&W R-2180-1 and

this secured an order for eighty fighters. It is understood that the P-43 and P-44 airframes were, apart from the powerplant, nearly identical and that, structurally, the only difference between them was a longer engine cowling for the more powerful engine together with the six machine guns. The XP-44 never made it to the mock-up stage and the additional weight of equipment and armament indicated that the modified type would not have the necessary speed performance. Fortunately, Republic's efforts with its AP-10 project (below) meant that this did not matter – once the potential of that design had become clear, the P-44 programme was abandoned.

The P&W R-2800 offered 2,000hp (1,491kW) and was considered as an alternative engine. A document from about April 1940, which appears to have assessed the P-44 for US Navy use, indicates that in this form the P-44 would have a span of 38ft 9in (11.81m), a length of 29ft 6.5in (9.00m) and a gross weight of 8,000lb (3,629kg). Its estimated ceiling appears to be 35,800ft (10,912m). With the R-2800 power unit the type was known as the P-44-2, the estimated maximum speed was 422mph (679km/h) at 20,000ft (6,096m) and large orders for production machines were planned. However, these contracts were changed once the P-47 became the favoured design.

LEFT The Republic XP-43 Lancer pictured at Farmingdale. *Mike Machat*

Curtiss XP-46

As a follow-on from the P-40, Curtiss's intention with the XP-46 was to draw on and incorporate some advanced features that had recently appeared on fighters developed in Europe, introducing such items as automatic leading-edge slots. Two prototypes were ordered in September 1939, and it was the second XP-46 prototype that was first to fly (as the XP-46A on 15 February 1941), the decision having been taken to get the aircraft into the air

ABOVE The well-known artwork that depicts the Republic XP-44 project. *Mike Machat*

without much of its equipment and armament. Unfortunately, in 'lightweight' form the second machine could only just reach the required maximum speed of 410mph (660km/h) (at 15,000ft/4,572m), and the first fully equipped XP-46 prototype made only

355mph (571km/h). This shortfall killed any plans for putting the fighter into production, and it became one of many Curtiss prototypes produced during the period covered by this book that failed to progress further.

BELOW A beautiful colour photo of the XP-46. *Alan Griffith*

XP-46 data	
Span	33ft 4in (10.16m)
Length	30ft 2in (9.19m)
Wing area	208sq ft (19.34sq m)
Maximum take-off weight	7,665lb (3,477kg)
Powerplant	one 1,150hp (858kW) Allison V-1710-39
Armament	two 0.50in (12.70mm) and eight 0.30in (7.62mm) machine guns
Maximum speed	355mph (571km/h) at 12,200ft (3,719m)
Service ceiling	29,500ft (8,992m)
Combat range	325 miles (523km)

XP-44 data (estimated)	
Span	36ft 0in (10.97m)
Length	28ft 4in (8.63m)
Wing area	386sq ft (35.90sq m)
Loaded weight	8,330lb (3,778kg)
Powerplant	one 1,400hp (1,044kW) P&W R-2180-1
Armament	two 0.50in (12.70mm) and four 0.30in (7.62mm) machine guns
Maximum speed	386mph (621km/h) at 15,000ft (4,572m)

P-44-2 data with R-2800 power unit	
Span	38ft 9in (11.81m)
Length	29ft 6.5in (9.00m)
Gross weight	8,000lb (3,629kg)
Ceiling (estimated)	35,800ft (10,912m)
Maximum speed (estimated)	422mph (679km/h) at 20,000ft (6,096m)

Republic AP-10/P-47 Thunderbolt

The original Republic AP-10 submission showed another lightweight fighter powered by a single Allison V-1710-39 and armed with just two 0.50in (12.7mm) machine guns placed in the engine housing. The armament was subsequently increased to six guns and a prototype was ordered as the XP-47 in November 1939. A second unarmed XP-47A prototype was ordered in the following January, but by then the events in Europe associated with Germany's advances had shown that, although speed and armament were vital, a fighter also needed to be tough and be capable of absorbing punishment. As a result, Republic chief designer Alexander Kartveli presented a new and much larger design in June 1940, which was powered by a P&W R-2800 radial. In September work on the XP-47 prototypes was terminated and the order switched to the new design, which was designated XP-47B (the Republic number was still AP-10); it was at this point that the P-44 programme was also stopped. The XP-47B's tubby appearance left many questioning its suitability as a fighter, but after flight testing had begun on 6 May 1941 a speed of 412mph (663km/h) was recorded, which exceeded the estimates by 12mph (19km/h) and did much to quieten the doubters.

The P-47 Thunderbolt was to be built in vast numbers and established Republic as a major player in fighter development.

ABOVE A wind tunnel model of the AP-10/XP-47 on test at Langley. *Alan Griffith*

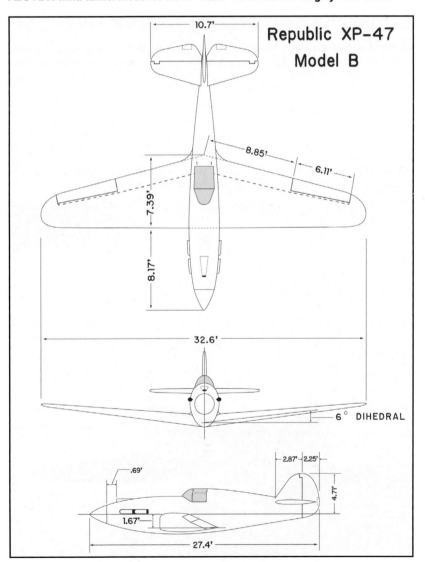

ABOVE This drawing shows Republic's AP-10 'Model B' lightweight fighter (8.39). It has a span of 32ft 7in (9.94m) and a length of 27ft 5in (8.35m). *Alan Griffith copyright*

ABOVE A picture showing a Republic P-47B production aircraft (serial 41-5931), the first version of the Thunderbolt to be manufactured in series. It has a sliding canopy.

BELOW This view of a P-47N Thunderbolt, the final version to be built in quantity, shows how the basic design had been altered and refined during the war.

AP-10/XP-47 data

Span	30ft 0in (9.14m)
Length	27ft 6in (8.38m)
Empty weight	4,790lb (2,173kg)
Powerplant	one 1,150hp (858kW) Allison V-1710-39
Armament	two 0.50in (12.70mm) machine guns
Maximum speed	415mph (668km/h)

XP-47B data

Span	40ft 9.75in (12.44m)
Length	35ft 0in (10.67m)
Wing area	300sq ft (27.90sq m)
Gross weight	11,600lb (5,262kg)
Maximum take-off weight	12,700lb (5,761kg)
Powerplant	one 2,000hp (1,491kW) P&W XR-2800-17
Armament	eight 0.50in (12.70mm) machine guns
Maximum speed	412mph (663km/h) at 25,800ft (7,864m)
Service ceiling	38,000ft (11,582m)
Range	575 miles (925km)

XP-47J data

Span	40ft 9.75in (12.44m)
Length	33ft 3in (10.13m)
Wing area	300sq ft (27.90sq m)
Gross weight	12,400lb (5,625kg)
Maximum take-off weight	16,780lb (7,611kg)
Powerplant	one 2,800hp (2,088kW) P&W XR-2800-57
Armament	six 0.50in (12.70mm) machine guns
Maximum speed	505mph (813km/h) at 34,430ft (10,494m)
Service ceiling	45,000ft (13,716m)
Range	765 miles (1,231km)

ABOVE The Republic XP-47J. In concept similar to North American's lightweight P-51 Mustang, the XP-47J achieved a world record speed of 505mph (813km/h) in August 1944. *Mike Machat*

Many examples would serve in Europe, and the P-47 would also become the Air Force's last radial-engine fighter, serving until 1955. Among the many versions were prototypes (but no production) of the XP-47H fitted with a 2,300hp (1,715kW) Chrysler XIV-2220-1 in-line engine (which really served as a testbed) and the XP-47J with a 2,800hp (2,088kW) R-2800-57. On 5 August 1944 the latter achieved 505mph (813km/h), making it the first propeller-driven aeroplane to pass the 500mph (805km/h) mark. Two XP-47J prototypes were ordered and the first flew on 26 November 1943, but in the end only this example was completed, as the design effort moved on to the XP-72 (below).

BELOW The Republic XP-47H. Two examples were built at Republic's auxiliary facility in Evansville, Indiana, but despite the new powerplant and a much modified airframe there was no significant improvement in performance. *Mike Machat*

Douglas XP-48

The final competitor thought to be involved in XC-616 was the Model 312 from Douglas Santa Monica (a company that had no previous fighter experience). This was to be powered by the Ranger SGV-770 driving a three-blade propeller with a diameter of 9ft 6in (2.90m), and the design featured a very slim high-aspect-ratio tapered wing and a tricycle undercarriage; in fact, in many respects it looked like a private pilot's light aeroplane. The designation XP-48 was allotted, but the project was abandoned pretty quickly, in part because it was considered that the manufacturer's performance estimates were to be regarded with some doubt. Little further background information has so far appeared in regard to the XP-48.

New Requirements – Advanced Configurations

The next major design competition was held in the winter of 1939/40 under a document called R40-C and Specification XC-622, and resulted in a series of projects that included several unconventional proposals, some for example using pusher engines. This step was intended to open the development of a fighter for Fiscal Year (FY) 1940, and one of the driving forces behind it was the fact that the previous 1939 competitions had failed to produce an outstanding aeroplane. In fact, a special Air Board headed by General Henry H. 'Hap' Arnold had produced a report in mid-September 1939 that stressed quite strongly that the Air Corps needed a serious research and development programme to ensure that the Service acquired new aircraft that would be a match for any potential enemy types. Arnold was also responsible for organising a separate Board in May 1939 led by Brig-Gen Walter G. Kilner, which had the task of establishing a full list of characteristics for aircraft types and other programmes to cover the next five years. It was the

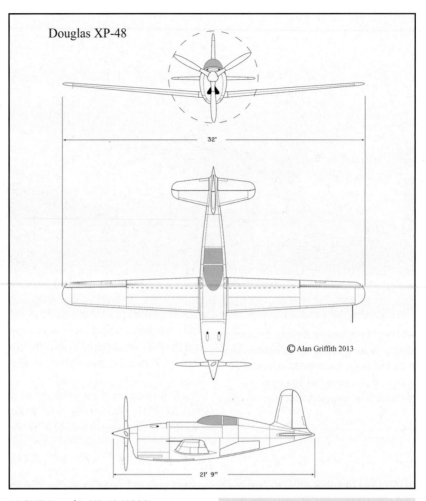

Douglas XP-48

32'

21' 9"

© Alan Griffith 2013

ABOVE Douglas XP-48 (1939).
Alan Griffith copyright

work of the Kilner Board that prompted the issuing of R40-C.

Funding was to be found to permit the ordering of two prototypes of several different designs, and the maximum speed for any all-new design was expected to be at least 425mph (684km/h) at altitudes of between 15,000ft and 20,000ft (4,752m and 6,096m), but with the remarkably high figure for 1939/40 of 525mph (845km/h) desired. At 5,000ft (1,524m) a maximum speed of at least 360mph (579km/h) was expected, with 460mph (740km/h) desired, and the fighter would take between 5 and 7 minutes to reach 20,000ft (6,096m). The first of the two prototypes or 'flying articles' was to be a flying shell, and after this had been flight-tested the second aircraft would be kitted out with full equipment to provide what was essentially a production prototype.

XP-48 data	
Span	32ft 0in (9.75m)
Length	21ft 9in (6.63m)
Wing area	92sq ft (8.56sq m)
Gross weight	3,400lb (1,542kg)
Powerplant	one 525hp (kW) Ranger SGV-770
Armament	one 0.50in (12.70mm) and one 0.30in (7.62mm) machine gun
Top speed	350mph (563km/h)

After further deliberations the 'Request for Data' (which more recently would be termed a Request for Proposals) was labelled R40-C and covered by Air Corps Type Specification XC-622 of 27 November 1939. The basic aircraft was to have a single engine and an armament of four guns with a mix of machine guns (0.50in/12.70mm and 0.30in/7.62mm) and cannon (20mm and 37mm) permitted. The document was approved in February 1940 and by early April the following designs had been submitted by industry.

RIGHT Bell Model 13 (3.40).
Gerald Balzer

Model 13 data	
Span	28ft 0in (8.53m)
Length	29ft 8.7in (9.06m) (possibly different on 'A' and 'B')
Wing area	143sq ft (13.30sq m)
Gross weight	7,096lb (3,219kg) (Model 13A); 7,104lb (3,222kg) (Model 13B)
Armament (on all)	two 0.50in (12.70mm), four 0.30in (7.62mm) machine guns, one 37mm cannon
Maximum speed at 5,000ft (1,524m)	430mph (692km/h) (Model 13 with V-1430-1); 440mph (708km/h) (Model 13 with V-1430-3); 375mph (603km/h) (Model 13A); 396mph (637km/h) (Model 13B)
Maximum speed at 15,000 to 20,000ft (4,752 to 6,096m)	475mph (764km/h) (Model 13 with V-1430-1); 487mph (784km/h) (Model 13 with V-1430-3); 425mph (684km/h) (Model 13A); 443mph (713km/h) (Model 13B)
Times to 20,000ft (6,096m)	4.7min (Model 13 with V-1430-1 and V-1430-3); 7min (Model 13A); 6,2min (Model 13B)

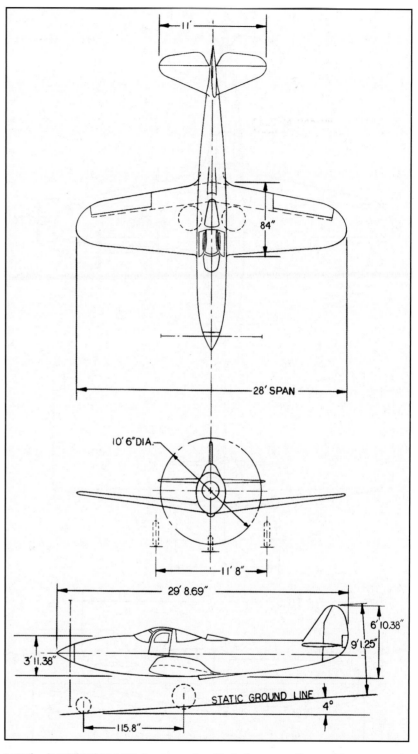

Bell Models 4G, 13, 13A and 13B

Bell's series of proposals were all variants of the P-39 above, but with different engines and a much reduced wingspan. There were in fact two versions of the Model 13, with either a Continental 1,600hp (1,193kW) V-1430-1 or a 1,700hp (1,268kW) V-1430-3 power unit driving a propeller with a diameter of 10ft 6in (3.20m), while the 13A had an Allison V-1710-E8 and the 13B a V-1710-E9, with a 10ft 2in (3.10m) propeller; the latter pair could use the P-39's extension shaft but the Continentals would need a new arrangement and all had a single three-bladed propeller. The tricycle undercarriage was retained and the Model 13 series had a low-position tapered wing with heavily rounded tips. There was also the Model 4G, which introduced a P&W X-1800 engine in a standard P-39B or P-39C airframe, but this was not looked on as a new design.

19

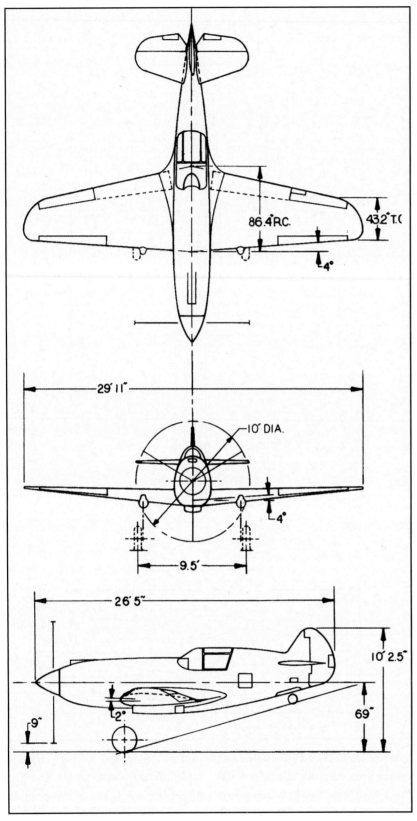

ABOVE Curtiss CP-40 (3.40). *Gerald Balzer*

Curtiss Model CP-40-1 and -2

The CP-40-1 and -2 were submitted by the Buffalo branch of Curtiss and used the same airframe but with different engines (which again may have affected the aircraft's length slightly against the figure quoted in the data). The -1 was to use an Allison V-1710-F6R with a single-speed supercharger, while the -2 had the Continental I-1430-3 and a two-stage supercharger. Armament was four 0.50in (12.7mm) machine guns, and the engines had single 10ft (3.05m)-diameter three- and four-blade propellers respectively. Clearly based around the P-40 but scaled down in size, the CP-40s were really somewhat more reminiscent of the XP-37 prototype flight-tested in April 1937, but with their cockpit position not so far to the rear in relation to the wing as on the earlier machine. The new designs were to have a conventional tail-wheel undercarriage and a tapered low wing with a rounded trailing edge.

CP-40 data	
Span	29ft 11in (9.12m)
Length	26ft 5in (8.05m)
Wing area	150sq ft (13.95sq m)
Armament	four 0.50in (12.70mm) machine guns

CP-40-1 data	
Gross weight	6,310lb (2,862kg)
Maximum speed at 5,000ft (1,524m)	400mph (644km/h)
Maximum speed at 15,000 to 20,000ft (4,752 to 6,096m)	460mph (740km/h)
Time to 20,000ft (6,096m)	6.5min

CP-40-2 data	
Gross weight	6,715lb (3,046kg)
Maximum speed at 5,000ft (1,524m)	430mph (692km/h)
Maximum speed at 15,000 to 20,000ft (4,752m and 6,096m)	485mph (780km/h)
Time to 20,000ft (6,096m)	in excess of 5min

RIGHT Curtiss P 248A (3.40).
Gerald Balzer

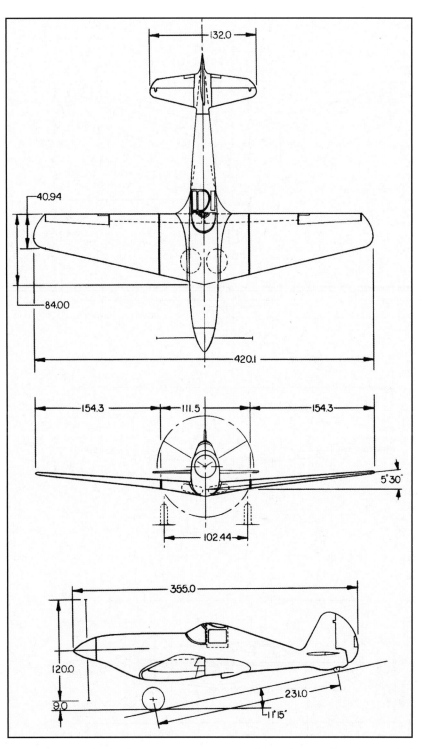

P-248 data

Span	35ft 1in (10.69m)
Length	29ft 7in (9.02m)
Wing area	174.3sq ft (16.21sq m)
Armament	four machine guns, two 0.30in (7.62mm) and two 0.50in (12.70mm)

P-248A single-prop data

Gross weight	5,477lb (2,484kg)
Maximum speed at 5,000ft (1,524m)	376mph (605km/h)
Maximum speed at 15,000 to 20,000ft (4,752 to 6,096m)	425mph (684km/h)
Time to 20,000ft (6,096m)	6.0min

P-248A dual-prop data

Gross weight	5,677lb (2,575kg)
Maximum speed at 5,000ft (1,524m)	378mph (608km/h)
Maximum speed at 15,000 to 20,000ft (4,752 to 6,096m)	432mph (695km/h)
Time to 20,000ft (6,096m)	5.8min

P-248C data

Gross weight	5,694lb (2,583kg)
Maximum speed at 5,000ft (1,524m)	388mph (624km/h)
Maximum speed at 15,000 to 20,000ft (4,752 to 6,096m)	445mph (716km/h)
Time to 20,000ft (6,096m)	5.0min

Curtiss P-248

The P-248 and P-249 (below) proposals, six designs in all, were the work of Curtiss's St Louis branch. The P-248 represented one airframe with three different powerplants: the P-248A would have an Allison V-1710 driving a single 10ft (3.05m)-diameter three-blade propeller, the P-248A had the same engine but was fitted with a 9ft (2.74m)-diameter dual three-bladed opposite-rotating (counter-rotating) propeller, while the P-248C would use a Continental I-1430-3 with a four-blade prop 9ft 6in (2.90m) in diameter; all had single-speed superchargers. The airframe was based on the firm's CW-21 lightweight interceptor fighter prototype flown in September 1938, which had been designed purely for export and not for the home air arms, and which was intended to offer a high rate of climb so that early attacks could be made against incoming enemy bombers. The CW-21 was not designed to be a dogfighting aircraft and examples were ordered by China and the Netherlands. The main alteration for the P-248 was the replacement of the CW-21's Wright R-1820 Cyclone radial power unit. Having a conventional undercarriage with a low-position wing, which had a small angle of sweep on the leading edge and a straight trailing edge, the P-248 was a higher-powered version of the CW-21 carrying four machine guns, two 0.30in (7.62mm) and two 0.50in (12.70mm).

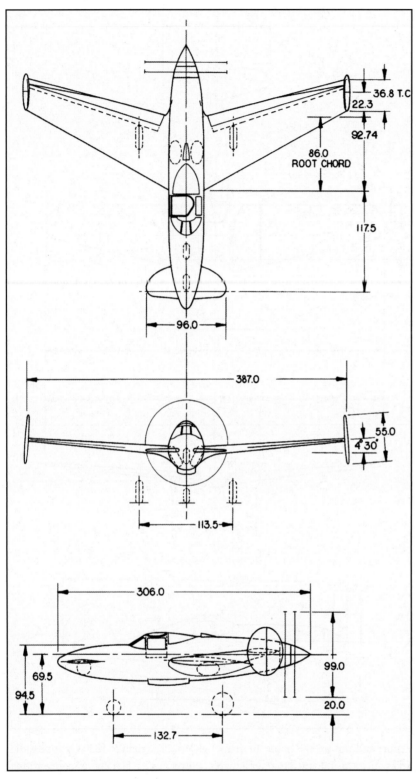

P-249 data

Span	32ft 3in (9.83m)
Length	25ft 6in (7.77m)
Wing area	173sq ft (16.09sq m)
Armament	one 37mm cannon plus one 0.30in (7.62mm) and two 0.50in (12.70mm) machine guns

P-249A data

Gross weight 5,727lb (2,598kg)	
Maximum speed at 5,000ft (1,524m)	425mph (684km/h)
Maximum speed at 15,000 to 20,000ft (4,752 to 6,096m)	480mph (772km/h)
Time to 20,000ft (6,096m)	5.6min

P-249C data

Gross weight	5,674lb (2,574kg)
Maximum speed at 5,000ft (1,524m)	445mph (716km/h)
Maximum speed at 15,000 to 20,000ft (4,752 to 6,096m)	510mph (821km/h)
Time to 20,000ft (6,096m)	4.8min

P-249T data

Gross weight	9,157lb (4,154kg)
Maximum speed at 5,000ft (1,524m)	485mph (780km/h)
Maximum speed at 15,000 to 20,000ft (4,752 to 6,096m)	525mph (845km/h)
Time to 20,000ft (6,096m)	4.4min

Curtiss P-249

The Curtiss P-249 is the first of the XC-622 proposals to be described here that was an all-new design, and again it was offered in three variants. In fact, with a pusher engine, a 'free-floating' foreplane and wings highly swept on both leading and trailing edges, it presented a most advanced concept, a compact aeroplane and a considerable contrast to the P-248. There was a tricycle undercarriage folding into the fuselage, and wingtip fins. The three versions were listed as the P-249A, P-249C and P-249T, the letters identifying their power units – the Allison V-1710-F3R, Continental I-1430-3 and Wright R-2160 Tornado. The Tornado brought a substantial increase to the P-249T's weight, but the estimated data also indicated that there would be a substantial increase in performance. The respective propeller arrangements were a dual three-blade opposite-rotating 8ft 6in (2.59m)-diameter example, a single four-blade of 9ft 0in (2.74m) diameter, and a dual three-blade opposite-rotating 10ft 0in (3.05m)-diameter, while the engines themselves had single-speed, two-stage and single-speed, two-stage superchargers respectively. The armament was one 37mm cannon together with one 0.30in (7.62mm) and two 0.50in (12.70mm) machine guns.

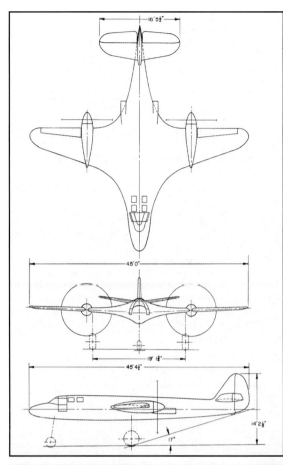

LEFT McDonnell Model 1 (3.40). *Gerald Balzer*

BELOW A wind tunnel model of the McDonnell Model 1. *David Stern*

Model 1 data	
Span	45ft 0in (13.72m)
Length	45ft 4.5in (13.83m)
Wing area	324sq ft (30.13sq m)
Armament	pair of 20mm cannon and two 0.30in (7.62mm) machine guns

Data with Allison V-3420-B2	
Gross weight	13,826lb (6,271kg)
Maximum speed at 5,000ft (1,524m)	383mph (616km/h)
Maximum speed at 15,000 to 20,000ft (4,752 to 6,096m)	448mph (721km/h)
Time to 20,000ft (6,096m)	7.0min

Data with P&W H-3130	
Gross weight	14,801lb (6,714kg)
Maximum speed at 5,000ft (1,524m)	385mph (619km/h)
Maximum speed at 15,000 to 20,000ft (4,752 to 6,096m)	454mph (730km/h)
Time to 20,000ft (6,096m)	7.0min

Data with P&W X-1800-A2G	
Gross weight	13,527lb (6,136kg)
Maximum speed at 5,000ft (1,524m)	347mph (558km/h)
Maximum speed at 15,000 to 20,000ft (4,752 to 6,096m)	406mph (653km/h)
Time to 20,000ft (6,096m)	9.3min

Data with Wright R-2160	
Gross weight	14,357lb (6,512kg)
Maximum speed at 5,000ft (1,524m)	368mph (592km/h)
Maximum speed at 15,000 to 20,000ft (4,752 to 6,096m)	421mph (677km/h)
Time to 20,000ft (6,096m)	8.5min

McDonnell Model 1

Another advanced all-new layout was presented by the new McDonnell Aircraft Corporation; indeed, the Model 1 was the company's first official proposal. Again there were four versions of the basic design, which differed in powerplant only, and these were officially submitted on 11 April 1940. The layout did look relatively conventional but it was heavily streamlined with airfoil-shaped fillets where the wing and fuselage were joined, and inside it was even more unconventional. No individual designation was given by McDonnell to each variant, and the engine choices (all liquid-cooled) were a single Allison V-3420-B2, a P&W H-3130, a P&W X-1800-A2G or a Wright R-2160 Tornado. Whichever type was installed it was to be housed in the fuselage to the rear of the cockpit with its power transmitted to a pair of two-speed, four-blade, pusher propellers using geared right-angle drive shafts; the 10ft 7in (3.22m)-diameter pusher propellers were to be mounted behind the wing trailing edges on the end of small nacelles (the prop dimensions were quoted for the V-3420-B2 and H-3130, but no information is available for the other units). Armament was a pair of 20mm cannon and two 0.30in (7.62mm) machine guns, and the Model 1 had a tricycle undercarriage, still a new feature at that time.

N-2 series data
Powerplant for N-2, N-2A, N-2B, N-2C and N-2D
was to become P&W R-2800-A5G, P&W X-1800-
A2G, X-1800-A3G, Allison V-1710-E9 or P&W R-
1830-C5G
Armament was to be two 0.50in (12.70mm) machine
guns and two 20mm cannon on the first three
designs, but with two 0.30in (7.62mm) machine guns
replacing the '50s' on the N-2C and N-2D

N-2/2A/2B data

Span	40ft 5in (12.32m)
Length	22ft 11in (6.99m)
Wing area	298sq ft (27.71sq m)

N-2C/2D data

Wing area	184sq ft (17.11sq m)

N-2 data

Gross weight	9,050lb (4,105kg)
Maximum speed at 5,000ft (1,524m)	405mph (652km/h)
Maximum speed at 15,000 to 20,000ft (4,752 to 6,096m)	472mph (759km/h)
Time to 20,000ft (6,096m)	5.15min

N-2A data

Gross weight	8,966lb (4,067kg)
Maximum speed at 5,000ft (1,524m)	406mph (653km/h)
Maximum speed at 15,000 to 20,000ft (4,752 to 6,096m)	474mph (763km/h)
Time to 20,000ft (6,096m)	5.2min

N-2B data

Gross weight	9,046lb (4,103kg)
Maximum speed at 5,000ft (1,524m)	415mph (668km/h)
Maximum speed at 15,000 to 20,000ft (4,752 to 6,096m)	486mph (782km/h)
Time to 20,000ft (6,096m)	5.0min

N-2C data

Gross weight	6,169lb (2,798kg)
Maximum speed at 5,000ft (1,524m)	400mph (644km/h)
Maximum speed at 15,000 to 20,000ft (4,752 to 6,096m)	442mph (711km/h)
Time to 20,000ft (6,096m)	6.8min

N-2D data

Gross weight	6,335lb (2,874kg)
Maximum speed at 5,000ft (1,524m)	389mph (626km/h)
Maximum speed at 15,000 to 20,000ft (4,752 to 6,096m)	437mph (703km/h)
Time to 20,000ft (6,096m)	7.0min

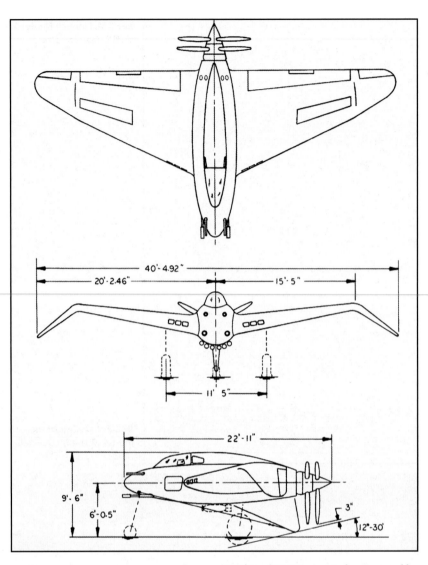

ABOVE Northrop N-2/N-2A/N-2B.
Gerald Balzer

Northrop N-2 Series

Another relatively new company, the Northrop Corporation's speciality was flying wings, and the N-2 reflected this. The design was proposed in five versions with different engines, although two (the N-2C and N-2D) appear to have been smaller airframes overall. The fuselage (really a nacelle) was short and stocky and the wing was swept at the leading edge and straight along the trailing edge; there was a considerable degree of droop or anhedral on the wingtips, which was introduced with the object of providing extra directional control. The short fuselage necessitated a tricycle undercarriage. The N-2, N-2A, N-2B,

N-2C and N-2D were to be powered by a P&W R-2800-A5G, X-1800-A2G or X-1800-A3G, an Allison V-1710-E9, and a P&W R-1830-C5G respectively, driving (in the first three cases) a 9ft 6in (2.90m)-diameter dual three-blade opposite-rotating propeller, or (for the last two) a single four-blade prop with the same diameter. Except for the Allison, each of these power units would need an extension shaft, while the X-1800-A3G would require a turbo-supercharger when all of the others would use two-speed superchargers. The guns were all housed in the nose: two 0.50in (12.70mm) machine guns and two 20mm cannon on the first three designs, and two 0.30in (7.62mm) machine guns replacing the '50s' on the N-2C and N-2D.

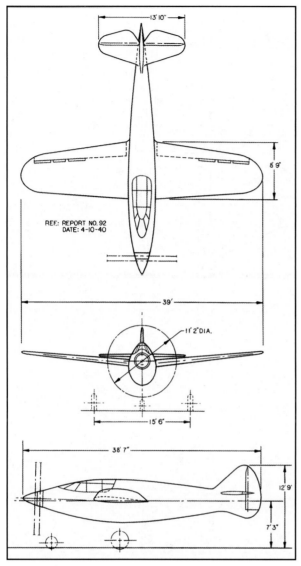

**LEFT Republic AP-12
(3.40).**
Gerald Balzer

Republic AP-12

Republic's answer to R40-C was the AP-12 project, of which there was just one version. Coupled with a mildly tapered wing was a supremely streamlined fuselage that housed a single Tornado with a two-speed single-stage supercharger. The extension shaft from the Tornado would drive a dual three-blade opposite-rotating tractor propeller 11ft 2in (3.40m) in diameter, and the aircraft featured a tricycle undercarriage.

AP-12 data	
Span	39ft 0in (11.89m)
Length	38ft 7in (11.76m)
Wing area	unknown
Gross weight	unknown
Powerplant	one Wright R-2160 Tornado
Armament	two 0.30in (7.62mm) and four 0.50in (12.70mm) machine guns, one 20mm cannon
Accurate performance currently unavailable	

BELOW AP-12 artwork. The AP-12 was also known as the 'Rocket', and this image illustrates well the design's powerplant arrangement. *Gerald Balzer*

Vultee Model V-70

With its V-70 proposal, of which there were three versions, Vultee offered a relatively conventional layout with twin booms and a pusher engine at the rear of the central fuselage/nacelle. The outer wings beyond the twin booms were tapered, while the leading edge of the centre section was swept. The power unit on all three variants was to be a P&W X-1800-A4G with a two-speed supercharger, the variations arising from either the propeller or the gross weight. The propeller diameter throughout was 10ft 0in (3.05m); one version had a dual three-blade opposite-rotating prop and the other (Version 2) a single four-blade prop. Once again there was a tricycle undercarriage, and the guns, a single 0.30in (7.62mm), two 0.50in (12.70mm) and two 20mm cannon, would all fit in the nose. The brochure indicated that the V-70's aerodynamics would be superior to current designs.

*

Bell's Model 4G and the McDonnell Model 1s, to be powered by the X-1800-A2G and the R-2160 Tornado, were

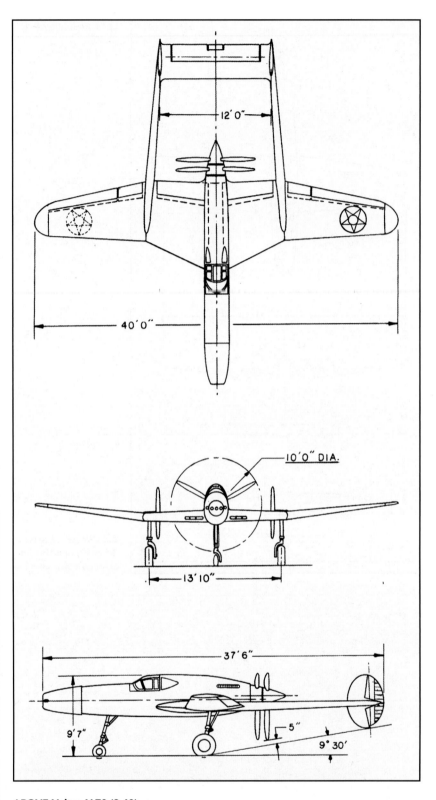

ABOVE Vultee V-70 (3.40).
Gerald Balzer

V-70 data

Span	40ft 0in (12.19m)
Length	37ft 6in (11.43m)
Wing area	244.6sq ft (22.75sq m)
Armament	single 0.30in (7.62mm), two 0.50in (12.70mm) and two 20mm cannon

Versions 1 and 3 data

Gross weight	9,000lb (4,082kg) and 9,055lb (4,107kg) respectively
Maximum speed at 5,000ft (1,524m)	443mph (713km/h)
Maximum speed at 15,000 to 20,000ft (4,752 to 6,096m)	525mph (845km/h)
Time to 20,000ft (6,096m)	5min

Version 2 data

Gross weight	8,788lb (3,986kg)
Maximum speed at 5,000ft (1,524m)	449mph (722km/h)
Maximum speed at 15,000 to 20,000ft (4,752 to 6,096m)	525mph (845km/h)
Time to 20,000ft (6,096m)	7min

ABOVE From certain angles the XP-54 did look quite unusual for a fighter aircraft.
Greater St Louis Air & Space Museum

XP-54 data	
Span	53ft 10in (16.40m)
Length	54ft 9in (16.69m)
Wing area	455.5sq ft (42.36sq m)
Gross weight	18,360lb (8,328kg)
Overload weight	19,735lb (8,952kg)
Powerplant	one 2,300hp (1,715kW) Lycoming XH-2470-1
Armament	two 0.50in (12.70mm) machine guns, two 37mm cannon
Maximum speed	304mph (489km/h) at sea level and 404mph (650km/h) at 28,000ft (8,534m)
Service ceiling	37,000ft (11,278m)
Range	500 miles (805km)

quickly rejected following a preliminary engineering analysis. At the end of May 1940 the appraisal of the other R40-C proposals was declared and the winners were Vultee, Curtiss (St Louis) with its P-249C, and Northrop; the three winning designs were to be ordered in prototype form as the XP-54, XP-55 and XP-56 respectively. Each of these very different layouts had a pusher engine and employed NACA laminar flow aerofoils. Close analysis had shown that the small wingspan of the Bell Model 13 series and the Curtiss CP-40s would have given a high wing loading, which would have had an adverse affect on the type's manoeuvrability at high altitude, while the Curtiss P-248 offered no real advance over current types. Although the radical Curtiss P-249 was favoured, it was considered that the counter-rotating propellers required for the 'A' and 'T' version would almost certainly require a long development time, in the case of the Tornado at least two and a half years. This long development period for the Tornado also counted against Republic's AP-12 and was the main reason behind that project's rejection.

Returning to McDonnell, only the V-3420 and H-3130 versions of the Model 1 were expected to achieve the XC-622 requirements (these engines had two-stage and two-stage two-speed geared superchargers respectively), but it was estimated that the type's sophisticated engine and power drives would take at least 42 months to develop, while the airframe itself was the heaviest of the different proposals. Indeed, this pair were placed twenty-first and twenty-second of the twenty-three submittals evaluated. However, the Model 1 still generated sufficient interest for the Air Corps to purchase engineering data and a wind tunnel model in June 1940, and the Model 1 would subsequently evolve into the Model 2 (XP-67) prototype described in Chapter Two.

Vultee XP-54

Although in general sharing the same configuration as the original V-70s, the Vultee XP-54 as built had in fact been redesigned and increased in size by a third (Vultee called the new form the V-84). The fighter's progress was delayed seriously by a switch from the original conception of a medium-altitude, high-speed aircraft embodying a low-drag aerofoil and the ultimate in aerodynamic refinement within a reasonably conventional arrangement, to a high-altitude, pressure-cabin fighter with a rated altitude of 40,000ft (12,192m). This change resulted in the complete redesign of the aeroplane after a great deal of time and money had been expended in an elaborate series of wind tunnel tests. In fact, by November 1942 it had moved much further away from the Air Corps's Pursuit Team's immediate desire for a fast-climbing interceptor than when originally conceived, in which version it would have had a rate of climb of more than 5,000ft/min (1,524m/min). In addition the X-1800 was subsequently abandoned and a liquid-cooled Lycoming XH-2470 was chosen to replace it.

Two prototypes were ordered and the first XP-54 'Swoose Goose' finally became airborne on 15 January 1943. In the air the fighter's handling characteristics were found to be good but its maximum speed fell short of the specified limits by a serious degree. The figures quoted below were achieved with the airframe having been given a waxed 'superfinish' to reduce drag, which in service would not have been practical – the best recorded with a normal factory finish was 380mph (611km/h) at 28,000ft (8,534m), which was the critical altitude for the engine turbo. The second machine flew on 24 May 1944, but by then Vultee had known for a year that no production orders would be forthcoming. The last flight was made in April 1945.

ABOVE & BELOW Ground views of the Vultee XP-54 prototype. *Gerald Balzer*

THIS PAGE Views of the Curtiss XP-55 lightweight flying model. *Gerald Balzer*

Curtiss XP-55 Ascender

The tail-first arrangement used by the Curtiss XP-55 was an effort to get the ultimate in aerodynamic cleanliness and high-speed performance, and the design represented a major departure from previous practice. However, just like the XP-54, the programme experienced considerable delays, although this time they were due more to the higher priority given to other production programmes in the Curtiss-Wright plant. In fact, poor wind tunnel results for the P-249C prompted the Army at one stage to decide against placing an order for the fighter, but Curtiss decided to fund privately a full-scale lightweight flying model of the aircraft, which was built of metal and wood with fabric covering and powered by a 275hp (205kW) Menasco C6S-5 engine. This was called the CW-24B, and it first flew on 2 December 1941, achieving a speed of 180mph (290km/h). It also prompted renewed interest in the full-scale fighter, and three examples were ordered, the first of which began flight-testing on 13 July 1943, but was then wrecked in an accident on 15 November during a stall test.

As a result of the first aircraft's loss, the second and third machines received modifications (the second retrospectively), particularly to the wingtips and elevators, which increased the span to 41ft 0in (12.50m) and the wing area to 217.2sq ft (20.20sq m). They flew on 9 January and 25 April 1944 respectively but, overall, it was considered that the type did not present a sufficient advantage over conventional fighters to take the design beyond the prototypes. Both the XP-55 and the Northrop XP-56 were also considered 'naturals' for the later installation of jet engines or rocket propulsion units since there was no rear empennage to interfere with their operation. Indeed, in March 1945 Curtiss proposed an XP-55 development powered by a General Electric TG-180 jet engine, which it called the P-304.

XP-55 data (first prototype)	
Span	40ft 6.9in (12.37m)
Length	29ft 7in (9.02m)
Wing area	208.9sq ft (19.43sq m)
Gross weight	6,885lb (3,123kg)
Overload weight	7,711lb (3,498kg)
Powerplant	one 1,125hp (839kW) Allison V-1710-95
Armament	four 0.50in (12.70mm) machine guns
Maximum speed	390mph (628km/h) at 19,300ft (5,883m)
Sea level rate of climb	2,350ft/min (716m/min)
Service ceiling	35,800ft (10,912m)
Range	635 miles (1,022km)

ABOVE AND PREVIOUS PAGE Like the other R40-C prototypes, the Curtiss XP-55 presented a very distinctive appearance.
Gerald Balzer

Northrop XP-56
Black Bullet

The decision to proceed with Northrop's project was seen as an opportunity to experiment further with flying wings (together with the scale models and XB-35 described later in this book), and to determine if such a planform (with a pusher engine and low-drag aerofoil) was suited to an

advanced fighter type of aeroplane – in the eyes of the Air Corps this was 'a truly experimental airplane if ever there as one', and in fact it had come third in the R40-C competition. Indeed, both the XP-55 and XP-56 were described as 'major engineering steps

forward', and another of the new features introduced by the XP-56 was the heavy utilisation of helium arc-welded magnesium in its primary structure. However, by early May 1941 the XP-56 had been classed as secondary in priority to Northrop's XP-61 night fighter (see

BELOW The Army Air Corps's Aircraft Laboratory completed this artwork for the Northrop XP-56 on 1 June 1942, more than a year before the type finally flew.
Greater St Louis Air & Space Museum

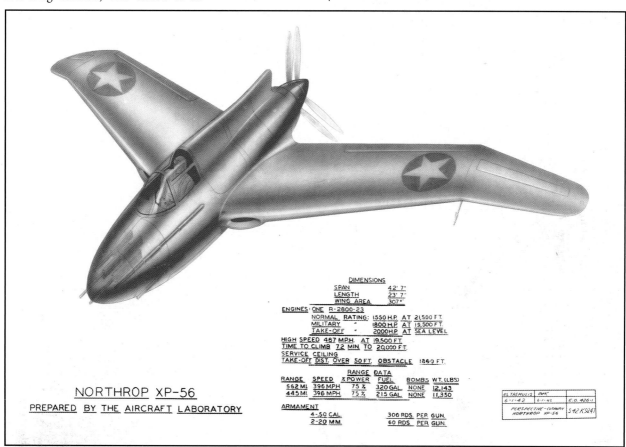

ABOVE & LEFT The Northrop XP-56 Black Bullet was a very stocky-looking aeroplane, and the first prototype, shown here, completed only a few hops. Note the early two-tone camouflage and early war roundels applied to the aircraft on the left.
Greater St Louis Air & Space Museum

Chapter Two) and was being continued with only ten engineers working on it to ensure that some progress was still made. Indeed the need to work on the XP-61 and XB-35 programmes delayed the prototype's completion considerably. The loss of the X-1800 chosen to power the XP-56 also meant that a replacement had to be found and the choice was the P&W R-2800-29.

The first prototype made a short hop on 6 September 1943 followed by several more before it toppled over during a ground run on 8 October and was wrecked. The second machine was consequently modified, but it did not fly until 23 March 1944 and in the end flew on just ten occasions, during which it experienced high levels of drag. In the end the XP-56 effort produced little in the way of flight data, but it did provide rather more information about the development of advanced aeroplanes.

Alternative Programmes and Ideas

More pursuit programmes were started during the war, which resulted in several sets of prototypes being ordered, although some did not go into production and others never flew. But there was one spectacular success, the P-51 Mustang, which has a claim to be the best piston fighter of the Second World War

XP-56 data (first prototype)

Span	42ft 7in (12.98m)
Length	23ft 7in (7.19m)
Wing area	306.5sq ft (28.50sq m)
Gross weight	11,350lb (5,148kg)
Powerplant	one 2,000hp (1,491kW) P&W R-2800-29
Armament	four 0.50in (12.70mm) machine guns and two 20mm cannon
Maximum speed	original guarantee 467mph (751km/h) at 25,000ft (7,620m), maximum speed estimate after flight test 340mph (547km/h) at 19,500ft (5,944m), maximum achieved in flight 320mph (515km/h)
Service ceiling (estimated)	33,000ft (10,058m)
Maximum range	660 miles (1,062km)

Data (second prototype)

Span	43ft 1in (13.13m)
Wing area	311.0sq ft (28.92sq m)
Gross weight	12,588lb (5,710kg)

ABOVE & LEFT The second XP-56
introduced a higher vertical tailfin, but
it still performed just ten full flights.
Gerald Balzer

ABOVE The North American NA-73X prototype. *Alan Griffith*

North American NA-73/ P-51 Mustang

The North American P-51 was not the result of a design competition. It was produced privately against an urgent UK requirement for new fighters issued in April 1940, with orders following in May, and it was not until 1942 that the Army Air Corps adopted the type for its own use. The time taken to develop the Mustang Mk 1 (which in America was called the P-51) was a record, and the NA-73X prototype made its maiden flight on 26 October 1940. At that stage it was powered by an Allison V-1710 and the early versions revealed themselves to be splendid aeroplanes to fly with a good speed at medium altitude. However, in April 1942 the British demanded that the P-51 should have the Rolls-Royce Merlin 61 engine installed in order to

ABOVE LEFT Serial 42-106767 was a USAAF P-51B Mustang with a Packard Merlin and the original cockpit canopy. LEFT P-51B Mustang 43-12102 was used to flight-test the later bubble canopy.

ABOVE The view that many enemy aircraft had of the later Merlin P-51s over Europe as they headed in to attack. The large ventral radiator is well seen.

improve its high-altitude performance, where it was felt that, together with the Spitfire Mk IX, it would be an adequate answer to the new and very impressive German Focke Wulf Fw 190. In due course Rolls-Royce converted five machines, the first flying on 13 October 1942, and the new variant demonstrated a great improvement on the earlier version's performance at altitude, a speed of 433mph (697km/h) at 33,000ft (10,058m) being recorded by the Aeroplane & Armament Experimental Establishment at Boscombe Down.

In the meantime the Air Corps had begun its own Merlin conversion with the XP-51B (which for a brief period was designated XP-78), and the first prototype flew on 30 November 1942. The quality and supreme performance of the new combination of engine and airframe was all too obvious and the Mustang was subsequently built in many versions (and with variations in appearance) to become a key element in winning the air war in Europe. The Mustang also went on to see service in the Korean War of 1950-53 and in many other air arms, and it put North American on the map as a major player in the development of top-quality fighter aircraft, a position that it held right through the 1950s. After the war a version was also proposed with forward-swept wings.

P-51A data

Span	37ft 0in (11.28m)
Length	32ft 3in (9.83m)
Wing area	233sq ft (21.67sq m)
Gross weight	8,600lb (3,901kg)
Maximum take-off weight	9,000lb (4,082kg)
Powerplant	one 1,200hp (895kW) Allison V-1710-81
Armament	four 0.50in (12.70mm) machine guns, 1,000lb (454kg) bombs
Maximum speed	390mph (628km/h) at 20,000ft (6,096m)
Service ceiling	31,350ft (9,555m)
Range	350 miles (563km)

P-51B data

Dimensions as P-51A	
Gross weight	9,800lb (4,445kg)
Maximum take-off weight	11,800lb (5,352kg)
Powerplant	one 1,380hp (1,029kW) Packard Merlin V-1650-3
Armament	four 0.50in (12.70mm) machine guns, 2,000lb (907kg) bombs
Maximum speed	440mph (708km/h) at 30,000ft (9,144m)
Service ceiling	42,000ft (12,802m)

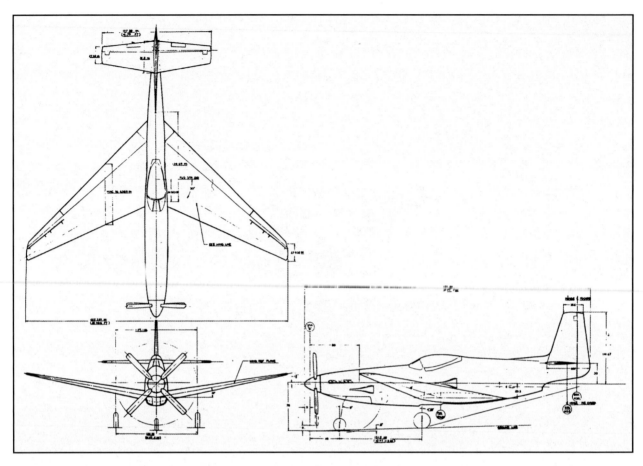

ABOVE A drawing showing the forward-swept-wing Mustang. This design had a span of 35ft 4in (10.77m), a length of 37ft 7in (11.45m), a gross wing area of 250sq ft (23.25sq m) and a gross weight of 11,100lb (5,035kg).

LEFT The original manufacturer's model of the FSW Mustang.
George Cox

ABOVE A mock-up of the Bell XP-59. Note the weapon positions – three machine guns in the boom noses, and a cannon to each side of the fuselage nose. *Jay Miller*

Bell Model 16/XP-52/ Model 20/XP-59

Numerous sources have indicated that the Bell Model 16 twin-boom design with pusher propeller was submitted to the above-mentioned R40-C but, despite showing a similar configuration to the Vultee offering, original documents indicate that this was not the case. The Model 16 was a separate project, work on which began in 1940

XP-52 data

Span	35ft 0in (10.67m)
Length	34ft 0in (10.36m)
Wing area	233sq ft (21.67sq m)
Gross weight	8,750lb (3,969kg)
Powerplant	one 1,250hp (932kW) Continental XIV-1430-5
Armament	six 0.50in (12.70mm) machine guns, two 20mm cannon.
Maximum speed (estimated)	425mph (684km/h) at 19,500ft (5,944m)
Service ceiling	40,000ft (12,192m)
Maximum range	960 miles (1,545km)

XP-59 data

Span	40ft 0in (12.19m)
Length	37ft 3in (11.35m)
Wing area	286sq ft (26.60sq m)
Gross weight	10,463lb (4,746kg)
Powerplant	one 2,000hp (1,491kW) P&W Double Wasp R-2800-23
Armament	as XP-52
Maximum speed (estimated)	450mph (724km/h) at 22,000ft (6,706m)
Service ceiling	38,000ft (11,582m)
Range	850 miles (1,368km)

with a contract for two prototypes placed in October, one to be powered by a Continental V-1430 (at the time an experimental engine then under development) and the other by an R-2800 from Pratt & Whitney. The design was quite handsome with a slightly swept wing, a large nose air intake and heavy glazing on the cockpit, but by the end of October the Continental version had been dropped while the P&W-powered aircraft was to be continued as the Model 20/XP-59. Again two prototypes were ordered (in February 1941), but in due course priority passed to other types and the project was finally abandoned in November 1942. The XP-59A designation was subsequently applied to America's first jet fighter programme (see Chapter Nine).

XP-53 data

Span	41ft 5in (12.62m)
Length	35ft 3in (10.74m)
Wing area	275sq ft (25.575sq m)
Gross weight	9,975lb (4,525kg)
Powerplant	one 1,600hp (1,193kW) Continental XIV-1430-3
Armament	eight 0.50in (12.70mm) machine guns
Maximum speed (estimated)	430mph (692km/h) at 18,000ft (5,486m)
Service ceiling	30,500ft (9,296m)

Curtiss XP-53

A further development of the XP-46, the Curtiss XP-53 was to have a laminar flow wing and one Continental XIV-1430-3, but retaining other elements of the earlier aircraft. A prototype was planned as the XP-53, but on 1 October 1940 the Army Air Corps asked if a Packard V-1650-1 Merlin could go into a second machine, so two airframes were ordered later that month. However, work on the Continental engine was slow and in addition it was soon clear that the XP-53 would not provide the performance originally hoped for. The first airframe was subsequently used as a static test specimen while the second (Merlin) aircraft received the new designation XP-60.

Curtiss XP-60 Series

The Curtiss XP-60 was started as a structural and aerodynamic study of a low-drag laminar flow aerofoil on a standard P-40D airframe with a Packard V-1650-1 engine. The XP-53 above was, apart from the powerplant, structurally identical to the first XP-60 from a point aft of the firewall. However, the parties involved (manufacturer and user) became interested in the type's production possibilities and it was

ABOVE **An air-to-air photo of the Curtiss XP-60.** *NARA II via Alan Griffith*

eventually turned into a completely new aircraft, designed to take either an Allison, Continental or Chrysler engine. Using the low-drag wing actually brought considerable delay to the project, but the XP-60's development did provide the solution to a current problem of adequate aileron control coupled with a low-drag aerofoil. In fact, Curtiss succeeded in applying the sealed-gap type of aileron to the XP-60, which resulted in unusually good aileron control and low stick forces throughout the flight range, a development that would of course now be available to all manufacturers of fighter-type

aeroplanes. The sole XP-60 performed its first flight on 18 September 1941, but suffered problems' and exhibited a shortfall in performance.

To begin with three further XP-60 versions were planned, the A, B and C. The first had a 1,425hp (1,063kW) Allison V-1710-75 engine fitted with a General Electric turbo-supercharger, the second the Allison with a Wright turbo (the aircraft was not completed in this form and eventually became the XP-60E), and the third was held

back for the later installation of the 16-cylinder 2,300hp (1,715kW) Chrysler XV-2220 liquid-cooled engine (which was also dropped because the engine was too heavy). The XP-60A first flew on 11 November 1942, but it lacked performance and at one stage the Air Corps Pursuit Project Unit did not feel that any of these three types had much to offer and recommended their cancellation. However, with the engineering so advanced and any

BELOW **A left rear view of the Curtiss XP-60A taken on 14 October 1942.** *NARA II via Alan Griffith*

ABOVE The Curtiss XP-60C pictured during a test flight.
NARA II via Alan Griffith

RIGHT & OVERLEAF BOTTOM XP-60E in flight. Originally to receive Allison V-1710 and designated XP-60B, but fitted instead with R-2800 and re-designated. First flight May 26, 1943.
NARA II via Alan Griffith

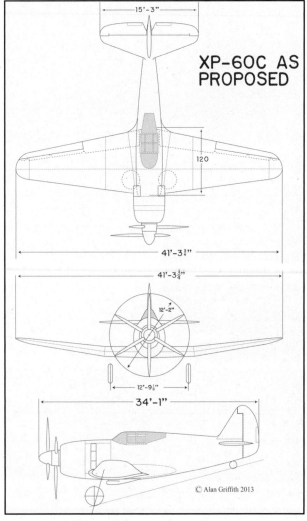

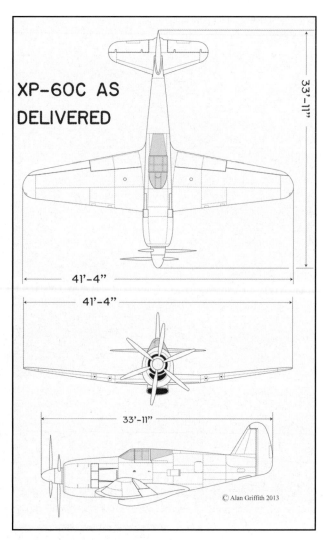

ABOVE A drawing of the XP-60C as it was first proposed, with a span of 41ft 3.75in (12.59m) and a length of 34ft 1in (10.39m).
Alan Griffith copyright

ABOVE A drawing of the XP-60C as delivered, with a span of 41ft 4in (12.60m) and a length of 33ft 11in (10.34m).
Alan Griffith copyright

termination saving only shop assembly time, this recommendation was never implemented. The P-60A was even considered for production, but that idea was killed when it became clear that the Republic P-47 was pretty well as good.

Then, during the second half of 1942, when pressure was exerted to find a new fast-climbing interceptor as a competitor to the Japanese Zero (Mitsubishi A6M) and the German Fw 190, it was decided to utilise the XP-60C for a quick

XP-60 data	
Span	41ft 5.25in (12.63m)
Length	33ft 4in (10.16m)
Wing area	275.4sq ft (25.61sq m)
Gross weight	9,350lb (4,241kg)
Powerplant	one 1,300hp (969kW) Packard RR V-1650-1 Merlin
Armament	eight 0.50in (12.70mm) machine guns (not fitted)
Maximum speed	380mph (611km/h) at 20,000ft (6,096m)
Service ceiling	29,000ft (8,839m)
Maximum range	995 miles (1,601km)

XP-60A data	
Span	41ft 4in (12.60m)
Length	33ft 11in (10.34m)
Gross weight	9,616lb (4,362kg)
Maximum take-off weight	10,160lb (4,609kg)
Powerplant	one 1,425hp (1,063kW) Allison V-1710-75
Armament	six 0.50in (12.70mm) machine guns
Maximum speed (estimated)	420mph (676km/h) at 25,000ft (7,620m)
Sea level rate of climb	2,560ft/min (780m/min)
Service ceiling	32,500ft (9,906m)
Range	375 miles (603km)

XP-60C data	
Span	41ft 4in (12.60m)
Length	33ft 8in (10.26m)
Gross weight	10,525lb (4,774kg)
Maximum take-off weight	11,835lb (5,368kg)
Powerplant	one 2,000hp (1,491kW) P&W R-2800-53
Armament	four 0.50in (12.70mm) machine guns
Maximum speed	324mph (km/h) at sea level, 414mph (666km/h) at 20,350ft (6,203m)
Sea level rate of climb	3,890ft/min (1,186m/min)
Service ceiling	35,000ft (10,668m)
Range	315 miles (507km)

installation of the two-stage 2,000hp (1,491kW) R-2800 engine. This aircraft, at a gross weight of 10,000lb (4,536kg) and with 'War Emergency' engine ratings, was expected to have a high speed of 430mph (692km/h) at 22,000ft (6,706m) and a rate of climb of 4,600ft/min (1,402m/min) at sea level. As such it would be a companion to the North American P-51B and the Republic XP-63 as a possible immediate answer to the Director of Pursuit's urgent plea for a fast-climbing interceptor. The XP-60C first flew on 27 January 1943. In due course the original XP-60 was fitted with a 1,350hp (1,007kW) Packard Merlin 61 as the XP-60D, while the XP-60E with a P&W R-2800-10 flew on 26 May 1943, and there was one YP-60E (taken from an order for twenty-six machines) with a bubble canopy. Despite plans in October 1941 for a large production order, these prototypes were to be the only examples to fly.

XP-63A data	
Span	38ft 4in (11.68m)
Length	32ft 8in (9.96m)
Wing area	248sq ft (23.06sq m)
Gross weight	7,525lb (3,413kg)
Maximum take-off weight	10,000lb (4,536kg)
Powerplant	one 1,325hp (988kW) Allison V-1710-47
Armament	two 0.50in (12.70mm) machine guns, one 37mm cannon

P-63A data	
Maximum speed	410mph (km/h) at 25,000ft (7,620m)
Service ceiling	43,000ft (13,106m)
Range	450 miles (724km)

Bell P-63 Kingcobra

The Bell XP-63 prototype was first designed to provide a drastic improvement over the standard P-39, and it embodied a low-drag aerofoil, extra fuel and numerous other improvements. The prototype first became airborne on 7 December 1942, and in due course the P-63 Kingcobra was successfully put into production in large numbers as a fighter-bomber.

Vultee P-66 Vanguard

In the late 1930s Vultee proposed the idea of producing four different aircraft types that would have a common set of wings, aft fuselages and tail assemblies – a single-seat fighter, a basic combat trainer, an advanced trainer, and a basic trainer. The P-66 fighter version first flew on 8 September 1939, and 144 were ordered by Sweden, although these eventually served with the USAAF and China.

P-66 data	
Span	36ft 0in (10.97m)
Length	28ft 4in (8.63m)
Wing area	197sq ft (18.32sq m)
Maximum take-off weight	7,384lb (3,349kg)
Powerplant	one 1,200hp (895kW) P&W R-1830-33
Armament	two 0.30in (7.62mm) and four 0.50in (12.70mm) machine guns
Maximum speed	340mph (547km/h) at 15,100ft (4,602m)
Absolute ceiling	29,750ft (9,068m)

BELOW An example of the P-63A-1-BE variant of the Bell Kingcobra, serial 42-68871.

General Motors/Fisher P-75 Eagle

ABOVE A photo taken on the ground of the original Fisher XP-75 Eagle prototype 43-46950. *Greater St Louis Air & Space Museum*

The Fisher XP-75 was an attempt to solve the problems incidental to the installation of an Allison V-3420 engine in a pursuit aircraft. The V-3420 was effectively two V-1710 units mated to a common crankcase, which at that time offered an excellent power-to-

weight ratio. It was also selected for the Lockheed XP-58 fighter and Boeing XB-39 bomber reviewed elsewhere, but none of these types went into service, so only about 150 engines were to be manufactured. In fact, the Air Corps Experimental Engineering Section had

previously tried to interest several of the pursuit aircraft manufacturers in an aeroplane mounting the V-3420, but at the time none of them showed any interest, saying in effect that it was not a pursuit engine and would never be of use as such. However, when former

BELOW the original Fisher XP-75 Eagle prototype 43-46950. *Greater St Louis Air & Space Museum*

**ABOVE A similar view for comparison of
XP-75A prototype 44-32162.**
Greater St Louis Air & Space Museum
**LEFT A splendid image of
P-75A 44-44550 in the air.**
Greater St Louis Air & Space Museum

XP-75 data	
Span	49ft 1in (14.96m)
Length	41ft 6in (12.65m)
Wing area	342sq ft (31.81sq m)
Gross weight	13,807lb (6,263kg)
Maximum take-off weight	18,210lb (8,260kg)
Powerplant	one 2,600hp (1,939kW) Allison V-3420-19
Armament	ten 0.50in (12.70mm) machine guns
Maximum speed	418mph (673km/h) at 21,600ft (6,584m)
Sea level rate of climb	c4,200ft/min (1,280m/min)
Maximum range	3,500 miles (5,632km)

Curtiss designer Donovan Berlin joined Fisher during 1942 (Berlin had been responsible for the P-40 and XP-55) he made some preliminary studies showing that a fighter could be built with an excellent ground-level rate of climb and a gross weight of between 12,000lb and 12,500lb (5,443kg and 5,670kg). Through Berlin's considerable drive, the XP-75 programme began to move forward rapidly, utilising parts of existing aircraft types to the maximum extent in order to get the first machine flying within the required deadline date of six months. Initially the airframe would use P-51 outer wing panels, a Vought F4U Corsair undercarriage and the empennage from a Douglas SBD Navy attack aircraft.

The first XP-75 prototype flew on 17 November 1943, but there were many development problems and plans for a 2,500-aircraft mass-production programme had to be put on hold. A considerable amount of redesign was undertaken, the updated aircraft was redesignated XP-75A, and the first example flew in February 1944, but delays, cost overruns and other problems ensured that only thirteen XP-75s and production P-75As were ever completed.

Tornado-engined Fighters

In 1940 the immensely powerful and quite gigantic six-row forty-two-cylinder turbo-supercharged Wright R-2160 radial engine was first proposed, which in due course would be selected for several fighter designs. For convenience most of them are grouped here, but none would fly (the use of the engine by Hughes is covered in the next chapter). The R-2160, which was named Tornado, was in fact a liquid-cooled radial engine and its power output at take-off was estimated to be 2,350hp (1,752kW). Its cylinders were arranged in six radial banks to provide a small overall engine diameter that would enable aircraft manufacturers to design fuselages with small cross-section areas. The Tornado project would end without any examples having flown, and that of course also killed the projects that had been designed to use it.

Lockheed L-131

The two-seat Lockheed L-131 pursuit design was drawn in 1941 and presented a rather clean and sleek aeroplane. Company reports indicate that the L-131's weight estimates were calculated using the structure, equipment and fittings used in the firm's XF-49 prototype variant of the P-38 Lightning (see Chapter Two). The powerplant was

RIGHT Lockheed L-131 (1941).
Peter Clukey

ABOVE The first P-75A, 44-44549, is shown here after having received the fin extension and also small tip finlets. *Greater St Louis Air & Space Museum*

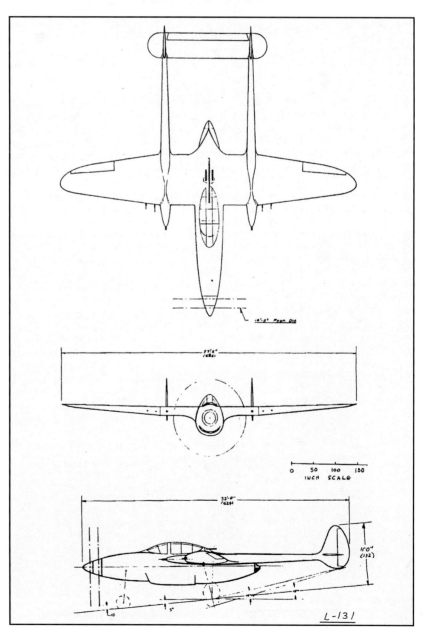

L-131 data

Span	57ft 2in (17.42m)
Length	52ft 0in (15.85m)
Gross take-off weight	20,000lb (9,072kg)
Powerplant	one 2,350hp (1,752kW) Wright R-2160
Armament	eight guns, four wing-mounted, another in 'nose' of each boom, and two more facing rearwards
Maximum speed at gross take-off weight	326mph (525km/h) at sea level, 418mph (673km/h) at 25,000ft (7,620m)
Sea level rate of climb	2,045ft/min (623m/min)
Absolute ceiling	37,880ft (11,546m)

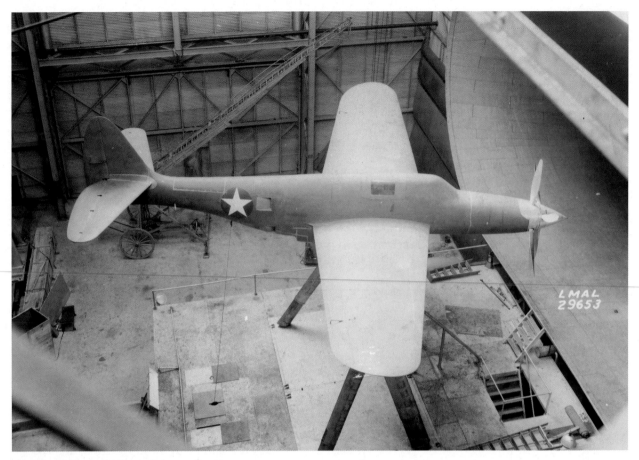

ABOVE & BELOW A three-quarter-scale model of the Republic XP-69 undergoes preparation for wind tunnel testing. *Langley Memorial Aeronautical Laboratory via Griffith*

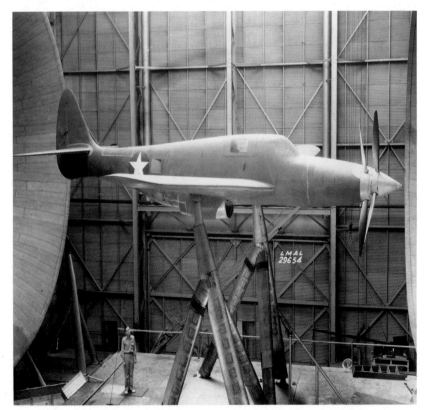

a single Tornado fed by a chin intake and driving a 14ft 0in (4.27m)-diameter contra-rotating propeller, and the armament included four wing-mounted guns, another in the 'nose' of each boom, and two more facing rearwards at the back of the cockpit canopy.

Republic AP-18/XP-69

The principal reason for proceeding with the development of the XP-69 project was to obtain a pursuit fighter as soon as possible designed around the Wright Tornado, which at the time of negotiation was the latest and most highly rated power unit to be made available for fighter-type aeroplanes. A secondary element was to acquire a fighter equipped with a pressure cabin that could fly at high altitude to intercept enemy bombers flying at such heights.

In July 1941 Republic submitted two proposals to Material Command for high-altitude fighters, the AP-18 around the Wright Tornado and the AP-19 to be built around the P&W Wasp Major (which some time later became the XP-72

– see below). The Tornado aircraft was considered to be the most logical choice to procure first, since the engine was expected to be available earlier. Republic submitted its proposals for building two experimental prototypes in September, an order was placed in December, and the type was assigned the designation XP-69. It was to have a Wright R-2160-3 fitted with two 13ft 8.5in (4.18m) three-blade counter-rotating propellers and the engine was to be mounted in the fuselage to the rear of the cockpit and connected to the propeller by a long extension shaft. This aircraft had an all-metal, stressed-skin, full cantilever wing of the laminar flow type, which was to be fitted with split flaps having 40° of travel. The wing consisted of a centre section and two panels with detachable tips, and the ailerons were of the NACA sealed-gap type; the left-hand one was provided with a trim tab, while both had a balance tab. The fuselage was of all-metal semi-monocoque construction composed of transverse bulkheads and continuous longitudinal stringers. The guns were all mounted in the wings outside the propeller disc, and the pressurised cockpit was designed to maintain a cabin pressure altitude of 10,000ft (3,048m) within the altitude range of 10,000ft to 35,000ft (3,048m to 10,668m).

By November 1942 this heavy high-altitude fighter remained the only aircraft of its type under development around the Tornado, although its gross weight was already in the region of 18,000lb (8,165kg). Nevertheless, the

Air Corps Experimental Engineering Section believed that this end of the weight scale should be adequately explored, just as it was trying to explore the other end of the scale of extreme lightness and low horsepower with the Bell XP-77 (see below). The mock-up was examined in June 1942 and building of the first prototype got under way during November, but the priority given to the XP-69 project was subsequently cut back so that Republic could handle its substantial wartime orders. This eventually resulted in work on the programme being discontinued before the prototype had flown, and the project was finally cancelled in May 1943.

Vultee V-84/XP-68

The XP-68 was to be a version of the Vultee XP-54 kitted out with a Tornado, which in fact meant that the XP-68 fighter itself was often given the same name. This short-lived programme was cancelled on 22 November 1941. Little data is available.

Ranger-engined Fighters

A relatively small engine that featured briefly in fighter design was the V-770 from the Ranger Engine Division of Fairchild. This was under development from 1931 and there were development problems, but an advanced version produced in 1941 went into the Fairchild AT-21 Gunner training aircraft, and was selected for the lightweight Douglas XP-48 mentioned above, and the Bell XP-77.

Bell XP-77

A project first given the go-ahead in May 1942, the Bell XP-77 was to be the ultimate in lightweight, small interceptor aircraft, and to reduce the pressure on industry and its supply of raw materials it was to be assembled using non-strategic materials; in fact, it was to be made primarily from wood. The Air Corps's engineering staff, however, were by November 1942 not showing much enthusiasm for the type since there were so many problems involved in the development of the Ranger engine, with its Szydlowski-Planiol supercharger, which was to provide the required horsepower at 25,000ft or 30,000ft (7,620m or 9,144m). In fact, a successful development was necessary to make the altitude performance of the XP-77 of any value. Designer Robert Woods put a lot of drive behind the project and it did offer an answer to General Arnold's frequently voiced desires for a really lightweight, simple and cheap interceptor. Some in the Air Corps also felt that it could make an excellent pursuit training aircraft, since it would be much cheaper to produce than standard pursuit types.

After long delays the first prototype made it into the air on 1 April 1944. However, by the time of this flight the supply of strategic materials such as aluminium alloys had become more secure, and the two examples completed were now really only of

BELOW The Bell XP-77 prototype.
Gerald Balzer

XP-69 data	
(Republic estimates, September 1942)	
Span	51ft 8.4in (15.76m)
Length	51ft 6.3in (15.70m)
Wing area	505sq ft (46.965sq m)
Gross weight	18,655lb (8,462kg)
Maximum take-off weight	26,164lb (11,868kg)
Powerplant	one 2,500hp (1,864kW) Wright R-2160-3
Armament	four 0.50in (12.7mm) machine guns, two 37mm cannon
Maximum speed (estimated)	450mph (724km/h) at 35,000ft (10,668m)
Service ceiling	48,900ft (14,905m)
Maximum range	1,800 miles (2,896km)

ABOVE The Bell XP-77 prototype. *Gerald Balzer*

BELOW The XP-77's lack of size is shown splendidly in this view of the aircraft parked between a B-25 and an A-20. *Gerald Balzer*

value for acquiring technical data. One of them was lost in a crash, overall the airframe proved to be overweight, the engine was delayed, meaning that an

XV-770-6 had to be installed, which did not have a supercharger, and the lack of power from the Ranger ensured that the aircraft was down on speed (original estimates had indicated 410mph/660km/h at 27,000ft/8,230m). There were no further examples, the original order for twenty-five having been cut back.

Fairchild Model 85

Rather later in timescale than the XP-77, Fairchild's Model 85 was prepared in May 1944 and was to be powered by two Ranger SGV-770-D-4B engines housed in individual wing nacelles. The problems of classifying and grouping together the fighters covered in this book were not helped by the Model 85, because here was a twin-engine naval fighter with folding wings

and an arrestor hook, but it seemed worthwhile to put the Ranger-powered pursuits together since the Model 85 did not appear to be part of a naval fighter competition. In plan view, the 85 resembled the Grumman F7F Tigercat described later, with a nicely tapered wing and a slim fuselage. The upper nose housed four machine guns, the lower nose two more, the wings folded just outboard of the engine nacelles, and there was a tricycle undercarriage. The engines had three-blade propellers 9ft 6in (2.90m) in diameter, and this neat design looks quite substantial until one notes just how large the cockpit canopy is in relation to the airframe. No weight or performance estimates are available for the Model 85.

XP-77 data	
Span	27ft 6in (8.38m)
Length	22ft 10in (6.96m)
Wing area	100sq ft (9.30sq m)
Gross weight	3,583lb (1,625kg)
Maximum take-off weight	4,028lb (1,827kg)
Powerplant	one 520hp (388kW) Ranger XV-770-6
Armament	two 0.50in (12.70mm) machine guns, one 20mm cannon, 300lb (136kg) bombs
Maximum speed	330mph (531km/h) at 4,000ft (1,219m)
Sea level rate of climb	c3,600ft/min (1,097m/min)
Service ceiling	30,100ft (9,174m)
Maximum range	550 miles (885km)

The Culmination of USAAF Piston Fighter Development

The following pair of prototypes represented pretty well the last gasp of piston fighter technology for the USAAF. Although neither entered production, each for its time was a highly sophisticated aeroplane.

Curtiss XP-62

In January 1941 an Army Air Corps requirement was raised for a powerful high-altitude interceptor designed around the new two-row, eighteen-cylinder Wright R-3350-17 Duplex Cyclone air-cooled radial engine, and Curtiss proposed a design on 29 April for which two prototypes were subsequently ordered as the XP-62 and XP-62A respectively. Curtiss had to provide the new fighter with a guaranteed maximum speed of 468mph (753kmh) at 27,000ft (8,230m) (during August this figure was reduced to 448mph/721kmh), and it was to be armed with either eight 20mm cannon or twelve 0.50in (12.70mm) machine guns. The mock-up was inspected during the following December, then on 1 January 1942 recommendations were made to cut the loaded weight from 15,568lb (7,062kg) to 14,000lb (6,350kg) by taking out four cannon, revising the airframe structure and removing some equipment (the prototype would have a six-blade contra-rotating propeller). A contract for 100 P-62s was cleared on 25 May 1942, but on 27 July this was dropped after it was made clear that production of the new fighter would get in the way of deliveries of P-47G Thunderbolts (which were also under contract from Curtiss), while the R-3350 units would be needed for other types. On 21 September 1943 the second prototype, the XP-62A, was also cancelled.

In general there was little enthusiasm for the XP-62 at the Experimental Engineering Section at Wright Field, the type having been 'sold' on the basis of its twelve 0.50in

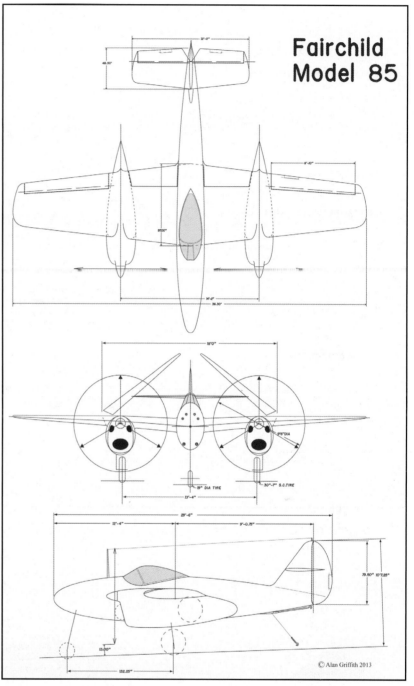

Fairchild Model 85

© Alan Griffith 2013

(12.70mm) machine guns and 468mph (753km/h) speed using turbo-superchargers and a pressure cabin. Once the general need for high rate of climb began to dominate proceedings in the second half of 1942, the XP-62's future looked bleak – even the manufacturer lost interest after the production contract had been cancelled. Nevertheless, the project did present Curtiss with an opportunity to deal with the problems of pressure

ABOVE Fairchild Model 85 (16.5.44).
Alan Griffith copyright

Model 85 data	
Span	36ft 3.5in (11.06m); folded 18ft 0in (5.49m)
Length	29ft 6in (8.99m)
Wing area	220sq ft (20.46sq m)
Powerplant	two 520hp (388kW) Allison XV-770
Armament	six machine guns

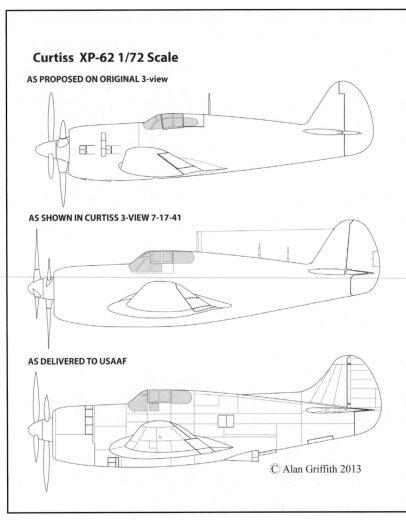

Curtiss XP-62 1/72 Scale

AS PROPOSED ON ORIGINAL 3-view

AS SHOWN IN CURTISS 3-VIEW 7-17-41

AS DELIVERED TO USAAF

© Alan Griffith 2013

LEFT Comparison side angle views of the Curtiss XP-62 as first proposed, as presented in a Curtiss document dated 17.7.41, and as built in prototype form. *Alan Griffith copyright*

cabins and low-drag aerofoils, and it was the first attempt to use the R-3350 engine in a pursuit aircraft coupled with a dual-rotation tractor propeller.

However, there were delays with the pressure cabin and the modifications that also had to be made to the engine, the consequence of which was that the prototype did not get airborne until 21 July 1943; indeed, the cabin was not in place for the first sortie and for the early limited flight-testing completed up until February 1944. Work then began on installing the pressure cabin for general trials work, but it was never completed and the prototype never flew again, being scrapped in September 1945. Other work at Curtiss received higher priority while the need for this type of pursuit fighter died away. Besides the XP-62, the R-3350 (one of the most powerful radial piston

BELOW The Curtiss XP-62 prototype pictured on 10 August 1943. *NARA II via Griffith*

XP-62 data

Span	53ft 7.75in (16.35m)
Length	39ft 6in (12.04m)
Wing area	420sq ft (39.06sq m)
Loaded weight	14,660lb (6,650kg)
Maximum take-off weight	16,651lb (7,553kg)
Powerplant	one 2,250hp (1,678kW) Wright R-3350-17
Armament	four 20mm cannon
Maximum speed	448mph (721km/h) at 27,000ft (8,230m)
Service ceiling	35,700ft (10,881m)
Normal range	900 miles (1,448km)

engines to be developed in the United States) also found its way onto all of the contenders in the B-29/B-32 bomber competition, the Curtiss XBTC-2 and Douglas BTD and AD attack types, the Curtiss XF14C naval fighter prototype, and the Lockheed Neptune patrol machine. The XP-62 itself did not complete sufficient flying to provide a full set of maximum performance data and the figures quoted in the accompanying table are estimates.

Republic AP-19/XP-72

The one-off Republic XP-72 was originally designed to operate as a long-range, high-altitude, high-speed fighter, the P-47 Thunderbolt airframe being big enough to handle virtually any reciprocating engine with relatively few changes to the overall structure. In late April 1942 Republic finished a redesign of the P-47B variant fitted with the R-3350-23, but to the authors' knowledge no part of this design was committed to metal as the Wright R-3350 Duplex Cyclone was not only trouble-prone but, as noted above, the production run was predominantly directed towards the B-29 and B-32 long-range bombers discussed later in the book.

In the meantime Pratt & Whitney had produced what would prove to be the final strictly reciprocating major engine to be used by the US military before it moved on to turboprops and jet engines, the massive four-row, twenty-eight-cylinder turbo-supercharged R-4360 Wasp Major. Design work on the R-4360 was authorized on 11 November 1940,

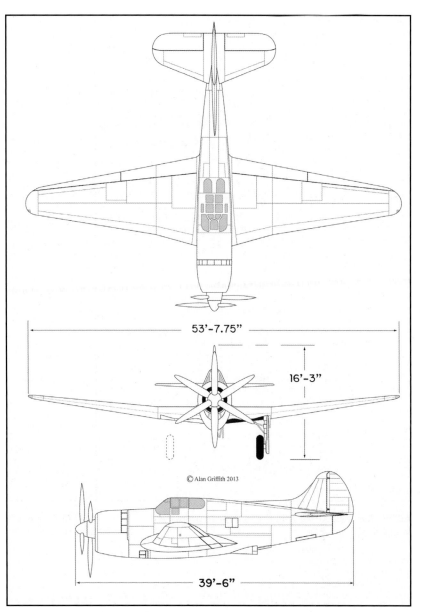

© Alan Griffith 2013

ABOVE A drawing showing the Curtiss XP-62 as delivered. *Alan Griffith copyright*
BELOW The Curtiss XP-62 prototype pictured 18 November 1943. *NARA II via Griffith*

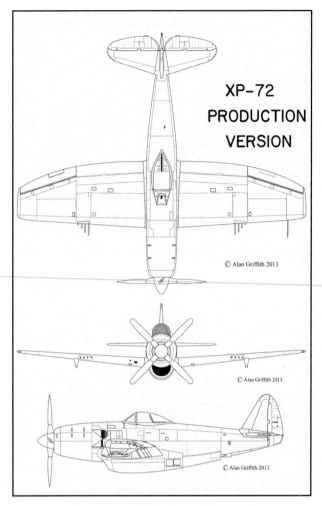

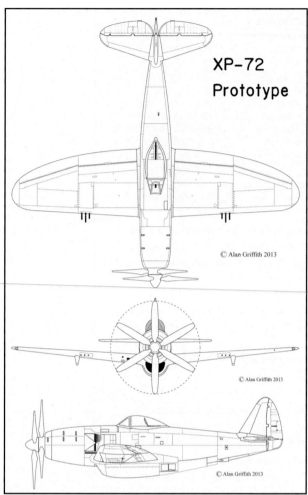

ABOVE Republic XP-72 with the four-blade propeller.
Alan Griffith copyright

ABOVE Republic XP-72 with the six-blade contra-rotating propeller. *Alan Griffith copyright*

ABOVE It was the second XP-72, 43-6599, that flew with the contra-rotating propeller. *Alan Griffith*

with the first example running on 28 April 1941. In 1943 ten of these engines were provided as experimental models for prototype aircraft, and the types relevant to this book that were to be powered by the R-4360 included the Boeing XF8B and Goodyear F2G naval

OPPOSITE BOTTOM The first prototype of the Republic XP-72 'Superbolt' carried the serial 43-6598.
NARA II via Griffith

fighters, the Northrop B-35 and Convair B-36 bombers, Curtiss XBTC, Douglas TB2D and Martin AM Mauler Navy attack aircraft, Martin's P4M Mercator patrol plane, Vultee's XA-41, and the Hughes XF-11.

Republic's AP-19 design was in essence a P-47 airframe mated to the new engine, and two prototypes were ordered in June 1943. It had a close-fitted engine cowling and used a version of the R-4360, which featured a remote-mounted, engine-driven auxiliary stage

supercharger behind the cockpit that was run by a long shaft passing from the engine back to the supercharger through the cockpit on the floor between the pilot's legs (it was a leaking seal on this shaft that sprayed hot oil on to test pilot Ken Jernstedt and brought about a forced landing that damaged the aircraft). The supercharger air inlet was placed in the wing root.

The XP-72 was known as the 'Super Thunderbolt' and it experienced relatively few delays. At the start it had a conventional four-blade propeller, but the second prototype received an Aero Products six-blade contra-rotating prop, while the type's excellent potential performance resulted in a contract for 100 P-72s. However, by the time the type made its first flight on 2 February 1944 versions of the P-47 and P-51 were already successfully flying operations at high altitude from England to Berlin, and this had removed the need for another high-altitude propeller-driven fighter; consequently the P-72 production order was cancelled.

Quoting Alan Griffith's exclusive interview with Ken Jernstedt regarding his experiences flying the prototype, the original mission for the XP-72 was switched from high-altitude fighter to mid-altitude fighter and ground attack, with the particular intention of using the aeroplane's superior speed to chase and kill the V-1 flying bombs being sent towards London from enemy-occupied territory during the second half of 1944. Jernstedt also stated that the ultimate production version was to have the much-improved wings of the P-47N variant of the Thunderbolt. Prospective armament ran between six 0.50in (12.70mm) machine guns (three per wing) to four 37mm cannon (two per wing). Ken Jernstedt made no comments about the difference between having the counter-rotating propeller fitted as against the original four-blade arrangement, but did say that the XP-72 'was exceptionally fast'. Other reports indicate that the fighter was quite responsive to the controls and apparently 'a joy to fly'. The second machine first flew on 26 June 1944 and, officially, the XP-72's top speed was given as 490mph (788km/h) at 25,000ft (7,620m), both prototypes achieving this figure; the projected top speed was apparently in excess of 500mph (805km/h). Forever a 'what-if' aeroplane, the XP-72 was full of unrealised promise and potential and in the end was a victim of the pace of developments in fighter design, with the turbojet becoming the primary power source.

XP-72 data	
Span	40ft 11in (12.47m)
Length	36ft 7in (11.15m)
Wing area	300sq ft (27.90sq m)
Gross weight	14,414lb (6,538kg)
Maximum take-off weight	17,492lb (7,934kg)
Powerplant	one 3,450hp (2,573kW) P&W R-4360-13
Armament	six 0.50in (12.7mm) machine guns (production four 37mm cannon), two 1,000lb (454kg) bombs
Maximum speed	490mph (788km/h) at 25,000ft (7,620m)
Service ceiling	42,000ft (12,802m)
Range	1,200 miles (1,931km)

*

The XP-72 and also the Republic XP-47J version of the Thunderbolt offered a pretty phenomenal speed performance, and this was only approximately 40 years after the Wrights had made their first powered flight. Referred to earlier, the XP-47J was begun in late 1942 as a high-performance lightweight variant of the Thunderbolt, fitted with a tightly cowled P&W R-2800-57 engine and a lighter wing. In August 1944 the sole example flown achieved 505mph (813km/h) in level flight (or 507mph/816km/h depending on the source). In addition, the later versions of the North American P-51 offered speeds approaching the magic 500mph (805km/h) barrier, yet all of these types were near obsolete – the jet fighter with the huge potential speed and performance offered by its new source of power made them out of date almost immediately. These final piston designs were incredibly impressive beasts and as a group certainly deserve to receive more recognition than they have often been given. The arrival of the contra-rotating propeller to accommodate such powerful engines also represented the cutting edge technology of the day and was just one element in the design of what were very complex pieces of machinery.

What is striking is that Curtiss, at one time the master US fighter designer, does not have an aircraft that features in any list of 'ultimate' Army Air Corps fighters, the XP-62 perhaps coming the closest. In fact, its progressive loss of position as a leading producer of top-quality fighters is reflected in several of the situations recorded in this text. There were a number of reasons for this demise. For example, Curtiss had to produce the P-47G version of Republic's Thunderbolt, and making room for that production line was one of many influences behind the P-62's cancellation. As it turned out, the Curtiss plant experienced severe problems and delays in producing the P-47G, the examples of which were relegated to advanced flying training. Even if the P-47 contract helped sow the seeds of the company's decline, Curtiss had already lost a lot of its organisational capability by that time. While not wishing to produce anything that it had not originated, its own new designs were mainly different iterations of the original P-36 Hawk fighter of the mid-1930s. In fact, if one looks at virtually any Curtiss wartime fighter design (bar the XP-55) one can see elements of earlier aircraft – landing gear, wings, cockpit and rear fuselage/tail. At the end, the team seemed almost bereft of ideas for new piston-powered fighters, although in fairness many studies for jet fighters had still to come.

It is tempting to wonder, had Donovan R. Berlin stayed at Curtiss, whether the story would have turned out differently. Berlin was born in 1898 and joined Curtiss in 1934, his first big success being the P-36, and in 1940/41 he was appointed Chief Engineer and Head of Design at Curtiss-Wright. However, he left in December 1941 having been disappointed by the lack of official backing for a new development of the P-40. After working with Fisher, Berlin joined McDonnell Aircraft in 1947 and directed the design of several jet fighters before moving into the field of helicopters. His last fighter design for Curtiss was the very radical XP-55, and nothing much followed.

Single-engine USAAF Fighter Designs in Perspective

Looking back, decades later, it may seem excessive that so many new fighters were commissioned from the industry as experimental prototypes. In addition to the designs described here, many other adaptations and refinements of models already in production also took place. Indeed, in the autumn of 1942 there were assertions that the Air Corps had too many experimental models of both fighter and bomber, with the result that on 6 November Colonel F. O. Carroll, Chief of the Experimental Engineering Section, sent a memorandum to General Arthur W. Vanaman, Commanding General of the Air Corps Materiel Center at Wright Field, to clarify the situation.

Carroll explained that 'the only way we can be certain of having two or three really good experimental airplanes, which will be reduced to quantity production at the earliest possible date after completion of flight tests, is to "shop around" to the greatest extent possible with existing engineering facilities in order to be certain that all possible fields are covered.' Having assessed the experimental types currently under contract, Carroll added that 'a number of airplanes, which may never be reduced to quantity production, have contributed very materially to the orderly experimental development of better airplanes, and have hence assisted in our maintaining a favourable competitive position.' He closed by saying that they had 'in some instances tended to drag out existing types too long [and] the P-40 is the best example of this tendency. We should consider with extreme care the decision on just when to stop building one type and to place an improved type in production [but] certainly should not wait until the enemy forces our hand, as appears to be the case with the Fw 190.'

The single-engine fighter types in service at the start of the Second World War filled an important role, but the P-39 and P-40 were not up to the task of countering the best that the enemy had to offer. Fortunately the service was to acquire two outstanding, if very different, single-engine fighters in the P-47 Thunderbolt and P-51 Mustang. En route there was a bold design competition that resulted in three very unorthodox prototypes, the XP-54, XP-55 and XP-56, and overall it was a very fertile period for design thinking with several other designs reaching the prototype stage. The period covered also saw the first appearance of the jet fighter, as discussed in the final chapter. However, the last of the types described in this chapter represented the pinnacle of US piston fighter design. Fighters like the XP-72 offered an extraordinary improvement in performance over the P-39 and P-40 from just a few short years earlier, yet any potential that they offered was already being outstripped by that of the first generation of jet fighters, with more capable jet types following on before the end of the decade.

However, this is only part of the piston-engine fighter story. At the same time as these single-engine fighters were being developed there were equivalent programmes under way for twin-engine types. These form the subject matter for Chapter Two.

Chapter Two
USAAF Twin-Engine Fighters

Relatively few twin-engine fighters were built and flown during the period covered by this book, though three did enter service. Only a limited number of drawings for relevant unbuilt projects have come to light, so this chapter is largely a review of the types that reached flight-testing. However, the opportunity has been taken to include new background information on some of them, which has been taken from recently discovered original documents.

While the previous chapter highlighted America's pursuit of the 'ultimate' single-engine piston fighter, the

Army Air Corps does not appear to have pushed for the 'last word' in twin-piston fighters. There appears to be no equivalent, for example, of the British de Havilland Hornet (unless one considers the P-82, which was really an adaptation of an earlier design). A further interesting observation, applicable to both this and Chapter One, is that unlike many other countries the Army Air Corps did not look closely at turret fighters – aircraft that used a gun turret as a main part of their armoury – for daytime operations. The turret-armed Northrop P-61 was, of course, a night fighter.

ABOVE An air-to-air photo of the only Lockheed XP-58 prototype to achieve flight-testing.
Greater St Louis Air & Space Museum

New requirements – the P-38 Lightning

To complement the single-engine Specification X-609 covered in Chapter One, which resulted in the Bell P-39, there was also a design competition for a twin-engine high-altitude interceptor covered by X-608 issued in February 1937. According to a 2010 article on

Hughes aircraft, is it understood that Chance Vought, Consolidated, Hughes, Lockheed and Vultee were all invited to bid, with only Consolidated declining to take part. However, an older 1988 piece on the Vultee proposal below indicates that only Curtiss, Lockheed and Vultee were involved (see the Bibliography). Little concrete information can be found currently for any of the submissions apart from Lockheed and Vultee, although the Curtiss offering is thought to have been a development of that company's twin-engine A-18 attack aircraft of 1937 (which was itself a development of the YA-14 of 1935).

Lockheed Model 22

It is known that Lockheed's design team had looked at several layouts before selecting its final choice, apparently working on concepts for the best part of a year. The alternative single-seat twin-engine fighter arrangements to be examined had embraced a conventional fuselage with conventional wing-mounted engines and a twin tailplane, two more had their engines buried in the fuselage (in tandem to the rear of the cockpit) and employed geared shafts to drive propellers mounted on the wings (in either pusher or tractor configuration), another had fuselage-mounted engines placed side-by-side driving pusher propellers, and there were three twin-boom layouts. The first of these had its engines fore and aft in a central fuselage, there was another with engines in each boom with a cockpit offset in the port boom, and finally a design with a separate short fuselage that contained both the pilot and his armament. It was this final configuration that offered the most promise and formed Lockheed's submission to X-608. The Model 22 was to be armed with four machine guns and one 20mm, but no performance data has been found for the fighter as proposed.

Vultee P-1015

The Vultee P-1015 was a conventional twin-Allison-engine single-seat fighter design and had a wing-shape that was very reminiscent of the later British de Havilland Mosquito. The two turbo-supercharged V-1710-C7 units would each drive a three-blade 11ft 2½in (3.415m) tractor propeller, and the oil coolers and coolant radiators were placed in the wings. The fuselage was very slim, a conventional retractable tailwheel undercarriage was provided with the main gears going into the wing, and there were five guns in the nose – four 0.50in (12.70mm) machine guns and a 20mm cannon. The project had a span of 54ft 0in (16.46m) and a length of 40ft 11in (12.47m).

Vultee had 'great expectations' for this design after wind tunnel testing performed by the Guggenheim Aeronautical Laboratory at the California Institute of Technology at Pasadena had provided some very encouraging data. According to Jerry Vought, who attending the awarding of the X-608 contract, Curtiss had bid a

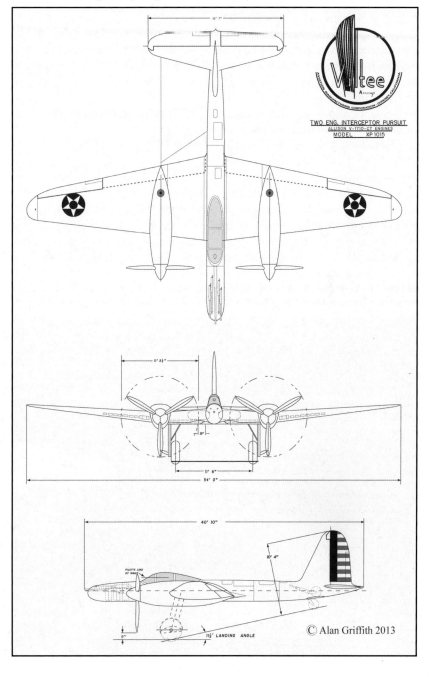

RIGHT Vultee V-35/XP-1015 (early 1937).
Alan Griffith copyright

cash figure for the fighter that was far too high (suggesting, therefore, that the firm did not want another new project on its hands), while Lockheed had bid lower than Vultee, and that of course had contributed to its win. Lockheed was announced as the winner on 23 June 1937.

Lockheed P-38 Lightning

Lockheed's successful design was given the designation XP-39 and named Lightning, and the prototype first flew on 27 January 1939. This was to be another aircraft whose progress was helped by orders from Britain and France. As has been commented already, it would become one of the best-known fighters of the Second World War, being manufactured in large numbers and serving in many theatres. Its performance also meant that in high-speed dives it suffered from the effects of compressibility – when the deflected airflow over part of the wing reaches supersonic speed, creating shockwaves and moving the centre of lift, affecting stability. A newly encountered phenomenon, this took a long time to cure. Thus, even before America had entered the war on 7 December 1941, the

XP-38 data	
Span	52ft 0in (15.85m)
Length	37ft 10in (11.53m)
Wing area	327.5sq ft (30.46sq m)
Gross weight	13,964lb (6,334kg)
Maximum take-off weight	15,416lb (6,993kg)
Powerplant	two 1,150hp (858kW) Allison V-1710-11/15
Armament	one 20mm cannon, four 0.30in (7.62mm) machine guns (not carried in prototype)
Maximum speed	413mph (665km/h) at 20,000ft (6,096m)
Service ceiling	38,000ft (11,582m)
Range	890 miles (1,432km)

future problems that were to be associated with jet-powered aircraft in the trans-sonic region had already begun to show themselves.

Two Engines from Hughes

Hughes D-2, D-3 and D-5

Hughes also tendered a design, possibly called the H-2, against X-608, but this was rejected and no information about it has been seen (in fact, there are suggestions that Hughes submitted a

single-engine fighter design to X-609 as well, which may have been called the H-1). However, the company went on to develop a small family of twin-engined aircraft that embraced fighter, bomber and reconnaissance types. Strictly speaking some of what follows probably belongs in the USAAF bomber and/or attack aircraft chapters, but it seems sensible to group them together here in a single section.

Work on the D-2 two-seat twin-engine fighter-bomber is thought to have started in early 1939, some official correspondence in fact describing it as an 'experimental bombardment airplane'. Progress was slow and the type's role was changed, while artist's renditions of the bomber (with a glass nose) were drawn in 1942. Two P&W R-2800-49 engines were to be installed until 2,350hp (1,752kW) Wright R-2160-3/5 Tornados became available, and in March 1941 the D-2 was reported as being a 'long range multi-gun fighter' with a normal weight of 27,500lb (12,474kg) and a tricycle undercarriage. By early 1942 the designation DX-2 was also being used for the aircraft, while D-2A appeared in documents from mid-1942. In March 1942 the aircraft was listed as a 'high-

BELOW The Lockheed P-38 Lightning was ordered in numbers by the RAF but only a few examples were delivered, all the remainder being retained for the USAAF. Serial AE979 was the second Lightning Mk I.

speed twin-engine, twin-boom, pressurised fighter' or interceptor, and either one or two crew could be carried. The definition of the D-2's primary role was cloudy to say the least.

In fact, only the one D-2 was built and when flown it was not described as a military aircraft because it had not been built to a military specification; perhaps it would be best to consider it as a demonstrator. In mid-1942 Material Division finally decided to purchase the airframe, and since that body at first considered it to be in the pursuit category it was designated XP-74 (other references state XP-73), although very quickly it was recognised that the machine might more accurately fall into the light bomber/attack category, and it then became the XA-37. The D-2 made its maiden flight on 20 June 1943 and in the air it performed poorly due to problems with high control forces. It was clear that the aircraft required substantial modifications, including a full redesign of the wings and a different airfoil section, but the airframe was to be destroyed by fire on 11 November 1944 having flown very few hours. Photographs of the complete aircraft are rarely seen.

In March 1942 there was much debate regarding the firm's ability to manufacture aircraft using the Duramold process. Hughes had purchased some rights to use this composite material, which was formed of birch ply impregnated with phenolic resin and laminated together in a mould under pressure and heat to provide a lightweight structural material. As such it offered some advantages over aluminium in terms of strength and weight, and most of the D-2 airframe was made in Duramold.

In August 1941 some 'military characteristics' for a Convoy Protector were released for an aircraft to be equipped with two four-gun turrets and capable of escorting bombers for distances of up to 2,000 miles (3,218km). In response Hughes produced the D-3, an airframe that

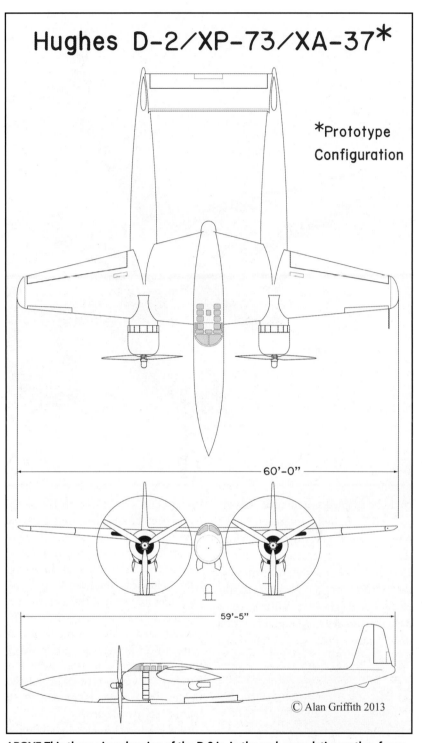

Hughes D-2/XP-73/XA-37*

***Prototype Configuration**

60'-0"

59'-5"

© Alan Griffith 2013

ABOVE This three-view drawing of the D-2 is, in the end, speculative as thus far no official Hughes Aircraft or USAAF three-views of the D-2 have been found by either author. However, both its layout and details are based upon existing reference materials, including dimensions found in various sources including patent drawings, photos of the prototype being assembled, original photos and drawings of the D-2 mock-up and assembly breakdown, Hughes three-view drawings of the D-5 in two different variations, and two known photographs of the prototype on the ground for detail and overall proportions. While the authors believe these drawings to be very close to the original aircraft, they must be viewed as speculative until original engineering drawings are located and thoroughly examined. *Alan Griffith copyright*

ABOVE Hughes D-2 artwork from 1942, showing the aircraft fitted with Wright Tornado engines. *NARA II via Buttler*

could be adapted as a bomber convoy-protector, fighter, interceptor and bomber convoy-destroyer, and which stayed under consideration during 1941 and 1942 (the timescale matches the XP-58 and XP-71 later in the chapter). Hughes submitted some design estimates to Material Division on 13 January 1942, which showed that

D-2 data	
Span	60ft 0in (18.29m)
Length	57ft 10in (17.62m)
Wing area	616sq ft (57.29sq m)
Gross weight	31,672lb (14,366kg)
Powerplant	two 2,000hp (1,491kW) P&W R-2800-49
Armament	none fitted, but at 22 April 1942 to be one 20mm cannon, four 0.50in (12.70mm) machine guns, all fixed, four 0.50in (12.70mm) machine guns in turrets
Maximum speed	433mph (697km/h) at 25,000ft (7,620m)
Service ceiling	36,000ft (10,973m)

the aircraft was indeed to be armed with a pair of four-gun turrets. Material Division replied that further study of the project was for the time being to be held in abeyance, although three days later Hughes followed up with proposals for two flight-test prototypes together with a static-test airframe. The aircraft was to be powered by two Allison V-3420 engines, and by March the four versions were listed as the D-3 bomber convoy-protector, D-3F fighter, D-3H interceptor and D-3R bomber convoy-destroyer.

The Hughes D-5 was a light bomber and bomber escort project development of the D-2, work on which was begun in early 1942. There were also some photo reconnaissance versions that would lead to the XF-11 below and, although planned from the beginning to be produced in Duramold, in due course the D-5's structure was switched to all-metal. Official documents show that the engineers at Wright Field

always felt that the Lockheed XP-58 (see below) would be a better choice than either the D-2 or D-5, but eventually support was forthcoming from Colonel Elliott Roosevelt (son of the US President) who stated that the D-2/D-5 was the only type to consider having in the reconnaissance role. In due course this project went ahead and was turned into the XF-11.

Hughes XF-11

The Hughes twin-engine story closes with the XF-11 two-seat high-speed reconnaissance aircraft developed from the D-5 and first flown with contra-rotating propellers in place on 7 July 1946. It crashed soon after taking off, but the second prototype was flown on 5 April 1947 and was subsequently passed to the Army Air Force, where it

ABOVE The Hughes D-2 prototype pictured during assembly. *NARA II via Griffith*

ABOVE & RIGHT These poor-quality photographs are thought to be the only images showing the (supposedly) complete Hughes D-2 prototype. *NARA II via Griffith*

XF-11 data	
Span	101ft 4in (30.89m)
Length	65ft 5in (19.94m)
Wing area	983sq ft (91.42sq m)
Loaded weight	47,500lb (21,546kg)
Maximum take-off weight	58,300lb (26,445kg)
Powerplant	two 3,000hp (2,237kW) P&W R-4360-31/37
Maximum speed	420mph (676km/h) at 30,000ft (9,144m)
Ceiling	48,000ft (14,630m)
Range	c5,000 miles (8,045km)

underwent evaluation fitted with single four-blade propellers; any plans for production were, however, abandoned. As an unarmed reconnaissance type the XF-11 really should not be here, but it has been included almost as a special case to round off the story, and it was a remarkable and very attractive aeroplane. In addition, an article by test pilot Lindell C. Hendrix (who flew the type) concluded that had the XF-11 gone into production it could have done so as an interceptor since it operated at altitudes that early jet aircraft had difficulty in reaching.

New Requirements – Advanced Configurations

In March 1939 Circular Proposal 39-775 and Specification XC-615 were raised for a twin-engine escort fighter

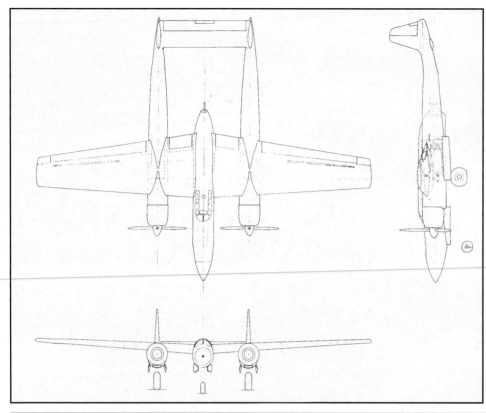

LEFT How the Hughes D-5
looked at 17 June 1943.
NARA II via Griffith
BELOW Manufacturer's
artwork for the D-5. Bombs
were to be carried in a bay
behind the forward
cockpit. Note the four-gun
rear turret.
NARA II via Griffith

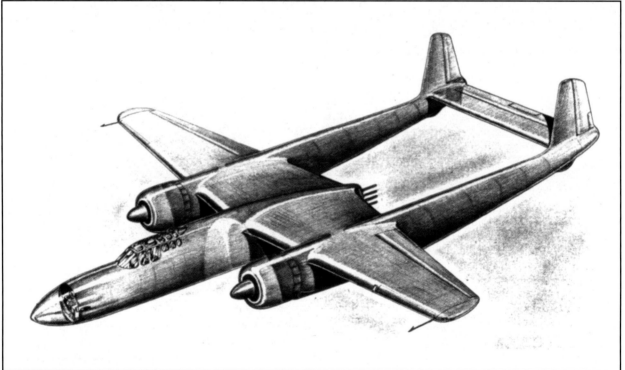

to be powered by a pair of Twin-Wasp engines and fitted with a conventional undercarriage. The competition was won by the Lockheed Model 222/Model 522/L-106/XP-49 and the Grumman G-41/G-45/XP-50, both developments of existing designs (a factor that had also formed part of the requirements), while Bellanca submitted its Model 33-220. The project lists provide little indication as to whether proposals were made by other manufacturers, although one source lists in all Bell, Brewster, Curtiss, Grumman, Lockheed and Vought. Neither of the winning prototypes, both ordered in November 1939, would enter production.

ABOVE The first Hughes XF-11 prototype fitted with contra-rotating propellers. *NARA II via Griffith*

BELOW The second XF-11, 44-70156, had four-blade propellers. *NARA II via Griffith*

Lockheed Model L-106/XP-49

ABOVE Views of the Lockheed XP-49. *Greater St Louis Air & Space Museum*

Lockheed's XP-49 made use of the Lightning's wing and fuselage but introduced new nacelles and booms for different engines, together with a pressurised cockpit. When the aircraft was first designed the objective was to use P&W X-1800 engines as substitutes for the Allisons (the estimated top speed here was 473mph/761km/h at 20,000ft/6,096m) or, for production machines, the Wright R-2160. The Continental XIV-1430 was then selected after P&W had dropped the X-1800, but the lower power rating of this engine (1,600hp/1,193kW as against

2,000hp/1,491kW for the X-1800) indicated that there could be a big drop in speed.

By early November 1942 the XP-49 had been listed in the experimental category by the Air Corps Experimental Engineering Section, but it was somewhat of a borderline case since it was really a direct 'improvement' of the standard P-38. The XP-49 was held back substantially by the troubles and delays experienced by the Continental engines; after extra horsepower had been made available to the P-38 itself by new versions of the Allison V-1710 engine,

which resulted in an enhanced performance, this alternative aircraft lost a good deal of its former attractiveness. In fact, it was now seen mainly as a test vehicle to get flight experience on the Continental power unit and to learn some of the problems associated with its installation. The XP-49 first flew on 14 November 1942 and flight-testing confirmed that its speed performance was indeed relatively poor. Despite having good manoeuvrability and handling, from an early stage the only XP-49 to be ordered was used purely as a testbed.

XP-49 data	
Span	52ft 0in (15.85m)
Length	40ft 1in (12.22m)
Wing area	327.5sq ft (30.46sq m)
Gross weight	19,948.5lb (9,049kg)
Maximum take-off weight	22,000lb (9,979kg)
Powerplant	two 1,540hp (1,148kW) Continental XIV-1430-13/15
Armament	two 20mm cannon, four 0.50in (12.70mm) machine guns
Maximum speed	347mph (558km/h) at sea level (one Lockheed report gives 372mph/599km/h at sea level), 406mph (653km/h) at 15,000ft (4,572m)
Sea level rate of climb	c3,200ft/min (1,000m/min)
Service ceiling	37,500ft (11,430m)
Range	680 miles (1,094km)

XP-50 data	
Span	42ft 0in (12.80m)
Length	31ft 11in (9.73m)
Wing area	303.5sq ft (28.23sq m)
Gross weight	11,990lb (5,439kg)
Maximum take-off weight	13,060lb (5,924kg)
Powerplant	two 1,200hp (895kW) Wright R-1820-67/69
Armament	two 20mm cannon, two 0.50in (12.70mm) machine guns
Maximum speed (estimated)	424mph (682km/h) at 25,000ft (7,620m)
Sea level rate of climb	c4,000ft/min (1,219m/min)
Service ceiling	40,000ft (12,192m)
Range	553 miles (890km)

Grumman Model G-46/XP-50

The Grumman XP-50 was a land-based version of the company's XF5F-1 naval fighter prototype first flown in April 1940 (see Chapter Six), and compared to the earlier machine it had a longer nose to house both the guns and the front wheel of its tricycle undercarriage. First flown on 18 February 1941, the only example ordered had achieved just 20 hours of flight time when on 14 May one of the engine turbo-superchargers exploded during a test flight and the airframe caught fire and crashed. This loss brought the XP-50 programme to an end.

Escort and Heavy Fighters

The rest of the twin-engine fighter programmes are grouped together. All of the following aircraft and designs fall into the 'medium' or 'heavy' category of fighter, again mostly to serve in the escort fighter role, which for almost all of the war was a much desired objective of the Army Air Corps and which seems to have run in two spells, first with the XP-58 and XP-71, then from autumn 1943 with the XP-81, XP-82 and XP-61E. And yet none of these aircraft appear to have been the result of a proper design competition, although the McDonnell XP-67 had begun its gestation as the Model 1

submitted to XC-622 as described in Chapter One. There was also the Grumman XP-65, an Army variant of the F7F Tigercat, which is reviewed in the relevant Navy fighter chapter.

Lockheed L-121/Model 20/XP-58 Chain Lightning

In its original conception the Lockheed XP-58 was seen as a high-altitude medium-range bomber escort fighter, but then Lockheed ran into compressibility troubles on its P-38 Lightning and the manufacturer became worried that similar difficulties might be experienced with the XP-58. In fact, Lockheed suggested that the engine's turbo-supercharger and its related equipment should be eliminated and that the XP-58 be redesigned as a low-altitude ground support aeroplane armed with a 75mm cannon. The Air Corps Experimental Engineering Section did agree to this, but then, as a result of a Conference held in Washington during the autumn of 1942, and the interjection of the Beech XA-38 attack aircraft (see Chapter Five), it was felt that the XP-58 in its high-altitude form represented an excellent immediate answer to the Air Corps's Pursuit Directorate's requirements for a bomber-destroyer type of aircraft. The later type was not conceived as one that would have to be employed in terminal velocity dives, so any troubles caused by

RIGHT & BELOW The Grumman XP-50 prototype. *Gerald Balzer*

compressibility should not be so serious. As a result of the Pursuit Board's recommendations, the Experimental Engineering Section went ahead with the procurement of two XP-58s in their original form as high-altitude aircraft. This was in spite of numerous attempts on the part of Lockheed and other parties to abandon the project.

The XP-58 was begun as a company-funded prototype, having been requested by the Air Corps in April 1940. The original L-121 proposal embraced both single- and twin-seat versions and, initially, the armament was to be four 37mm cannon mounted in the nose, together with defensive turrets. However, firing tests revealed that the trajectory of the 37mm shells saw them drop more quickly than any other type of weaponry and ammunition, which of course reduced the 37mm's effective range. Eventually, the combination of the 75mm cannon and two 0.50in (12.70mm) machine guns provided a solution. The original engine choice was the Continental IV-1430, but it subsequently became clear that this would not provide sufficient power, and a list of substitutes was worked through before in 1943 the Allison V-3420 became the favoured option. However, other factors, including the various changes of role, meant that the first and only XP-58, named Chain Lightning, did not become airborne until 6 June 1944, by which time it was no longer required. The only prototype completed was scrapped in 1946 after having accumulated only around 25 hours flying time.

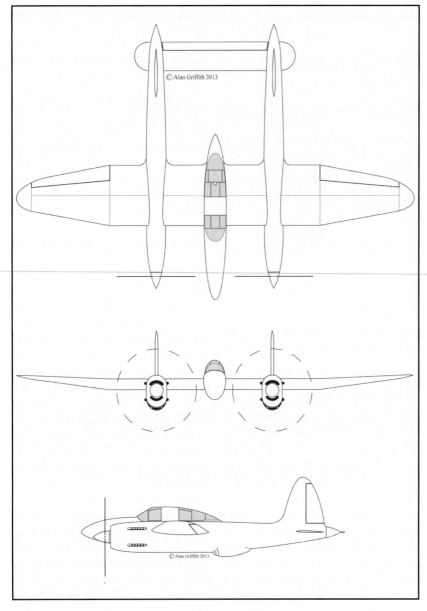

ABOVE An intermediate configuration for the Lockheed L-121/XP-58 design prior to the prototype's construction. *Alan Griffith copyright*

BELOW & OPPOSITE Images showing the Lockheed XP-58 prototype, which was quite a handsome aeroplane. *Greater St Louis Air & Space Museum*

XP-58 data	
Span	70ft 0in (21.34m)
Length	49ft 5.5in (15.08m)
Wing area	600sq ft (55.80sq m)
Gross weight	39,192lb (17,777kg)
Maximum take-off weight	43,000lb (19,505kg)
Powerplant	two 2,6000hp (1,939kW) Allison V-3420-11/13
Armament	four 37mm cannon, or one 75mm cannon plus four 0.50in (12.70mm) machine guns, 4,000lb (1,814kg) bombs.
Maximum speed at gross take-off weight	430mph (692km/h) at 20,000ft (6,096m)
Service ceiling	38,200ft (11,643m)
Sea level rate of climb	2,582ft/min (787m/min)
Range	1,250 miles (2,011km)

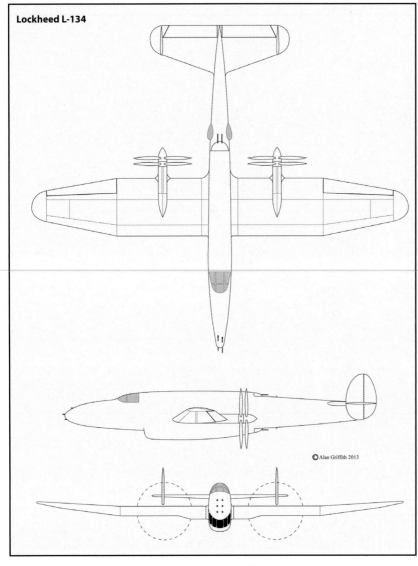

Lockheed L-134

© Alan Griffith 2013

ABOVE Lockheed L-134-3 project (1942). *Alan Griffith*

Lockheed L-134

Lockheed's two-seat L-134 project of 1942 was a redesign of the XP-58, which was in fact carried out while the XP-58 prototype was being built. The only known drawing to survive shows the L-134-3 variant, but Lockheed documents indicate that a canard version also existed. No dimensions are given, but the L-134-3 was a heavy machine and carried six guns in three pairs in the nose (apparently two machines guns, two cannon underneath, then two machine guns at the bottom). It had a tricycle undercarriage with the main gear folding into the inner wings, and the two engines were mounted in the fuselage between the pilot and the rearwards-facing gunner (who had upper and lower defensive turrets each with two more machine guns). The engines were to drive contra-rotating pusher propellers fitted on small nacelles attached to the wing trailing edges, and there were four fuel tanks in each wing holding 240, 308, 40 and 45 gallons (908, 1,166, 151 and 170 litres) respectively, to give a total capacity of 1,266 gallons (4,792 litres).

Northrop N-8/P-61 Black Widow

The Northrop P-61 was the first American aircraft to be designed as a dedicated night fighter, which meant that it was also the first to be radar-equipped, and as such it was a pioneering and impressive aeroplane. The experience of the RAF, with its efforts to defend its airspace during the German Blitz bombing campaign in 1940, had highlighted the need for such a type and the P-61 became a priority project brought about by the urgent British requirement for an immediate solution to the night fighter problem.

LEFT A close-up of a Northrop P-61C Black Widow night fighter. The cannon were fitted inside a ventral tub beneath the cockpit. *Gerald Balzer*

ABOVE & BELOW Two photos of an early production Northrop P-61A-1, serial 42-5507. *Gerald Balzer*

ABOVE The Douglas XA-26A prototype 41-19505 served as a prototype night fighter and is seen here on 5 February 1944 with its radar nose and the 20mm gun tray immediately behind the nose gear doors. *Alan Griffith*

During 1940 American officials in the UK were briefed on the British work with radar for detecting enemy aircraft, the briefings including the ongoing efforts to develop airborne intercept (AI) radar, whereby a self-contained unit could be installed in a fighter, which would then permit it to operate independently of ground stations. At the same time the British Purchasing Commission, a body based in New York that was responsible for arranging the production and purchase of armaments from North American manufacturers, declared an urgent need for a high-altitude, high-speed

aircraft to intercept German bombers flying in British airspace at night. Such a type would have to carry an AI radar set (the early forms of which were quite heavy) and the British conveyed the requirements to all of the aircraft designers and manufacturers with which they were working. Air Technical Service Command at Wright Field put together some basic requirements as well, and Northrop responded after having realised that any suitable turret-armed aircraft would need to be large and powered by twin engines to ensure that it had sufficient performance. Vladimir H. Pavlecka, Northrop Chief of Research, and Jack Northrop handed over their preliminary design on 5 November, and this was accepted. The only competition would come from Douglas with its XA-26A two-seat night fighter prototype of the Invader attack aircraft (see Chapter Five), the sole prototype of which flew on 27 January 1943.

The XP-61 Black Widow prototype first flew on 26 May 1942 and deliveries began at the end of 1943. It is often forgotten that the P-61 represented a brand-new category of fighter aircraft, which of course required the development of a whole range of new operating techniques. In November 1942 the Experimental Engineering Section noted that the

early P-61s 'should be followed by the development of a higher altitude version and probably by the parallel development of a completely new type, as soon as sufficient tactical experience had been gained with the service test machines to answer the question of the relative efficiency of fixed and flexible calibre guns (turrets) on such a type and the minimum number of crew necessary to carry out the night fighter mission.' The night fighter would go on to form a completely new element in the inventory of major air arms. The number of P-61s built eventually exceeded 1,000, and there was also the F-15 Reporter photo reconnaissance variant.

McDonnell Model 2A/XP-67

Although McDonnell's Model 1 was rejected as an R40-C competitor, the design had proved of sufficient interest to warrant the purchase of engineering information by the Army. On 30 June 1941 the company submitted a revised proposal in a design known as the Model 2, but exactly a month later this too was turned down. Then the team made a series of design changes that resulted in the more conventional twin-engine Model 2A layout of 24 April 1941, based around two Continental I-1430 units with four-blade tractor propellers.

XP-61 data	
Span	66ft 0in (20.12m)
Length	48ft 10in (14.88m)
Wing area	662sq ft (61.57sq m)
Gross weight	25,150lb (11,408kg)
Maximum take-off weight	28,870lb (13,095kg)
Powerplant	two 2,000hp (1,491kW) P&W R-2800-10
Armament	four 20mm cannon, four 0.50in (12.70mm) machine guns
Maximum speed	370mph (595km/h) at 20,900ft (6,370m); 430mph (692km/h) at 30,000ft (9,144m) for turbo-supercharged P-61C
Service ceiling	33,100ft (10,089m); 41,000ft (12,497m) for turbo-supercharged P-61C
Range	1,200 miles (1,931km)

ABOVE McDonnell's XP-67 prototype was from most angles quite an unorthodox machine. *Greater St Louis Air & Space Museum*

Formal approval and a contract followed in October 1941 for two XP-67 aircraft (the designation was assigned on 29 July), together with mock-ups and all of the other required development materials and testing, such as wind tunnel work. The latter was in fact to take more than two years to clear (the mock-up was inspected in mid-April 1942), and the first XP-67 did not fly until 6 January 1944 (at one stage the Air Defence Branch in Washington had requested that the XP-67, the XP-71 (see below) and the Republic XP-69 should be discontinued, but the plan was rejected by Material Division). The second XP-67 was intended to have dual-rotation propellers, which were expected to add 7-10mph (11-16km/h) to the maximum speed, but this airframe's construction was held in abeyance pending flight performance test results from aircraft number 1, although a go-ahead was finally given on 10 April.

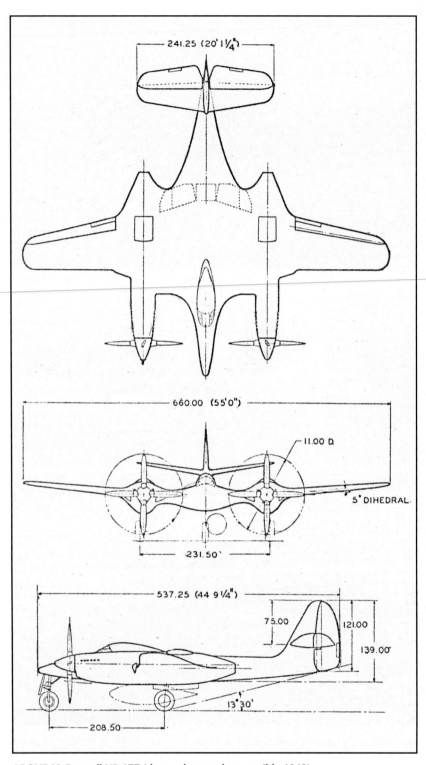

XP-67 data

Span	55ft 0in (16.76m)
Length	44ft 9.25in (13.66m)
Wing area	414sq ft (38.50sq m)
Gross weight	22,114lb (10,031kg)
Maximum take-off weight	25,400lb (11,521kg)
Powerplant	two 1,600hp (1,193kW) Continental XI-1430-17/19
Armament	six 37mm cannon (not fitted)
Maximum speed	405mph (652km/h) at 25,000ft (7,620m)
Sea level rate of climb	c2,600ft/min (792m/min)
Service ceiling	37,400ft (11,400m)
Maximum range	2,384 miles (3,836km)

ABOVE McDonnell XP-67E (date unknown, but possibly 1943).
Robert A. Burgess Collection, Greater St Louis Air & Space Museum

continuing with the second machine, the XP-67 programme was terminated on 24 October (the second prototype was apparently 15% complete at this point). In November 1942 the XP-67 was described by the Experimental Engineering Section as another 'true experimental model representing the ultimate in aerodynamic refinement of a conventional arrangement with the fuselage and nacelles merging smoothly into the wing itself.' The interface between fuselage, wings and nacelles on an aeroplane usually created turbulence (interference drag) and many designs had their wings curved in gracefully to try and reduce this problem. The streamlining of the centre wings on the XP-67 between the fuselage and nacelles in particular was some of the most extreme yet seen, but it did not provide the hoped-for benefit. The names 'Bat' and 'Moonbat' given to the XP-67 were both unofficial.

The XP-67E was a proposed version with a mixed powerplant – two Packard Rolls-Royce V-1650-11 units giving 1,925hp (1,435kW) at their war emergency rating and driving four-blade propellers, together with two 2,300lb (10.2kN)-thrust General Electric I-20 jets, one in the rear of each engine nacelle. The aircraft's dimensions were unchanged and the maximum fuel load consisted of 1,290 gallons (4,883 litres) internally, together with another 300 gallons (1,136 litres) carried externally. The variant was not built.

Taxi tests had commenced on 4 December 1943, but were stopped four days later due to fires in both engine nacelles, and the first machine was to be destroyed by a fire that started during a flight on 6 September 1944 and spread after the machine had landed. It had completed some 43 flight hours and, in view of the relatively small benefit that would accrue from

Curtiss XP-71

Curtiss's XP-71 was a very heavy escort fighter and bomber-destroyer design, the project having been taken on by the Army Air Corps with an order for two examples after a first proposal had been made in early November 1941. The early drawing shown here (created from an original) shows rather more sweep angle on the wings than has previously been acknowledged, when company artworks for the revised and developed layout have sweep only on the inner wing with the outer sections nearly straight. In November 1942 the Air Corps Experimental Engineering Section considered that the XP-71 was the solution to the Air Corps's Tactical Aircraft team's latest desires for a bomber-destroyer aircraft. In fact, many months previously the Experimental Engineering Section had attempted to get a destroyer type of aircraft designed around the 75mm gun, primarily as a result of the astonishingly accurate firing tests that had been conducted with the original 75mm installation (a hand-loaded weapon) in a Douglas B-18 bomber some years previously. To begin with Curtiss-Wright had been somewhat lukewarm regarding the XP-71 project, but the Experimental Engineering Section finally succeeded in getting the type under contract.

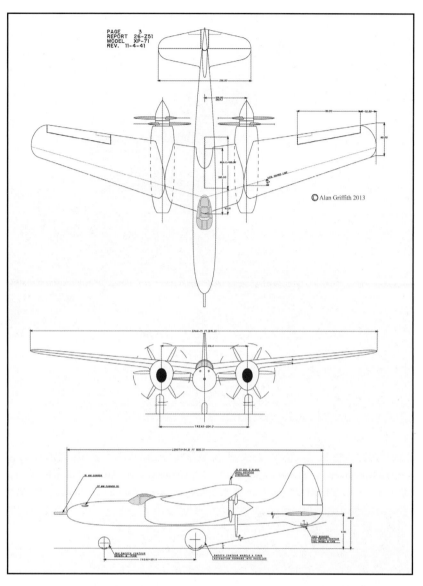

ABOVE The Curtiss XP-71 as first proposed, with swept wings – and published, it is believed, for the first time (drawing dated 11.11.41). It is thought that a quite dramatic redesign of at least the wing and tail had taken place by 1943. *Alan Griffith*

BELOW The XP-71 wind tunnel model showing the form in which the aircraft was to be built. *Alan Griffith*

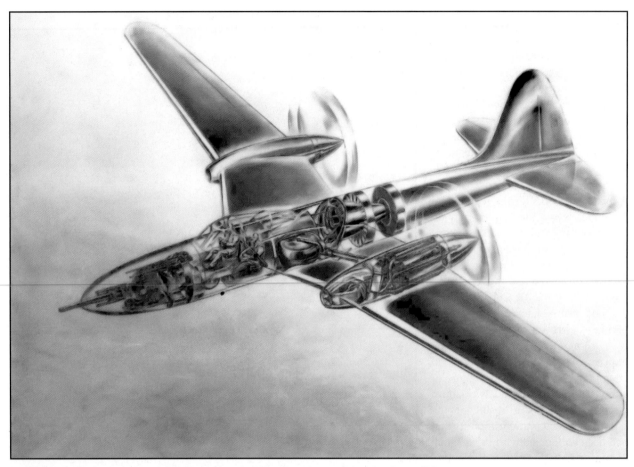

ABOVE Manufacturer's artwork for the XP-71, showing some internal detail. *Alan Griffith*

ABOVE The Curtiss XP-71 mock-up at St Louis photographed on 26 January 1943. Note the 75mm cannon in the nose.

XP-71 data (straight wing form based on data from wind tunnel test)	
Span	83ft 0in (25.30m)
Length	60ft 8in (18.49m)
Wing area	903.2sq ft (84.00sq m)
Gross weight	39,578lb (17,953kg)
Powerplant	two 3,450hp (2,573kW) P&W R-4360-13
Armament	two 37mm and one 75mm cannon
Maximum speed	428mph (689km/h) at 25,000ft (7,620m)
Service ceiling	40,000ft (12,192m)

ABOVE **Convair XP-81 'mixed powerplant' escort fighter.** *Terry Panopalis*

As one of the largest fighters to be planned during the war – indeed, probably the largest (this aircraft would have been bigger than some medium bombers) – the XP-71 was to be powered by a pair of P&W R-4360 engines, each of which would drive 13ft 6in (4.11m)-diameter contra-rotating pusher propellers. To perform its role the type needed a range in excess of 3,000 miles (4,827km). As such the XP-71 would be a most complex piece of machinery (although not necessarily particularly advanced) requiring, most likely, a long period of development. Moreover, armed with two 37mm and one 75mm cannon in the nose and with two crew (in a pressurised cockpit), it would not have been especially nimble (the 75mm installation was the same as that used for the Lockheed XP-58 above). Consequently, by early December 1942 the concept of this 'convoy fighter' had lost much of its appeal to the Army Air Corps, so some thought went into adapting it as a photo reconnaissance aeroplane; this too, however, came to nought. By mid-February 1943 the XP-71's design was pretty well finished, and it would progress little further, then in mid-October Curtiss and the Air Corps agreed to abandon the programme so that the manufacturer could concentrate on more important work. A good deal of wind tunnel testing had been completed together with partial mock-ups when the XP-71 finally came to a halt before any airframe fabrication had started. In truth, the aircraft was probably just too big!

Convair Model 102/XP-81

The Convair XP-81 was a design prepared in order to satisfy new Army Air Force escort fighter requirements produced in September 1943, and two prototypes were ordered in November 1944. Since the early jets consumed fuel at such a vast rate, Convair opted to use a 'mixed powerplant' of a jet in the rear fuselage and a turboprop to ensure that the aeroplane would have sufficient range to escort bombers on their operations across the Pacific – the jet was there primarily to supply the extra power required for take-off and combat. However, the turboprop was not available for the fighter's maiden flight on 11 February 1945 and a Packard V-1650-7 Merlin piston engine had to be installed instead. Testing with

XP-81 data	
Span	50ft 6in (15.39m)
Length	44ft 8in (13.62m)
Wing area	425sq ft (39.525sq m)
Gross weight	19,500lb (8,845kg)
Maximum take-off weight	24,650lb (11,181kg)
Powerplant	one 2,300hp (1,715kW) General Electric XT31-GE-1 (TG-100) turboprop and one 3,750lb (16.7kN) Allison J33-GE-5 jet
Armament	six 0.50in (12.70mm) machine guns or six 20mm cannon, 3,200lb (1,452kg) bombs
Maximum speed (estimated)	507mph (816km/h) at 30,000ft (9,144m)
Sea level rate of climb	c5,300ft/min (1,615m/min)
Service ceiling	35,500ft (10,820m)
Range	2,500 miles (4,023km)

XP-82 data	
Span	51ft 3in (15.62m)
Length	39ft 1in (11.91m)
Wing area	408sq ft (37.94sq m)
Gross weight	19,100lb (8,663kg)
Maximum take-off weight	22,000lb (9,979kg)
Powerplant	two 1,860hp (1,387kW) Packard Merlin V-1650-23/25
Armament (not in prototype)	six 0.50in (12.70mm) machine guns, 4,000lb (1,814kg) bombs
Maximum speed	468mph (753km/h) at 22,800ft (6,949m)
Service ceiling	40,000ft (12,192m)
Range	1,390 miles (2,237km)

the turboprop began on 22 December 1945, but the engine did not supply anything like the expected level of power, which put the XP-81's performance below estimate. Consequently the programme did not progress beyond the prototypes. The mixed powerplant experienced a short period of popularity during the mid-to-late-1940s, but the concept was taken on more seriously by the US Navy (see later).

North American P-82 Twin Mustang

North American's P-51 Mustang proved excellent as an escort fighter over Europe, but even that aircraft's considerable range was not sufficient to allow it escort Army Air Force bombers over the Pacific Ocean. Consequently, in October 1943 North American made a proposal to join two P-51 fuselages together with a common centre wing and tailplane, an extraordinary idea that proved a success and resulted in the P-82. Whether this was tied in with the same requirements that led to the XP-81 above is uncertain. The first of two prototype XP-82s became airborne on 16 June 1945, but the engines had to be swapped over before a 'proper' first flight could be made on the 26th (attempts to get the aircraft flying had begun in mid-April, but the handed engines affected the airflow over the centre wing and this was not cured until they were installed the other way around). Production aircraft introduced after the war included long-range and night fighter variants.

ABOVE The first prototype North American XP-82 was serial 44-83886, pictured here in 1948 at NACA's Langley facility. *Richard Curtiss*

RIGHT Serial 42-83887 was the second XP-82 Twin Mustang prototype.

Northrop XP-61E

In the case of the XP-82 there may have been another competitor for a long-range escort day fighter (although any direct competition is not confirmed), and that was the XP-61E prototype from Northrop, a streamlined version of the night fighter that had the dorsal turret removed and replaced by four more machine guns in the nose with a bubble canopy covering the two crew. There was extra fuel in the rear of the fuselage pod in place of the radar operator's cockpit, but the project came to nothing and just the two prototypes were produced. These were modified from P-61B airframes, the first flying on 3 January 1945. The North American P-82 was a more suitable choice since it had the superior performance, and one of the XP-61Es was later adapted as a prototype for the XF-15 Reporter photo reconnaissance aircraft, with cameras replacing the nose guns.

XP-61E data	
Span	66ft 0in (20.12m)
Length	49ft 7in (15.11m)
Wing area	662sq ft (61.57sq m)
Gross weight	31,425lb (14,254kg)
Maximum take-off weight	40,181lb (18,226kg)
Powerplant	two 2,000hp (1,491kW) P&W R-2800-65
Armament	four 20mm cannon, four 0.50in (12.70mm) machine guns
Maximum speed	376mph (605km/h) at 17,000ft (5,182m)
Service ceiling	30,000ft (9,144m)
Range	2,550 miles (4,103km)

ABOVE The first Northrop XP-61E
prototype carried the serial 42-39549.
Gerald Balzer

LEFT & BELOW More photos of the first
XP-61E. *Gerald Balzer*

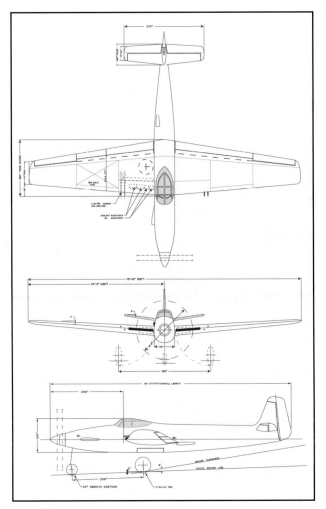

ABOVE Martin Model 207-1 (23.8.43). *Alan Griffith copyright*

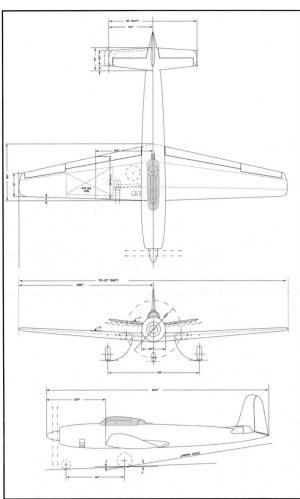

ABOVE Martin Model 207-5 (23.8.43). *Alan Griffith copyright*

Martin Model 207

Finally, there was the Model 207 'Convoy Fighter' from Martin, for which several different configurations were drawn, nearly all of them dated 23 August 1943. Standard almost throughout were two V-3420 engines mounted in the fuselage, one in front and one to the rear of the cockpit, and driving a contra-rotating propeller; since this type was classed by the manufacturer as a 'Convoy Fighter' one assumes that one of the engines could have been shut down during cruise and patrol flying. Other common features were two 20mm cannon in each wing and a tricycle undercarriage.

The single-seat Model 207-1 had a 550-gallon (2,082-litre) fuel tank in each

wing and two 360-gallon (1,363 litre) tanks beneath the cockpit, although the rear of these could be replaced by a bay to hold either two 1,000lb (545kg) or three 500lb (227kg) bombs. Model 207-1A was the same except for the addition of a rear-facing twin 0.50in (12.70mm) turret at the back of the cockpit; one assumes that this was controlled remotely because the 207-1A still appeared to be a single-seater. The two-seat Model 207-2 had a kink in the wing leading edge, while the 207-5, a two-seat project with a rear cockpit turret together with a 675-gallon (2,555-litre) tank in each wing, had a radial engine powerplant, of a type unspecified by the surviving documentation. Models 207-10 and -11 were appreciably smaller designs, while

the single-engine -7 looked briefly at swept wings and a V-tail. No performance data is available for any Model 207 configuration, but other Martin documentation gives 'gross weight 35,000lb (15,876kg)'.

Model 207-1 data

Span	75ft 10in (23.11m)
Length	64ft 2in (19.56m)
Powerplant	two Allison V-3420
Armament	four 20mm cannon

Model 207-5 data

Span	75ft 10in (23.11m)
Length	62ft 9in (19.13m)

Model 207-10 data

Span	56ft 2in (17.12m)
Length	52ft 4in (15.95m)

ABOVE Martin Model 207-1 artwork. *Alan Griffith copyright*

ABOVE Martin Model 207-1 artwork. *GLMMAM via Piet and Griffith*

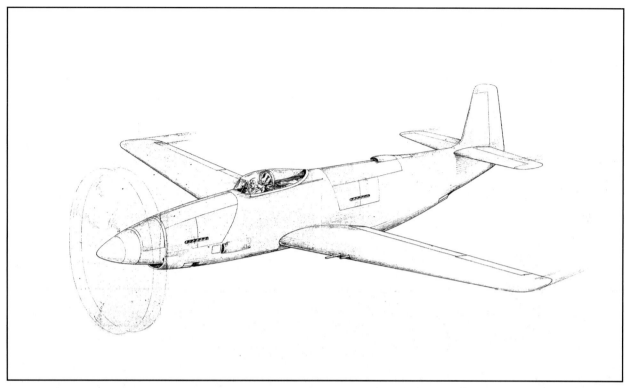

ABOVE Manufacturer's artwork for the smaller Martin Model 207-10. *GLMMAM via Piet and Griffith*

Twin-engine USAAF Fighter Designs in Perspective

Despite the limited effort put into the development of twin-engine fighters over the period in question, the US aircraft industry still managed to produce three outstanding examples: the P-38, P-61 and P-82. In addition, spurred by the perceived need for a long-range escort fighter, a handful of other fascinating designs were produced, a few of which got as far as flight-testing. As ever, these developments took place against a background of changing military philosophy, and it is interesting to note that the USAAC's desire for an

escort fighter or 'convoy-protector' was put on hold for a time while the idea of fitting out B-17 and B-24 bombers with exceptionally heavy armament was explored. Known as the B-40 and B-41 respectively, these aircraft are referred to later in the book. The twin-engine fighter category also embraced 'mixed-powerplant' aeroplanes, which for a short period were seen as a possible direction for the future.

Fighter aircraft were principally designed either for 'dog-fighting' – aerial combat with similar enemy

aircraft – or for intercepting enemy bombers. As a consequence, the design emphasis focused on speed, climb rate and manoeuvrability. The next chapter begins a review of the parallel development of bombers for the Army Air Force: aircraft designed to fly longer distances, and carry much heavier loads, while attempting to survive the attention of those fighters. It was part of a design struggle between offensive and defensive capabilities that would continue for decades.

Chapter Three
USAAF Light and Medium Bombers

ABOVE The serial number 40-2344 signifies that this is a B-25B version of the North American Mitchell bomber.
Gerald Balzer

In terms of light and medium bombers, the USA was fortunate in having two very capable aircraft already in production at the time of its entry into the war. These aircraft – the B-25 and B-26 – also possessed considerable development potential. Nonetheless, considerable effort was devoted to the examination of other designs, and these developments form the subject of this chapter.

However, before examining them it is worth pointing out that it is difficult to be too rigid in assigning military aircraft to specific categories. The USAAC's light and medium bomber categories are at times difficult to split away from the attack aircraft section covered in Chapter Five, and certain designs would fit quite comfortably into either chapter. By 1945 the 'light bombardment' category had pretty well replaced the 'attack aviation' class, although the 'A' series of designations did continue to be used after the war and was not finally eliminated until 1948. Consequently, for this book those attack aircraft that were really light bombers have been held back for Chapter Five.

Early Requirements – Douglas B-23

ABOVE An example of the Douglas B-23 Dragon.

Douglas B-23 Dragon

The B-23 was the result of a major redesign by Douglas of its earlier B-18 bomber, and was ordered as a new type without any design competition, the first example making its maiden flight on 27 July 1939. In all only thirty-eight B-18s were built and their service career was pretty short, primarily because more modern developments left the type behind.

B-23 data	
Span	92ft 0in (28.04m)
Length	58ft 4in (17.78m)
Wing area	993sq ft (92.35sq m)
Gross take-off weight	26,500lb (12,020kg)
Powerplant	two 1,600hp (1,193kW)
	Wright R-2600-3 Cyclone
Armament	one 0.50in (12.70mm)
	and three 0.30in
	(7.62mm) machine guns,
	4,400lb (1,996kg) bombs
Maximum speed	282mph (454km/h) at
	12,000ft (3,658m)
Best rate of climb	1,493ft/min (455m/min)
Service ceiling	31,600ft (9,632m)
Range with 4,000lb	1,400 miles (2,253km)
(1,814kg) load	

The Next Step

The first full twin-engine medium bomber design competition for the period covered by this book was held against Circular Proposal 39-640 of March 1939 and Army Air Corps Performance Specification XC-213 of 25 January 1939, to which designs were submitted as below. Martin documents indicate that its Model 178 was also covered by CP 39-640; here, however, the only surviving basic drawings (including a blended fuselage/wing layout) do not provide further information. A Request for Proposals was issued on 11 March and the listed requirements included a 3,000lb (1,361kg) bomb load to be carried at more than 300mph (483km/h) for a range of 2,000 miles (3,218km); the powerplant choice could be either the P&W R-2800, or the R-2600 or R-3350, both from Wright. On 10 August 1939 North American's NA-62 and Martin's Model 179 were selected as the B-25 and B-26 respectively.

Burnelli XBA-1

The preliminary specification brochure for Burnelli's six-crew XBA-1 project was dated 1 July 1939. Apart from the central lifting fuselage, in its appearance this Burnelli offering was rather more conventional than many of his other bomber and transport designs. The primary engine choice was a pair of Wright R-2600 units, although the R-3350 from the same manufacturer was an alternative, with both driving four-blade Curtiss propellers. The engine nacelles were angled out slightly (at 3°) to provide better single-engine control, and cooling air came through inlets in the lower section of the fuselage leading edge. Defensive guns were placed in both trailing edge corners of the lifting fuselage, which, together with a retractable dorsal turret, covered the whole of the XBA-1's rear. There was another gun in the nose firing forward, and finally one more in the fuselage floor; bombs were carried in the lifting fuselage, and a total of 1,670 gallons (6,322 litres) of fuel was available internally.

RIGHT Burnelli XBA-1 (29.6.39). *Alan Griffith copyright*
BELOW A manufacturer's model of the Burnelli XBA-1.
Dave Ostrowski

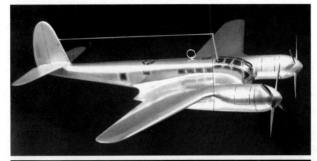

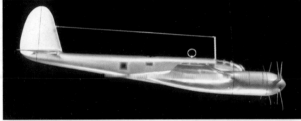

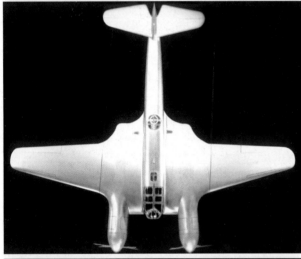

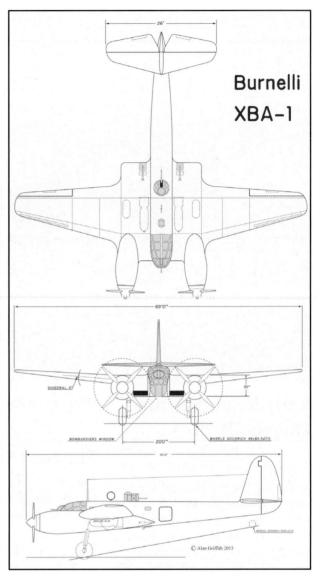

Burnelli
XBA-1

© Alan Griffith 2015

XBA-1 data	
Span	69ft 0in (21.03m)
Length	60ft 10in (18.53m)
Wing area	442sq ft (41.11sq m)
Fuselage (lifting) area	418sq ft (38.87sq m)
Gross weight	28,300lb (12,837kg)
Powerplant	two Wright R-2600 or R-3350
Armament	six machine guns plus bombs
Maximum speed at 15,000ft (4,572m)	'300' with R-2600 and '337' with R-3350 (unknown if figures are mph or knots)
Service ceiling	33,100ft (10,090m) with R-2600; 30,200ft (9,205m) with R-3350

LEFT It is thought that the Burnelli XBA-1 mock-up was never 'complete'. This view showed the bomb aimer's position.
Dave Ostrowski

Chance Vought VS-302

Vought's submission against CP 39-640, dated 30 June 1939, was the VS-302A and VS-302B versions of the same airframe. This had a high wing with twin engines driving three-blade propellers up to 14ft 6in (4.42m) in diameter. The inner wings were completely straight while the outer portions were tapered, and the design had twin fins as well as a tail-wheel undercarriage with the tail wheel itself right at the very end of the rear fuselage. For defence there was a single nose gun, guns in the lower rear fuselage and also in blisters on each side of the middle fuselage. The VS-302A was to be powered by a pair of Wright R-2600 engines, while the VS-302B had P&W R-2800s.

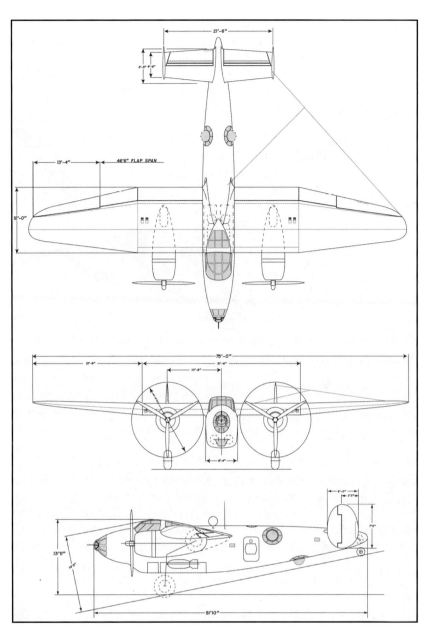

ABOVE Chance Vought VS-302 (24.5.39). *Alan Griffith copyright*

VS-302 data

Span	75ft 0in (22.86m)
Length	51ft 10in (15.79m)
Wing area	738sq ft (68.63sq m)
Gross weight	with four 600lb (272kg) bombs 25,749lb (11,680kg); with same warload and increased fuel 27,660lb (12,547kg); with one 2,000lb (907kg) bomb 25,317lb (11,484kg); with extra fuel 27,228lb (12,351kg)
Armament	Normal offensive load included one 2,000lb (907kg), two 1,100lb (499kg), four 500lb (227kg) or twenty 100lb (45kg) bombs

VS-302A data

Maximum speed	293mph (471km/h) at sea level, 348mph (560km/h) at 27,000ft (8,230m)
Service ceiling	35,600ft (10,851m)

VS-302B data

Maximum speed	350mph (563km/h) at 25,000ft (7,620m)
Service ceiling	30,000ft (9,144m)

Convair LB-22 and LB-24

The Convair LB-22 design was certainly submitted against XC-213 in a brochure dated 7 May 1939. This design is thought to have been a twin-engine version of the company's XB-24 heavy bomber (see Chapter Four), which first flew at the end of 1939. The new version was to be powered by two Allison V-3420 units and would weigh roughly the same as the B-24.

The six-seat LB-24 was first put together in a brochure in February 1939, then revised in June, and there is evidence that it may also have been presented against C-213. The fact that it was offered with the Wright R-2600-B655 with two-speed supercharger as a baseline powerplant, then backed up with either the R-2600-B657 with a turbocharger or the P&W two-speed R-2800-A4G or the turbo R-2600-AG,

ABOVE Consolidated LB-22 concept artwork with Allison engines.
Alan Griffith Collection

BELOW LB-24 manufacturer's artwork.
Alan Griffith Collection

supports this view (in fact, the LB-22's powerplant and weight appear to put that design outside XC-213's parameters). Again there is no drawing, but there is a little more information and data for the project – for example, the aircraft's circular fuselage had a rounded nose and there were forward, dorsal, ventral and tail gun positions. The LB-24's estimated gross weight was 27,053lb (12,271kg).

Martin Model 179

Martin put together quite a selection of Model 179 configurations, most of them showing the same general layout and using twin power units. However, the final submission dated 1 July 1939 had twin fins, when the B-26 as flown would use a single vertical surface. This chunky design would employ two 1,700hp (1,268kW) Wright R-2600 or two 1,850hp (1,380kW) P&W R-2800-5 engines with four-blade propellers. The following September the brochure was revised and the data quoted here comes from that document (back in July the length had been 56ft 0in/17.06m and the top speed 317mph/510km/h). At normal load the five-seat Model 179 could carry one 2,000lb (907kg), two 1,100lb (499kg) or eight 300lb (136kg) bombs and, in the overload condition, eight 600lb (272kg) bombs.

Model 179 proposal data	
Span	65ft 0in (19.81m)
Length	57ft 3.75in (17.46m)
Wing area	600sq ft (55.80sq m)
Normal gross take-off weight	26,625lb (12,077kg)
Overload take-off weight	29,122lb (13,210kg)
Performance ('guaranteed values'):	
Maximum speed	323.5mph (521km/h)
Service ceiling	26,440ft (8,060m)
Maximum range	3,000 miles (4,827km)

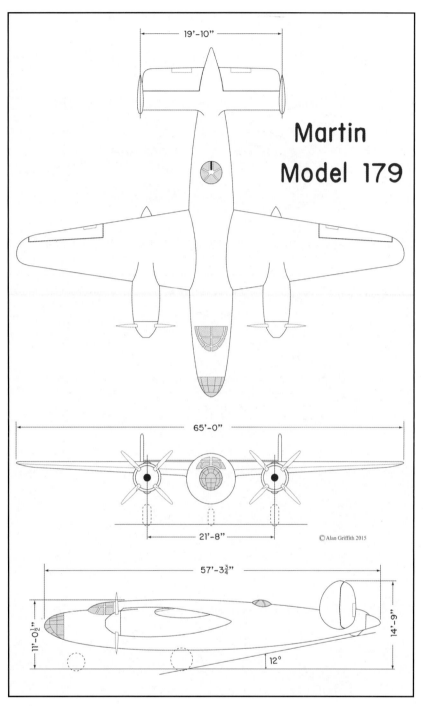

ABOVE Martin Model 179 (1.7.39). *Alan Griffith copyright*

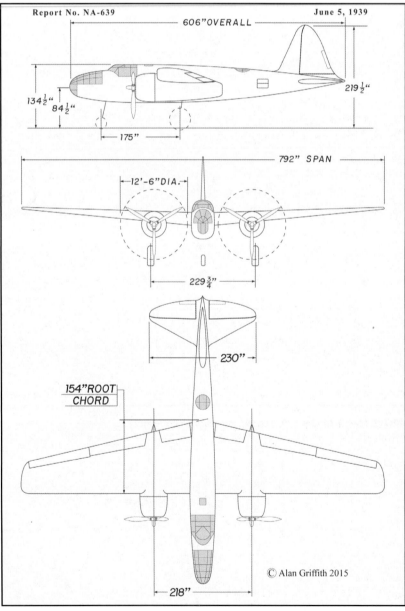

ABOVE Manufacturer's sketch impression of the Model 179.
Stan Piet, GLMMAM

North American NA-62

The North American NA-62 design was a development of the company's NA-40 attack aircraft prototype listed in Chapter Five. However, the company's XC-213/CP 39-640 proposals came under the P-442 designation within a report entitled NA-639, and multiple variations of the twin-engine format had been examined (prior to this there had also been studies under P-439 as illustrated). The main brochure was completed on 5 June 1939 and appears to have pushed the single-fin P-442-17 as the company's official proposal, but artwork was also prepared for the twin-tail P-442-41. P-442 as proposed was a single-fin, five-seat aircraft powered by two 1,700hp (1,268kW) Wright R-2600s (several other alternative powerplants were listed) driving three-blade 12ft 6in (3.81m)-diameter Curtiss full-feathering controllable-pitch propellers.

LEFT North American P-442 proposal (5.6.39). *Alan Griffith copyright*

**RIGHT
Manufacturer's
artwork for the
North American
P-439 (1939).**
Dave Ostrowski

**RIGHT
Manufacturer's
artwork for the
North American
P-439 (1939).**
Dave Ostrowski

BELOW Original artist's concept for the North American P-442-17. *Air Force Historical Research Agency (AFHRA) via Griffith*

ABOVE Original artist's concept for the North American P-442-41. *Air Force Historical Research Agency (AFHRA) via Griffith*

P-442-17 data

Span	66ft 0in (20.12m)
Length	50ft 5in (15.39m)
Wing area	unknown
Gross take-off weight with four 600lb (272kg) bombs	21,378lb (9,697kg)
Armament	normal offensive load of one 2,000lb (907kg), two 1,100lb (499kg), four 600lb (272kg) or six 300lb (136kg) bombs; possibility of external wing racks for another two 1,100lb (499kg) or 600lb (272kg) bombs; defensive machine guns in retractable upper rear turret, lower rear gun position and in nose

Lockheed Model 29A

There is no confirmation at the time of writing as to whether the Model 29A was part of the XC-213/CP 39-640 competition, but the aircraft's size and performance figures (and its appearance) compare well with other submissions. The choice of engines is unknown but the Model 29A had a tricycle undercarriage and appears to have four fixed forward-firing guns in the sides of the nose together with a twin-gun tail turret for rear defence. Curiously, this project does not feature in the normal 'L' series of Temporary Design Designations, and the fact that it has a full Model number indicates that a lot of work was done on the project.

*

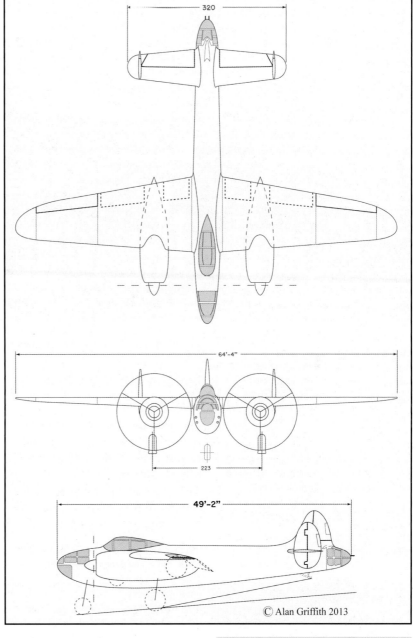

© Alan Griffith 2013

ABOVE The Lockheed Model 29A (c1939/40). *Alan Griffith*

Model 29A data

Span	64ft 4in (19.61m)
Length	49ft 2in (14.99m)
Wing area	550 sq ft (51.1sq m)
Gross take-off weight	21,000lbs (9979 kgs)
Maximum speed	328mph (528km/h) at sea level, 386mph (621km/h) at 'design altitude' of 20,000ft (6,096m)
Service ceiling	32,300ft (9,845m)
Absolute ceiling	33,800ft (10,302m); on one engine 22,800ft (6,949m)
Maximum sea level rate of climb	3,180ft/min (969m/min)
Range with 550 gallons (2,082 litres) fuel	1,543 miles (2,483km)

ABOVE A splendid view of North American B-25J Mitchell 43-3889.

B-25C data	
Span	67ft 7in (20.63m)
Length	52ft 11in (16.13m)
Wing area	610sq ft (56.73sq m)
Gross take-off weight	34,000lb (15,422kg)
Powerplant	two 1,700hp (1,268kW)
	Wright R-2600-13 Cyclone
Armament	six 0.50in (12.70mm)
	machine guns, maximum
	5,200lb (2,359kg) bombs
Maximum speed	284mph (457km/h) at
	15,000ft (4,572m)
Sea level rate of climb	1,375ft/min (419m/min)
Service ceiling	24,000ft (7,315m)
Range with 3,200lb	1,525 miles (2,454km)
(1,452kg) bombs	

North American B-25 Mitchell

The first production North American B-25 made its maiden flight on 19 August 1940 and the new bomber was named Mitchell in honour of the country's famous aviation pioneer, General William 'Billy' Mitchell, who is considered to be the father of the US Army Air Force. There were no XB-25 prototypes, the less-elegant NA-40 having essentially performed that role, and the Mitchell joined its first unit in February 1941, going on to operate in many wartime theatres. In all, a little less than 10,000 B-25s were produced.

BELOW This photo shows a B-25 in RAF service; it is serial FL218, which was a Mitchell Mk II, the equivalent to the B-25C.

Martin B-26 Marauder

Martin's B-26 introduced several interesting features in its construction, such as spot-welding, while the bomber's span was unusually small. Again, there was no XB-26 prototype and the first production machine flew on 25 November 1940. The name Marauder came from the UK (which also ordered the aircraft), and in the end this was preferred to Martin's own suggestion of 'Martian'. After numerous early problems and quite a number of fatal crashes due to the B-26's high wing loading and high landing speed, the maturing aircraft began to leave its mark in both Europe and the Pacific. In due course it became the Martin type to be manufactured in the highest numbers, and after it had been retired from American service in 1947/48 the Douglas A-26 Invader described later in the book assumed the B-26 designation.

B-26A data	
Span	65ft 0in (19.81m)
Length	56ft 0in (17.07m)
Wing area	602sq ft (55.99sq m)
Gross take-off weight	27,200lb (12,338kg)
Powerplant	two 1,850hp (1,380kW) P&W R-2800-9 Double Wasp
Armament	two 0.50in (12.70mm) and three 0.30in (7.62mm) machine guns, maximum 3,000lb (1,361kg) bombs or one 2,000lb (907kg) torpedo
Maximum speed	315mph (507km/h)
Service ceiling	25,000ft (7,620m)
Range with 3,000lb (1,361kg) bombs	1,000 miles (1,609km)

BOTTOM This photograph provides close-up detail for a Martin B-26.
BELOW The serial number for this British Martin B-26 Marauder is FK111.

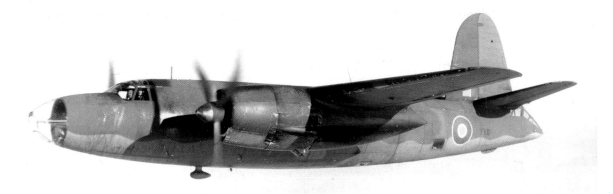

ABOVE A very early production Martin B-26, serial 40-1373, is seen armed with torpedoes at Adak on 5 November 1942. *NARA II via Ryan Crierie*
LEFT Martin Model 182 (1939). *Alan Griffith copyright*

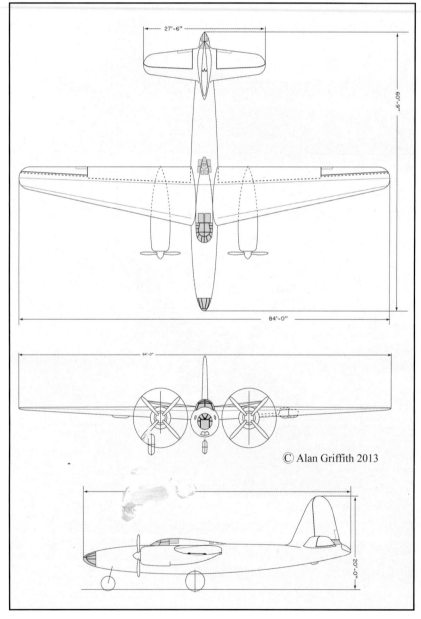

© Alan Griffith 2013

New Specification

In August 1939 Specification XC-214 was raised for a new high-altitude medium bomber, and once again projects from Martin (the Model 182) and North American (with its NA-63) were submitted, the latter being ordered as the XB-28, this time as a prototype. In fact, these designs were the only submissions made and the XB-28 failed to pass beyond the prototype stage. One key objective here was the development of pressure cabins, but the value of the XB-28 at high altitude would be compromised by a situation where its roles could also be performed by other types.

Martin Model 182/XB-27

The rather sleek-looking seven-seat Martin Model 182 had in its appearance more similarities with a fighter than a bomber. Its defensive armament comprised nose, dorsal, ventral and tail positions, with a 0.50in (12.70mm) machine gun in the tail and 0.30in (7.62mm) weapons in the other three positions. The engines had turbo-superchargers and four-blade propellers and the pressurised cockpit filled the

Model 182 data	
Span	84ft 0in (25.60m)
Length	60ft 9in (18.52m)
Wing area	750sq ft (69.75sq m)
Gross take-off weight	32,970lb (14,955kg)
Powerplant	two 2,100hp (1,566kW) P&W R-2800-9 Double Wasp
Armament	one 0.50in (12.70mm) and three 0.30in (7.62mm) machine guns, maximum 4,000lb (1,814kg) bombs
Maximum speed	376mph (605km/h) at 25,000ft (7,620m)
Service ceiling	33,500ft (10,211m)

entire fuselage apart from the bomb bay. No prototype was ordered, but during 1940 the Army Air Corps did put up the money for a more in-depth study of the design, and at that point the Model 182 was given the designation XB-27. It was never close to being built.

ABOVE Artwork from North American that is thought to show the NA-63 project in an early form. *Gerald Balzer*

North American NA-63/XB-28

At the start of this project North American's NA-63 was essentially a version of the B-25 mentioned above fitted with new engines and a pressure cabin, but as the design process moved forward the layout was to change and the resulting XB-28 looked quite different. Prototypes were first ordered in February 1940, but by 5 May 1941 the first XB-28 was still only 4%

complete, and did not make its maiden flight until 26 April 1942. In a review dated 6 November 1942 the five-seat XB-28 was stated as being two years late because of unavoidable delays due to precedence being given to problems with the company's other production programmes. That same report also described it as the first pressure cabin military aircraft fitted with remote fire control equipment. The XB-28's four-

XB-28 data	
Span	72ft 7in (22.12m)
Length	56ft 5in (17.19m)
Wing area	676sq ft (62.87sq m)
Gross weight	35,763lb (16,222kg)
Maximum take-off weight	39,135lb (17,752kg)
Powerplant	two 2,000hp (1,491kW) P&W R-2800-27
Armament	six 0.50in (12.70mm) and three 0.30in (7.62mm) machine guns, maximum 4,000lb (1,814kg) bombs
Maximum speed	372mph (599km/h) at 25,000ft (7,620m)
Service ceiling	34,800ft (10,607m)
Range with 600lb (272kg) load	2,040 miles (3,282km)

BELOW A photo of the North American XB-28 as first built.

**THIS PAGE A series
of walk-around
views of the XB-28.**
*NARA II via
Ryan Crierie*

blade propellers were 'handed' (rotated in opposite directions) to reduce torque, and a third example (designated XB-28A) was ordered to look into the aircraft's obvious potential in the high-altitude photographic reconnaissance role (the performance of the XB-28 was well in advance of current types). However, in August 1943 this machine was lost in a crash, and the second XB-28 was never completed.

Separate Designs

There are a number of other light and medium bomber projects for which drawings exist but which appear not to fall into any specific design competitions or requirements. These include offerings from Consolidated taken from its LB-series, two very different Douglas twin-engine bombers, and some ideas from Martin. Of these only the Douglas XB-42 was flown, but they make a fascinatingly varied collection.

Consolidated LB-26

It appears that Consolidated's four-seat LB-26 medium bomber project of 1 February 1940 was a scaled-down version of the LB-24 above. Four fixed guns were housed in the wings (one in each wing root and one in each outer wing, all just outside the propeller arc) while more were to go in a tail turret or, alternatively, top and bottom fuselage mounts. The design had a high wing, twin fins, a tricycle undercarriage and three-blade propellers with a diameter of 13ft 6in (4.11m).

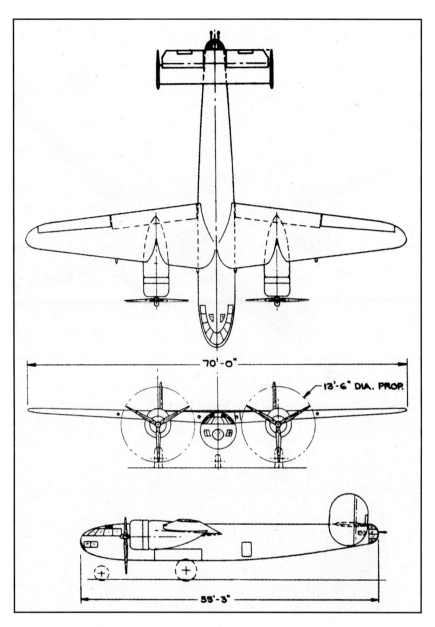

ABOVE Consolidated LB-26 (1.2.40). Note the tail turret. *SDASM via Griffith*

LB-26 data

Span	70ft 0in (21.34m)
Length	55ft 3in (16.84m)
Wing area	579sq ft (53.85m)
Gross weight	22,500/23,000lb (10,206/10,433kg)
Powerplant	two Wright R-2600 (P&W R-2800 and R-1830 also assessed)
Armament	bomb load not given
Maximum speed	326mph (525km/h)

Consolidated LB-28

A further Consolidated medium bomber to be considered on its own, although again a development of a previous project, was the LB-28 of 7 March 1940. The LB-27 had been offered as an export aircraft at a weight of 20,759lb (9,416kg), and the LB-28 was a refinement of this project with a stretched fuselage, the front of which was different with heavy glazing; there was also more fuel for a considerable increase in range and twin Wright R-3350 two-speed powerplants. The gun arrangement was unchanged from the LB-27 (a fixed gun on each side of the forward fuselage together with a defensive gun at the rear of the cockpit), but the bomb load was doubled to 2,400lb (1,089kg). The LB-28 had a high tapered wing and its gross weight was given as 24,443lb (11,087kg).

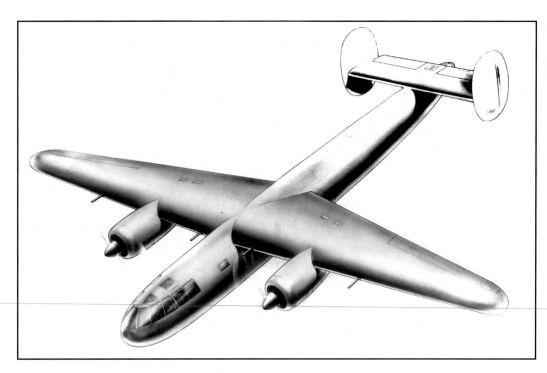

**LEFT
Manufacturer's
artwork for the
LB-26.**
*Alan Griffith
Collection*

BELOW Manufacturer's rendition of the Model 9 (5.10.38). *Alain Pelletier*

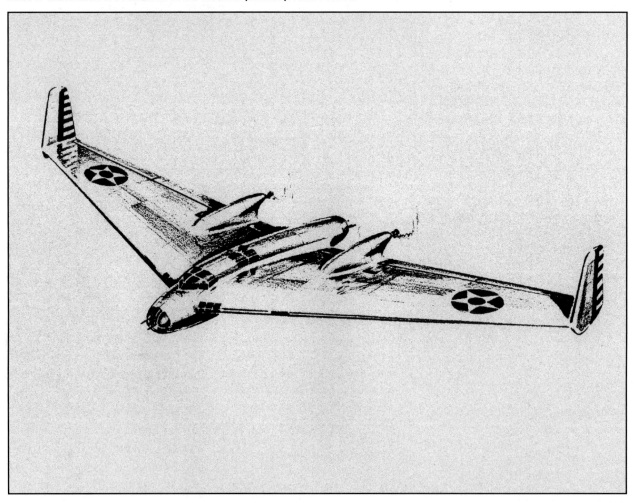

Douglas El Segundo Model 9

It is understood that 'Model 9' or 'Project 9' relates to this bomber being the ninth design produced by Jack Northrop while he was working for Douglas in the late 1930s. It seems pretty certain that the Model 9 was much influenced by Northrop and, like so many of the offerings to come from his own independent company, it was a flying wing. The preliminary design was produced in 1938 and did not progress beyond the drawing board, but an 8%-scale wind tunnel model with a high-quality finish was tested thoroughly by the Guggenheim Aeronautics Laboratory at the California Institute of Technology. This was assessed with and without a large central fin and with different shapes of nacelle and ducting, and the report was completed on 20 October 1938. The full-scale Model 9 was to have had a span of 84ft 0in (25.60m) and a length of 31ft 8in (9.65m).

Douglas XB-42 Mixmaster

The Douglas XB-42 resulted from unsolicited private venture studies opened in 1943, and was designed to meet an Army Air Force need, which in fact recurred throughout the war, for a smaller, faster and longer-range tactical bomber that would remove the

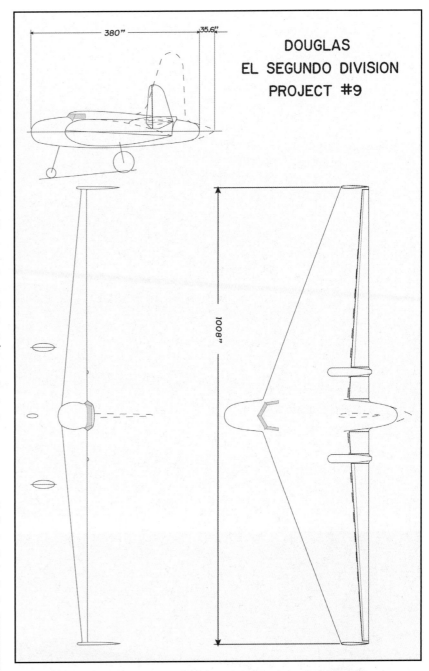

ABOVE **The Douglas Model 9 (5.10.38).**
Alan Griffith copyright

XB-42 data	
Span	70ft 6in (21.49m)
Length	53ft 7.5in (16.35m)
Wing area	555sq ft (51.615sq m)
Gross take-off weight	32,702lb (14,834kg)
Design gross weight	35,700lb (16,194kg)
Powerplant	two 1,460hp (1,089kW) Allison V-1710-129
Armament	six 0.50in (12.70mm) machine guns, 8,000lb (3,629kg) bombs
Maximum speed	410mph (660km/h) at 23,440ft (7,145m); original estimated maximum speed 470mph (756km/h) at 25,000ft (7,620m)
Sea level rate of climb	1,050ft/min (320m/min)
Service ceiling	29,400ft (8,961m)
Range with 2,000lb (907kg) warload	1,800 miles (2,896km)

AAF's need to use expensive strategic bombers in a purely tactical role. In fact, the XB-42 was designed as an inexpensive substitute for the Boeing B-29 (see Chapter Four), and it was also the first bomber to achieve flight status with pusher rather than tractor engines. The first proposal was submitted in April 1943, two prototypes were ordered and the type was designated XA-42 until 25 November of that year. The first example became airborne on 6 May 1944, but in general the flight test programme gave disappointing results and in due course the first machine had additional Westinghouse 19XB-2A jet engines installed in nacelles under each wing. As the XB-42A it performed a second maiden flight on 27 May 1947. The programme was abandoned in August 1948, but a prototype all-jet version had followed in 1946 and this flew as the XB-43.

THIS PAGE AND OPPOSITE TOP
**Views of the Douglas XB-42 prototype
43-50224.**
Alain Pelletier/Terry Panopalis (colour)

Martin Model 161

Martin's Model 161 series of projects embraced several different layouts covering twin-engine medium bombers, a twin-engine high-speed transport, and a four-engine 'Transoceanic Express'. The two bomber designs, which appear to have received the most consideration, are reproduced here. The Model 161D was dated March 1937 and showed a design with a high tapered straight wing and twin fins, a tricycle undercarriage (a very modern feature for its time) and three-blade propellers 12ft 0in (3.66m) in diameter.

The Model 161D3 possessed a generally similar configuration but less information is available for this design. Its span was 90ft 0in (27.43m) and its length 54ft 7in (16.64m), and the engines drove three-blade 14ft 0in (4.27m)-diameter propellers.

Model 161D data

Span	87ft 6in (26.67m)
Length	52ft 10in (16.10m)
Wing area	816sq ft (75.89sq m)
Gross take-off weight	42,380lb (19,224kg)
Powerplant	either two Wright R-2600 Twin Cyclones, P&W R-2180s or Allison V-1710s
Maximum speed (estimated)	357, 349 and 340mph (574, 562 and 547km/h) with above engines respectively
Armament	unknown
Service ceiling	28,100ft (8,565m)
Sea level rate of climb	1,410ft/min (430m/min)

RIGHT One of the various Model 161 designs was the 161D-1 (3.37).
Stan Piet, GLMMAM

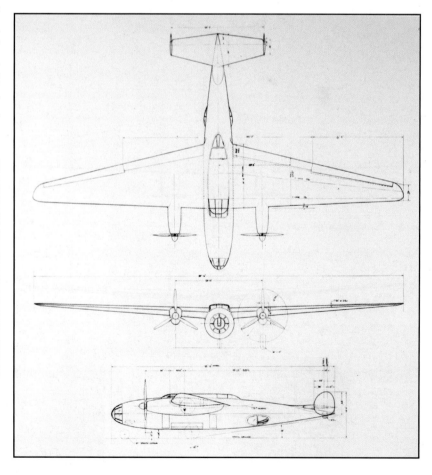

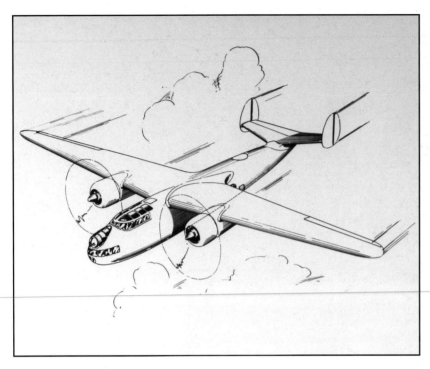

LEFT Manufacturer's sketch showing the Martin 161D3-1. *Stan Piet, GLMMAM*

USAAF Light and Medium Bombers in Perspective

Before America entered the Second World War in December 1941 the Army Air Corps had already been able to put two excellent twin-engine medium bombers into service – the B-25 and B-26 – and these would operate throughout the conflict. The efforts to produce a further specialist twin-engine bomber, the XB-28, were overtaken by the realisation that the type was no longer really required. Its proposed high-level role could be carried out by the new four-engine heavy bombers that were entering service, while at low level the Douglas A-26 Invader (covered in Chapter Five) already offered the required capability. Moreover, the A-26 did not have the added complexity of needing a pressurised cabin (in practice, twin-engine bombers were mostly employed at low altitudes throughout the war). Incidentally, when the 'A' category was dropped in 1948 the A-26 was redesignated B-26. Nonetheless, the search for other potential light bombers led to some very interesting designs, most notably the XB-42, which flew in prototype form, together with others that never got beyond the drawing board.

The next chapter looks at the heavyweight contemporaries to these aircraft, some of which would rank among the largest aircraft to be designed anywhere in the world during the era.

BELOW Martin Model 161D3-1 (4.38). *Stan Piet, GLMMAM*

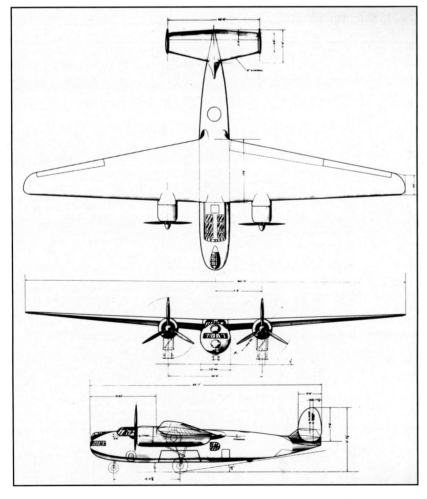

Chapter Four
USAAF Heavy Bombers

ABOVE A splendid photograph of a Boeing B-29 Superfortress in flight. *USAF*

The whole concept of the term 'heavy bomber' was to change during the Second World War. This was partly in response to bombing becoming a major element of offensive military strategy and partly due to the fact that war was now being waged over vast distances. As a consequence, there would be a huge increase in aircraft size, in load-carrying capacity and in the range these machines could cover. The search for the transcontinental bomber would result in some of the biggest aircraft projects yet seen anywhere in the world, starting a trend that would continue for decades.

At the start of the period covered by this book the Army Air Corps already had under development the Boeing B-17 Flying Fortress – later to become one of the legendary aircraft of the war – with the Consolidated B-24 Liberator not far behind. If one ignores the largely experimental XB-15, these can be considered the Service's first true modern heavy bombers. Two major development programmes were to follow, together with a number of other significant studies. It should be noted that, although these aircraft are nowadays universally referred to as 'bombers', the great majority of American official documents of the time used the term 'bombardment aircraft'.

ABOVE Serial 42-5234 was a Boeing B-17F that eventually joined the RAF as Fortress Mk II FA707.

B-17G data	
Span	103ft 9in (31.62m)
Length	73ft 10in (22.50m)
Wing area	1,420sq ft (132.06sq m)
Gross weight	54,000lb (24,494kg)
Maximum take-off weight	65,500lb (29,711kg)
Powerplant	four 1,200hp (895kW) Wright R-1820-97
Armament	thirteen 0.50in (12.70mm) machine guns, (normal load) 8,000lb (3,629kg) bombs
Maximum speed	287mph (462km/h)
Rate of climb	900ft/min (274m/min)
Service ceiling	35,600ft (10,851m)
Range, typical	2,000 miles (3,218km)

Boeing Model 299/B-17 Flying Fortress

The Boeing B-17 was first flown on 28 July 1935, which of course takes the bomber outside the parameters of this volume, but it was to prove one of the key aircraft of the conflict and by the time of the outbreak of war the basic design had in fact matured. From the first Model 299 the type was modified quite considerably, and the B-17E, which appeared in September 1941 and would be the first mass-produced variant, presented an extensive revision of the original design. The fuselage had been extended with the rear section made larger and a new and bigger vertical tail fin, rudder and horizontal tailplane. There just is not space here to record any of the Flying Fortress's phenomenal operational career, but 12,725 examples were built.

However, there were some further developments that do need to be recorded. One B-17 was kitted out with four Allison V-1710-89 engines and flown on 19 May 1943 as the prototype XB-38, but there was to be no production. This work was undertaken by Lockheed's subsidiary company Vega as its V-134 project, and during 1942 (under the V-139 designation) the same organisation converted another B-17F into the prototype XB-40 gunship. This was a very heavily armed aircraft carrying up to eighteen 0.50in (12.70mm) machine guns and was to be used to help protect the bomber stream. Thirteen more were converted into YB-40s in an effort that preceded the arrival of long-range escort fighters. Air Corps documents from early November 1942 show that the interest in the XB-40 and the similar conversion of a standard B-24 into the XB-41 (see below) was considerable, yet despite its promise the idea was not a success and the programme did not progress very far.

RIGHT Only the one Consolidated XB-24 prototype was built.

B-24J data	
Span	110ft 0in (33.53m)
Length	67ft 8in (20.63m)
Wing area	1,048sq ft (97.46sq m)
Gross weight	55,000lb (24,948kg)
Maximum take-off weight	65,000lb (29,484kg)
Powerplant	four 1,200hp (895kW) P&W R-1830-35
Armament	ten 0.50in (12.70mm) machine guns, 8,800lb (3,992kg) bombs
Maximum speed	290mph (467km/h)
Rate of climb	1,025ft/min (312m/min)
Service ceiling	28,000ft (8,543m)
Range	2,100 miles (3,380km)

Consolidated B-24 Liberator

The first example of the Consolidated B-24 Liberator became airborne on 29 December 1939. Like the B-17, the new type was to be built in huge numbers; in fact, more B-24s were produced than any other American bomber type (18,482). However, the design itself did not go through the same degree of external modification as its Boeing companion. With the same objective as the XB-40 above, one B-24D was armed with fourteen 0.50in (12.70mm) machine guns as the XB-41 'flying destroyer gunship' and was test-flown during February 1943. However, problems with stability stopped any further examples from being converted.

A New Heavy Bomber

In 1938 the Army Air Corps had begun to consider acquiring a new type of heavy bombardment aircraft that could hit targets with high accuracy. From late 1939 a competition was held to find this new 'superbomber', opening a line that would eventually lead to the Boeing B-29 Superfortress, the aircraft that would drop the world's first nuclear weapons. Boeing's path towards this truly impressive aircraft extended over several years and embraced a number of different projects, dating right back to the

XB-15. (Note: the weights on some of the designs between the Models 222 and 341 below must be regarded with a little doubt. Quoted ranges are for a 2,000lb/907kg bomb load.)

Boeing Model 316/Y1B-20/XB-20

Boeing's Model 316 project of 4 March 1938 was in some respects a revision and updating of the XB-15 with more powerful engines. It had nine crew and sharply tapered outer wings, it used a tricycle undercarriage (apparently the first Boeing design to incorporate this feature), and was to carry 4,450 gallons (16,845 litres) of fuel internally with another 880 gallons (3,331 litres) described as 'droppable'. However, the 316's heavy gross weight would have required very large main wheels, which could not retract completely into the engine nacelles, so each main undercarriage leg was to have two proportionately smaller wheels that could fit totally within the nacelles. The Army Air Corps appraisal of the Model 316, dated 12 May 1938, declared that in regard to its structural and aerodynamic design the aircraft's general arrangement as proposed was considered excellent, although several modifications were suggested including some aerodynamic refinements to the gun blisters. With the

chosen diameters of the three-blade propellers (14ft 0in/4.27m) and the engine gear ratio, however, it was considered that the propeller tip speeds would be excessive, resulting in an appreciable loss of effectiveness. It was considered that a diameter of 13ft 6in (4.11m) would be better and would improve both efficiency and propeller noise, but the AAC's best recommendation was actually to reduce the gear ratio and use a 15ft 0in (4.57m)-diameter propeller. Although an order was placed for prototypes of what was being described as a 'superbomber' (they were given the designation Y1B-20 or XB-20), the project was cancelled before construction had begun.

Model 316 data	
Span	157ft 0in (47.85m)
Length	109ft 2in (33.27m)
Wing area	2,920sq ft (271.56sq m)
Gross weight	87,600lb (39,735kg)
Powerplant	four 1,650hp (1,230kW) Wright GR-2600-A73
Armament	three 0.30in (7.62mm) and four 0.50in (12.70mm) machine guns, eight 2,000lb (907kg), sixteen 1,100lb (499kg), twenty 600lb (272kg) or forty-two 100lb (45kg) bombs
Maximum speed	258mph (415km/h) at 25,000ft (7,620m)
Service ceiling	31,200ft (9,510m)
Range	4,000 miles (6,436km)

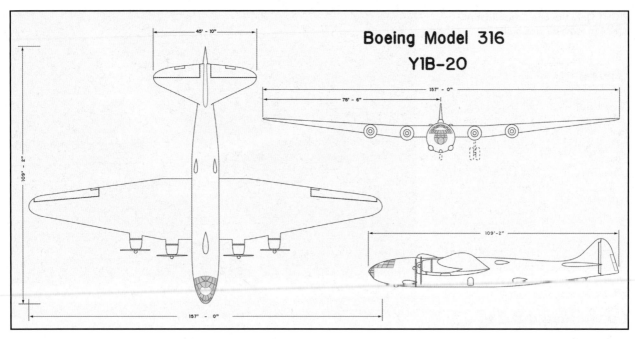

ABOVE Boeing Model 316/Y1B-20/XB-20 (4.3.38). *Alan Griffith copyright*

Boeing Model 322

In the meantime the Air Corps had requested that Boeing might look at a variant of the B-17 fitted with a pressure cabin, and the result was the six-seat Model 322 of June 1938. This took the standard B-17 wings, engines and empennage and coupled them with a new circular large-diameter pressurised fuselage. Again, a tricycle undercarriage was used with a new twin wheel nose leg joining the standard B-17 main gears (as a result of the new fuselage the CofG would have moved forward considerably). The main weakness here was that the pressure cabin restricted the defensive armament to just four guns, an insufficient number for a heavy day bomber, and the design did not proceed.

Model 322 data

Span	108ft 7in (33.10m)
Length	75ft 5in (22.98m)
Gross weight	53,100lb (24,086kg)
Powerplant	four 1,400hp (1,044kW) P&W R-2180
Armament	four machine guns, maximum 9,928lb (4,503kg) bombs
Maximum speed	307mph (494km/h) at 25,000ft (7,620m)
Range	3,600 miles (5,792km)

Boeing Model 333

Boeing's Model 333 of January 1939 had four in-line Allison engines in tandem inside two wing nacelles (tractor and a pusher engine in each), which produced a very clean design. It had a single-wheel tricycle undercarriage and, for the first time, a rearward-facing defensive tail-mounted machine gun. In addition, the pressurised sections of the fuselage were connected by a narrow crew communication tunnel, a feature that would stay in all succeeding projects through to the B-29. Nevertheless, the Model 333 had its weaknesses, the tandem engine arrangement being particularly questionable, and in due course work moved on to the Model 333A, which was near identical in almost every respect to the 333. It had the same Allison powerplant except that the engines were now submerged entirely within the wing and drove airscrews that were taken forward of the wing leading edge on extended shafts. However, the outer engine stumps protruded below the wing skin, so had to be encased in streamlined blisters, and when it was found that the V-1710's power dropped rapidly with height it was clear that an alternative was required.

In the meantime both Pratt & Whitney and Wright had begun work on what they called 'flat' engines, which were to be narrow enough to allow to them be buried fully within a large aircraft's wing; thus in February work moved on to the Model 333B, which

Model 333 data

Span	109ft 0in (33.22m)
Length	80ft 8in (24.59m)
Gross weight	48,600lb (22,045kg)
Powerplant	four 1,150hp (858kW) Allison V-1710
Armament	maximum 5,800lb (2,631kg) bombs
Maximum speed	307mph (494km/h) at 15,000ft (4,572m)
Range	3,420 miles (5,503km)

Model 333A data

Span	108ft 6in (33.07m)
Length	80ft 8in (24.59m)
Gross weight, powerplant and bomb load as Model 333	
Maximum speed	328mph (528km/h) at 15,000ft (4,572m)
Range	3,000 miles (4,827km)

Model 333B data

Span	111ft 0in (33.83m)
Length	80ft 8in (24.59m)
Gross weight	52,180lb (23,669kg)
Powerplant	four 1,850hp (1,380kW) Wright '1800'
Armament	maximum 5,800lb (2,631kg) bombs
Maximum speed	364mph (586km/h) at 20,000ft (6,096m)
Range	2,500 miles (4,023km)

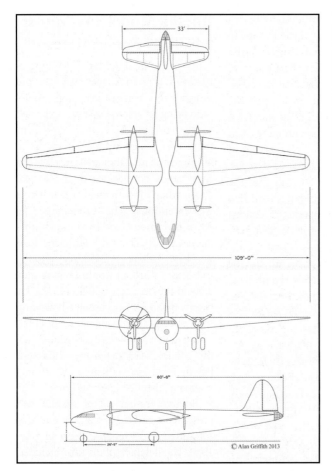

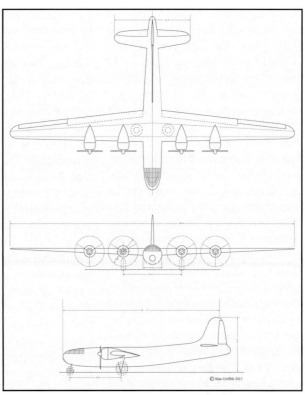

ABOVE Boeing Model 334A (7.39). *Alan Griffith copyright*
LEFT Boeing Model 333 (26.1.39). *Alan Griffith copyright*

retained the airframe of the 'A'. Although the new powerplant increased the top speed markedly, the range was reduced to an unsatisfactory level because fuel space in the wings had been lost to accommodate the engines.

Boeing Model 334

Boeing continued its studies with the Model 334 of March 1939, which was basically similar to the 333B but had the wing redesigned to take more fuel. The flat '1800' engines were still encased inside the wings and the 334 also introduced twin fins and rudders to provide a greater arc of fire for its eight machine guns. This resulted in an even more streamlined design that offered a higher speed and greater bomb load. However, by now the concept of having submerged engines was seen to be flawed in that it had failed to improve the aerodynamic efficiency sufficiently to justify having the more complex wing structure and the loss of fuel space. This was the last time Boeing looked at a buried powerplant (which always required wide chord inner wings), and the design team also dispensed with the twin fins because any structural gain from this arrangement did not compensate for the reduction in arc of fire.

What was required was an entirely new wing, and the next project, produced in July, was called the Model 334A. This time the degree of alteration was substantial and the result showed little similarity to the 334 in that it had a narrow-chord tapered wing not unlike that of the B-24, four engine nacelles and a large single fin. In addition there was a new type of engine and a tricycle undercarriage. For the first time the design began to look like the eventual B-29, but there were still some steps to take. The next design in this series, the Model 341, was submitted against the XC-218/R40-B design competition of January 1940.

*

Model 334 data	
Span	120ft 0in (36.58m)
Length	83ft 4in (25.40m)
Gross weight	66,000lb (29,938kg)
Powerplant	four 1,850hp (1,380kW) Wright '1800'
Armament	maximum 7,830lb (3,552kg) bombs
Maximum speed	390mph (628km/h) at 20,000ft (6,096m)
Range	4,500 miles (7,241km)

Model 334A data	
Span	135ft 0in (41.15m)
Length	80ft 0in (24.38m)
Gross weight	66,000lb (29,938kg)
Powerplant	four 2,200hp (1,641kW) Wright R-3350
Armament	maximum 7,830lb (3,552kg) bombs
Maximum speed	390mph (628km/h) at 16,000ft (4,877m)
Range	5,333 miles (8,581km)

One of the most important features for any new bomber was its ability to fly at high speed and high altitude. The problem with the latter was that it would require the development of suitable pressure cabins. On 9 May 1937 Lockheed flew its twin-engine Lockheed XC-35 transport with an experimental pressurised cabin. In fact, this was the first American aircraft to feature cabin pressurisation with all its associated complications, and it was used to perfect the relevant operating techniques. The XC-35 was flown at heights of between 20,000 and 35,000 feet (6,096 and 10,668 metres), and on 8 April 1938 Brig-Gen Henry H. 'Hap' Arnold wrote that 'a military bomber should be designed and constructed as the next logical step in the development'. He added that the bomber should be designed for altitudes in excess of 35,000ft (10,668m) with fully supercharged engines and pressurised cabins. One of the complications of the latter was that it would require remotely controlled defensive guns to maintain crew compartment sealing. Such a bomber would be capable of flying beyond the range of anti-aircraft guns, and beyond the altitude of any contemporary pursuit aircraft, in addition to being difficult, if not impossible, to detect from the ground.

However, it was not until the arrival of the Specification XC-218 and R40-B competition that it became possible for

this objective to be fulfilled, by which time the early months of the European war had revealed that the USAAF's existing bombers were badly out of date. The request for data was issued on 29 January 1940, but on 8 April the requirements were revised as XC-218A and showed in particular an increase in the defensive weaponry; a series of resubmittals followed the spec changes. One element of XC-218 was that the range with a 2,000lb (907kg) load had to be more than 5,300 miles (8,528km) and the data quoted for the different designs are for this load. Four manufacturers took part and in due course the Air Corps took the unusual step of allocating each of them an 'XB' designation. For the initial series it is understood that the designs to receive a full evaluation by the various Air Corps research laboratories (before the resubmittals) were the Boeing 341, Consolidated LB-25-2, Douglas 332B, and Lockheed 51-58-01, the remainder apparently being assessed in part only. Lockheed would subsequently withdraw from the contest in September, and Douglas did not win a development contract, leaving Boeing and Consolidated to move on to the prototype stage with the XB-29 and XB-32 respectively.

BELOW Boeing Model 345 artwork.
NARA II via Alan Griffith

Boeing Model 341/Model 345/B-29 Superfortress

Work on the Boeing Model 341 appears to have started in August 1939, and the design had a wing of very high aspect ratio using an aerofoil that was expected to give better results than any form previously designed for a bomber. The layout was all new, though its fuselage did show some similarities to the Model 334A, while the estimated performance was exceptional. The turbocharged R-2800s had three-blade 14ft 6in (4.42m)-diameter propellers, the internal fuel load was 4,170 gallons (15,785 litres), and the maximum warload would include four 2,000lb (907kg), ten 1,000lb (454kg) or twenty 500lb (227kg) bombs. Following the specification changes Boeing's submission was revised as the Model 345, the Model 341's defensive armament having been just six 0.50in (12.70mm) manually operated machine guns.

Boeing's rather larger Model 345 presented a revised armament and was submitted to Wright Field on 11 May 1940. The defensive guns now included ten 0.50in (12.70mm) machine guns mounted in five paired turrets, and there was also a single 20mm cannon in the tail. A big step made here was that the gunners were no longer inside their turrets – because of the difficulties of pressurising the whole body, the gunners now operated their turrets remotely from

Model 341 data	
Span	124ft 7.4in (37.98m)
Length	85ft 6in (26.06m)
Wing area	1,332sq ft (123.88sq m)
Design gross weight	76,000lb (34,474kg)
Powerplant	four 2,000hp (1,491kW) P&W R-2800
Armament	maximum 10,000lb (4,536kg) bombs
Maximum speed	405mph (652km/h) at 25,000ft (7,620m)
Service ceiling	35,420ft (10,796m)
Range	5,100 miles (8,206km)

Model 345 data	
Span	141ft 3in (43.05m)
Length	93ft 0in (28.35m)
Wing area	1,710sq ft (159.03sq m)
Design gross weight	97,774lb (44,350kg)
Maximum take-off weight	111,490lb (50,572kg)
Internal fuel	5,440 gallons (20,593 litres)
Powerplant	four 2,200hp (1,641kW) Wright R-3350
Armament	maximum 16,000lb (7,258kg) bombs
Maximum speed	382mph (615km/h) at 25,000ft (7,620m)
Service ceiling	34,950ft (10,653m)
Range	5,333 miles (8,581km)

B-29 data	
Span	141ft 3in (43.05m)
Length	99ft 0in (30.18m)
Wing area	1,736sq ft (161.45sq m)
Maximum take-off weight	134,000lb (60,782kg)
Powerplant	four 2,200hp (1,641kW) Wright R-3350-23
Armament	twelve 0.50in (12.70mm) machine guns, one 20mm cannon, maximum 20,000lb (9,072kg) bombs
Maximum speed	358mph (576km/h) at 25,000ft (7,620m)
Rate of climb	900ft/min (274m/min)
Service ceiling	31,850ft (9,708m)
Range	3,250 miles (5,229km)

ABOVE The last of three Boeing XB-29s was serial 41-18335, seen here during a test flight.

BELOW Serial 42-93844, flying with open bomb doors, was the first of a batch of Boeing B-29A-5-BN Superfortresses.

inside the pressurised compartment and used periscopes for sighting (remote turrets also featured in some of the competing designs). The three-blade props were 17ft 0in (5.18m) in diameter and the maximum loads were eight 2,000lb (907kg), twelve 1,000lb (454kg) or eighteen 500lb (227kg) bombs.

The six-crew Model 345 proved successful and a contract was awarded in August 1940 for XB-29 prototypes. The full-size mock-up was inspected late that year and the new bomber was named Superfortress, making its maiden flight on 21 September 1942. The subsequent manufacturing and production programme was to be the largest yet devoted to a single aircraft type, with Bell, Boeing, Fisher and Martin all building airframes. Indeed, the type with its new features presented a big step forward in bomber development and in the end the build total was only thirty short of 4,000. The first YB-29 was later converted by Fisher Body to receive Allison V-3420-11 power units as the one-off prototype XB-39, which first flew as such on 9 December 1944. Post-war the B-29 was revised and upgraded as the Model 345-2, and this became the B-50, first flown on 25 June 1947. The changes here included the introduction of a stronger structure, a taller fin and a switch to Pratt & Whitney R-4360 engines.

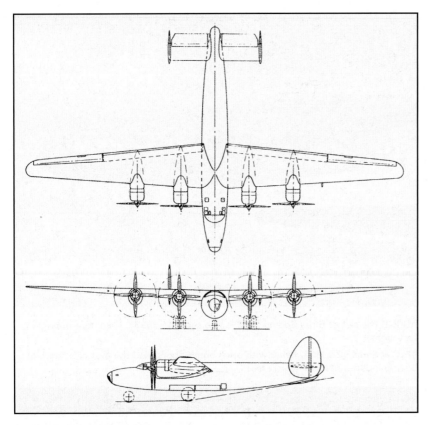

ABOVE Consolidated LB-25 (c5.40).

Consolidated LB-25/ Model 33/B-32 Dominator

After wind tunnel testing had commenced back in October 1939, the first Consolidated LB-25 studies were completed in early March 1940, and four variants were submitted in the first instance with variations in powerplant seemingly the only change. Details for defensive guns appear to be one 20mm tail gun, and eight 0.50in (12.70mm) and two 0.30in (7.62mm) machine guns, although these are not shown on the drawing. The LB-25-1 was to have four-blade 15ft 0in (4.57m) propellers.

Consolidated's revision for the updated XC-218A was known as the Model 33 (with a second version called the Model 33A having alternative engines), and drawings indicate that the design was pretty similar to the XB-32 as built. The Model 33 had six crew (with provision for three relief crew), and used 15ft 2in (4.62m)-diameter four-blade propellers (the 33A's were 14ft 2in/4.32m). The project was ordered for prototype development on 6 September

1941 as the Air Corps XB-32, and the first example made its maiden flight on 7 September 1942 with twin fins, but production machines would feature a different nose and cockpit shape and a very tall single fin. As a planned back-up to the B-29, in all only 188 B-32 Dominators were built, flying operations relatively briefly right at the end of the Pacific war.

LB-25-1 data

Span	135ft 0in (41.15m)
Length	77ft 8in (23.67m)
Wing area	1,422sq ft (132.25sq m)
Design gross weight	85,619lb (38,837kg)
Internal fuel	4,650 gallons (17,602 litres)
Powerplant	four 2,200hp (1,641kW) Wright R-3350 (turbo)
Armament	maximum four 2,000lb (907kg), eight 1,000lb (454kg) or sixteen 500lb (227kg) bombs
Maximum speed	390mph (628km/h) at 25,000ft (7,620m)
Service ceiling	32,000ft (9,754m)
Range	5,333 miles (8,581km)

LB-25-2 data

Design gross weight	83,875lb (38,046kg)
Internal fuel	4,550 gallons (17,224 litres)
Powerplant	four 2,000hp (1,491kW) P&W R-2800-A6G (turbo)
Maximum speed	375mph (603km/h) at 25,000ft (7,620m)
Service ceiling	30,000ft (9,144m)
Range	5,333 miles (8,581km)

LB-25-3 data

Design gross weight	90,964lb (41,261kg)
Internal fuel	4,950 gallons (18,738 litres)
Powerplant	four 2,350hp (1,752kW) Wright R-2160 Tornado (turbo)
Maximum speed	398mph (640km/h) at 25,000ft (7,620m)
Service ceiling	31,000ft (9,449m)
Range	5,333 miles (8,581km)

LB-25-4 data

Design gross weight	96,070lb (43,577kg)
Internal fuel	5,250 gallons (19,873 litres)
Powerplant	four 2,650hp (1,976kW) P&W H-3130 (turbo)
Maximum speed	415mph (668km/h) at 25,000ft (7,620m)
Service ceiling	31,000ft (9,449m)
Range	5,333 miles (8,581km)

Model 33 data

Span	as LB-25 series
Length	77ft 0in (23.47m)
Wing area	as LB-25 series
Design gross weight	92,500lb (41,958kg)
Internal fuel	4,840 gallons (18,321 litres)
Powerplant	four 2,200hp (1,641kW) Wright R-3350-B670-2 (turbo)
Armament	as LB-25 series; defensive weaponry of one 20mm tail cannon and twelve 0.50in (12.70mm) machine guns
Maximum speed	386mph (621km/h) at 25,000ft (7,620m)
Service ceiling	31,400ft (9,571m)
Range	5,333 miles (8,581km)

Model 33A data

Design gross weight	90,000lb (40,824kg)
Internal fuel	4,980 gallons (18,851 litres)
Powerplant	four 2,000hp (1,491kW) P&W R-2800-A6G (turbo)
Maximum speed	374mph (602km/h) at 25,000ft (7,620m)
Service ceiling	30,000ft (9,144m)
Range	5,333 miles (8,581km)

ABOVE A beautiful photo of the first Consolidated XB-32 prototype 41-142.

BELOW The production B-32 Dominator presented a rather different appearance from the XB-32, the biggest external change being an enormous single fin. 42-108472 was the first production B-32 to be delivered, in September 1944.

XB-32 data	
Span	135ft 0in (41.15m)
Length	83ft 0in (25.30m)
Wing area	1,422sq ft (132.25sq m)
Maximum take-off weight	113,500lb (51,484kg)
Powerplant	four 2,200hp (1,641kW) Wright R-3350-23A
Armament	ten 0.50in (12.70mm) machine guns, maximum 20,000lb (9,072kg) bombs
Maximum speed	379mph (610km/h) at 25,000ft (7,620m)
Average rate of climb	1,105ft/min (337m/min)
Service ceiling	30,700ft (9,357m) with 2,000lb/907kg bombs
Range	4,450 miles (7,160km)

Douglas Model 332/XB-31

It is thought that most of Douglas's Model 332 designs were essentially the same airframe but with different powerplants (drawings are not available for the various versions); however, judged from the weight data the 332D and 332E might have been a bit larger than the others. The 332B had three-blade 15ft 1in (4.60m)-diameter propellers, while the four-bladers on the 332C and 332D were 15ft 2in (4.62m) in diameter and on the 332E 16ft 6in (5.03m) in diameter. The Air Corps review and assessment papers for this series stated that for all designs apart from the Model 332 itself the wing loading would be excessive. It was also thought that the horizontal tail would fall within the wing wake.

The follow-on Model 332F proposed against the revised XC-218A was a larger and heavier design, although it was still to be crewed by only six people. Four-blade 18ft 1in (5.51m)-diameter propellers were to drive the R-3350 power units, and the maximum bomb load was unchanged. It is understood that a total of six twin 0.50in (12.70mm) machines were carried in turrets (four of them went in pairs facing rearwards in the rear of the outer nacelles), together with another machine gun and a 20mm cannon in the tail. Again, the Air Corps assessment declared that the wing loading and also the CofG travel were excessive and that the gross weight would increase (the 332F was described as a 'heavy airplane'), but the detail design was considered to be 'excellent'. Douglas's study contract was not followed by a development contract, and work on the XB-31 soon came to an end. (Note: the Model D-423 designation [see below], given as the XB-31 in some published sources, is dated October 1941 – far too late for this competition. All of Douglas's R40-B proposals came under the Model 332 series, and exactly when the XB-31 designation was allocated is not known.)

Model 332 data

Span	127ft (38.71m)
Wing area	1,500sq ft (139.50sq m)
Design gross weight	74,500lb (33,793kg)
Internal fuel	4,271 gallons (16,167 litres)
Powerplant	four 1,700hp (1,268kW) Wright R-2600 (turbo)
Armament	could include four 2,000lb (907kg), eight 1,000lb (454kg) or sixteen 500lb (227kg) bombs
Maximum speed	368mph (592km/h) at 25,000ft (7,620m)
Service ceiling	33,500ft (10,211m)
Range	5,490 miles (8,833km)

Model 332A data

Design gross weight	80,500lb (36,515kg)
Internal fuel	4,866 gallons (18,420 litres)
Powerplant	four 2,000hp (1,491kW) P&W R-2800 Double Wasp (two-stage, two-speed)
Maximum speed	368mph (592km/h) at 25,000ft (7,620m)
Service ceiling	30,600ft (9,327m)
Range	5,360 miles (8,624km)

Model 332B data

Design gross weight	82,000lb (37,195kg)
Internal fuel	4,911 gallons (18,590 litres)
Powerplant	four 2,000hp (1,491kW) P&W R-2800 (turbo)
Maximum speed	384mph (618km/h) at 25,000ft (7,620m)
Service ceiling	32,500ft (9,906m)
Range	5,430 miles (8,737km)

Model 332C data

Design gross weight	86,000lb (39,010kg)
Internal fuel	5,326 gallons (20,161 litres)
Powerplant	four 2,200hp (1,641kW) Wright R-3350 (two-stage)
Maximum speed	386mph (621km/h) at 25,000ft (7,620m)
Service ceiling	30,600ft (9,327m)
Range	5,340 miles (8,737km)

Model 332D data

Design gross weight	90,000lb (40,824kg)
Internal fuel	5,619 gallons (21,270 litres)
Powerplant	four 2,200hp (1,641kW) Wright R-3350 (turbo)
Maximum speed	403mph (648km/h) at 25,000ft (7,620m)
Service ceiling	32,500ft (9,906m)
Range	5,470 miles (8,801km)

Model 332E data

Design gross weight	91,000lb (41,278kg)
Internal fuel	5,373 gallons (20,339 litres)
Powerplant	four 2,350hp (1,752kW) Wright R-2160 Tornado (turbo)
Maximum speed	425mph (684km/h) at 25,000ft (7,620m)
Service ceiling	33,400ft (10,180m)
Range	5,360 miles (8,624km)

Model 332F data

Span	140ft 6in (42.82m)
Length	88ft 8.5in (27.04m)
Wing area	1,780sq ft (165.54sq m)
Design gross weight	106,994lb (48,532kg)
Internal fuel	6,383 gallons (24,162 litres)
Maximum take-off weight	120,000lb (54,432kg)
Powerplant	four 2,200hp (1,641kW) Wright R-3350 (turbo)
Maximum speed	377mph (607km/h) at 25,000ft (7,620m)
Service ceiling	31,600ft (9,632m)
Range	5,370 miles (8,640km)

Lockheed L-117/ Model 51-58/XB-30

Lockheed's L-117/Model 51-58 offering was a variant of its Constellation airliner and was the same size as that design except that the fuselage had been extended for a new glass nose. There were four versions (apparently with the same engines but with different weights and fuel loads), but here another design was also listed, the Model 51-18-01. The bomber had a crew of seven and the four engines would drive three-blade propellers, which at least on the initial Model 51-58-01 were 15ft 2in (4.62m) in diameter. The resubmitted Design 51-58-01 used the same powerplant and propellers and carried the same bomb loads, and in fact appears to have shown minimal changes, with the same span and wing area as before. This work was given the Air Corps designation XB-30.

Design 51-58-01 data

Design gross weight	81,370lb (36,909kg)
Internal fuel	4,600 gallons (17,413 litres)
Powerplant	four 2,200hp (1,641kW) Wright R-3350-B670 Duplex-Cyclone (turbo)
Armament	four twin 0.50in (12.70mm) machine gun turrets, all remotely controlled, plus a 20mm cannon and two more machine guns in tail; maximum bomb load 16,000lb (7,258kg), comprising eight 2,000lb (907kg), twelve 1,000lb (454kg) or sixteen 500lb (227kg) bombs
Maximum speed	385mph (619km/h) at 25,000ft (7,620m)
Service ceiling	35,000ft (10,668m)
Range	5,333 miles (8,581km)

51-58-02 data

Design gross weight	81,304lb (36,879kg)
Internal fuel	4,600 gallons (17,413 litres)

51-58-03 data

Design gross weight	84,520lb (38,338kg)
Internal fuel	4,800 gallons (18,170 litres)
Maximum speed	384mph (618km/h) at 25,000ft (7,620m)
Service ceiling	34,000ft (10,363m)

51-58-04 data

Design gross weight	86,100lb (39,055kg)
Internal fuel	4,920 gallons (18,624 litres)
Maximum speed	383mph (616km/h) at 25,000ft (7,620m)
Service ceiling	33,500ft (10,211m)

51-18-01 data

Design gross weight	86,120lb (39,064kg)
Internal fuel	4,920 gallons (18,624 litres)
Powerplant	four 2,500hp (1,864kW) P&W H-3130-A26 (two-stage, two-speed)
Maximum speed	415mph (668km/h) at 25,000ft (7,620m)
Service ceiling	30,000ft (9,144m)

51-58-01 re-submittal data

Span	123ft 0in (37.49m)
Length	104ft 9in (m)
Wing area	1,650sq ft (153.45sq m)
Design gross weight	85,961lb (38,992kg)
Maximum take-off weight	90,000lb (40,824kg)
Internal fuel	4,800 gallons (18,170 litres)
Maximum speed	385mph (619km/h) at 25,000ft (7,620m)
Service ceiling	33,500ft (10,211m)
Range	5,333 miles (8,581km)

Martin Studies

Separate from the above competition, but concurrent, was a long-term project from Martin, which almost resulted in another four-engine 'heavy' being built. Although reflecting some of the elements required by XC-218, the Martin XB-33 'Super Marauder' was referred to as an interim type between the B-17/B-24 category and the larger B-29/B-32. However, the project began as a smaller twin-engine type.

Martin Model 189/XB-33 Super Marauder

Work on the Martin Model 189 was opened in October 1940 as a high-altitude medium bomber with a pressurised cabin, and the type was to be ordered in prototype form as the XB-33. However, as the development process moved forward the aircraft's weight rose and it eventually reached a point where the design had to be turned into a four-engine machine. In all, this part of the work, which stretched into January 1941, brought eighteen twin-engine designs, including an unusual foreplane variant (Design No 4). Design No 8A of 23 December 1940 had a single fin but one of the final efforts, which appeared in model form and apparently represented the XB-33, was twin fin Design No 16.

Design No 4 had two bomb bays; the forward bay took twenty-two 100lb (45kg) bombs but nothing larger than 300lb (136kg) in size, while the rear bay could hold two 2,000lb (907kg), four 1,000lb (454kg), eight 500lb (227kg) or forty-two 100lb (45kg) bombs. The foreplane was placed high on the fuselage while the two engine nacelles stretched back to produce booms for the twin fins. There were twin remote-control dorsal, ventral and tail turrets, but the powerplant for this design is unknown. Design No 4 is included here because its advanced appearance is of

BELOW Martin Model 189 (XB-33) Super Marauder (late 1940). *Stan Piet, GLMMAM*

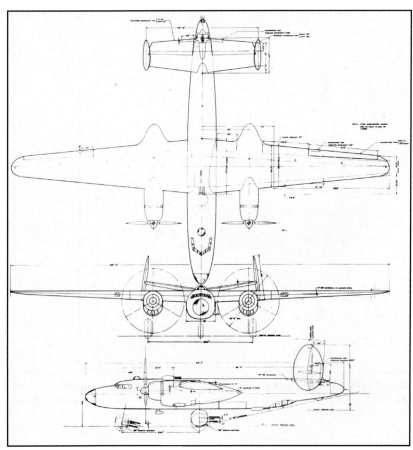

ABOVE Manufacturer's artwork for the Martin Model 189 Super Marauder. *Stan Piet, GLMMAM*

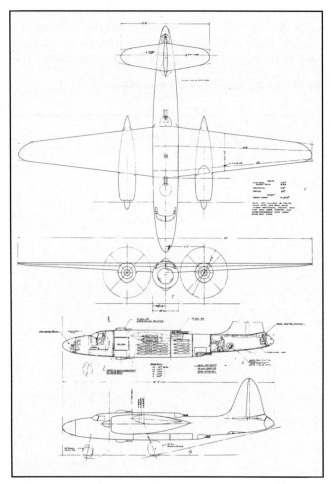

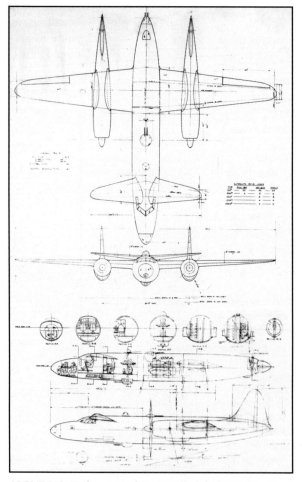

ABOVE LEFT A drawing of the single-fin Martin Model 189 (12.40).
Stan Piet, GLMMAM

ABOVE RIGHT The unusual Martin Model 189 Design No 4 used a foreplane rather than a conventional tailplane (c11.40). *Stan Piet, GLMMAM*

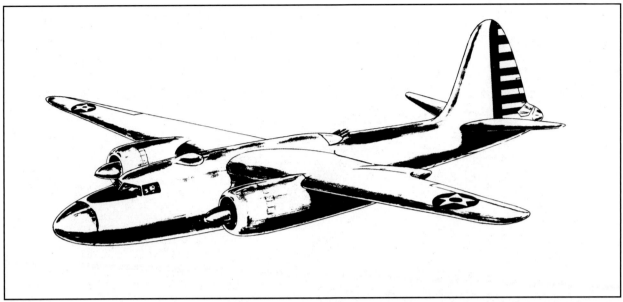

TOP The single-fin Model 189 was also represented by this piece of artwork. *Stan Piet, GLMMAM*
ABOVE Artwork for the Model 189 Design No 4. *Stan Piet, GLMMAM*

considerable interest. Design No 8A had upper and lower forward twin 0.50in (12.70mm) machine gun turrets and upper and lower rear-firing quadruple 0.50in (12.70mm) turrets, four crew, and twin bomb bays for a total carrying capacity of two 2,000lb (907kg), four 1,100lb (499kg), ten 600lb (272kg), or sixty 100lb (45kg) bombs. Finally, Design No 16 had a four-gun dorsal turret and twin ventral and tail turrets, all with 0.50in (12.70mm) machine guns. Here the bomb load was the same as Design No 8A, and 16ft 6in (5.03m)

four-blade propellers were to have been fitted. All these designs used a tricycle undercarriage and the data reflects how the Model 189 gradually grew in size. Each of these three designs had a relatively high wing, but alternatives with a low wing were also considered, and the 190/XB-33's powerplant was to be two 2,200hp (1,641kW) turbo-supercharged R-3350s. Quoted data for the 'Model 190' also includes a maximum speed of 340mph (547km/h) and ceiling 30,000ft (9,144m).

Design 4 data

Span	73ft 8in (22.45m); foreplane 31ft 2in (9.50m)
Length	62ft 10.5in (19.16m)
Wing area	615sq ft (57.195sq m); foreplane 160sq ft (14.88sq m)

Design 8A data

Span	85ft 0in (25.91m)
Length	61ft 3in (18.67m)
Wing area	755sq ft (70.215sq m)
Gross weight	41,200lb (18,688kg)

Design 16 data

Span	100ft 0in (30.48m)
Length	68ft 0in (20.73m)
Wing area	950sq ft (88.35sq m)
Powerplant	two Wright R-3350 (either turbo or two-stage)

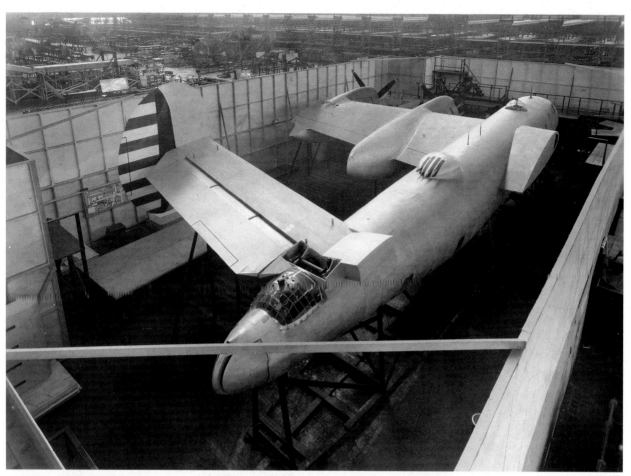

ABOVE & BELOW Photos of the mock-up of the Martin XB-33. *Alan Griffith*

Model 190-9/XB-33 data	
Span	122ft 4in (37.29m)
Length (not including rear gun barrels)	78ft 9in (24.00m)

B-33 data	
Span	134ft 0in (158.00m)
Length (not including nose and rear gun barrels)	79ft 10in (24.33m)
Wing area	1,500sq ft (139.50sq m)
Gross weight	84,060lb (38,130kg)
Powerplant	four 1,800hp (1,342kW) Wright R-2600-15 Cyclone 14 (Twin Cyclone),
Armament	maximum 12,000lb (5,443kg) bombs
Maximum speed (estimate at end of programme)	330mph (531km/h)
Rate of climb	1,135ft/min (346m/min)
Service ceiling	39,800ft (12,131m)
Range	2,000 miles (3,218km)

Martin Model 190/XB-33

In late April 1941 the twin-engine Model 189 was enlarged to a four-engine type as Martin's Model 190, and this now became the XB-33 (published sources have reported that the four-engine version was the XB-33A, but the manufacturer's drawings appear to use XB-33 and B-33 only). The Model 190 was a handsome aircraft and eventually embraced some nine different designs. The twin fins were retained and the horizontal tailplane had 15° of dihedral, rather than the 8° of the Model 189 Design No 16. At one point the normal bomb load was to have been four 2,000lb (907kg), eight 1,000lb (454kg), sixteen 500lb (227kg) or fifty-six 100lb (45kg), all carried in a central bomb bay except for some of the smaller sizes, which would go in small bays in the rear of the inner engine nacelles.

The first drawing reproduced here shows the Model 190-9/XB-33 as revised on 16 October 1941 (the XB designation had been assigned in August). It had eight 0.50in (12.70mm) defensive guns in remote-controlled turrets – four in a dorsal position and two in both ventral and tail turrets – the three-blade propellers had a diameter of 14ft 2in (4.32m), and the tricycle undercarriage main gears had twin wheels. The original second drawing (dated 5 May 1942) was marked as 'B-33' and presumably shows how production machines would have appeared. There was a new nose, which now had two guns, the rear-facing dorsal turret had just two 0.50in (12.70mm) guns, and the increase in the aircraft's overall size was reflected by the nose gear also having twin wheels; the three-blade propellers were 15ft 8in (4.78m) in diameter. A total of 402 production B-33s was planned and the assembly of two prototypes got moving during 1942, but they were never completed and the project was abandoned towards the end of the year. Continued increases in weight had by then eroded the bomber's performance, while the B-29 and new variants of other types would clearly be sufficient to fill any gaps. Martin subsequently began working with Northrop on the XB-35 (see below).

BELOW A drawing showing how the Martin Model 190 XB-33 would have appeared. Although work on the aircraft began in April 1941, this revision is dated 16 October 1941. *Stan Piet, GLMMAM*

BELOW revised Model 190 design, which the drawing states would have been the production B-33. It is dated 5 May 1942. *Stan Piet, GLMMAM*

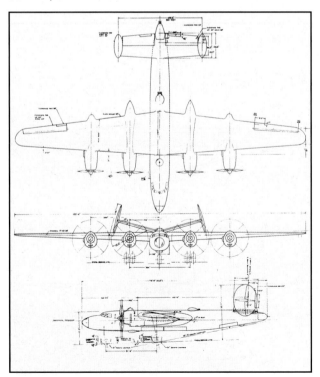

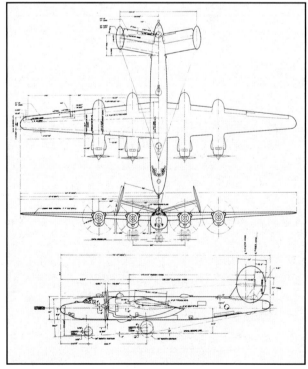

Transcontinental Capability

The effort to find a very heavy bombardment aircraft, a true intercontinental bomber, was opened in April 1941 and continued past the end of the war in 1945. After the start of the war in Europe the Army Air Corps realised that it would need a long-range bomber to carry the war to the enemy, an opinion that was strengthened by Japan's attack on Pearl Harbor in December 1941. Had Britain fallen in 1940, the US would have been left with no European allies and no bases outside the Western Hemisphere, so Air Corps bombers would have to attack the enemy from bases within America itself. The outcome was the phenomenal Consolidated B-36 Peacemaker, the flying career of which belongs entirely to the post-war period, but its beginning and gestation were very much a Second World War programme. Although some urgency was placed behind this project, the unsatisfactory level of technology in the early phases (all of the manufacturers experienced difficulties in defining aircraft that could

meet the stringent requirements), then the shortage of materials due to wartime demands, meant that progress was slow.

The requested long-range bomber was to be capable (after the initially very high requirements had been relaxed) of a maximum speed of 450mph (724km/h) at 25,000ft (7,620m), a ceiling of 40,000ft (12,192m), an overall range of 10,000 miles (16,090km), and a combat radius with a 10,000lb (4,536kg) bomb load of 4,000 miles (6,436km). Initially Boeing, Consolidated and Douglas responded, but Lockheed and Northrop also produced long-range bomber studies during the 1941/42 period, which, although seemingly not directly part of the competition, must have been designed because of it. Northrop's flying wing design eventually became the separate B-35 programme. After making revisions to their projects following the relaxation of the requirements, the three main contenders submitted their proposals in the early part of September 1941. On 3 October Consolidated's work was endorsed ahead of that of Boeing and Douglas, and later that month plans were worked out to build two experimental prototypes of the firm's Model 35.

Consolidated Models 35 and 36 and Flying Wing

Consolidated produced a set of designs, all of which at one stage appear to have come under the Model 35 designation. However, the six-engine pusher arrangement that came close to the eventual B-36 was renumbered Model 36. The Model 35 drawings included a design with four engines arranged unconventionally, having both tractor and pusher propellers of 19ft 0in (5.79m) diameter on each wing nacelle, together with three bomb bays. There was also a six-engine version of this layout with a further trailing edge outer nacelle and pusher propeller on each wing. The larger Model 36 had six pusher engines and its fuselage was longer than that of the Model 35, but quite similar in shape (a tractor version of this was also assessed). The display model (which has XB-36 marked on its fins) showed undernose and tail turrets each with four guns, together with two twin-gun upper and one lower fuselage turrets. Both designs had high-position wings, twin fins and a tricycle undercarriage.

BELOW The four-engine version of the Consolidated Model 35 (11.8.41). *Dennis R. Jenkins*

BELOW The six-engine version of the Consolidated Model 35, which in due course was developed into the XB-36 (1941). *Dennis R. Jenkins*

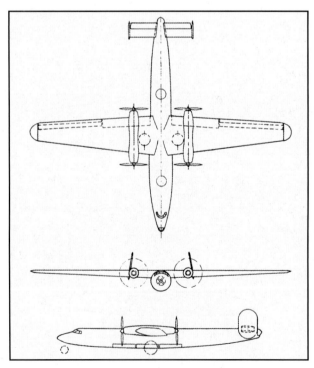

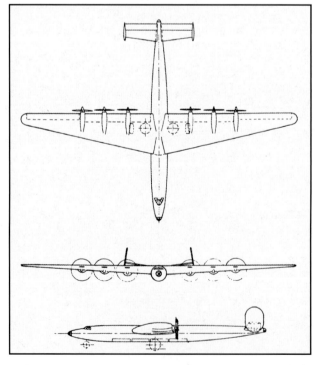

Model 35 data	
Span	164ft 5in (50.11m)
Length	128ft 0in (39.01m)
Wing area	2,700sq ft (251.10sq m)

Model 36 data	
Span	230ft 0in (70.10m)
Length	163ft 0in (49.68m)
Wing area	4,800sq ft (446.40sq m)

During 1942 Consolidated also looked at a flying wing with six pusher engines, specifically as a comparison to the XB-36 but more generally to try and ascertain what benefits and what penalties an all-wing aircraft would provide. This work seems to have been stimulated by Northrop's efforts with its B-35 (see below). The powerplant was the same as the XB-36 (six Pratt & Whitney R-4360s), and the flying wing's estimated top speed was found to be 394mph (634km/h), rather better than the 378mph (608km/h) then quoted for the XB-36. However, its cruising speed (an important element of the specification, which had set a figure between 240 and 300mph/386 and 483km/h) was 210mph (338km/h) compared to the 270mph (434km/h) offered by the XB-36. The design would use eight-blade 15ft 0in (4.57m)-diameter propellers and had twin main undercarriage wheels.

Consolidated flying wing data	
Span	288ft 0in (87.78m)
Length	78ft 0in (23.77m

Douglas Model 423

The Douglas submission was the Model 423, but late in 1941 this manufacturer declared that it did not wish to produce an 'out-and-out 10,000-mile [16,090km] airplane project', preferring instead the 423, with a range of 6,000 miles (9,654km). The Model 423 project has been presented in previous publications as the Douglas XB-31 competitor to R40-B, but this is not correct; it was a much bigger aircraft than the Boeing B-29. The design had a massive straight tapered wing and huge vertical fin, together with four tractor engines. The proposal was rejected.

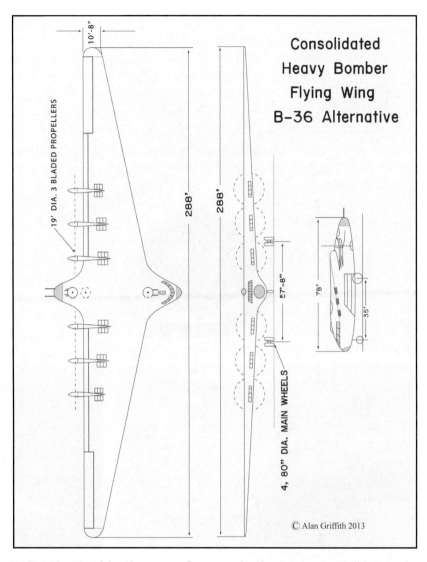

ABOVE The Consolidated six-engine flying wing bomber (1942). *Alan Griffith copyright*

Model 423 data	
Span	207ft 0in (63.09m)
Length	117ft 3in (35.74m)
Wing area	3,300sq ft (306.90sq m)
Maximum take-off weight	198,000lb (89,813kg)
Powerplant	four 3,000hp (2,237kW) P&W R-4360 Wasp Major
Armament	six 0.50in (12.70mm) machine guns, two 37mm cannon, maximum 25,000lb (11,340kg) bombs
No performance data available	

Consolidated/ Convair B-36 Peacemaker

Consolidated's winning design was designated XB-36. A mock-up was inspected on 20 July 1942 but due to various difficulties the programme's timescale slipped badly and the first prototype did not fly until 8 August 1946. Nevertheless, 384 examples were built and they equipped the Air Force until the end of the 1950s, having become the world's first manned bomber to possess an unrefuelled intercontinental range. One reason why the B-36 survived so long after the Second World War was that in 1947 the new United States Air Force needed a long-range aircraft to deliver its atomic bomb.

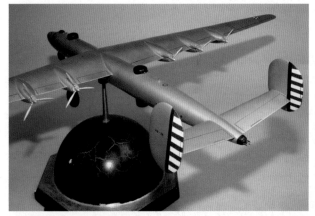

BELOW RIGHT & BOTTOM RIGHT
Colour images of the Consolidated/
Convair XB-36 serial 42-13570. *Jay Miller*

RIGHT & BELOW Manufacturer's display
model of the Convair XB-36. *Jim Keeshen*

B-36B data	
Span	230ft 0in (70.10m)
Length	162ft 1in (49.40m)
Wing area	4,772sq ft (443.80sq m)
Powerplant	four 3,500hp (2,610kW)
	Wright R-3350-41
Armament	sixteen 20mm cannon,
	maximum 86,000lb
	(39,010kg) bombs
Maximum speed	381mph (613km/h)
Rate of climb	1,510ft/min (460m/min)
Service ceiling	42,000ft (12,802m)
'Extreme' range	10,000 miles (16,090km)

B-36A data	
Maximum take-off weight with maximum 72,000lb (32,659kg) bombs	310,380lb (140,788kg)

Model 385 data	
Span	251ft 0in (76.50m)
Length	161ft 0in (49.07m)
Wing area	4,500sq ft (418.50sq m)
Gross weight	315,000lb (142,884kg)
Maximum take-off weight	335,000lb (151,956kg)
Powerplant	six P&W Wasp Major
Armament	fourteen 0.50in (12.70mm) machine guns, one 20mm cannon, four 10,000lb (4,536kg), eight 4,000lb (1,814kg), thirty-two 2,000lb (907kg), thirty-six 1,600lb (726kg), forty-eight 1,000lb (454kg) or ninety-six 500lb (227kg) bombs
Maximum speed	267mph (430km/h) at sea level, 329mph (529km/h) at 30,000ft (9,144m)
Sea level rate of climb	650ft/min (198m/min)
Service ceiling	not given
Range	8,210 miles (13,210km)

Boeing Models 384 and 385

Boeing's original 1941 projects are currently unidentified (although the Air Corps reported in April 1942 that Boeing had been 'overly conservative' with its proposals, stating that the firm had not tackled these long-range projects 'with the necessary degree of enthusiasm'). Some sources have indicated that the Models 384 and 385 were the submissions, but these date from later in 1942, which clouds the issue. The 384 had a four-engine tractor powerplant with a narrow-chord tapered wing and three-blade propellers. It used a tailwheel undercarriage with twin main wheels (the rear wheels actually went underneath the mid-rear section of the fuselage), and there were defensive turrets under the nose, behind the cockpit canopy, on both the upper and lower rear fuselage, and in the tail.

The quite different Model 385 was dated 29 August 1942 and was larger, with a six-engine tractor arrangement using four-blade propellers of 24ft 0in (7.32m) diameter, a longer fuselage and a tricycle undercarriage. It was to have had a crew of between nine and fifteen, and its defensive armament comprised two upper and two lower fuselage turrets and a pair of tail guns, together with two single mounts in each side of the fuselage, all with machine guns, and also a solitary 20mm cannon.

Lockheed L-130

Temporary Design Designation L-130 covered Lockheed's 1941 studies for a long-range bomber, and there were at least five different versions. However, the work may not have gone into too much detail since the drawing for the first layout was not dimensioned and the powerplant was six to eight 3,000hp (2,237kW) engines, but no details were provided for the choice of engine. Lockheed's report indicated that only Design 1 would have achieved all of the specified requirements, while the other four projects had maximum gross weights of between 194,500 and

BELOW Boeing Model 384 (4.41). *Dennis R. Jenkins*

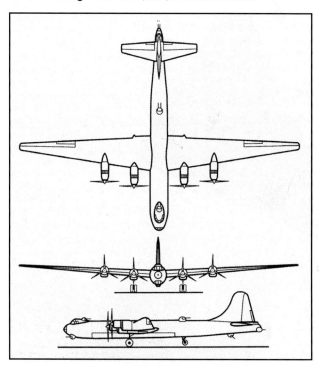

BELOW Boeing Model 385 (4.41). *Dennis R. Jenkins*

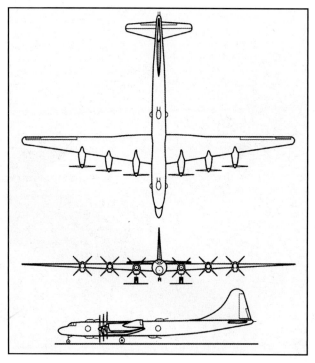

RIGHT This rough manufacturer's drawing shows the first version of the Lockheed L-130 (1941). *Peter Clukey*

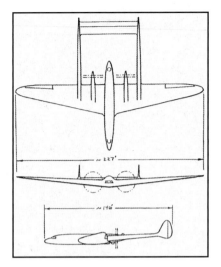

L-130 Design 1 data	
Span	227ft 0in (69.19m)
Length	146ft 0in (44.50m)
Wing area	unknown
Gross weight	250,000lb (113,400kg)
Maximum speed	380mph (611km/h)
Maximum range	8,160 miles (2,487km)

279,000lb (88,225 and 126,554kg), with top speeds between 340 and 377mph (547 and 607km/h).

Northrop Flying Wings

The 'flying wing' became the focus of Jack Northrop's design work from the 1930s onwards and he advocated this configuration because he considered that it would remove any structural weight from an airframe that was not directly responsible for producing lift. It would also reduce the parasitic drag, and theoretically a flying wing bomber could transport a greater payload faster and further than a conventional aeroplane. Although the resulting B-35

programme ran concurrent with the transcontinental bomber project, it appears to have been an altogether separate initiative. Martin had declined to take part in the long-range bomber competition but did become involved with the B-35.

Northrop N-9/XB-35

The first prototype of Northrop's flying wing was ordered in November 1941 as

the XB-35. However, this aeroplane would break so much new ground that in addition an order was placed for a series of one-third-scale models of the bomber called the N-9M (M for 'Model'). First flown on 27 December 1942, the N-9Ms were used to collect data and to provide aircrew with flight experience in this new wing planform. Previously, on 3 July 1940, Northrop had also flown its N-1M, another scale model research aircraft that was built for an earlier twin-engine flying wing medium bomber proposal. Consequently, by the time the first XB-35 became airborne on 25 June 1946 the company had collected a considerable volume of knowledge and experience in flying wings. However, in the air substantial problems were experienced with the bomber's powerplant and, together with other technical issues, this put the programme well behind schedule. The two XB-35s were followed by an order for thirteen pre-production YB-35s (in the event only one of these flew), and a production order for 200 aircraft to be built by Martin was dropped.

BELOW One of the Northrop N-9M scale model test aircraft. *Gerald Balzer*

ABOVE The Northrop XB-35 seen during its maiden flight. *Gerald Balzer*
BELOW The extraordinary XB-35 comes in to land. *Gerald Balzer*

In early November 1942 the Northrop XB-35 was described by Air Corps representative Colonel F. O. Carroll as being 'off the scale completely' in terms of its role as an experimental aircraft, embodying as it did the tailless arrangement. He added that it would probably not be advisable (even if engineers were available) to have another organisation working independently on such a design, 'since Mr Northrop is well ahead of the field in this respect'. However, Carroll stressed the need that they should have, if at all possible, a second source for 'an airplane of the Consolidated B-36 type'. In the end the XB-35 did not prove a success, but postwar it was followed by jet-powered versions called the YB-49 and YRB-49, which were conversions of YB-35 airframes. These projects too, however, did not progress to the production phase.

LEFT This is the first YB-35, which first flew on 15 May 1948. *Gerald Balzer*

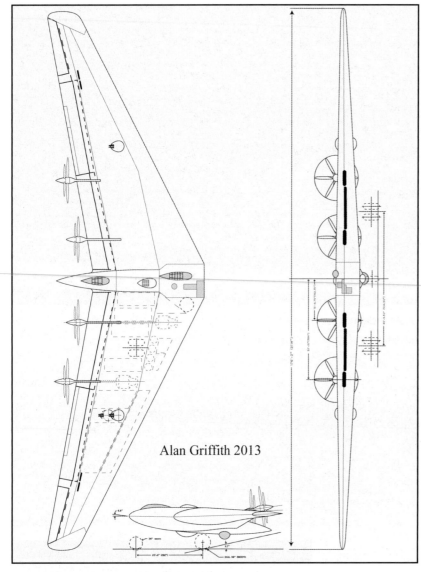

N-9M data

Span	60ft 0in (18.29m)
Length	17ft 9.5in (5.42m)
Wing area	490sq ft (45.57sq m)
Gross weight	6,326lb (2,869kg)
Powerplant	two 260hp (194kW) Menasco C6S-4
Maximum speed	257mph (414km/h)
Service ceiling	21,500ft (6,553m)

XB-35 data

Span	172ft 0in (52.43m)
Length	53ft 1in (16.18m)
Wing area	4,500sq ft (418.50sq m)
Gross weight (with turrets)	154,000lb (69,854kg)
Powerplant	four P&W R-4360
Armament	eighteen 0.50in (12.70mm) machine guns, maximum 52,200lb (23,814kg) bombs
Maximum speed	391mph (629km/h)
Service ceiling	40,000ft (12,192m), but restricted to 20,000ft (6,096m)
Range	7,500 miles (12,068km)
Rate of climb (YB-35)	625ft/min (191m/min)

Alan Griffith 2013

ABOVE Northrop XB-35 as modified for by Bell Aircraft engineers for their production.
Copyright Alan Griffith

1943 Studies

In August 1943 representatives of several manufacturers visited Material Command to propose new bomber aircraft. The last to visit were North American Aviation and Consolidated Vultee Aircraft (Consolidated and Vultee having now merged as Convair), and each company apparently presented several designs for consideration. It was practice for any new design proposals to be evaluated by the various Material Command laboratories. In this case information is available for two designs.

Consolidated/ Convair flying wing

The Consolidated proposal was for a four-engine tailless tractor heavy bomber with turbo-supercharged P&W R-4360 engines completely submerged in the wing and connected by extension shafts to two dual counter-rotating propellers 20ft 0in (6.10m) in diameter. Each engine would drive its own propeller, which could be feathered independently. The flight compartment was pressurised and the armament consisted of a nose turret (four 0.50in/12.70mm machine guns), an identical tail turret, and

upper and lower aft fuselage turrets each with two 37mm cannon, all of which were locally operated and pressurised. Integral tanks were provided for 7,000 gallons (26,498 litres) of fuel, and removable bomb bay tanks were also available to hold another 6,000 gallons (22,712 litres). There were nine crew members and the Air Corps review noted that the principal unconventional features for this design were:

1. It was a tailless design, permitting large increases in the lift drag ratio
2. The use of full-span flaps permitted a high lift coefficient
3. Longitudinal trim was obtained at the stall by using extending trailing edge and leading edge trim surfaces
4. Wingtip leading-edge slots were also provided

The project was examined by Convair at the same time as its smaller twin-engine patrol types covered in Chapter Eight. It was really just a study, and once this and the patrol aircraft research had been concluded Convair abandoned the concept of flying wings, on which its design teams had been working, together with blended wings, since at least 1937.

Consolidated/Convair flying wing data	
Span	190ft 0in (57.91m)
Length	62ft 0in (18.90m)
Wing area	3,600sq ft (334.80sq m)
Gross weight	180,000lb (8,165kg)
Powerplant	four 3,250hp (2,424kW) P&W R-4360 (3,630hp/2,707kW on War Emergency Power)
Armament	ten 4,000lb (1,814kg), twenty 2,000lb (907kg), thirty-five 1,000lb (454kg) or forty-six 500lb (207kg) bombs; see text for guns
Maximum speed	395mph (636km/h) at 30,000ft (9,144m), 407mph (655km/h) on War Emergency Power
Service ceiling (half fuel)	45,000ft (13,716m)
Range with 8,000lb (3,629kg) bomb load	7,500 miles (12,068km)

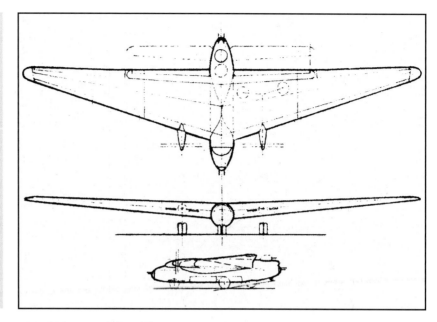

ABOVE The Consolidated flying wing bomber project (8.43). *Gerald Balzer*

North American NA-116

North American's four-engine heavy bomber was a midwing design with the engines mounted in side-by-side nacelles and driving four tractor six-blade counter-rotating propellers. The two inboard nacelles were extended to form booms that supported twin fins and rudders together with a single stabiliser and elevator. A short tailless fuselage was mounted between the booms and there was a tricycle undercarriage with three dual wheels. The 'design bomb load' was 10,000lb (4,536kg), and carrying this gave a range when flying at an altitude of 10,000ft (3,048m) (and with no bomb drop) of 5,000 miles (8,045km). The centre fuselage and both booms contained bomb bays, and the defensive

North American bomber data	
Span	154ft 0in (46.94m)
Length	85ft 9in (26.14m)
Wing area	unknown
Gross weight	132,000lb (59,876kg)
Powerplant	four 3,000hp (2,237kW) P&W XR-4360-SSG21-5 (3,450hp/2,573kW on War Emergency Power at sea level)
Armament	maximum 23,000lb (10,433kg) demolition or 34,000lb (15,422kg) armour-piercing bombs, fourteen 0.50in (12.70mm) machine guns, six 20mm cannon
Maximum speed	372mph (599km/h) at 25,500ft (7,772m)
Service ceiling (normal engine power at 2,200hp/1,641kW)	30,400ft (9,266m)

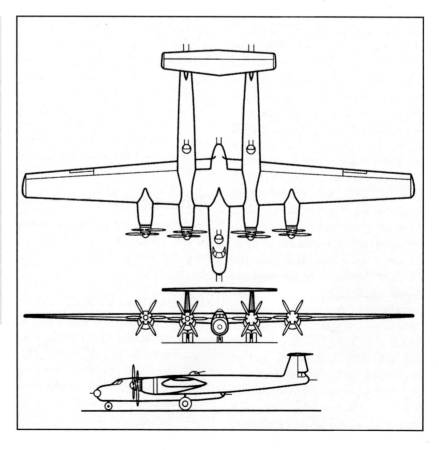

LEFT The North American NA-116 (8.43). Note that the design's defensive guns as described in the text from an Air Corps document do not match the arrangement shown in this drawing. *Dennis R. Jenkins*

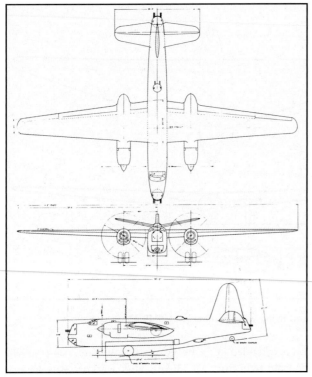

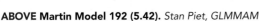

ABOVE Martin Model 192 (5.42). *Stan Piet, GLMMAM*

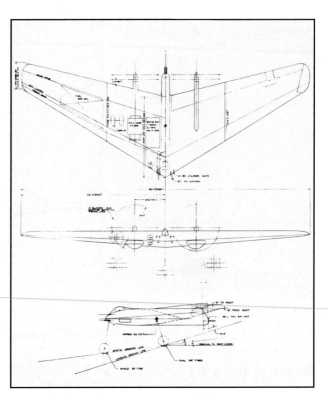

ABOVE Flying wing design that was considered under Martin's Model 192 designation. This is the Model 192-5, but the drawing is not dated (mid-1942). *Stan Piet, GLMMAM*

armament embraced four machine guns in a nose turret, two more in a fuselage upper turret, and two in each of four boom upper turrets, together with two cannon in the fuselage tail turret and two in a pair of boom tail turrets. Internal fuel totalled 6,100 gallons (23,091 litres), and the crew included a commander-pilot, co-pilot-engineer, navigator-bombardier, radio-operator-gunner and eight gunners.

On 30 August Colonel Turner A. Sims, Air Corps Deputy Chief of Staff, wrote a review of the Convair and North American projects, in the latter case providing most of the data to be found for the design to date. He declared that the most interesting of the proposals submitted so far had come from Consolidated Vultee, adding 'we feel that there is a definite advantage to tailless aircraft if the wing loading can be kept high and a high C/L [lift coefficient] can be obtained for the landing condition.' This had been accomplished on the design by the use of a retractable horizontal tail surface (at the time the

Aircraft Laboratory was studying this design as a two-engine version weighing approximately 80,000lb/36,288kg). Meanwhile the North American proposal, except for its armament arrangement, did not appear to offer any very definite advantages for the period 2½ years ahead, and it was felt that the B-29, with more horsepower and two years of intensive development, would be almost an equal. In the event, neither of the proposals was ordered.

Other Studies

This final section pulls together a few one-off studies, including a further Army Air Corps request for a new heavy bomber.

Martin Model 192

This type fell within a new category because the Martin Model 192 of 1942 was designed to be a dedicated land-based torpedo bomber and a conventional bomber. It would have been quite a large aeroplane with a long bomb bay, seven crew and the ability to

carry a considerable quantity of bombs. The original design appears to have been produced in April 1942 and was then revised on 2 May; it shows a large fuselage, a mid-position wing, a single fin and a tailwheel undercarriage with twin main wheels. The engines are unidentified, but they drove 16ft 0in (4.88m) four-blade propellers and the bomber itself had a span of 114ft 0in (34.75m) and a length of 74ft 3in (22.63m). There were four 0.50in (12.70mm) machine guns in the nose, another four in the end fuselage and two each in retractable dorsal and ventral turrets. The offensive loads were impressive – one 10,000lb (4,536kg) bomb, two Mk XV 3,400lb (1,542kg) torpedoes, eighteen 1,600lb (726kg) armour-piercing bombs, and six 2,000lb (907kg), fifteen 1,000lb (454kg) or twenty-one 300lb (136kg) bombs. In mid-November the design was revised again, following which it showed just two guns in the nose and tail, its span was unchanged but the length had been reduced slightly.

There may have been several other layouts because one alternative design has survived, the flying wing Model 192-5 from around the middle of 1942. Powered by a pair of P&W Wasp Majors, this aircraft had pusher contra-rotating 14ft 0in (4.27m)-diameter four-blade propellers and its span was to be 90ft 0in (27.43m). There was a 37mm cannon and two 0.50in (12.70mm) machine guns just to each side of the nose, and a further pair of defensive guns in a tail sting (eight guns in all), while the bomb load was not quite as substantial as the main project: one 2,000lb (907kg), two 1,000lb (454kg) or four 500lb (227kg) bombs in each of two bays just to either side of the centreline. The main gears had twin wheels and the fuel included an 800-gallon (3,028-litre) tank in each outer wing.

Martin Model 194

Towards the end of 1942 Martin produced a long-range bomber design, the Model 194, which fell between the sizes represented by the B-29 and B-36; in fact, Martin called it the 'Long Ranger' heavy bomber. The main layout (Design 1) had pusher engines driving contra-rotating propellers of 15ft 2in (4.62m) diameter, its span was 171ft 0in (52.12m), and its length (not including the barrels of the twin 37mm tail turret) 119ft 10in (36.52m). Besides the tail gun there were two upper fuselage and one lower fuselage turrets, each with four 0.50in (12.70mm) machine guns. All of the guns were remote controlled and, although no details are available, the bomb load appeared to have been considerable, borne out by each undercarriage leg having twin wheels. Two other designs considered were a tractor engine version of Design 1 (Design 3), together with another pusher type with about 21° of sweep on the wing leading edge; all three had the same wingspan and a similar fuselage.

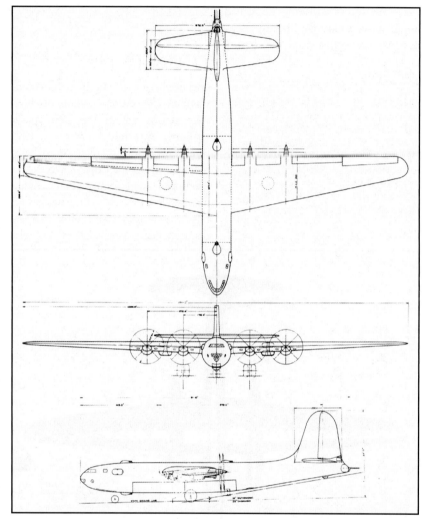

**ABOVE RIGHT
Martin Model 194
(12.42).**
Stan Piet, GLMMAM

**RIGHT Model 194
artwork.**
Stan Piet, GLMMAM

＊

During the latter part of 1942 there was a further AAC request for a twin-engine bombardment aircraft about which very little is known. In fact, to date the only concrete reference to it has been found in some Lockheed notes; it is unknown if any other designs were proposed and the identity

L-137-8 data

Span	122ft 6in (37.34m)
Length	87ft 0in (26.52m)
Wing area	1,500sq ft (139.50sq m)
Gross take-off weight	75,000lb (34,020kg)
Powerplant	two P&W Wasp Majors
Armament	4,000lb (1,814kg) bombs
Maximum speed at gross take-off weight	360mph (579km/h)
Service ceiling	37,000ft (11,278m)
Range with full bomb load	4,000 miles (6,436km)

of any covering specification has still to be discovered. It is possible that the Martin Models 195, 196 and 197 might have been involved because their dates slot into the timescale quite nicely, but no complete three-view drawings of those projects appear to exist, although a good number of internal detail drawings have survived.

Lockheed L-137

Lockheed's response to the requirement was the L-137, several variations of which were drawn within the same basic airframe. The only known surviving three-view drawing (reproduced here, redrawn) shows the L-137-8, which had a long slim tapered wing with the engine nacelles close inboard to the fuselage and fitted with propellers of 15ft 0in (4.57m) diameter. When assessed, the L-137 fell a

little short of the (currently unknown) stated limits for top speed and ferry range, but in all other respects the requirements were fulfilled.

USAAF Heavy Bombers in Perspective

The development of the heavy bomber during the years embraced by the Second World War saw the creation of some incredibly powerful machines, offering the capability to deliver heavy quantities of bombs over huge distances. The B-17s and B-24s based in England, together with British aircraft like the Avro Lancaster, dropped vast amounts of high explosive over enemy-held territory in Europe. A little later, B-29s carried the Pacific war to the Japanese homeland, and eventually concluded hostilities by dropping the atom bombs on Hiroshima and Nagasaki. This latter event would change the whole face of military strategy, setting a pattern for years to come, while the search for bigger and faster intercontinental bombers would continue. The B-29 would in turn be dwarfed by the massive B-36, the last word in piston engine bombers that would in time be replaced by the even heavier eight-jet B-52, an aircraft that remains in service to this day.

But while aircraft like the B-17 brought the capability for wide-scale destruction of enemy-held territories, there was another military requirement to which they were not well suited. That was the need to provide tactical support for battlefield or naval engagements. Between 1937 and 1945 the Army Air Corps looked at several widely differing attack types to meet this requirement, and these form the subject of the next chapter.

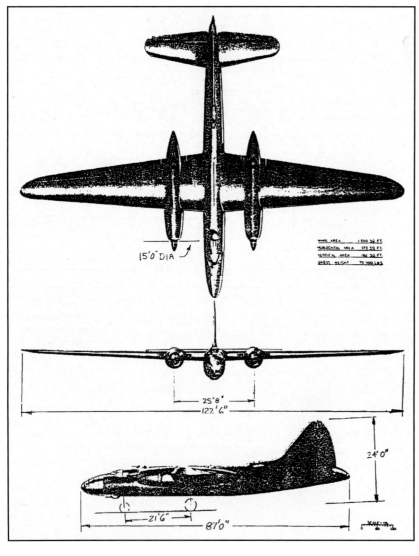

15'0" DIA

WING AREA 1,500 SQ FT
HORIZONTAL AREA 175 SQ FT
VERTICAL AREA 140 SQ FT
GROSS WEIGHT 75,000 LBS

25'8"
122'6"

24'0"

21'6"

87'0"

LEFT Lockheed L-137-8 (late 1942).
Peter Clukey

Chapter Five
USAAF Attack Aircraft

ABOVE One of the best of the attack aircraft types covered in this chapter was the Douglas A-26 Invader. This image shows 41-39158 undergoing assessment by the Aeroplane & Armament Experimental Establishment at Boscombe Down, UK, during August 1944.

Attack aircraft – aircraft designed for the specific role of supporting naval or land-based military campaigns – grew in importance as the Second World War progressed. Indeed, it became increasingly clear that both land and sea campaigns were heavily reliant on effective air support. As a consequence, considerable effort – by all the combatant nations – was put into the development of such aircraft. In the US this resulted in a wide range of designs, both large and small, some single-engine and some multi-engine.

In the years leading up to the war, the designs under consideration by the Air Corps were relatively modest in their capabilities, but five years later this had changed completely. Indeed, a number of impressive proposals had to be rejected simply because the industry was producing more high-potential designs than were needed. The records of many of these projects remain to be discovered. This chapter deals with USAAF types – the Navy equivalents are covered in Chapter Seven.

Multi-engine Programmes

The first competition for a new twin-engine attack aircraft spawned a series of prototypes. In December 1937 a specification was issued with very similar limits to 98-102 below, except that the requested bomb load was 1,200lb (544kg). However, by the time the surviving prototypes had reached the end of a fly-off competition (two had been lost in crashes) it was clear that in the face of new advances in technology and weaponry they were already becoming obsolescent.

RIGHT In the first view the Stearman X-100 is seen with its original nose, then with the amended later arrangement. *NARA II via Griffith*

Bell Model 9

There is little information for Bell's Model 9 proposal except that it is thought to have been a derivative of the YFM-1 Airacuda and that it was to be powered by Allison V-1710 inline engines. The project was withdrawn from the competition.

Model 9 data	
Gross weight	19,500lb (8,845kg)
Armament	includes two 37mm cannon
Maximum speed	255mph (410km/h) at 3,000ft (914m)

Douglas Model 7B

The Douglas Model 7B project was a revision of an earlier private venture light attack design from 1936 called the Model 7A. The 7B introduced more powerful engines to replace the units earmarked for the Model 7A (450hp/336kW Pratt & Whitney R-985 Wasp Juniors), and it had optional solid or transparent noses. The prototype first flew on 26 October 1938, and Douglas's own testing of the Model 7B proceeded satisfactorily; however, on 23 January 1939 the only example was destroyed in a crash before the Air Corps evaluation tests had got under way.

Stearman X-100/XA-21

The Stearman X-100 prototype first flew in March 1939 and took part in the Air Corps evaluation held later that month. Following assessment, the aircraft was fitted with a new and more conventional nose to replace its original streamlined glass version, but the type was not ordered into production and, as the XA-21, was subsequently used for trials flying. The experimental Pratt & Whitney Twin Hornet radial engines used by this aircraft did not enter production either.

XA-21 data	
Span	65ft 0in (19.81m)
Length	53ft 1in (16.18m)
Wing area	607sq ft (56.45sq m)
Gross weight	18,230lb (8,269kg)
Maximum weight	20,200lb (9,163kg)
Powerplant	two 1,400hp (1,044kW) P&W R-2180-7 Twin Hornet
Armament	five 0.30in (7.62mm) machine guns, 2,700lb (1,225kg) bombs
Maximum speed	257mph (414km/h) at 5,000ft (1,524m)
Service ceiling	20,000ft (6,096m)
Maximum range	1,200 miles (1,931km)

Model 7B data	
Span	61ft 0in (18.59m)
Length	45ft 5in (13.84m)
Wing area	464sq ft (43.15sq m)
Gross weight	15,200lb (6,895kg)
Powerplant	two 1,100hp (820kW) P&W R-1830 S3C3-G Twin Wasp
Armament	solid 'attack' nose: six 0.30in (7.62mm) and two 0.50in (12.70mm) machine guns; transparent 'bomber' nose: six 0.30in (7.62mm) machine guns, four fixed and two flexible; 2,000lb (907kg) bombs
Maximum speed	304mph (489km/h) at 5,000ft (1,524m)
Service ceiling	27,600ft (8,412m)
Combat range	1,555 miles (2,502km)

BELOW The Douglas Model 7B prototype, fitted with what was termed the 'B' nose. *NARA II via Griffith*

Martin Model 167F/XA-22

Martin's Model 167F first flew on 13 March 1939. This design was also rejected after the Air Corps's evaluation exercises, but it went on to win orders from the UK and France; in British service the type was named Maryland. The production run eventually stretched to 450 aeroplanes and when the prototype was acquired by the Air Corps it was designated XA-22.

BOTTOM A close-up view of the Martin 167F (XA-22) prototype, taken on 12 March 1939. *NARA II via Griffith*

BELOW LEFT A rare colour picture of a Martin Maryland. *Alan Griffith*

BELOW RIGHT A British official photograph of the Martin Maryland Mk I, taken in November 1941.

Maryland Mk I data	
Span	61ft 4in (18.69m)
Length	46ft 8in (14.23m)
Wing area	538.5sq ft (50.08sq m)
Gross weight	15,297lb (6,939kg)
Maximum take-off weight	16,809lb (7,625kg)
Powerplant	two 1,050hp (783kW) P&W R-1830-S1C3-G Twin Wasp
Armament	six 0.303in (7.70mm) machine guns, 2,000lb (907kg) bombs
Maximum speed	304mph (489km/h) at 13,000ft (3,962m)
Service ceiling	29,500ft (8,992m)
Range	1,300 miles (2,092km)

ABOVE Few photographs were taken of the North American NA-40 prototype. *Mark Nankivil*

North American NA-40

A single North American NA-40 prototype was also produced, and this first flew on 28 January 1939. However, its top speed fell short of what was needed, so Wright R-2600-A71 engines were installed as replacements for the original 1,100hp (820kW) P&W R-1830-S6C3-G Twin Wasps to produce what was called the NA-40B or NA-40-2 (the original engines gave a maximum speed of 265mph/426km/h). The only prototype was lost in a crash on 11 April, not surviving long enough to be given an Air Corps 'A' designation, but the design contributed much to the development the B-25 Mitchell covered in Chapter Three.

Douglas A-20

Douglas's DB-7 (Douglas Bomber 7) was a revision of the Model 7B and made its maiden flight on 23 January 1939. In due course the Army Air Corps placed an order for what was now designated the A-20, and as the 'Boston' this light bomber became very successful, with examples going to France, the UK and the Soviet Union. Variants included the Havoc night intruder and the P-70 night fighter, and nearly 7,500 examples of all versions were built.

NA-40-2 data	
Span	66ft 0in (20.12m)
Length	48ft 3in (14.71m)
Wing area	598.5sq ft (55.66sq m)
Gross weight	21,000lb (9,526kg)
Powerplant	two 1,600hp (1,193kW) Wright R-2600-A71
Armament	five 0.30in (7.62mm) machine guns, 1,200lb (544kg) bombs
Maximum speed	285mph (459km/h)
Service ceiling	25,000ft (7,620m)
Range	1,200 miles (1,931km)

DB-7 data	
Span	61ft 4in (18.69m)
Length	47ft 0in (14.33m)
Wing area	464.8sq ft (43.23sq m)
Maximum gross weight	17,031lb (7,725kg)
Powerplant	two 1,350hp (1,007kW) Wright R-2600-A5B
Armament	seven 0.30in (7.62mm) machine guns, maximum 2,080lb (943kg) bombs
Maximum speed	305mph (491km/h) at 9,650ft (2,941m)
Sea level rate of climb	2,440ft/min (744m/min)
Service ceiling	25,800ft (7,864m)
Range with 1,760lb (798kg) bombs	869 miles (1,398km)

LEFT A Douglas Boston serving with the Royal Air Force. The British involvement in a number of the aircraft programmes in this chapter (and this book) was considerable.

LEFT An example of the Martin A-30, which the RAF called the Baltimore.

Baltimore Mk V data	
Span	61ft 4in (18.69m)
Length	48ft 6in (14.78m)
Wing area	538.5sq ft (50.08sq m)
Gross weight	23,185lb (10,517kg)
Maximum weight	27,800lb (12,610kg)
Powerplant	two 1,700hp (1,268kW)
	Wright GR-2600-A5B
Armament	up to fourteen 0.303in
	(7.70mm) machine guns,
	2,000lb (907kg) bombs
Maximum speed	320mph (515km/h) at
	15,000ft (4,572m)
Average rate of climb	c2,080ft/min (634m/min)
Service ceiling	25,000ft (7,620m)
Range with 1,000lb/	980 miles (1,577km)
454kg bombs	

Martin Model 187/A-30 Baltimore

Martin's experience with the XA-22 and Maryland allowed the company to produce a successful follow-up aircraft, which was initially designated XA-23 but later became the A-30. It flew for the first time on 14 June 1941 and 1,575 were built, all destined for the RAF, which used the type extensively as the Baltimore.

Burnelli BX-AB-3

Published works have stated that the Burnelli BX-AB-3 was designed in competition with the Douglas Model 7B or the A-20, but this has not been confirmed. The design itself was typical Burnelli with a large central lifting fuselage/body between twin booms, the latter having twin fins and a single central horizontal tailplane in between. There was a long glass cockpit canopy (which looked large enough to cover a crew of three and had two defensive machine guns mounted at the rear), a tailwheel undercarriage, and four-blade propellers of a diameter of approximately 13ft (3.96m) driving liquid-cooled engines. The BX-AB-3's span was about 64ft (19.51m) and its length 47ft 6in (14.48m).

Multiple Proposals

In 1938 a new Specification 98-102, accompanied by Circular Proposal 38-385, called for a maximum speed of at least 250mph (402km/h) at 5,000ft (1,524m), with 280mph (451km/h) desired, a service ceiling of 20,000ft (6,096m), with 25,000ft (7,620m) desired, a range when flying at 5,000ft (1,524m) of 1,200 miles (1,931km), a 1,400lb (635kg) bomb load, six 0.30in (7.62mm) machine guns for defence, and a crew of three. The original Martin Model 167 (which became the XA-22 – see above) is one of the designs marked as having been submitted to 98-102, as was the Boeing Model 329, while the Curtiss Model 83 (about which nothing is known) was presented to CP 38-385.

The relationship between Specifications 98-102 and C-103 and C-104 that followed shortly afterwards has not been established, but there is every possibility that they were all linked. Indeed, most of the proposals in the early part of this chapter were

BELOW Burnelli BX-AB-3 (c1939). *Dave Ostrowski*

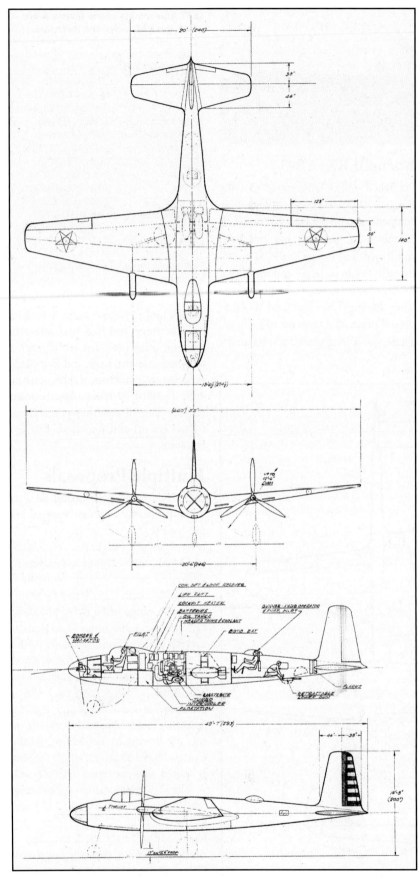

ABOVE Douglas DB-10 (11.8.38). *NARA II*

multi-engine designs that all appear to fall within a reasonably similar size and weight bracket.

Douglas DB-10

The Douglas DB-10 was a compact design with a mid-position tapered wing, and it was to be powered by two twelve-cylinder Lycoming XO-1230-1 'flat-type' engines enclosed in the wing and driving three-blade propellers up to 12ft 6in (3.81m) in diameter through shafts and right-angle gearboxes (the O-1230 was designed in the 1930s but was not especially successful due to problems with reliability). There was a tricycle undercarriage and the cabin was not pressurised, although the fuselage was of circular shape in order that 'supercharging' (pressurising) could be adopted at some stage with a minimum increase in weight. Internal fuel totalled 978 gallons (3,702 litres), and the six machine guns were arranged with four fixed (two in each side of the nose facing forward) and two flexible (in a rear-facing lower rear fuselage turret). At the overload weight the maximum range was given as 3,250 miles (5,229km), although the 'normal' range at 5,000ft (1,524m) was 1,260 miles (2,027km).

✳

DB-10 data	
Span	55ft 0in (16.76m)
Length	49ft 7in (15.11m)
Wing area	467sq ft (43.43sq m)
Gross weight	17,000lb (7,711kg)
Overload weight	20,800lb (9,435kg)
Powerplant	two 1,150hp (858kW) Lycoming XO-1230-1
Armament	six 0.30in (7.62mm) machine guns, maximum 1,400lb (635kg) bombs including one 1,100lb (499kg), two 600lb (272kg), four 300lb (136kg) or twelve 100lb (45kg) bombs
Maximum speed	302mph (486km/h) at 5,000ft (1,524m), 367mph (591km/h) at 25,000ft (7,620m) (or 385mph/ 619km/h at this height on take-off power)
Service ceiling	33,700ft (10,272m)
Time to 15,000ft (4,572m)	9.2min

A new series of studies was covered by Specification C-103 of July 1938, which in early 1939 was updated to C-103A. Among other increases in capability, C-103 requested a higher maximum speed of 350mph (563km/h) and the designs known to have been prepared to the first issue of the document are as follows.

Consolidated LB-8, LB-9 and LB-12

The first two of Consolidated's LB-8, LB-9 and LB-12 offerings were definitely presented against C-103, and the three-seat LB-8 had for its defence two fixed and four 'flexible' machine guns. It was joined by the LB-9 version, which added a third engine but which had the same armament. The LB12, powered by Rolls-Royce Merlin engines, was a little larger, and it has not been confirmed whether this was submitted officially against C-103.

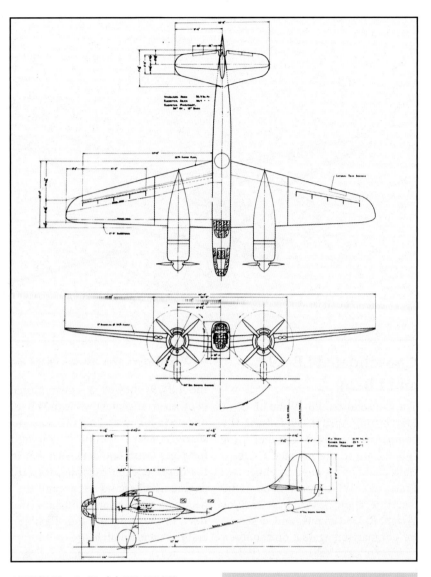

ABOVE Martin Model 175 (10.38).
Stan Piet, GLMMAM

LB-8 data	
Span	60ft 0in (18.29m)
Wing area	450sq ft (41.85sq m)
Gross weight	17,334lb (7,863kg)
Powerplant	two 1,000hp (746kW) Allison V-1710-F1
Armament	four 0.30in (7.62mm) machine guns, two 600lb (272kg) bombs
No performance data available	

LB-9 data	
Span	65ft 0in (19.81m)
Wing area	527sq ft (49.01sq m)
Gross weight	22,350lb (10,138kg)
Powerplant	three 1,000hp (746kW) Allison V-1710-F1
Armament	four 0.30in (7.62mm) machine guns, two 600lb (272kg) bombs
No performance data available	

LB-12 data	
Span	66ft 4in (20.22m)
Wing area	550sq ft (51.15sq m)
Gross weight	20,200lb (9,163kg)
Powerplant	two 1,050hp (783kW) RR Merlin
Armament	seven 0.30in (7.62mm) machine guns, 2,040lb (925kg) bombs
Maximum speed	352mph (566km/h) at 16,000ft (4,877m)
Range	1,580 miles (2,542km)

Martin Model 175

The Model 174 (below) and 175 light bombers were both based on Martin's Model 167/A-22 Maryland attack aircraft (see above) and were submitted to Specifications C-104 and C-103 respectively on the same day in late October 1938. The Model 175 was the smaller and lighter design and had a new wing low on the fuselage with a small degree of dihedral. The crew comprised the pilot, bombardier and rear gunner, the latter operating both single dorsal (in a retracting turret) and

Model 175 data	
Span	61ft 4in (18.69m)
Length	46ft 8in (14.23m)
Wing area	538.5sq ft (50.08sq m)
Gross take-off weight	21,587lb (9,792kg)
Powerplant	two P&W R-2800

single ventral rear-facing 0.30in (7.62mm) machine guns; the bomb load may have been a little less than that for the Model 174. The propeller diameter (four blades) was to be 12ft 0in (3.66m). No performance data is available for either type.

*

Later designs to C-103A (and CP 39-460 that went with it) are known to include the following, as well as the Martin 167A version of the above project.

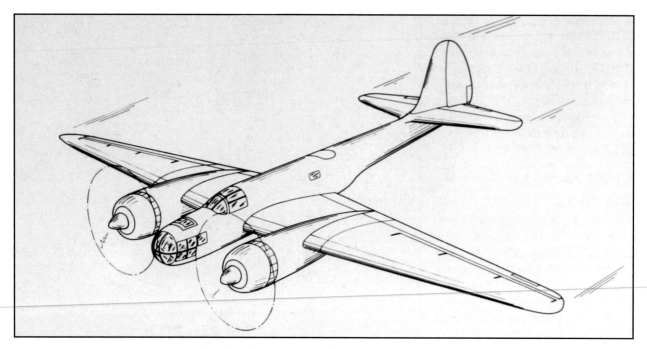

ABOVE **Martin's own artwork of the Model 175.** *Stan Piet, GLMMAM*

Consolidated LB-19 and LB-20

The Consolidated LB-19 and LB-20 of March and April 1939 formed the company's revised studies for submission to the updated C-103A. Both could be powered by either two Pratt & Whitney R-2800 (the 'baseline' choice), Wright R-2600 or Wright R-3350 engines and, designed for comparison against one another,

the LB-19 showed a conventional twin-fin arrangement while the LB-20 had twin booms. The two designs shared near identical forward fuselages (with one defensive gun in the nose), cockpit canopies, forward engine nacelles and wings, and they had the same wing area and guns (two fixed in the wing and four flexible), and the same bomb loads.

LB-19 data	
Span	60ft 0in (18.29m)
Length	42ft 5in (12.93m)
Wing area	530sq ft (49.29sq m)
Gross weight	21,083lb (9,563kg);
	21,147lb (9,592kg) (LB-20)

BELOW **Manufacturer's artwork for the Consolidated LB-19 (3.39).** *Alan Griffith*

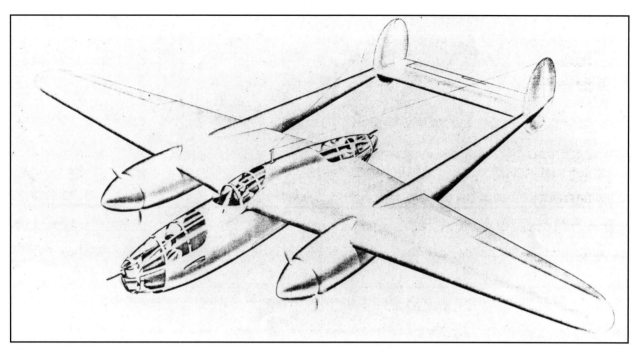

ABOVE Artwork for the Consolidated LB-20 (4.39). *Alan Griffith*

Martin Model 177

Martin's Model 177 light attack bomber of April 1939 looked quite different from the Models 174 and 175 in its general appearance, but was similar in terms of crew and weaponry. The aircraft had a heavily glazed nose, twin fins, a mid-position wing and a tailwheel undercarriage. Its powerplant is unknown but there were three-blade propellers having a diameter of 12ft 6in (3.81m). Two offensive guns were fixed in each outer wing outside the propeller arc, in addition to a retractable defensive dorsal turret with a 0.30in (7.62mm) machine gun, and a 0.50in (12.70mm) machine gun right at the end of the rear fuselage. The offensive load was a single 1,100lb (499kg) bomb or two 600lb (272kg), four 300lb (136kg) or eight 100lb (45kg) bombs, and the aircraft had a crew of three. The Model 177's span was 61ft 4in (18.69m) and its length 46ft 7in (14.20m).

The Model 177A project presented a very similar airframe fitted with two unidentified in-line piston engines and three-blade propellers of 11ft 0in

RIGHT Martin Model 177 (4.39). *Stan Piet, GLMMAM*

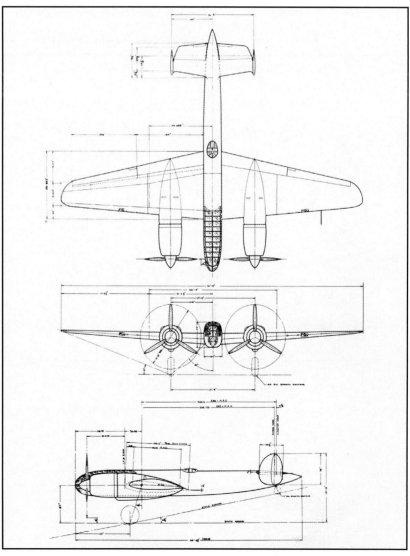

ABOVE Artwork for the Model 177. *Stan Piet, GLMMAM*

(3.35m) diameter. However, the airframe as a whole was scaled down to a span of 50ft 0in (15.24m) and a length of 41ft 5in (12.62m).

*

C-103 was matched by the issue of Specification C-104 in September 1938, which appears to have requested a similar category of aeroplane. The known designs to this requirement were submitted in January 1939 and, like all of the C-103 efforts, none were built.

Consolidated LB-14 and LB-15

Consolidated's three-seat twin-fin LB-14 project was another design to offer alternative powerplants (either two Allison V-3420s, or Pratt & Whitney X-1300s or Wright A617s), and in appearance it was fairly similar to but larger than the LB-12. The LB-14 used Fowler flaps and flush riveting to help provide an excellent speed performance; it had a tricycle undercarriage, and for defence there were two fixed nose guns together with a twin-gun tail turret. The LB-15 was a version powered by 'flat' engines.

BELOW Consolidated LB-14 (1.39).

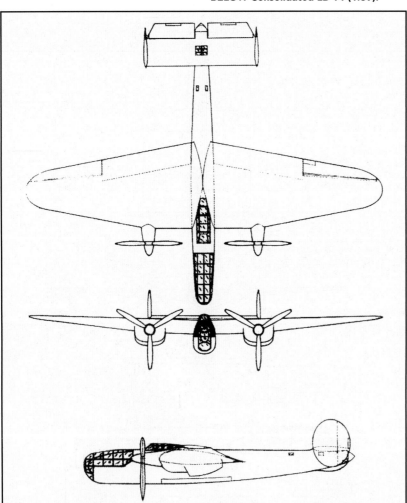

LB-14 data	
Span	60ft 0in (18.29m)
Wing area	600sq ft (55.80sq m)
Gross weight	22,650lb (10,274kg)
Powerplant	two 2,000hp (1,491kW) Allison V-3420-A3
Armament	four machine guns, 2,000lb (907kg) bombs
Maximum speed	430mph (692km/h) at 15,000ft (4,572m)
Range	1,200 miles (1,931km), or 1,960 miles (3,154km) with extra fuel

ABOVE Manufacturer's model of the Curtiss P-241 bomber project. The photo is dated 30 January 1939. *Dave Ostrowski* **RIGHT Curtiss P-241 (15.1.39).** *NARA II*

Curtiss P-241

The brochure for the Curtiss P-241 actually described it as a light bomber, and it was certainly a most unusual-looking design. Its elliptical wing was to employ a new aerofoil type and structure consisting of a specially developed symmetrical section with a maximum thickness 'at the 40% station', the aerofoil having been designed to reduce the possibility of entering the compressibility range at very high speeds. Its wing structure was a Curtiss-Wright neo-geodetic form based on an experimental wing design that had been statically tested for the earlier single-engine Curtiss 19R civil utility aircraft. This new and novel structure consisted primarily of equally spaced hat-section stiffeners nested into cross hats to reinforce the skin in a lattice-like manner. There were two spars of equal depth with no ribs, which, combined with a heavy-gauge surface skin, provided the capability to cope with higher stresses. The wing included a 'special flap' with the characteristics of the Fowler flap, designed for the Curtiss Model 20 transport (later the C-46), and it also had a full-span automatic built-in slot.

The P-241's fuselage was of monocoque construction and had a circular cross-section (again similar to the Model 20) so that it could withstand 'supercharging' (pressurisation – the crew

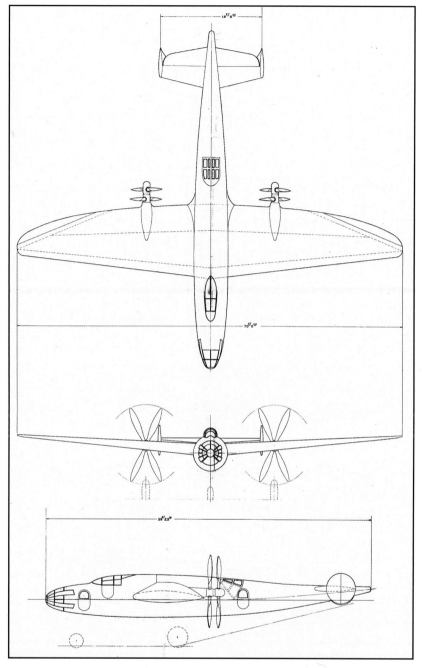

compartment forward of the engines was a pressurised cell). Its powerplant was to be two Wright R-3350s mounted face-to-face and connected by a 1:1 gearbox; on either side of the fuselage were ducts, one to provide engine cooling, the other engine supercharging; and the propellers were opposite-rotating to eliminate the effects of torque. The aircraft had a tricycle landing gear and twin fins, and

its bombs were to be carried in a compartment placed beneath and between the engines. There were front, wing and rear defensive guns, all of which were to be operated by remote control.

P-241 data	
Span	70ft 0in (21.34m)
Length	59ft 2.5in (18.04m)
Gross weight with	20,000lb to 22,000lb
full military load	(9,072kg to 9,979kg)
Armament (probable)	at least four machine guns, 2,000lb (907kg) bombs

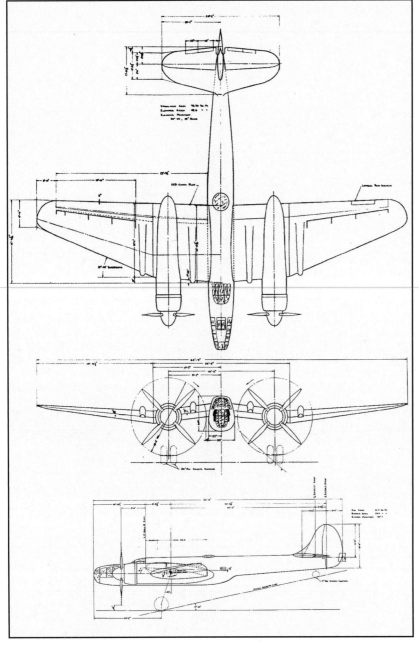

LEFT Martin Model 174 (10.38). *Stan Piet, GLMMAM*

Model 174 data	
Span	62ft 9in (19.13m)
Length	52ft 8in (16.05m)
Wing area	610sq ft (56.73sq m)
Gross take-off weight	c24,440lb (11,086kg)
Powerplant	two Allison XV-3420

Martin Model 174 (and 176)

Once more the Model 174 light bomber was based on the Maryland, but with a slimmer, more streamlined fuselage than the older aircraft; it also introduced a new inverted gull wing, which was swept outboard of the engine nacelles. Four-blade 12ft 9in (3.89m)-diameter props were fitted and the aircraft retained a conventional tailwheel undercarriage, here with twin main wheels. In internal layout the design was similar to the Model 175 above, with the same crew and defensive guns, while drawings showed an offensive load of one 2,000lb (907kg) or one 1,100lb (499kg) bomb, or two 600lb (272kg), four 300lb (136kg) or ten 100lb (45kg) bombs. In addition, again to C-104, Martin produced brief drawings for a Model 176, which had a heavily blended wing, but this appears not to have been submitted to the Air Corps.

Early Single-engine Programmes

Vultee V-72/A-31 and A-35 Vengeance

Work on the Vultee Vengeance began in 1940 in response to an order from France, but with that country's fall the deliveries were switched to the UK. No examples would be employed operationally by American air arms, but some were used for training, while the eventual number of A-31s and A-35s built exceeded 1,900. The prototype A-31 made its maiden flight on 30 March 1941, while the A-35 with a modified wing first appeared in September 1942.

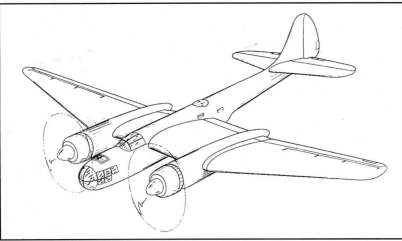

LEFT Manufacturer's artwork showing the Model 174. *Stan Piet, GLMMAM*

ABOVE This Vultee A-31 Vengeance is painted with US markings but carries a British serial number – EZ856. It was built by Northrop.

A-31 data	
Span	48ft 0in (14.63m)
Length	39ft 9in (12.12m)
Wing area	332sq ft (30.88sq m)
Maximum take-off weight	14,300lb (6,486kg)
Powerplant	one 1,600hp (1,193kW) Wright R-2600-A5B-5 Twin Cyclone
Armament	six 0.30in (7.62mm) machine guns, 1,000lb (454kg) bombs
Maximum speed	275mph (442km/h) at 11,000ft (3,353m)
Service ceiling	22,500ft (6,858m)
Range	700 miles (1,126km)

Brewster XA-32

The need for a type like the Brewster XA-32 dive bomber had been anticipated by the Air Corps before the war had started, and one problem that was apparent by November 1942, before the aircraft had flown, was to find a way of producing it in quantity – Brewster was a Navy facility and it could not handle this new type after having already won a great deal of priority Navy work. (In fact, according to an AAC report, the initiation by the Air Corps of a single-seat dive bomber like this did in fact change the view of the Navy, which had held to two-seat dive bombers for many years but now had several single-seaters under development.) The new Air Corps type, however, proved to be a poor aeroplane. Having been designed in 1941, the first of two XA-32 prototypes did not achieve a first flight until 22 May 1943; by then the aircraft had become substantially overweight and in the air its performance fell short of most of the estimated figures. Without bombs and flying in level flight, the

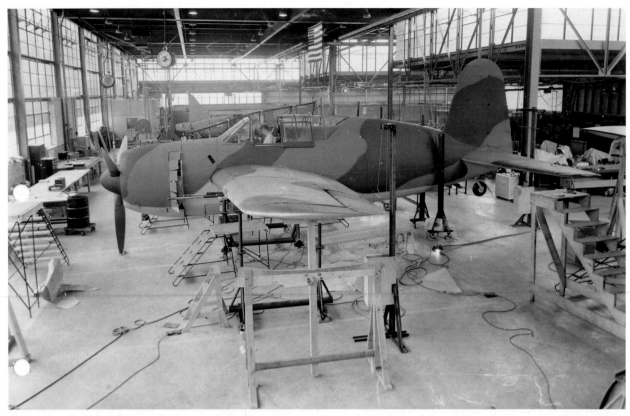

ABOVE The Brewster XA-32 mock-up seen in British camouflage.
NARA II via Griffith

XA-32 could manage a reasonable speed (279mph/449km/h according to AAC flight test reports), but the addition of external stores reduced the figure to 248mph (399km/h) and buffeting also now appeared at the maximum speed. These problems ensured that the XA-32 would never enter series production.

North American NA-97/ A-36 Apache

The A-36 was a ground attack version of North American's P-51 Mustang (see Chapter One) and was powered by the fighter's original Allison engine (the type was also known as Invader). In all, 500 were built and the variant could be

BELOW The XA-32 prototype is seen in 1943 during a test flight.
NARA II via Griffith

distinguished by the presence of rectangular, slatted dive brakes placed both below and above the wings. In fact, this feature apparently presented some problems in that the dive brakes had to be raised before entering a dive, because if they opened asymmetrically during a high-speed descent the differing airflow over the wings could produce damage and even tear off a wing. The first example flew in September 1942 and the type began its combat service in the middle of the following year.

XA-32 data	
Span	45ft 1in (13.74m)
Length	40ft 7in (12.37m)
Wing area	425sq ft (39.525sq m)
Gross weight	19,960lb (9,054kg)
Powerplant	one 2,100hp (1,566kW) P&W R-2800-37
Armament	six 0.50in (12.70mm) machine guns, four 20mm cannon, 1,000lb (454kg) bombs in bay, plus 2,000lb (907kg) under wings
Maximum speed	to be 311mph (500km/h) at 13,200ft (4,023m)
Sea level rate of climb	1,754ft/min (535m/min)
Service ceiling	26,000ft (7,925m)
Range with 3,000lb (1,361kg) bombs	300 miles (483km)

A-36A data	
Span	37ft 0in (11.28m)
Length	32ft 3in (9.83m)
Wing area	236sq ft (21.95sq m)
Maximum weight	10,700lb (4,854kg)
Powerplant	one 1,325hp (988kW) Allison V-1710-87
Armament	six 0.50in (12.70mm) machine guns, two 500lb (227kg) bombs
Maximum speed	356mph (573km/h) at 5,000ft (1,524m)
Best rate of climb	2,700ft/min (823m/min)
Service ceiling	25,100ft (7,650m)
Range	550 miles (885km)

ABOVE Serial 41-39108 was a production A-26B Invader.

Later twin-engine attackers

Finding a demarcation line between twin-engine attack aircraft and the twin-engine light bombers in Chapter Three has proved difficult, and some of the programmes described in this text could equally well have been placed in the earlier section. Indeed, after the war the A-26 described below was redesignated B-26.

Douglas A-26 Invader

Air Corps documents from late 1942 described the A-26 from Douglas as a light bomber or attack bomber. It was designed originally to fill the need for a type to be used by support aviation in roles that were visualised by the Air Board well before war had broken out. The original XA-26 was to have an 800-mile (1,287km) radius of operation, but

BELOW The Douglas XA-26B Invader prototype was serial 41-19588.
NARA II via Griffith

the initial requirements were raised in 1940 and Douglas was given first priority to design and develop the new type – there was no design competition and the firm's proposals were submitted in early 1941. However, the advent of war and the needs of ground air support aviation switched the emphasis to the XA-26B with a 'solid' nose, which to begin with could take anything from 0.50in (12.70mm) machine guns, 20mm or 37mm cannon, or even a 75mm howitzer. However, in time the normal solid-nose A-26 would contain six or eight machine guns.

The first example flew on 10 July 1942 and in their early stages both versions appeared to be unusually attractive projects, the flight test programme showing excellent performance and handling and a top speed that exceeded the original guaranteed figure. The two versions were followed by the A-26C with a glass bombardier's nose, and the A-26 (later B-26) did prove to be quite a

success, operating in several theatres of the war from 1944, and continuing in service for many years afterwards. In fact, it became a veteran of three major conflicts – the Second World War, Korea and Vietnam. The last American Air National Guard examples lasted until the early 1970s, and many other countries also acquired the type. Altogether more than 2,450 were built.

XA-26 data	
Span	70ft 0in (21.34m)
Length	51ft 2in (15.60m)
Wing area	540sq ft (50.22sq m)
Normal weight	26,700lb (12,111kg)
Maximum take-off weight	31,000lb (14,062kg)
Powerplant	two 2,000hp (1,491kW) P&W R-2800-27
Maximum speed	370mph (595km/h) at 17,000ft (5,182m)
Service ceiling	31,300ft (9,540m)

A-26C bomber data	
Armament	six 0.50in (12.70mm) machine guns, maximum load 6,000lb (2,722kg) bombs; could also carry two 2,000lb (907kg) torpedoes

ABOVE A three-quarter left front image of the imposing XA-38. *Alan Griffith*

Beech Model 28/XA-38 'Grizzly'

During the late autumn of 1942 the Air Corps reported that the only current project that it had for what was called the 'destroyer type' category was the Beech XA-38. This had a two-man crew, a 75mm gun and two 0.50in (12.70mm) machine guns in the nose, and two twin 0.50in (12.70mm) turrets, top and bottom, for rear defence. The XA-38 was begun in 1942 as a 'bomber-destroyer' aeroplane, but later became an attack type in the effort to find a replacement for the Douglas A-20. What was required by then was a powerful ground attack machine that could hit 'hardened' targets

such as bunkers and armour, and in December 1942 a contract was awarded for two prototypes. The original Model 28 layout showed a three-seater, which looked like a scaled-up Model 18 Twin Beech training and utility aircraft, but by the time the first prototype flew on 7 May 1944 the design had been thoroughly revised. However, no orders were placed beyond the two prototypes, despite the aircraft showing a good performance with a top speed higher than predicted. One reason behind the

lack of orders was that the XA-38's engine type was required for the Boeing B-29 production run. In addition, the AAF did not get its hands on a prototype until the war was nearly over, by which time the need for Beech's attacker had passed. There were four underwing hardpoints. The XA-38's name was unofficial.

BELOW One of the XA-38 prototypes is seen during a test flight. *Ryan Crierie*

XA-38 data	
Span	67ft 4in (20.52m)
Length	51ft 9in (15.77m)
Wing area	626sq ft (58.22sq m)
Design gross weight	29,900lb (13,563kg)
Maximum take-off weight	35,265lb (15,996kg)
Powerplant	two 2,300hp (1,715kW) Wright R-3350-43
Maximum speed	376mph (605km/h) at 4,800ft (1,463m)
Sea level rate of climb	2,170ft/min (661m/min)
Service ceiling	27,800ft (8,473m)
Combat range	1,070 miles (1,722km)

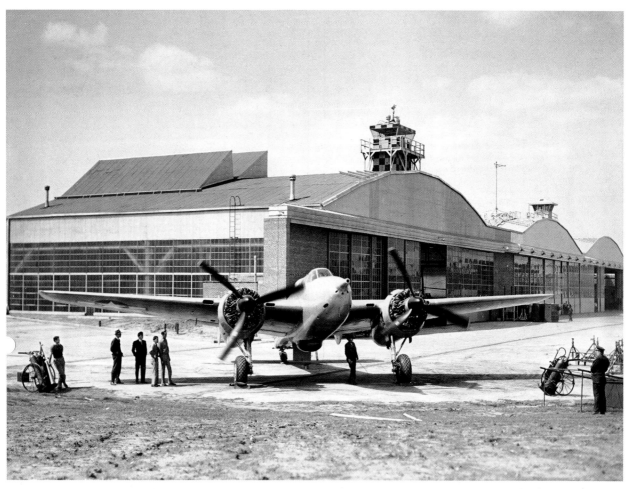

Final Single-engine Projects

The wartime attack aircraft story is rounded off by a series of powerful single-engine designs, and those that follow in the 'A' series were apparently started off by new requirements drafted in October 1941 (Ryan's Model 26 may also have been a rival to the three resulting 'XAs'). These requested a single-seat close support Army co-operation aircraft, and speeds of the order of

ABOVE The first engine run of the prototype Beech XA-38. *Alan Griffith*

340mph (547km/h) at 16,000ft (4,877m) were envisioned. A maximum speed at sea level in excess of 300mph (483km/h) was considered essential, the desired service ceiling was 30,000ft (9,144m), with 25,000ft (7,620m) the minimum requirement, and the desired range was to be 1,200 miles (1,931km), with 800 miles (1,287km) the minimum. Fixed forward-firing wing-mounted 37mm,

20mm or 0.50in (12.70mm) guns were stated (all outside the propeller disc area), and at least one 1,000lb (454kg) or two 500lb (227kg) bombs would be carried. There was also to be provision for one 2,000lb (907kg) bomb or torpedo. In due course the XA-39, XA-40 and XA-41 were all killed off after it was established that single-seat fighters such as the P-47 Thunderbolt and P-51 Mustang were good enough to perform ground support duties as well. The XA-41 prototype was retained for technical reasons.

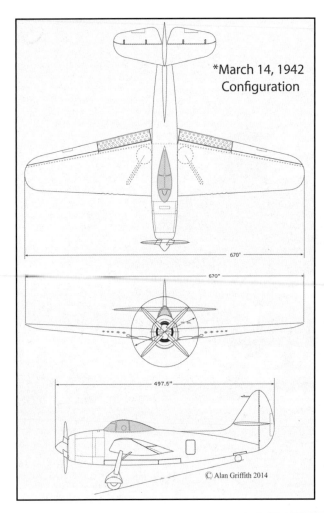

*March 14, 1942 Configuration

ABOVE The original configuration for the Kaiser-Fleetwings XA-39 (14.3.42).
Alan Griffith copyright

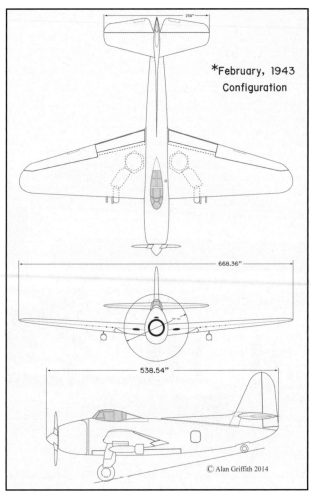

*February, 1943 Configuration

ABOVE The Kaiser-Fleetwings XA-39 as it looked in February 1943.
Alan Griffith copyright

Kaiser-Fleetwings H-60/ XA-39

By November 1942 the single-seat Fleetwings XA-39 was looked upon as a parallel development to the XA-32, with improvements in speed coming from an improved cowling around the engine as well as from aerodynamic refinements; it also had an increased bomb load. The bombs would have been carried externally and the guns were in the wings outside the propeller arc. There is not too much other information currently available concerning the XA-39, but it failed to progress to hardware and in the end only a mock-up was constructed. The 14 March 1942 drawing is considered to be the original proposal, while the last known drawing is dated 23 July 1943.

XA-39 data (at February 1943)

Span	55ft 8.25in (16.98m)
Length	44ft 10.5in (13.68m)
Wing area	513sq ft (47.71sq m)
Gross weight	16,160lb (7,330kg)
Maximum overload	21,772lb (9,876kg)
Powerplant	one 2,000hp (1,491kW) P&W R-2800-27
Armament	four 0.50in (12.70mm) machine guns and two 37mm cannon (alternatives six and four or eight and two respectively), one 2,000lb (907kg), two 1,600lb (726kg) or 1,000lb (454kg), six 500lb (227kg) bombs or six 325lb (147kg) depth bombs in fuselage bay, two 1,600lb (726kg), 1,000lb (454kg), 500lb (227kg) or 325lb (147kg) on wing racks
Maximum speed	332mph (534km/h) at sea level, 357mph (574km/h) at 16,600ft (5,060m)
Rate of climb	not given
Service ceiling	27,050ft (8,245m)
Maximum range	1,580 miles (2,542km)

XA-39 data (at 14 March 1942)

Span	55ft 10in (17.02m)
Length	41ft 5.5in (12.62m)
Wing area	504.5sq ft (46.92sq m)
Normal gross weight	15,670lb (7,108kg)
Powerplant	one P&W R-2800
Armament	ten guns, bomb load unknown

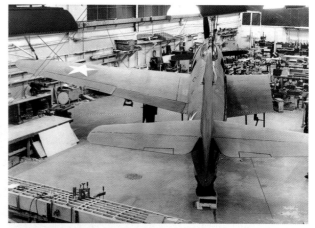

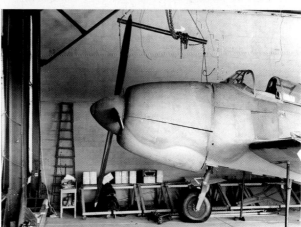

ABOVE The Kaiser-Fleetwings XA-39 mock-up, photographed on 11 August 1943.
NARA II via Griffith

Curtiss XA-40

The Curtiss XA-40 was begun as an attempt to standardise with the Navy on the single-seat XTBC-1, which was being engineered at Columbus (see Chapter Seven). By November 1942 this picture had changed a little, with the Air Corps version of the Navy's basic design being engineered at St Louis, although it would still use as many standard features as possible in order to save engineering time and effort. It was

understood, however, that Curtiss was also using this change of location as an attempt to stop having to build the Brewster XA-32 at its St Louis plant. The XA-40 was abandoned in October 1943 with just the mock-up completed.

BELOW The XA-40 project actually began with the Curtiss SB3C which the AAC planned to obtain. However, when the Navy didn't pick it up Curtiss made subsequent proposals such as the P-276 (followed by the P-279), neither of which were accepted as the entire classification of Single-engine, Single-seat Army Cooperation Aircraft (read Dive Bombers) was eliminated in October, 1943. *Alan Griffith*

XA-40 data	
Span	48ft 0in (14.63m)
Length	36ft 4in (11.07m)
Gross weight	17,120lb (7,766kg)
Powerplant	two Wright R-3350-8
Armament	six 0.50in (12.70mm) machine guns, four 20mm cannon, 2,000lb (907kg) bombs or torpedoes
Maximum speed	358mph (576km/h) at 16,000ft (4,877m)

Vultee V-90/XA-41

Vultee's single-seat XA-41 was based around the Wasp Major engine, the extra horsepower provided by this unit resulting in improved performance, particularly in the number and sizes of the various bombs that could be carried, but not necessarily also with a great increase in speed. In fact, in late 1942, well before the aircraft had flown, the Air Corps considered the XA-41 to be a particularly interesting project because it would be an opportunity to find out just what could be done with an attack/support aircraft fitted with the powerful 3,000hp (2,237kW) engine. Two prototypes of the XA-41 were ordered as dive bombers in

XA-41 data	
Span	54ft 0in (16.46m)
Length	48ft 8in (14.83m)
Wing area	540sq ft (50.22sq m)
Gross weight	18,800lb (8,528kg)
Maximum take-off weight	23,359lb (10,596kg)
Powerplant	one 3,000hp (2,237kW) P&W R-4360-9
Armament	four 0.50in (12.70mm) machine guns, four 37mm cannon, up to 6,500lb (2,948kg) bombs or stores
Maximum speed	353mph (568km/h) at 15,500ft (4,724m)
Sea level rate of climb	c2,300ft/min (701m/min)
Service ceiling	27,000ft (8,230m)
Range with 3,000lb (1,361kg) bombs	800 miles (1,287km)

ABOVE The sole Vultee XA-41 prototype to fly was serial 43-35124.

November 1942, but their role was soon altered to low-altitude attack. However, as noted, by the time the first of them flew on 11 February 1944 a decision had been taken to fly only the one XA-41 because the Air Corps had realised that its existing fighter types were performing ground attack operations well enough to remove any need for a new specialised aeroplane. The first prototype was completed to allow it to serve as a testbed aircraft, a role that it performed (mainly with Pratt & Whitney) until 1950; the second machine was cancelled outright.

Ryan Model 26

Ryan's Model 26 from February 1942 sported a very distinct inverted gull wing and had an all-metal fuselage covered in stressed skin. The forward fuselage behind the power unit incorporated the bomb bay and the cockpit, and was made from two deep beams with heavy longerons forming chord members and curved external skins stiffened by transverse frames. The aft portion of the fuselage was an approximately conical full monocoque structure consisting of curved sheet covering stiffened by transverse channel-type bulkheads. The wing comprised a centre section built integrally with the fuselage together with two outer panels having detachable wingtips; basically its construction was of the two-spar box-type with flat sheet, corrugations and/or stringers and extruded beam chord members. Aluminium alloy was to be used throughout, although heat-treated steel fittings would be introduced for highly stressed parts. There were 20% chord slotted flaps extending from the fuselage to the inner end of the ailerons, and dive

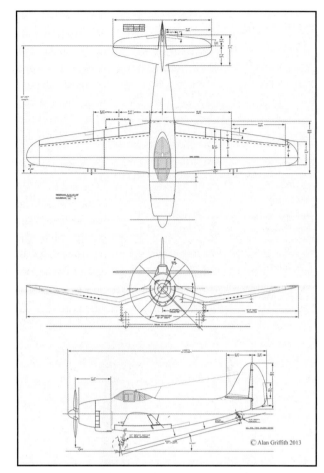

RIGHT Ryan Model 26 (15.2.42). *Alan Griffith copyright*

BELOW Manufacturer's sketch showing the Model 26. *NARA II via Alan Griffith*

Model 26 data	
Span	55ft 0in (16.76m)
Length	40ft 8in (12.40m)
Wing area	400sq ft (37.20sq m)
Gross weight	14,800lb (6,713kg)
Powerplant	one 2,100hp (1,566kW) P&W R-2800-37
Armament	see text
Maximum speed	297mph (478km/h) at sea level, 318mph (512km/h) at 16,000ft (4,877m)
Sea level rate of climb	2,820ft/min (860m/min)
Service ceiling (full power)	30,400ft (9,266m)
Absolute ceiling	31,400ft (9,571m)
Maximum range (normal fuel)	868 miles (1,397km)
Range with 750 gallons (2,839 litres) fuel	3,420 miles (5,503km)

BELOW **Martin Model 201 (24.5.43).** *NARA II via Stan Piet*

brakes were in place to limit the Model 26's speed in a dive for bomb-dropping or to reduce its speed in readiness to release a torpedo. The dive brakes operated independently from the slotted flaps, and the 26's dive speed limit was 510mph (821km/h).

The Model 26's normal internal fuel load was 200 gallons (757 litres), but for the overload condition this could be increased to 750 gallons (2,839 litres). Its bomb bay could take one 1,000lb (454kg), two 500lb (227kg) or two 300lb (136kg) bombs, while also having provision to take one 2,000lb (907kg) bomb or a 2,000lb (907kg) torpedo as overload, and

the underwing load (one per wing) was two 500lb (227kg) or 300lb (136kg) bombs. The wing-mounted guns could be either two 37mm cannon, five 0.50in (12.70mm) machine guns, or a combination of three 0.50in (12.70mm) machine guns and two 20mm cannon, in each outer wing. A four-blade 13ft 2in (4.01m)-diameter propeller was fitted, and the aircraft had a tailwheel undercarriage. It is unknown if the Model 26 was designed in competition with any of the above single-engine types or if it was just an unsolicited proposal. Nevertheless, the design was not accepted.

Martin Model 201

Martin's Model 201 was described as a high-performance low-level attack bombardment airplane and the brochure was submitted to the Air Corps Engineering Division in mid-June 1943. The aircraft was designed primary to perform tactical missions as part of a large strike force and to destroy targets on land and sea in close support of air, ground and naval forces. It was considered to be particularly outstanding with respect to its speed, which was achieved primarily by using very powerful engines installed in the fuselage in such a manner as to eliminate wing nacelles completely. This in turn reduced the aircraft's frontal area and permitted the use of an uninterrupted flap area from the side of the fuselage to the aileron. The dual Allison V-3420 powerplant embedded in the nose of the aircraft would drive dual-rotation fully-feathering quick-reversing constant-speed propellers of 15ft 6in (4.72m) diameter, eight blades in all.

The aircraft had straight tapered mid-position wings and a dihedral tailplane. Its fuselage used a semi-monocoque structure, a tricycle undercarriage was fitted, and there were three crew members – two pilots and a rear gunner. The defensive firepower comprised two 0.50in (12.70mm) machine guns in a tail turret, and for its offensive role the Model 201 had provision in its wings for twelve 0.50in (12.70mm) machine guns or six 20mm cannon. Self-sealing fuel tanks in the wing provided a total of 1,180 gallons (4,467 litres) of fuel, while the bomb bay

ABOVE This artwork of the Model 201 in flight shows what an attractive and balanced design it was. *NARA II via Stan Piet*

BELOW Although essentially the same image, this view shows the Martin 201 fitted with a dorsal turret for additional defence together with another single gun in the main cockpit. No information is available for this variant. *GLMMAM*

MODEL ⊛ 201...
HIGH PERFORMANCE
MEDIUM BOMBER
The Glenn L. Martin Company

ABOVE This is a further version of the Martin 201 with a mid-position wing and other subtle differences, but retaining twelve wing guns. Unfortunately, nothing is known about this design and whether it preceded or followed the layout shown in the May 1943 brochure. *NARA II via Stan Piet*

ABOVE Artwork for the later Model 201 version. *NARA II via Stan Piet*

Model 201 data

Span	78ft 0in (23.77m)
Length (not including tail gun barrels) 63ft 4in	
	(19.30m)
Wing area	760sq ft (70.68sq m)
Tactical gross weight	40,264lb (18,264kg)
with four 1,000lb	
(454kg) bombs	
Powerplant	two 2,850hp (2,125kW)
	Allison V-3420-A21
Armament	one 4,000lb (1,814kg), two
	2,000lb (907kg), four
	1,000lb (454kg), six 500lb
	(227kg), ten 250lb (113kg)
	or fifteen 100lb (45kg)
	bombs, two Navy MK 13-2
	torpedoes, fifteen
	fragmentation clusters,
	eight non-rotating or
	eighteen MK-241-type
	rocket projectiles (by
	August 1943 weapon
	choice included one
	8,000lb/3,629kg or six
	1,600lb/726kg bombs)
Maximum speed	425mph (684km/h) at sea
	level (441mph/710km/h
	when using War
	Emergency Power)
Service ceiling	at least 23,000ft (7,010m)
Sea level rate of climb	3,100ft/min (945m/min)
at light weight	
Range with 4,000lb	2,740 miles (4,409km)
(1,814kg) bombs	

beneath the cockpit could take an additional two 500-gallon (1,893-litre) fuel cells for ferry operations. The Model 201 had a design minimum/maximum terminal velocity with and without dive brakes respectively of 300mph (483km/h) and 520mph (837km/h). The detail given in the brochure (and the fact that there appears to have been more than one version of the design) indicates that a lot of work was undertaken on this project, and it appears to have attracted a good deal of interest. However, the Model 201 was not ordered and the Martin list notes that the project was 'inactive' at 10 December 1943.

USAAF Attack Aircraft in Perspective

Surprisingly, the development of attack aircraft (known in some official documents as the 'support class') appears to have been somewhat neglected in books on aviation history – certainly by comparison with the larger category of light bombers. This is a pity because the final generation of USAAF piston-powered attack types – the A-26, XA-38

to XA-41 series, the Martin 201 and Ryan 26 – represents a fascinating group of aeroplanes. They could perhaps be described as the ultimate in piston-powered attack aircraft, equivalent to the de Havilland Mosquito, which the British now classified as a bomber.

The Air Corps also subsequently dropped the 'A' category. The XA-42 (covered in Chapter Three) was redesignated XB-42 and the first jet-powered attack aeroplanes – the XA-43, XA-44 and XA-45 – were all given new 'B' numbers. This brought the old attack aircraft sequence to an end – at least until its resurrection in the 1960s. Having now covered all US Army Air Corps combat types except for certain patrol aircraft, the next chapters move on to deal with the US Navy's equivalents in the search for new fighters and bombers.

Chapter Six
US Navy Fighters

While the Air Corps was making the huge strides to improve its capability, resulting in the multitude of proposals that led to the outstanding aircraft described in the earlier chapters, the Navy was taking similar steps – and the outcome was no less impressive. One interesting difference revealed during the research for this book, however, was the greater effort spent exploring the potential offered by mixed-powerplant engines. This was an attempt to improve on the performance of piston-engine fighters – which was approaching its limit –

While the Air Corps was making the huge strides to improve its capability, resulting in the multitude of proposals that led to the outstanding aircraft described in the earlier chapters, the Navy was taking similar steps – and the outcome was no less impressive. One interesting difference revealed during the research for this book, however, was the greater effort spent exploring the potential offered by mixed-powerplant engines. This was an attempt to improve on the performance of piston-engine fighters – which was approaching its limit –

before sufficiently powerful jet engines were available to permit effective carrier operations.

This chapter looks at the studies and competitions that would give rise to some of the most successful and impressive fighters – on land or sea – of the war.

Early Studies

A 1935 design competition for a single-seat single-engine fighter resulted in two new types for the Navy, the Grumman Wildcat and Brewster Buffalo.

ABOVE One of the dominant fighter aircraft of the Second World War was the Vought F4U Corsair. This example, serial 57707, was in fact an F4U-1D variant.

Brewster F2A Buffalo

Brewster's XF2A-1 prototype made its maiden flight on 2 December 1937 and the Buffalo went on to serve with several air arms. It was the US Navy's first monoplane fighter to enter service, but its performance and handling suffered through increases in weight, and in the end only 500 were manufactured.

ABOVE The F2A Buffalo was a disappointing aircraft. The identity of this F2A-1 is not visible.

LEFT This Grumman F4F-3 Wildcat was photographed on 1 April 1943.
Tommy Thomason

XF2A-1 data	
Span	35ft 0in (10.67m)
Length	25ft 6in (7.77m)
Wing area	209sq ft (19.44sq m)
Gross weight	5,017lb (2,276kg)
Powerplant	one 950hp (708kW) Wright XR-1820-22
Armament	one 0.30in (7.62mm) and one 0.50in (12.70mm) machine gun
Maximum speed	278mph (447km/h) at 15,200ft (4,633m)
Sea level rate of climb	2,750ft/min (838m/min)
Service ceiling	30,900ft (9,418m)

F2A-2 data	
Maximum speed	323mph (520km/h) at 16,500ft (5,029m)
Service ceiling	34,000ft (10,363m)

Grumman F4F Wildcat

The Grumman F4F Wildcat was produced as a new design after Brewster's proposal had been favoured over Grumman's back-up G-16/XF4F-1 biplane prototype, the latter subsequently being abandoned before its completion since it was clearly inferior. The monoplane G-18/XF4F-2 prototype first flew on 2 September 1937 and proved superior to the Buffalo. By the start of the war the Wildcat had become one of the very best of the world's naval fighters and nearly 7,900 were eventually built. In Royal Navy service the F4F was called the Martlet.

XF4F-2 data	
Span	34ft 0in (10.36m)
Length	26ft 5in (8.05m)
Wing area	232sq ft (21.58sq m)
Gross weight	5,231lb (2,373kg)
Powerplant	one 900hp (671kW) P&W R-1830-66
Armament	two or four 0.50in (12.70mm) machine guns, 200lb (91kg) bombs
Maximum speed	288mph (463km/h) at 10,000ft (3,048m)
Sea level rate of climb	2,650ft/min (808m/min)
Service ceiling	29,540ft (9,004m)
Range	740 miles (1,191km)

ABOVE The Grumman XF6F-1 Hellcat prototype was serial 02981. *Tommy Thomason*

Grumman G-50/F6F Hellcat

Grumman's F6F Hellcat was designed in 1940 as an in-house successor to the F4F and the prototype contract for the XF6F-1 was signed in June 1941. Some sources state that the F6F resulted from a December 1940 design competition, but the George Spangenberg references indicate that the new type came from informal studies with Grumman. The first example flew on 26 June 1942 with a 1,700hp (1,268kW) Wright R-2600-10, but a decision was made to fit the more powerful Pratt & Whitney R-2800, which became standard. The fighter went on to serve with the US, British and French navies; more than 12,000 were produced, and it became a dominant force in the Pacific theatre and responsible for destroying more enemy aircraft than any other Allied naval aeroplane.

Single- and Twin-engine Competitions

In February 1938 the Navy's Bureau of Aeronautics (BuAer) issued Requests for Proposals for both single-engined and twin-engined fighter designs under Specifications SD-112-13 and SD-112-14 respectively. The first type was to have the highest maximum speed that could be obtained, together with a range of 1,000 miles (1,609km), and proved to be the starting point for the highly successful Chance Vought F4U Corsair. Overall, little information is available for the designs produced against these competitions, but it is possible that Martin's Model 168

project would have been involved here.

Bell Model 5/XFL-1 Airabonita

The Bell XFL Airabonita looked like a navalised version of the Army Air Force's P-39 from Chapter One, the biggest change being the use of a tailwheel undercarriage instead of the former's tricycle arrangement, together with the introduction of a tailhook. However, in fact it was close to being an all-new design that happened to look very like the P-39. One prototype was requested, and it first flew on 13 May 1940, but the early test results were not very good: there were development problems with both

XF6F-3 data

Span	42ft 10in (13.05m)
Length	33ft 10in (10.31m)
Wing area	334sq ft (31.06sq m)
Gross weight	12,179lb (5,524kg)
Powerplant	one 2,000hp (1,491kW) P&W R-2800-10
Armament	six 0.50in (12.70mm) machine guns
Maximum speed	398mph (640km/h) at sea level
Rate of climb	3,200ft/min (975m/min)
Service ceiling	39,900ft (12,162m)
Range (F6F-3)	1,090 miles (1,754km)

BELOW The prototype Bell XFL-1 Airabonita is seen on 3 October 1940. *Mark Nankivil*

XFL-1 data

Span	35ft 0in (10.67m)
Length	29ft 9in (9.07m)
Wing area	232sq ft (21.58sq m)
Gross weight	6,742lb (3,058kg)
Powerplant	one 1,150hp (858kW) Allison XV-1710-6
Armament	two 0.30in (7.62mm) machine guns plus one 0.50in (12.70mm) or one 37mm cannon
Maximum speed	281mph (452km/h) at sea level, 333mph (536km/h) at 12,000ft (3,658m)
Rate of climb	2,630ft/min (802m/min)
Service ceiling	33,000ft (10,058m)
Range	1,127 miles (1,813km)

V-166B XF4U-1 data

Span	40ft 0in (12.19m)
Length	30ft 0in (9.14m)
Wing area	314sq ft (29.20sq m)
Gross weight	9,357lb (4,244kg)
Maximum take-off weight	10,500lb (4,763kg)
Powerplant	one 1,800hp (1,342kW) P&W XR-2800-4
Armament	one 0.30in (7.62mm) and three 0.50in (12.70mm) machine guns, 200lb (91kg) bombs
Maximum speed	405mph (652km/h) at 9,600ft (2,926m)
Sea level rate of climb	2,260ft/min (689m/min)
Service ceiling	31,000ft (9,449m)
Maximum range	1,071 miles (1,723km)

engine and undercarriage, and there would be no production orders.

Chance Vought V-166/ F4U Corsair

Vought's winning Corsair was first proposed in two forms as the V-166A and V-166B (the same airframe but with different engines), and two prototypes were ordered; the first XF4U-1 became airborne on 29 May 1940. Unlike its rival from Bell, the F4U was manufactured in great numbers, with more than 12,500 eventually produced. It is remembered primarily for operations in the Pacific theatre, but in fact the Corsair was used by other services like the Royal Navy; it also took part in the Korean War of 1950-53 and served with minor air forces into the 1970s.

*

Proposals to the twin-engine SD-112-14 specification may have included a radial engine version of the P-38 Lightning (see Chapter Two) from Lockheed, as well as

a twin-engine project from Brewster. In fact, sources indicate that there were requests for bids from thirteen companies including Brewster, Seversky and Lockheed, although it is unlikely that they all would have responded. The winner was the design submitted by Grumman.

Grumman G-34/XF5F-1 Skyrocket

Grumman's XF5F-1 Skyrocket was a most peculiar-looking design with wing-mounted engines but having no fuselage forward of the wing leading edge (later a longer nose was fitted). Only the one prototype was ordered, around which Specification SD-260 of May 1938 was written, and the machine flew on 1 April 1940. It had propellers that were designed to rotate in opposite directions, which on take-off virtually removed the effects of torque generated by each engine, while the performance proved to be excellent. Nevertheless, the type did not enter production although the prototype was used for trials until

BELOW The prototype Vought XF4U-1 Corsair was serial 1443, seen here in 1940. Note the different canopy to the forms used for production.
Dick Atkins, Vought Archive

ABOVE Designed by Grumman around the time of the work on the XF5F-1 was another twin-engine Navy fighter project called the SP-1. This manufacturer's model may show the SP-1 or a version of it. *David Ostrowski*
RIGHT Grumman's XF5F-1 Skyrocket prototype pictured in its original form. *Tommy Thomason*

ABOVE Later the XF5F-1 was fitted with an extended nose. This picture is dated 28 August 1941.
BELOW A further view the XF5F-1 with its longer nose. *Tommy Thomason*

XF5F-1 data	
Span	42ft 0in (12.80m)
Length	28ft 8.5in (8.75m)
Wing area	303.5sq ft (28.23sq m)
Gross weight	10,021lb (4,546kg)
Maximum take-off weight	10,892lb (4,941kg)
Powerplant	two 1,200hp (895kW) Wright XR-1820-G231
Armament	four 0.50in (12.70mm) machine guns, four 165lb (75kg) bombs
Maximum speed	312mph (502km/h) at sea level, 358mph (756km/h) at 17,300ft (5,273m)
Rate of climb	4,000ft/min (1,219m/min)
Service ceiling	34,500ft (10,516m)
Range	1,170 miles (1,883km)

December 1944, much of the work being done in support of Grumman's follow-on F7F programme (see below).

Major Design Competition

A major competition run in early 1941 is thought to have been the last for a US Navy fighter held in the piston era. From this point onwards, and until there was no longer any doubt about the war's outcome, no full design competitions were opened by BuAer. Instead (according to the George Spangenberg website) new aircraft programmes were initiated by direct negotiation with BuAer's aircraft producers (it is not known if this statement included the mixed-powerplant types covered later). The 1941 effort resulted in the submission of the following designs against covering specification SD-112-18 of 21 December 1940, which requested a single- or twin-engine type for operation aboard carriers. The maximum possible speed was desired (a minimum of 400mph/644km/h was listed in a draft, but this was not repeated in the full issue), the ceiling had to be at least 35,000ft (10,668m), and the range 1,000 miles (1,609km). Part span flaps and conventional ailerons were requested, the maximum span had to be 46ft (14.02m), and the required armament was six 0.50in (12.70mm) machine guns but with provision for four 20mm cannon. The submissions all had to be in by 10 March 1941 and the data given here is thought to come from the manufacturer's brochures, although the sea level speeds may be revised BuAer estimates (which were generally lower).

Bell Model 22

Clearly a variant of Bell's XP-52 and XP-59 projects in Chapter One, the Model 22 was a twin-boom pusher design with a tricycle undercarriage and a six-blade contra-rotating propeller of 9ft 6in (2.90m) diameter. There was a small amount of sweep on the wings (18° on the leading edge), and three machine guns were housed in the nose of each boom.

Model 22 data	
Span	44ft 4in (13.51m); folded 22ft 4in (6.81m)
Length	37ft 3in (11.35m)
Wing area	315sq ft (29.295sq m)
Gross weight	11,500lb (5,216kg)
Powerplant	one 2,000hp (1,491kW) P&W R-2800
Armament	six 0.50in (12.70mm) machine guns
Maximum speed	339mph (545km/h) at sea level, 401mph (645km/h) at 22,000ft (6,706m)
Service ceiling	34,250ft (10,439m)
Combat range	1,008 miles (1,622km)

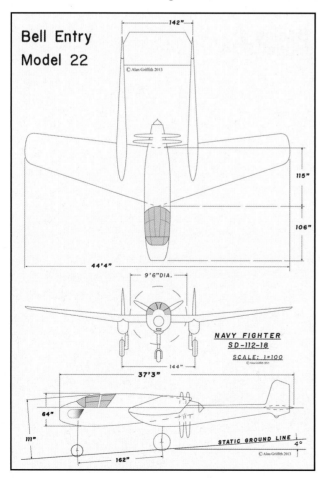

ABOVE A model of the Bell Model 22 VF proposal to SD-112-18. *Jay Miller*

LEFT The Bell Model 22 (1.41). *Alan Griffith copyright*

Boeing Models 352 and 374

The Boeing 352 was a twin-engine tractor design with three-blade propellers, a mid-position wing and a rather large vertical fin, together with a tricycle undercarriage. Its armament of six machine guns was installed entirely within the nose.

Published sources have previously indicated that the later Boeing Model 374 powered by two 1,350hp (1,007kW) Wright R-1820 Cyclone engines was the company's submission

to the SD-112-18 competition. This is not actually the case (the project is not mentioned in any paperwork and its date is too late), but it was clearly a follow-on to the Model 352, having a very similar configuration and wing but with an altogether heavier appearance to its fuselage. The Model 374 had three guns housed in each inner wing, the drawing indicating that they were all positioned outside the propeller arc.

Model 352 data	
Span	43ft 6in (13.26m); folded 23ft 0in (7.01m)
Length	39ft 0in (11.89m)
Wing area	337sq ft (31.34sq m)
Gross weight	13,500lb (6,124kg)
Powerplant	two c1,350hp (1,007kW) P&W R-2000 Twin Wasp
Armament	six 0.50in (12.70mm) machine guns
Maximum speed	324mph (521km/h) at sea level, 411mph (661km/h) at 19,000ft (5,791m)
Service ceiling	35,000ft (10,668m)
Combat range	1,021 miles (1,643km)
Model 374 data	
Span	46ft 0in (14.02m)
Length	42ft 0in (12.80m)
Gross weight	18,971lb (8,605kg)

BELOW Boeing Model 352 (1.41). *Alan Griffith copyright*

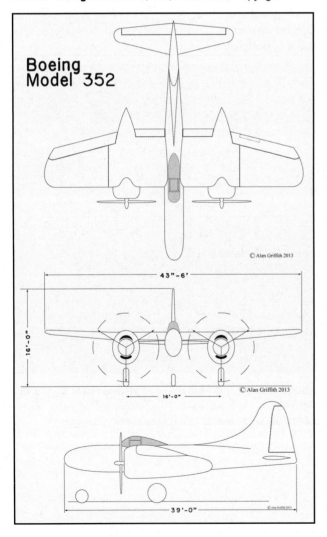

BELOW Boeing Model 374 (1942). *Alan Griffith copyright*

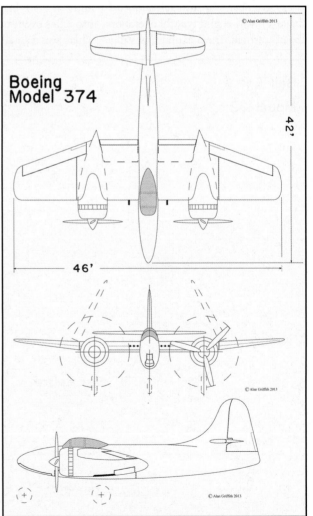

Brewster Model 33

Brewster's Model 33 designation covered four main versions – A, B, C and D – but there was also a Model E, which was a C fitted with an R-2800 engine and three-blade propeller. Model A was a twin-boom single-engine pusher with a three-blade single-rotation propeller, a central fin placed on top of the horizontal tailplane that connected the boom ends, and a tricycle undercarriage. In contrast, Model B was a stocky single-engine tractor design with the cockpit set well back from the nose, a four-blade propeller, and a tricycle undercarriage all the wheels of which retracted into the fuselage. Another one-engine tractor type, Model C looked a little sleeker, the reason being that its R-3350 was now buried inside the fuselage, which gave the nose and four-blade prop the appearance of a liquid-cooled in-line installation. Air was supplied to the engine by a slim inlet that essentially surrounded the fuselage at a point just to the rear of the cockpit. Finally, Model D returned to the twin-boom arrangement, quite similar in fact to Model A but now with two engines, a tractor unit in the nose and a pusher at the rear of the body, each with three-blade propellers. Its wing, tail and single fin were all very similar to Model A. For armament, Model A had all six machine guns in the nose, B and C both had four in the nose synchronised to fire through the propeller, together with two in the wings, while D had two synchronised nose guns and four wing guns.

BELOW Manufacturer's model of the Brewster Model 33A.

BELOW Brewster Model 33A (1.41). *Alan Griffith copyright*

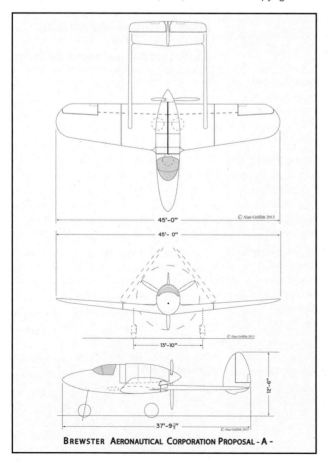

BELOW Brewster Model 33B (1.41). *Alan Griffith copyright*

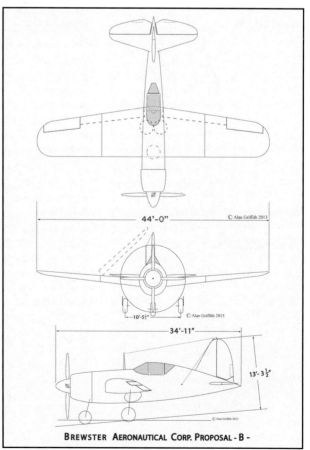

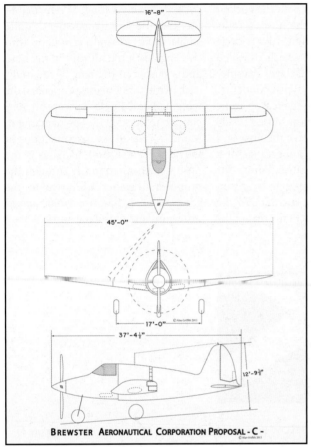

BREWSTER AERONAUTICAL CORPORATION PROPOSAL - C -

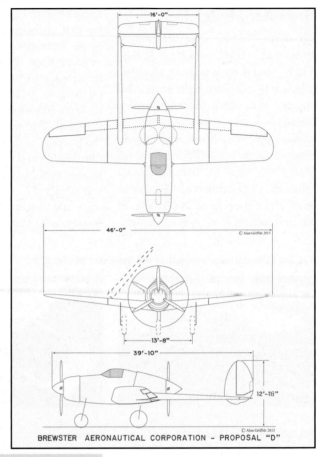

BREWSTER AERONAUTICAL CORPORATION - PROPOSAL "D"

Model 33A data

Span	45ft 0in (13.72m); folded 18ft 4in (5.59m)
Length	37ft 9.5in (11.52m)
Wing area	350sq ft (32.56sq m)
Gross weight	11,450lb (5,194kg)
Powerplant	one c2,200hp (1,641kW) Wright R-3350 Duplex Cyclone
Armament	six 0.50in (12.70mm) machine guns
Maximum speed	348mph (560km/h) at sea level, 430mph (692km/h) at 27,500ft (8,382m)
Service ceiling	36,100ft (11,003m)
Combat range	1,010 miles (1,625km)

Model 33B data

Span	44ft 0in (13.41m); folded 18ft 9in (5.715m)
Length	34ft 11in (10.64m)
Wing area	328sq ft (30.50sq m)
Gross weight	11,380lb (5,162kg)
Powerplant	one c2,200hp (1,641kW) Wright R-3350
Armament	six 0.50in (12.70mm) machine guns
Maximum speed	339mph (545km/h) at sea level, 422mph (679km/h) at 27,500ft (8,382m)
Service ceiling	37,200ft (11,339m)
Combat range	1,002 miles (1,612km)

Model 33C data

Span	45ft 0in (13.72m); folded 19ft 6in (5.94m)
Length	37ft 4.5in (11.39m)
Wing area	340sq ft (31.62sq m)
Gross weight	11,780lb (5,343kg)
Powerplant	one c2,200hp (1,641kW) Wright R-3350
Armament	six 0.50in (12.70mm) machine guns
Maximum speed	343mph (552km/h) at sea level, 431mph (693km/h) at 27,500ft (8,382m)
Service ceiling	36,700ft (11,186m)
Combat range	1,007 miles (1,620km)

Model 33D data

Span	46ft 0in (14.02m); folded 21ft 6in (6.55m)
Length	39ft 10in (12.14m)
Wing area	360sq ft (33.48sq m)
Gross weight	15,350lb (6,963kg)
Powerplant	one c2,200hp (1,641kW) Wright R-3350
Armament	six 0.50in (12.70mm) machine guns
Maximum speed	372mph (599km/h) at sea level, 459mph (739km/h) at 27,800ft (8,382m)
Service ceiling	39,700ft (12,101m)
Combat range	1,004 miles (1,615km)

ABOVE Brewster Model 33C (1.41).
Alan Griffith copyright

ABOVE LEFT Brewster Model 33C (1.41).
Alan Griffith copyright

Model 33E data

Gross weight	12,000lb (5,443kg)
Maximum speed	421mph (677km/h) at 25,800ft (7,864m)
Service ceiling	35,900ft (10,942m)
Combat range	1,005 miles (1,617km)

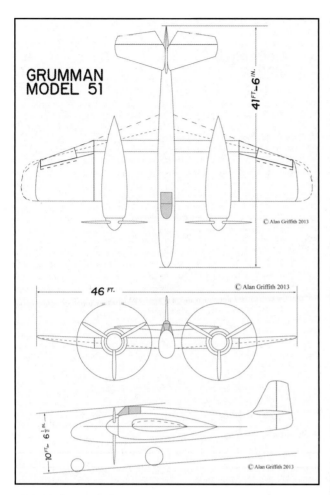

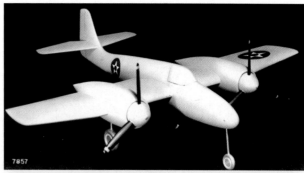

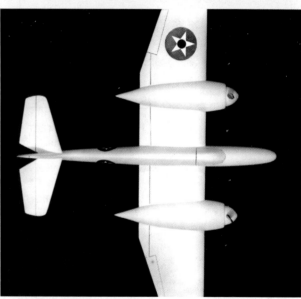

ABOVE The original Grumman G-51 proposal (1.41). Note the alternative wing shape as suggested by BuAer's assessors. *Alan Griffith copyright*

RIGHT A model of the Grumman G-51.

Grumman Model 51

The brochure drawing for the twin-engine Model 51 tractor design from Grumman held in the US National Archives has been modified by hand to show two different wings. For interest, both of these are included in the accompanying drawing, although the data relates to the original version with a straight trailing edge on the wing centre section. The design featured a smooth fuselage and streamlined engine nacelles, two guns in the fuselage nose and four in the wings, three-blade propellers, and a tricycle undercarriage.

Model 51 data	
Span	46ft 0in (14.02m); folded 26ft 0in (7.92m)
Length	41ft 6in (12.65m)
Wing area	441.4sq ft (41.05sq m)
Gross weight	16,277lb (7,383kg)
Powerplant	two c1,700hp (1,268kW) Wright R-2600
Armament	six 0.50in (12.70mm) machine guns
Maximum speed	351mph (565km/h) at sea level, 437mph (703km/h) at 27,100ft (8,260m)
Service ceiling	35,000ft (10,668m)
Combat range	1,000 miles (1,609km)

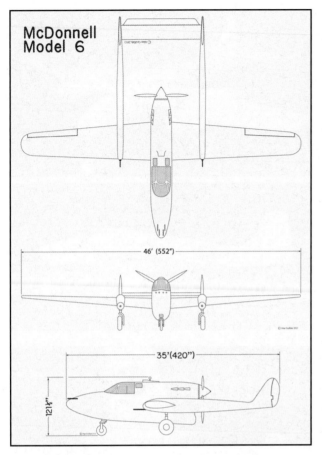

McDonnell Model 6

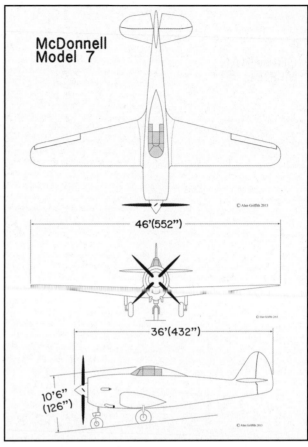

McDonnell Model 7

McDonnell Models 6, 7 and 8

Three different designs were submitted by McDonnell, Models 6, 7 and 8. The first of these was a twin-boom design with a single pusher engine and three-blade propeller. It had a rather narrow chord wing and for its armament four of the guns were placed in the nose with one more in each boom nose. The Model 7 was a conventional single-engine tractor type, again with a relatively narrow tapered low-position wing and with all of the armament mounted in the wing. A four-blade propeller of 13ft 0in (3.96m) diameter was used, and the Model 7's fuel capacity was 328 gallons (1,242 litres). Model 8 returned to the pusher configuration with a single engine and twin booms; it had a low wing and a six-blade contra-rotating propeller. All of the guns were housed in the nose and the tricycle undercarriage main gears folded inwards.

ABOVE LEFT
McDonnell Model 6 (2.41).
Alan Griffith copyright

ABOVE RIGHT
McDonnell Model 7 (2.41).
Alan Griffith copyright

RIGHT
McDonnell Model 8 (2.41).
Alan Griffith copyright

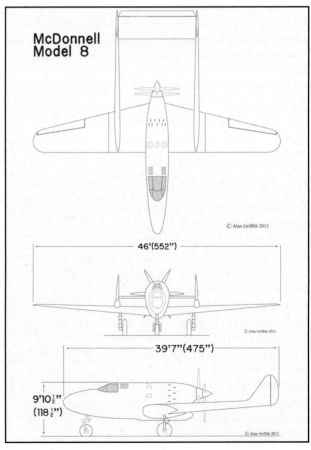

McDonnell Model 8

Model 6 data	
Span	46ft 0in (14.02m); folded 19ft 4in (5.89m)
Length	35ft 0in (10.67m)
Wing area	215sq ft (19.995sq m)
Gross weight	8,628lb (3,914kg)
Powerplant	one c1,150hp (858kW) Allison V-1710
Armament	six 0.50in (12.70mm) machine guns
Maximum speed	303mph (488km/h) at sea level, 389mph (626km/h) at 22,000ft (6,706m)
Service ceiling	35,210ft (10,732m)
Combat range	1,000 miles (1,609km)

Model 7 data	
Span	46ft 0in (14.02m); folded 19ft 6in (5.95m)
Length	36ft 0in (10.97m)
Wing area	282sq ft (26.23sq m)
Gross weight	11,060lb (5,017kg)
Powerplant	one 2,000hp (1,491kW) P&W R-2800
Armament	six 0.50in (12.70mm) machine guns
Maximum speed	332mph (534km/h) at sea level, 420mph (676km/h) at 28,000ft (8,534m)
Service ceiling	35,040ft (10,680m)
Time to 15,000ft (4,572m)	4.63min
Combat range	1,000 miles (1,609km)

Model 8 data	
Span	46ft 0in (14.02m); folded 19ft 8in (6.00m)
Length	39ft 7in (12.07m)
Wing area	282sq ft (26.23sq m)
Gross weight	11,907lb (5,401kg)
Powerplant	one 2,000hp (1,491kW) P&W R-2800
Armament	six 0.50in (12.70mm) machine guns
Maximum speed	331mph (533km/h) at sea level, 424mph (682km/h) at 23,000ft (7,010m)
Service ceiling	35,100ft (10,698m)
Combat range	1,000 miles (1,609km)

Naval Aircraft Factory Models A and B

The Naval Aircraft Factory (NAF) Model A was a very 'modern-looking' single-piston-engine tractor fighter and, with its inverted gull wing, appeared rather similar to the Vought F4U, although the Corsair had a tailwheel when the Model A was another type to employ a tricycle undercarriage. There was a four-blade single-rotating propeller and a bubble canopy, and the guns went in the wings. Even sleeker in appearance was the Model B twin-boom design with tandem tractor and pusher in-line liquid-cooled engines. In some respects this looked far more modern than many of its rivals: it had small twin fins, three-blade propellers for each power unit, three guns in each inner wing just inboard of the booms, and the now almost standard tricycle undercarriage (which here may have retracted rearwards into the booms).

BELOW Naval Aircraft Factory Model A (1.41).
Alan Griffith copyright

BELOW Naval Aircraft Factory Model B (1.41).
Alan Griffith copyright

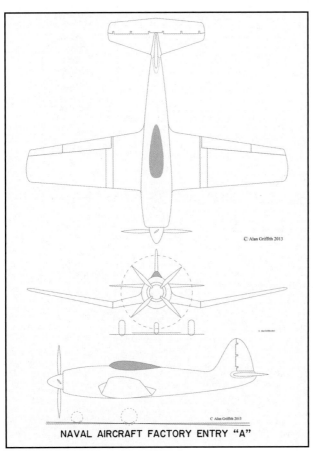

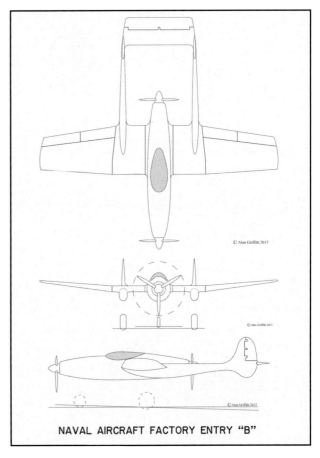

Model A data	
Span	46ft 0in (14.02m); folded 21ft 6in (6.55m)
Length	c38ft 8in (11.79m)
Wing area	375sq ft (34.875sq m)
Gross weight	10,685lb (4,847kg)
Powerplant	one c2,200hp (1,641kW) Wright R-3350
Armament	six 0.50in (12.70mm) machine guns
Maximum speed	340mph (547km/h) at sea level, 420mph (676km/h) at 28,000ft (8,534m)
Service ceiling	37,200ft (11,339m)
Combat range	1,080 miles (1,738km)

Model B data	
Span	46ft 0in (14.02m); folded 20ft 8in (6.30m)
Length	c40ft 6in (12.34m)
Wing area	370sq ft (34.41sq m)
Gross weight	10,655lb (4,833kg)
Powerplant	two c1,150hp (858kW) Allison V-1710
Armament	six 0.50in (12.70mm) machine guns
Maximum speed	346mph (557km/h) at sea level, 462mph (743km/h) at 22,000ft (6,706m)
Service ceiling	41,000ft (12,497m)
Combat range	1,315 miles (2,116km)

Vultee Models 79A and 79C

Vultee's Models 79A and 79C were developments of the manufacturer's XP-54 featured in Chapter One. They were twin-boom pusher designs, and the 79A had a cranked wing, six guns in the nose (although a BuAer data sheet states four in the nose, two in the wings), and a six-blade contra-rotating propeller; its twin fins were canted inwards, and there was a strange arrangement running underneath the propeller to accommodate and operate the arrester hook. Model 79C was very similar but had a larger wing and dispensed with the contra-rotation propeller, using instead a four-blade single-rotation prop of 10ft 2in (3.10m) diameter. Its six guns were arranged in a line across the upper nose. The Model 79A is something of a mystery since it does not appear in any BuAer assessment documents, which suggests that the design was possibly rejected very early on or even withdrawn by Vultee. The 79C also gets little mention and is listed very low in the scoring system used to grade the various SD-112-18 designs. One gets the impression that it was not highly rated at all by BuAer.

BELOW LEFT The Vultee Model 79A (1.41). Note the rather unusual arrangement used to accommodate an arrestor hook. *Alan Griffith copyright*

BELOW The Vultee Model 79C (1.41). One cannot help but wonder if it would have been difficult to put sufficient strength in the tail and the long thin boom to enable the structure to withstand carrier landings. *Alan Griffith copyright*

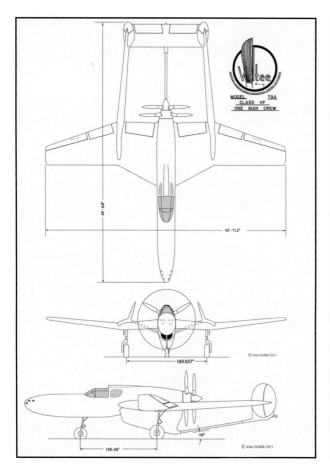

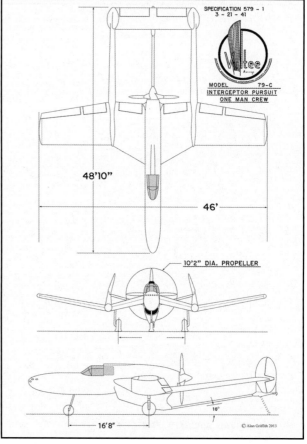

ABOVE Manufacturer's artist's concept for the Vultee Model 79A.
Alan Griffith

Model 79A data	
Span	42ft 11in (13.08m); folded not given
Length	44ft 9in (13.64m)
Wing area	293sq ft (27.25sq m)
Gross weight	12,800lb (5,806kg)
Powerplant	one 2,200hp (1,641kW) Lycoming XH-2470-4
Armament	six 0.50in (12.70mm) machine guns
Maximum speed	460mph (740km/h) at 16,500ft (5,029m)
Service ceiling	36,100ft (11,003m)
Combat range	1,002 miles (1,612km)

Model 79C data	
Span	46ft 0in (14.02m); folded 20ft 2in (6.15m)
Length	48ft 10in (14.88m)
Wing area	390sq ft (36.27sq m)
Gross weight	12,100lb (5,489kg)
Powerplant	one 2,200hp (1,641kW) Lycoming XH-2470-4
Armament	six 0.50in (12.70mm) machine guns
Maximum speed	328mph (528km/h) at sea level, 436mph (702km/h) at 16,500ft (5,029m)
Service ceiling	37,200ft (11,339m)
Combat range	1,007 miles (1,620km)

Wallace-Martin Model A

The Wallace-Martin Model A was a tractor/pusher type with a twin-boom configuration and two engines in tandem. The aircraft had twin fins, there were three-blade propellers for each engine, and a tricycle undercarriage. Two of the guns went in the upper nose where they were synchronised with the forward propeller, and there were two more in each wing beyond the propeller arc. The fighter appears to have had a 'car-door'-type entry to the cockpit.

✳

The above selection presents a fascinating mix of layouts with one/two engines and tractor or pusher arrangements, all offering advantages and disadvantages in terms of control, view out, weight, etc. For example, a pusher type offered

excellent vision for the pilot, but if an air-cooled engine was used a considerable design effort would be needed to effect sufficient cooling. A single-engine tractor type was simple and straightforward to design but needed the guns in the wings or synchronised with the propellers, while a tractor twin offered excellent performance and closely grouped guns but would be heavy and possess relatively poor manoeuvrability. A key factor in the assessment was the powerplant. BuAer's experts noted that the air-cooled engines available for use in the tractor position were the Wright R-2600 and R-3350 and the Pratt & Whitney R-2800. The R-2600 was probably the largest engine that could be used in the twin-engine types submitted without a very great increase in weight, while this same engine in a single-engine aircraft would result in too low a performance. The other pair when employed for a single-engine tractor type would give approximately the same results when operating under normal power, the R-3350's higher power being

167

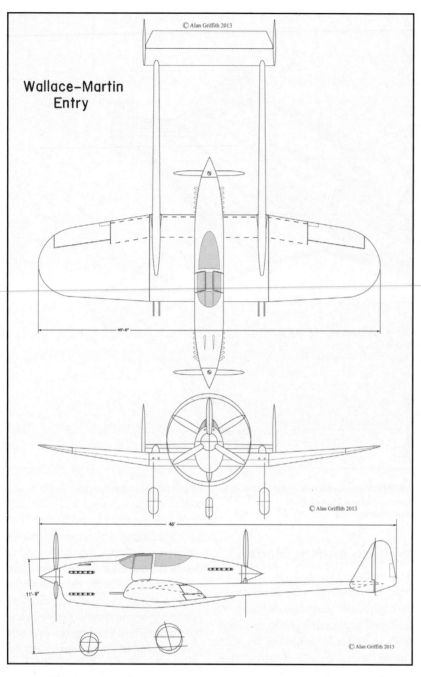

Wallace–Martin Entry

© Alan Griffith 2013

© Alan Griffith 2013

© Alan Griffith 2013

© Alan Griffith 2013

LEFT The Wallace-Martin Model A (1.41).
Alan Griffith copyright

Model A data	
Span	46ft 0in (14.02m); folded 19ft 6in (5.94m)
Length	45ft 6in (13.87m)
Wing area	442sq ft (41.11sq m)
Gross weight	15,000lb (6,804kg)
Powerplant	two 2,200hp (1,641kW) Lycoming XH-2470-4
Armament	six 0.50in (12.70mm) machine guns
Maximum speed	371mph (597km/h) at sea level, 430mph (692km/h) at 16,000ft (4,877m)
Service ceiling	38,100ft (11,613m)
Combat range	1,021 miles (1,643km)

offset by its greater weight and lower critical altitude (the maximum attitude at which, in standard atmosphere, it was possible to maintain a specified power). Under the higher 'military power' rating, however, the R-3350's performance would be much better thanks to its rather higher critical altitude – 24,000ft (7,315m) against 19,500ft (5,944m) for the R-2800.

For the other types and for the rear engine in the tandem twins there were but two liquid-cooled engines then

available or under development. The Allison V-1710 had too little power and its critical altitude, even under two-stage supercharging, was low at only 18,000ft (5,486m). The only other liquid-cooled type then under development that could be considered was the Lycoming XH-2470-4 but, given the fact that this design provided for only two-speed and not for two-stage supercharging, its critical altitude of 12,500ft (3,810m) was too low to give an attractive altitude performance. However, its 2,200hp (1,641kW) would provide for the greatest speed of any type in the 14,000 to 15,000ft (4,267 to 4,572m) height band, although above that the speeds would fall below the more highly supercharged types. Development of two-stage supercharging, then under way, would make this latter engine much more attractive.

Looking at the specific designs, Grumman's Model 51 was considered the outstanding twin-engine type in having high performance and good armament. Its one real weakness was its weight (too high for carrier decks) and consequent lower manoeuvrability – a smaller version would have been preferred by the Navy. The Brewster 33D offered flight on either engine with fewer complications than for normal twin-engine types, but here both the pilot's view over the nose and the armament were poor. The NAF's Model B had poor take-off and altitude performance, while the organisation's Model 'A' offered the best performance of the single-engine types, but had a canopy that required some redesign. In fact, the best two single-engine tractor fighters were the McDonnell Model 7 and NAF Model A, the view for the pilot in both (with their tricycle undercarriages) showing a great improvement over the Vought F4U. Although offering good performance, the Wallace-Martin was very heavy and had a poor performance and armament, while McDonnell's Model 7 had good armament but lower performance than the NAF 'A'. The McDonnell Model 8's pusher configuration would require a costly and time-consuming development, although its armament was considered to be the best; the Bell 22 also had good armament, but its performance was little better than the Vought F4U-1; and the Brewster 33A offered the best performance of any of the pushers. The Brewster 33A, B and C, however, all had faults and each of them exhibited poor spin recovery characteristics.

It was noted that specifying a span limitation for the competition of 46 feet (14.02 metres) had resulted in all of the designs having ceilings under 35,000ft (10,668m) (in the estimates as corrected by BuAer staff), and the review added that this limit must be removed if the desired service ceiling was to be obtained. It was estimated that at least 5ft 6in (1.68m) would have to be added to the Grumman 51's span in order for it to meet the desired figure (which is presumably why BuAer had added the higher-span wing to the brochure drawing). The reports concluded that at least one of five designs – the Brewster 33B, Grumman 51, McDonnell 7, and the pair from the NAF – should be contracted for immediately. However, since the NAF 'A' was 'simply another F4U-1', it was thought to be unwise to follow that design. Of the four types left it was believed that any one could make a perfectly satisfactory fighter, 'with the possible exception of the Grumman 51 due to its excessive weight'. In addition, wind tunnel tests on the Army Grumman XP-50 (see Chapter Two), which used nacelles of about the same size, had shown four distinct stalls prior to the final break in the lift curve, though an increase in span would help alleviate this condition and improve the ceiling. It the end it was recommended that an award be made for two prototypes from Grumman and, if enough funding was available, an award should also be made for a single-engine type, either the Brewster Model 33B or McDonnell 7. In the event, only the Model 51 was ordered.

Grumman F7F Tigercat and XP-65

The first of two XF7F-1 Tigercat prototypes made its maiden flight on 3 November 1943, but the type arrived too late to see combat operations during the war, although it did contribute to the conflict in Korea. Altogether 364 Tigercats were built and, because of the fighter's considerable weight, the great majority only served with land-based units. The F7F Tigercat was the US Navy's first twin-engine fighter to reach service, but the end of the war meant that it never really had a chance to use its full potential.

The plans for the F7F also included an Army Air Corps version called the XP-65, to succeed the XP-50 and run in parallel with the Navy type. Two XP-65 prototypes were ordered in May 1941 and were essentially to be the same aircraft; however, the differing needs of the two Services, Air Corps and Navy, produced a number of conflicting requirements that were discussed at a meeting held on 2 December 1941. In fact, at that point the Army Air Corps seemed willing to accept the aircraft practically in its naval version, the main differences being the powerplant – the Army desired a turbo-supercharged engine, which the Navy could not

ABOVE A side view of the Grumman XF7F-1 prototype. *Gerald Balzer*
BELOW Splendid photos that appear to show the same unidentified Grumman F7F Tigercat.

accept due to its higher weight – and a pressurised cockpit. The Army would accept the six 0.50in (12.70mm) machine guns but preferred four 20mm cannon, but again the Navy could not accept cannon because of their greater weight. Indeed, BuAer was very concerned about the XF7F's weight and understandably could not accept another rise since, from a carrier landing standpoint, the aircraft was already very heavy. For the Army there would still be an inherent penalty for having folding wings, arresting gear and provision for catapulting.

It was becoming clear that the compromises required to produce the Army version would require a considerable engineering effort from Grumman, and the problems with the project made the anticipated advantages of the original plan somewhat questionable. By January 1942 the Army wanted a multiple 37mm cannon and also appreciated that Grumman was a major supplier of Navy aircraft and might struggle to find the capacity to fulfil further orders for the Air Corps. The decision was taken, therefore, to discontinue the XP-65 project, and Grumman was officially informed of this move on 16 January 1942.

XF7F-1 data

Span	51ft 6in (15.70m)
Length	45ft 6.5in (13.88m)
Wing area	455sq ft (42.315sq m)
Gross weight	20,107lb (9,121kg)
Powerplant	two 2,100hp (1,566kW) P&W R-2800-22W Double Wasp
Armament	four 0.50in (12.70mm) machine guns, four 20mm cannon, 2,000lb (907kg) bombs
Maximum speed	429mph (690km/h)
Sea level rate of climb	4,200ft/min (1,280m/min)
Service ceiling	42,200ft (12,863m)
Range	1,160 miles (1,866km)

XP-65 data

Span	52ft 6in (16.00m)
Length	46ft 5in (14.15m)
Gross weight	21,425lb (9,718kg)
Powerplant	two 1,700hp (1,268kW) Wright R-2600-10
Armament	four 20mm cannon
Maximum speed	427mph (687km/h)

BELOW Sketch artwork for the Model 376. *NARA II*

The Wasp Major Fighters

The designs in this section make a fascinating series and show how much progress had been made since the Wildcat and Buffalo featured at the start of the chapter. Pratt & Whitney's development of the R-4360 Wasp Major engine prompted several manufacturers to produce single-seat, single-engine Navy fighter designs powered by it, and projects from Boeing, Chance Vought and Curtiss all appeared between December 1942 and March 1943, although seemingly not in direct competition with one another. The engine's use in new Army fighters such as the Republic XP-72 has already been described in Chapter One; Goodyear also tested a Corsair with an R-4360 as described briefly below, and in August 1943 Grumman drew its G-59 project, which was to be an F6F Hellcat fitted with a two-speed R-4360 power unit. It should be noted that (according to George Spangenberg) the Boeing line of fighter projects described here was begun as a series of unsolicited proposals, the manufacturer believing that no military specs were required, Boeing itself setting the configuration.

RIGHT Boeing Model 376 (5.12.42).
NARA II

Boeing Model 376

Boeing stated that its single-engine carrier-based Model 376 of December 1942 represented the minimum aeroplane, both in size and weight, for which a Wasp Major could be used. A variable-speed engine was selected because of its lighter weight, and the aircraft used a four-blade propeller 15ft 0in (4.57m) in diameter, dual-rotation propellers being considered unnecessary here because, since the fighter was designed primarily for low-level operation, it was possible to utilise a large-diameter propeller without

Model 376 data	
Span	53ft 0in (16.15m); folded 34ft 4in (10.46m)
Length	39ft 4.5in (12.00m)
Wing area	not available
Gross weight	13,740lb (6,232kg), overload 16,800lb (7,620kg)
Powerplant	one 3,000hp (2,237kW) P&W R-4360 Wasp Major
Armament	four 20mm cannon
Maximum speed	384mph (618km/h) at sea level, 401mph (645km/h) at 13,500ft (4,115m), 377mph (607km/h) at 25,000ft (7,620m)
Sea level rate of climb (full power)	4,450ft/min (1,356m/min)
Service ceiling	c35,000ft (10,668m)
Normal range	1,000 miles (1,609km)

involving unreasonable tip speed losses. The exhaust system was designed to be of the 'propulsive jet' type, but this meant that if the 376 was to be used as a night fighter some flame suppression would be required for the exhaust. Its wing was semi-monocoque and used a single main spar and slotted-type flaps, and the low-drag aerofoil had a thickness/chord ratio of 14%. Two 20mm guns were mounted in each outer wing outboard of the landing gear. The brochure declared that the Model 376's performance was exceptional for an aircraft of its size

Boeing Model 386

At the same time Boeing produced a preliminary brochure and study for another single-Wasp Major design, which it called the Model 386. This was similar to the Model 376 with a very similar wing and the same 14% t/c ratio and armament, but it was designed for medium-altitude operation. The two-stage engine would again employ a 'propulsive jet' exhaust with a separate manifold and jet for each bank of four cylinders, the thrust tending to compensate for the reduction in power at altitude. However, dual-rotating three-blade 13ft 6in (4.11m)-diameter propellers (six blades) were to be employed here because it was not possible to use a larger size without a high equivalent tip speed and the consequent loss in propulsive efficiency thereby produced. The range figures were the same as for the 376 and, like the earlier type, it had the same ferry range (3,000 miles/4,827km), which was accomplished with overload internal fuel carried in the wings as well as one 75-gallon (284-litre) droppable tank. An arrestor hook was fitted at the mid-rear fuselage position.

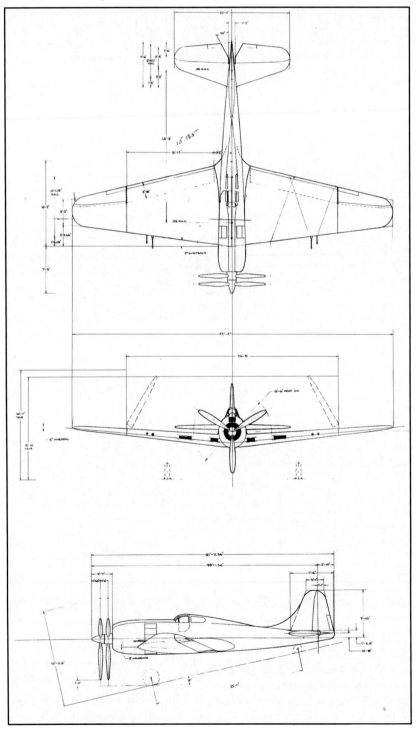

Model 386 data	
Span	55ft 4in (16.86m); folded 36ft 8in (11.18m)
Length	41ft 11.33in (12.78m)
Wing area	not available
Gross weight	15,456lb (7,011kg), overload 16,800lb (7,620kg)
Powerplant	one 3,000hp (2,237kW) P&W R-4360 Wasp Major
Armament	four 20mm cannon
Maximum speed	374mph (602km/h) at sea level, 434mph (698km/h) at 23,000ft (7,010m), 429mph (690km/h) at 30,000ft (9,144m)
Sea level rate of climb (full power)	3,840ft/min (1,170m/min)
Service ceiling	c46,000ft (14,021m)
Normal range	1,000 miles (1,609km)

LEFT Boeing Model 386 (7.12.42).
NARA II

ABOVE Sketch for the Model 386. *NARA II*

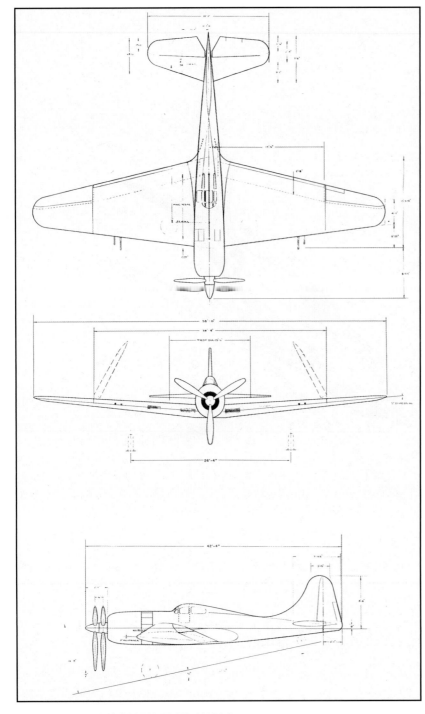

ABOVE Boeing Model 387 (8.12.42). *NARA II*

Boeing Model 387

Completing a trio of concurrent designs from Boeing was the Model 387. This was a high-altitude fighter and would use a Wasp Major equipped with an exhaust-driven turbo-supercharger, which would give a critical altitude with full military power of more than 25,000ft (7,620m). Boeing stressed that the advantage of the exhaust-driven turbo-supercharger was shown by the machine's speed and rate of climb at altitude (at 35,000ft/10,668m the rate of climb on full power was still more than 2,300ft per min/701m per min). The optimum operating altitude for the Model 387 was given as between 20,000 and 35,000ft (6,096 and 10,668m), but fighter performance was available right from sea level to more than 40,000ft (12,192m). The ferry range was again given as 3,000 miles (4,827km). A 13ft 6in (4.11m) dual-rotation propeller was used, the main wing spar was positioned at 35% chord, and there was an auxiliary spar to pick up the flap and aileron loads and to carry the wing torsion into the fuselage. None of these designs was ordered, but Boeing pressed on with its Navy fighter studies.

Model 387 data	
Span	58ft 0in (17.68m); folded 38ft 4in (11.68m)
Length	42ft 4in (12.90m)
Wing area	not available
Gross weight	16,602lb (7,531kg), overload 20,432lb (9,268kg)
Powerplant	one 3,000hp (2,237kW) P&W R-4360 Wasp Major
Armament	four 20mm cannon
Maximum speed	364mph (586km/h) at sea level, 450mph (724km/h) at 26,000ft (7,925m), 473mph (761km/h) at 31,900ft (9,723m)
Sea level rate of climb (full power)	3,840ft/min (1,170m/min)
Service ceiling	well in excess of 40,000ft (12,192m)
Normal range	1,000 miles (1,609km

ABOVE Manufacturer's Model 387 artwork. *NARA II*

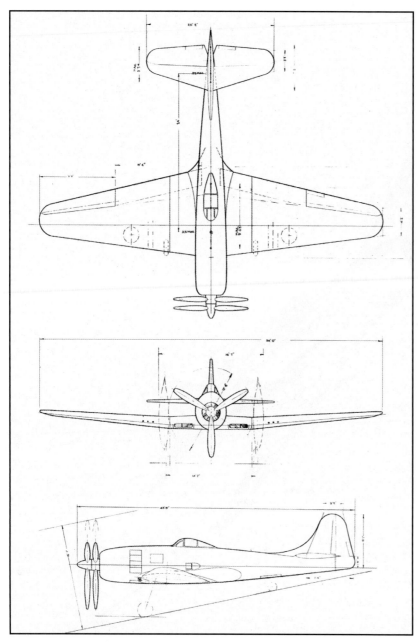

Model 398 data

Span	54ft 0in (16.46m); folded 16ft 7in (5.06m)
Length	43ft 9in (13.34m)
Wing area	not given
Gross weight	fighter 13,820lb (6,269kg)
Powerplant	one 3,000hp (2,237kW) P&W R-4360 Wasp Major (War Emergency Power rating 3,450hp/2,573kW)
Armament	six 0.50in (12.70mm) machine guns
Maximum speed	military power 376mph (605km/h) at sea level, 445mph (716km/h) at 25,700ft (7,834m); War Emergency Power 392mph (631km/h) at sea level, 456mph (734km/h) Mach 0.65 at 22,500ft (6,858m), 406mph (653km/h) at 26,200ft (7,986m)
Sea level rate of climb	military power 4,450ft/min (1,356m/min); War Emergency Power 5,150ft/min (1,570m/min)
Service ceiling	in excess of 35,000ft (10,668m)
Maximum range	1,130 miles (1,818km)

Model 398 data as fighter-bomber

Gross weight	16,285lb (7,387kg)
Maximum speed	375mph (603km/h) at sea level, 442mph (711km/h) at 25,700ft (7,834m)
Sea level rate of climb	4,310ft/min (1,314m/min)

LEFT Boeing Model 398 (5.3.43). *NARA II*

Boeing Model 398

The Model 398 was a revised version of Boeing's Model 386, which was designed for medium- and high-altitude operations and powered by a two-stage variable-speed supercharged version of the Wasp Major. It would have 'unusually high performance at all altitudes up to 26,000ft [7,925m],' but above this altitude both its speed and rate of climb would decrease. Although the 398 was primarily a fighter, the internal arrangement would permit, without any increase in body contour size, the addition of a bay below the pilot's floor

and aft of the front spar to take one 2,000lb (907kg) bomb instead of the 65-gallon (246-litre) fuel tank normally in that space. For the fighter-bomber there would be four extra wing fuel cells, one of 73 gallons (276 litres) and one of 59 gallons (223 litres) in each wing (details for any other fuel are unknown). Each outer wing panel housed three 0.50in (12.70mm) machine guns, the diameter of the six-blade contra-rotating propeller was 13ft 6in (4.11m) and, unlike the above projects where they folded upwards (but like the Model 394 below), the wings here would rotate and fold to

the rear along the length of the aircraft. The semi-monocoque wing had a t/c ratio of 15% and was essentially a monospar structure with the main bending resistant spar located at 35% of the wing chord. An auxiliary shear spar was located at 75% of the chord to carry the aileron and flap loads, and slotted flaps were to be employed. The fuselage was of conventional construction.

Boeing stressed that the system used on this aircraft to supply cooling air to the intercoolers and oil coolers as well as air to the blower was unique. Relatively large leading-edge wing ducts located in each wing stub adjacent to the fuselage would supply air through a 90° turn in the duct to a pressure chamber in the engine section. The ducts were located entirely forward of the front wing spar and would spill air into the pressure chamber through openings in the engine cowl, which were approximately the size and shape of the wing leading edge at its junction with the fuselage. From the face of each intercooler, ducts would carry the exit cooling air to flapped openings in the upper cowling, and a similar type of duct carried the exit cooling air from the faces of the oil coolers to a flapped opening in the bottom of the engine cowl. The oil coolers were located below the intercoolers and just forward of the front spar bulkhead, while the exit air flap was placed just below the oil coolers.

Boeing Model 400/XF8B-1

Boeing's Model 400 was another unsolicited proposal that brought the culmination of this series of projects and resulted in an order for three XF8B-1 prototypes. The brochure was submitted on 1 April 1943 and described the type primarily as a single-seat single-engine high-performance fighter-bomber, but in due course this aircraft would be known as the 'five-in-one' fighter since it was to operate either as a fighter or interceptor or as a dive, torpedo or level-height bomber. Maximum emphasis was placed on rate of climb, manoeuvrability and high speeds at altitudes up to 25,000ft (7,620m), and besides the wing guns provision was still made to carry up

to 2,000lb (907kg) of bombs internally. With overload fuel, and without carrying any bombs or gun ammunition, the Model 400 had a ferry range of 3,000 miles (4,827km). A go-ahead was given on 10 April against Specification SD-349 and the first XF8B-1 prototype flew on 27 November 1944. However, the George Spangenberg website states that the aircraft was inferior as a naval carrier airplane in all of its possible uses, and it would be expensive to produce. In truth, by the time of the prototype's arrival its time had passed. The war was soon to end and jet-powered aircraft would be the way forward; in fact, the XF8B-1 proved to be the Navy's last piston-engine fighter.

Chance Vought V-334

The single-seat V-334 fighter/torpedo-fighter project from Chance Vought had a straight leading edge to its tapered wing and a short stocky fuselage. It was actually described in the original drawing as a 'land-based' fighter, and no wing fold or arrestor hook are visible, but the drawing also shows two torpedoes carried side by side beneath the forward fuselage, and the Vought project list gives

Model 400 brochure data	
Powerplant	one 3,000hp (2,237kW) P&W R-4360 Wasp Major
Armament	six 0.50in (12.70mm) machine guns
Maximum speed	351mph (565km/h) at sea level, 435mph (700km/h) at 23,000ft (7,010m)
Sea level rate of climb (full power)	4,460ft/min (1,359m/min)
Service ceiling	in excess of 35,000ft (10,668m)
Range on normal fuel	1,200 miles (1,931km)

XF8B-1 data	
Span	54ft 0in (16.46m); folded 29ft 5in (8.97m)
Length	43ft 3in (13.18m)
Wing area	489sq ft (45.48sq m)
Gross weight	20,580lb (9,335kg)
Powerplant	one 2,500hp (1,864kW) P&W R-4360 Wasp Major
Armament	six 0.50in (12.70mm) machine guns, one 500lb (227kg), 1,000lb (454kg), 1,600lb (726kg) armour-piercing or 2,000lb (907kg) bomb
Maximum speed	351mph (565km/h) at sea level, 435mph (700km/h) at 26,500ft (8,077m)
Rate of climb	3,660ft/min (1,116m/min)
Service ceiling	37,500ft (11,430m)
Range	1,305 miles (2,100km)

RIGHT Boeing XF8B-1 prototype 57984 is pictured just after taking off, with the undercarriage in the process of retracting. *NARA II via Ryan Crierie*

BELOW The XF8B-1 prototype taxis past the cameraman. *NARA II via Ryan Crierie*

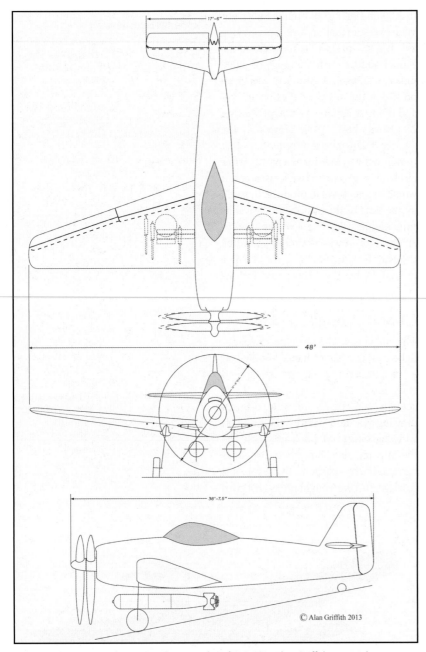

V-334 data

Span	48ft 0in (14.63m)
Length	38ft 7.5in (11.77m)
Wing area	365sq ft (33.945sq m)
Gross weight as normal fighter (no torpedo)	13,733lb (6,229kg)
Overload weight	14,368lb (6,517kg)
Powerplant	one 3,000hp (2,237kW) P&W R-4360 Wasp Major
Armament	six 20mm cannon
No performance data available at time of writing	

ABOVE Chance Vought V-334 (drawing dated 8.5.43). *Alan Griffith copyright*

fighter in the world'. Its advantages were listed as 'performance, particularly climb and high speed, striking power, manoeuvrability, easy and safe flying and landing characteristics, a minimum of vulnerable component parts and exceptional vision' for the pilot. The basic layout was conventional in arrangement, with the exception of the dual-rotation six-blade 14ft 2in (4.32m) propeller and the pilot's location, the dual-rotation prop enabling the aircraft to climb at steeper angles at slower speeds than those for best climb. Steep climbing angle performance had been shown by war experience to be a decided tactical advantage, the brochure adding that the turning radius and time to turn would also be improved considerably through the use of dual-rotation propellers; the contra-prop also eliminated engine torque for carrier take-offs.

The 'X-Wasp'/Wasp Major represented the maximum power that was then available from either an air-cooled or liquid-cooled engine type. A conventional arrangement with the powerplant in the nose had been selected because combat experience had shown that the majority of bullets or cannon projectiles that strike an aircraft during battle hit that part of the airframe behind the pilot's cockpit. For this reason the engine had been located forward and under the pilot, and an air-cooled power unit was chosen in preference to a liquid-cooled engine because of its lower vulnerability in combat, and its simpler installation. A carrier take-off within a minimum distance was helped by the incorporation of full-span Fehn ailerons and high-lift flaps. The aircraft's fuel totalled 295 gallons

the type as a Navy 'VF design'. Gun armament was to be six 0.50in (12.70mm) machine guns, all in the wings, with four outside the 14ft 6in (4.42m) six-blade contra-rotating propeller arc and two inside it, housed within the air intakes. The normal internal fuel load was 250 gallons (946 litres), rising to 331 gallons (1,253 litres) for overload. Inner wing flaps and outer wing ailerons stretched along the full length of the wing trailing edge.

Curtiss Wasp Major Studies

The papers found to date covering the efforts by the Curtiss-Wright Airplane Division to produce Wasp Major Navy fighters have revealed two drawings. When the brochure was prepared in March 1943, the R-4360 was known as the 'X-Wasp' and Curtiss declared that the favoured 'Cab over Engine' design was 'believed to be the superior of any American fighter and probably of any

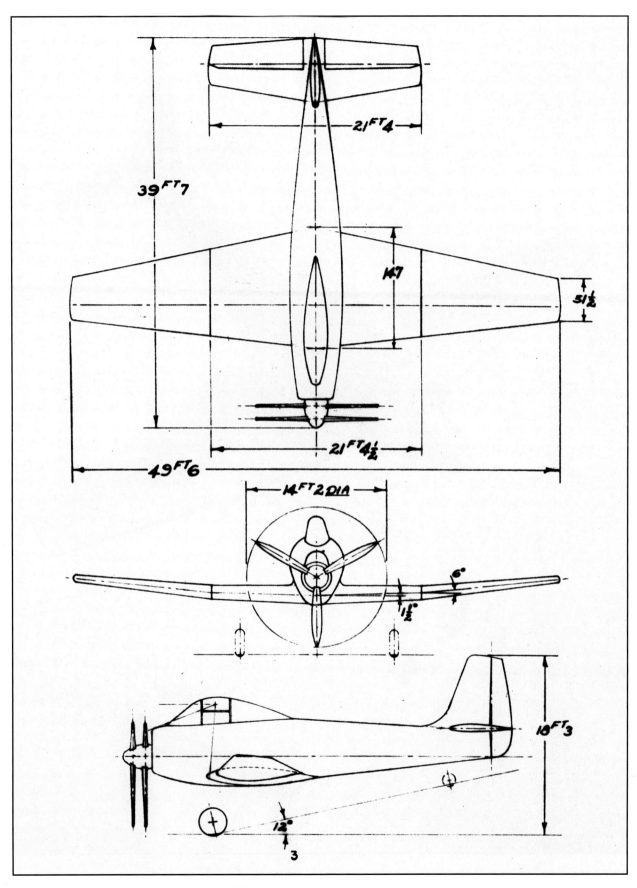

ABOVE Curtiss 'Cab over Engine' Wasp Major fighter (3.43). *NARA II*

ABOVE Manufacturer's rendering for the Curtiss 'Cab over Engine' fighter. *NARA II*

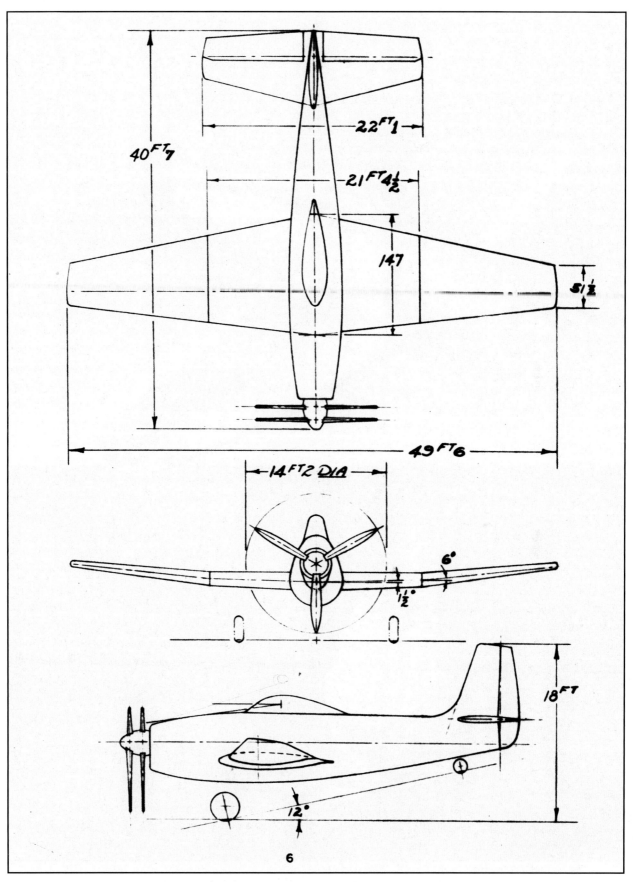

6

ABOVE Curtiss Wasp Major fighter with a more conventional cockpit position (3.43). *NARA II*

ABOVE An artist's rendering of the second Curtiss Wasp Major fighter design. *NARA II*

'Cab over Engine' data	
Span	49ft 6in (15.09m)
Length	39ft 7in (12.07m)
Wing area	410sq ft (38.13sq m)
Gross weight	16,600lb (7,530kg)
Powerplant	one 3,300hp (2,461kW) P&W R-4360-10
Armament	four 0.50in (12.70mm) machine guns, two 20mm cannon
Maximum speed	368mph (592km/h) at sea level, 431mph (693km/h) at 25,000ft (7,620m), 440mph (708km/h) at 27,000ft (8,230m), critical altitude, with two-speed gear ratio weight = 16,800lb (7,620kg); maximum speed 445mph (716km/h) at 27,000ft (7,620m)
Sea level rate of climb	3,460ft/min (1,055m/min); War Emergency Power 3,950ft/min (1,204m/min)
Service ceiling	40,800ft (12,436m)
Maximum range	1,500 miles (2,011km)

(1,341 litres) and there was provision for drop tanks under each wing to give a range of 1,500 miles (2,414km). The armament, two 20mm cannon and four 0.50in (12.70mm) machine guns, was housed in the wings, with the cannon just inboard of the 50s; alternatives were four 20mm or six machine guns. The 'War Emergency Power' rating for the engine was at this time assumed, so the performance figures for that rating given here were not guaranteed. No information was provided for wing folding or for an alternative design where the cockpit was moved rearwards to a more conventional position, except that is for its dimensions (span 49ft 6in/15.09m and length 40ft 7in/12.37m), and that it used the same engine and size of propeller. Both designs had a similar heavily tapered wing and tailwheel undercarriage.

Goodyear F2G-1 'Super Corsair'

The land-based F2G-1 and carrier-based F2G-2 were low-altitude versions of the Vought F4U Corsair (which Goodyear also produced as the FG-1), developed and manufactured by Goodyear and equipped with an R-4360 engine instead of the usual R-2800. The

F2G-2 data	
Span	41ft 0in (12.50m); folded 17ft 0.5in (5.19m)
Length	33ft 10in (10.31m)
Wing area	314sq ft (29.02sq m)
Gross weight	13,346lb (6,054kg)
Maximum take-off weight	15,422lb (6,995kg)
Powerplant	one 3,000hp (2,237kW) P&W R-4360-4 Wasp Major
Armament	four 0.50in (12.70mm) machine guns, 3,200lb (1,452kg) bombs
Maximum speed	399mph (642km/h) at sea level, 431mph (693km/h) at 16,900ft (5,151m)
Rate of climb	4,400ft/min (1,341m/min)
Service ceiling	38,800ft (11,826m)
Range	1,000 miles (1,609km)

ABOVE Views of the Goodyear XF2G-1 prototype. *NARA II via Ryan Crierie*

prototype XF2G-1, an extensively modified FG-1 airframe, first flew on 26 August 1944, but only ten examples had been completed before production was stopped by the close of the war, despite orders having been placed for more than 400 machines. In addition, flight-testing revealed a lack of speed as well as weaknesses in lateral control.

One-offs

The Boeing series of single-seat fighter/fighter-bomber studies included the Model 394, and there was also the F8F Bearcat from Grumman and the XF14C prototype from Curtiss.

Boeing Model 394

The small, lightweight carrier-based Boeing Model 394 of early March 1943 was a change of direction from the powerful aircraft described above. This aeroplane was designed to provide protection for its carriers and would utilise the excellent low-altitude performance of the latest Wright XR-1820-56 nine-cylinder engine with a two-speed single-stage supercharger, giving 1,500hp (1,119kW) when set at its 'War Power' rating. A single-rotation three-blade 13ft 6in (4.11m)-diameter propeller was used, there was a two-spar wing with the spar and inter-spar wing skin continuous through the fighter's body, and the outer wing panels (which housed only the guns) were capable of being folded aft manually. The flaps were of the slotted type and the main flap extended across the wing stub and body so that the total 'flapped' area was approximately 20% of the gross wing area. Armament was four machine guns – two in the upper nose synchronised to fire through the propellers, and another in each outer wing – and a 78.5-gallon (297-litre) fuel tank was placed ahead of the cockpit. The main undercarriage could retract, but the tailwheel was fixed. Boeing considered that the

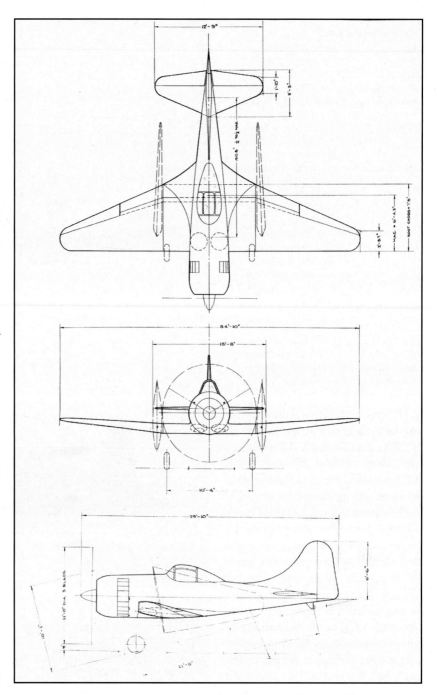

ABOVE Boeing Model 394 (5.3.43). *NARA II*

Model 394 would become 'the standard aircraft of its class', noting that an 'outstanding characteristic of the design is the practically negligible CofG travel', which would help ease of control for the pilot when performing every phase of the fighter mission.

Model 394 data	
Span	34ft 10in (10.62m); folded 13ft 8in (4.17m)
Length	29ft 10in (9.09m)
Wing area	206sq ft (19.16sq m)
Gross weight	6,202lb (2,813kg)
Powerplant	one 1,500hp (1,119kW) Wright XR-1820-56
Armament	four 0.50in (12.70mm) machine guns
Maximum speed	377mph (607km/h) at sea level (War Emergency Power), 401mph (645km/h) at 15,000ft (4,572m), 434mph (698km/h) at 24,200ft (7,376m)
Sea level rate of climb	5,230ft/min (1,594m/min) (War Emergency Power)
Service ceiling (BuAer estimate)	33,800ft (10,302m)
Normal range	770 miles (1,239km); with external tanks 1,450 miles (2,333km)

ABOVE Artwork for the Model 394. *NARA II*

ABOVE Curtiss XF14C-1 fighter prototype. *Tommy Thomason*

Curtiss Model 94A/XF14C-1

Two prototypes of the Curtiss Model 94A high-altitude fighter were ordered as the XF14C-1 in June 1941, and they were to be powered by a liquid-cooled Lycoming XH-2470 engine with a four-blade 14ft 2in (4.32m)-diameter single-rotation propeller. However, it eventually became clear that the engine would not be ready in time for the airframe, so by the end of 1943 work on the first machine had come to a halt. In due course a turbo-supercharged Wright R-3350 and a contra-rotating propeller were fitted to the second prototype as the XF14C-2, but this did not achieve a maiden flight until July 1944 (the delay was compounded by problems with the volume of war work being undertaken by the company). In the air it showed a performance that was no better than other fighters, while the need for this

high-altitude aircraft had in the meantime disappeared, so no production orders were forthcoming. George Spangenberg, who was responsible for the Design Requirements for many new naval aircraft and much of their evaluation from the 1940s onwards, did not rate the XF14C-2; in fact, he was

particularly critical, describing the aircraft as 'a dog'.

XF14C-1 data (estimated, November 1942)	
Span	46ft 0in (14.02m); folded 22ft 6in (6.86m)
Length	38ft 4in (11.68m)
Wing area	375sq ft (34.875sq m)
Gross weight	12,691lb (5,757kg)
Maximum take-off weight	13,868lb (6,291kg)
Powerplant	one 2,200hp (1,641kW) Lycoming XH-2470-4
Armament	four 20mm cannon
Maximum speed	344mph (553km/h) at 3,500ft (1,067m), 374mph (602km/h) at 17,000ft (5,182m)
Sea level rate of climb	2,810ft/min (856m/min)
Service ceiling	30,500ft (9,296m)
Maximum range	1,520 miles (2,446km)

XF14C-2 data	
Span	46ft 0in (14.02m); folded c22ft 6in (6.86m)
Length	37ft 9in (11.51m)
Wing area	375sq ft (34.875sq m)
Gross weight	13,405lb (6,081kg)
Maximum take-off weight	14,582lb (6,614kg)
Powerplant	one 2,300hp (1,715kW) Wright XR-3350-16 Duplex Cyclone
Armament	four 20mm cannon
Maximum speed	317mph (510km/h) at sea level, estimated 424mph (682km/h) at 32,000ft (9,754m), best achieved 398mph (640km/h)
Sea level rate of climb	2,700ft/min (823m/min)
Service ceiling	39,500ft (12,040m)
Maximum range	1,355 miles (2,180km)

ABOVE The Grumman XF8F-1 Bearcat prototype, pictured in 1945. *Gerald Balzer*

Grumman Model 58/F8F Bearcat

The Grumman Model 58 was a company-funded study and unsolicited proposal designed to provide Navy pilots with a higher-performance fighter than the currently available F6F and F4U, manoeuvrability and a very high rate of climb being key objectives. The Model 58 was a small single-seat high-performance carrier-based fighter designed primarily for use aboard the Navy's smaller 'converted' carriers; the concept was first suggested in a memorandum sent by Roy Grumman on 28 July 1943 to his chief engineer Bill Schwendler. His concern was the emphasis currently being given to twin-engined fighter types, and the increase in the size of new fighter designs overall. Every effort was made to keep the Model 58's weight to a minimum, aluminium monocoque being used for the body and aluminium panels for the wings. The latter had slotted-type flaps, the propeller was a four-blade of 12ft 6in (3.81m) diameter, and the internal fuel capacity was 140 gallons (530 litres), while droppable fuel took the overload figure to 265 gallons (1,003 litres). The XF8F-1 Bearcat prototype first flew on 21 August 1944 and altogether 1,265 examples were built. This type did not achieve combat during the Second World War, but those Bearcats acquired by France took part in the French Indochina War of 1946-54.

ABOVE Production Bearcat F8U-1 serial 94881.

Model 58 data (estimated, 20 September 1943)

Span	34ft 9in (10.59m); folded 22ft 2in (6.76m)
Length	27ft 6in (8.38m)
Wing area	221sq ft (20.55sq m)
Gross weight	8,400lb (3,810kg)
Powerplant	one 2,400hp (1,790kW) P&W R-2800-22 (War Emergency Power rating)
Armament	four 0.50in (12.70mm) machine guns
Maximum speed	408mph (656km/h) at sea level, 444mph (714km/h) at 20,000ft (6,096m)
Maximum rate of climb	6,600ft/min (2,012m/min)
Service ceiling	39,000ft (11,887m)

F8F-1 data

Span	35ft 6in (10.82m); folded 23ft 9.5in (7.25m)
Length	27ft 8in (8.43m)
Wing area	244sq ft (22.69sq m)
Gross weight	9,672lb (4,387kg)
Maximum take-off weight	12,740lb (5,779kg)
Powerplant	one 2,750hp (2,051kW) P&W R-2800-34W Double Wasp
Armament	four 0.50in (12.70mm) machine guns, 2,000lb (907kg) bombs
Maximum speed	382mph (615km/h) at sea level, 428mph (689km/h) at 18,800ft (5,730m)
Sea level rate of climb	5,610ft/min (1,710m/min)
Service ceiling	38,700ft (11,796m)
Range	1,416 miles (2,278km)

ABOVE The Curtiss XF15C-1 prototype with the horizontal tail in the original low position. *Tommy Thomason*

BELOW The second Curtiss XF15C-1 prototype, with the horizontal tail now placed on top of the fin. The exhaust pipe for the jet engine shows clearly.

XF15C-1 data	
Span	48ft 0in (14.63m); folded 20ft 5in (6.23m)
Length (original tail position)	43ft 8.5in (13.32m)
Wing area	400sq ft (37.20sq m)
Gross weight	16,630lb (7,543kg)
Maximum take-off weight	18,698lb (8,481kg)
Powerplant	one 2,100hp (1,566kW) Pratt & Whitney R2800-34W piston and one 2,700lb (12.0kN) Allis-Chalmers-de Havilland H1-B Goblin jet
Armament	four 20mm cannon
Maximum speed (both engines running)	432mph (695km/h) at sea level, 469mph (755km/h) at 25,300ft (7,711m)
Sea level rate of climb (both engines)	5,020ft/min (1,530m/min)
Service ceiling	41,000ft (12,497m)
Maximum range	1,385 miles (2,228km)

Mixed Powerplant

The US Navy looked closely at composite piston/turbojet powerplants for fighters and produced a specification calling for design submissions. A BuAer Request for Proposals of December 1942 apparently produced nine designs, but little is known about these, and of the projects listed below only the Ryan Fireball was involved. The value of the mixed powerplant, with piston and turbojet operated independently, was that the jet could augment the piston and boost the available speed for combat; in addition, the piston would work efficiently at low and medium altitudes while the jet offered better performance at high altitudes. However, when the jet was shut down the fighter had to carry it as dead weight. The main reason for having both types of engine, however, was that the very first turbojets did not provide sufficient power on their own – once new types had been developed with much higher thrust ratings, the need for mixed powerplants was passed.

Curtiss Model 99/XF15C-1

Thought to have been started in late 1943 or early 1944, three prototypes of Curtiss's Model 99 project were ordered in April 1944 as the XF15C-1, and the first of them become airborne on 27 February 1945 before its jet had been installed. The first machine was lost in a crash and a big change to be introduced subsequently was moving the horizontal tailplane from its original low fuselage position up to the top of the fin. However, the test programme experienced other problems and no production orders were placed, the Navy's contract with Curtiss for this type being terminated in October 1946.

G-67 data	
Span	51ft 6in (15.70m)
Length	45ft 4.5in (13.83m)
Wing area	455sq ft (42.315sq m)
Gross weight (fighter)	25,364lb (11,505kg)
Gross weight (bomber),	29,546lb (13,402kg)
with two 1,000lb/	
454kg bombs	
Powerplant	two 2,800hp (2,088kW)
	Pratt & Whitney R2800-
	22W piston and two
	2,000lb (8.9kNkN) thrust
	General Electric I-20 jets
Armament	four 0.50in (12.7mm)
	machine guns and four
	20mm cannon
Maximum speed	386mph (621km/h) at sea
	level on piston power only,
	473mph (761km/h) with jets
Sea level rate of climb	3,830ft/min (1,167m/min)
	pistons only, 6,290ft/min
	(1,917m/min) with jets

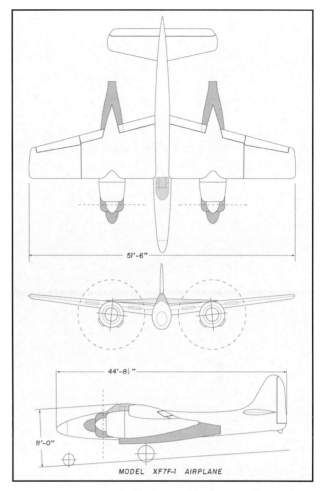

RIGHT
**Grumman G-67
(6.44).**
Tommy Thomason

51'-6"

44'-8½"

11'-0"

MODEL XF7F-1 AIRPLANE

Grumman G-57 and G-67

Grumman's G-57 project was a July 1943 design study for a Navy fighter with a mixed powerplant of a single R-2800 piston engine and a turbojet, but no details are available. This was followed by the G-67 started in June 1944, for which a brochure was submitted to BuAer in August. The proposal saw the installation of two General Electric I-20 jet engines into an F7F's engine nacelles behind the piston units. Some alteration of the engine mounts, nacelles and wing flaps would have been required, but the project was not taken up.

McDonnell Model 18J

McDonnell's Model 18 designation of 1944 covered a variety of Army fighter designs fitted with different powerplants, but the Model 18J, with both an R-2800-C piston engine and an I-40 jet, was proposed to the Navy on 13 September of that year. Only a tiny sketch has been seen, but some papers and data survive in the archives. The design appears to have been a conventional fighter layout with a tapered low-position wing, it would use a 12ft 0in (3.66m)-diameter propeller, it had a tricycle undercarriage, and could carry 317 gallons (1,200 litres) of fuel internally together with another 150 gallons (568 litres) externally. As usual the estimated data given here was

supplied by the manufacturer, but BuAer's speed and climb estimates came out considerably lower, as in their calculations the assessors took into account several different elements of jet engine performance that McDonnell's had not – for example, the loss of jet thrust along the exhaust pipe.

Ryan Model 28/FR-1 Fireball

Ryan's FR-1 Fireball was the only American mixed-powerplant fighter to reach production, having won the design competition held in late 1942/early 1943. Three XFR-1 prototypes were ordered in February 1943 and the first flew on 25 June 1944, although without its jet engine. It was the second prototype that made the first flight with the jet in position, on 20 September, and trials indicated that the two power units worked together well. The close of the war, however, saw a 700-aircraft

Model 18J data	
Span	45ft 4in (13.82m); folded 18ft 8in (5.69m)
Length	41ft 6in (12.65m)
Wing area	310sq ft (28.83sq m)
Gross weight	14,865lb (6,743kg)
Overload weight (external fuel)	15,925lb (7,224kg)
Powerplant	one 2,325hp (1,734kW) P&W R-2800-18W and one 4,000lb (17.8kN) General Electric I-40
Armament	six 0.50in (12.70mm) machine guns
Maximum speed	524mph (843km/h) at sea level, 568mph (914km/h) at 25,000ft (7,620m)
Sea level rate of climb	7,700ft/min (2,347m/min)
Service ceiling	at least 45,000ft (13,716m)
Combat radius (overload fuel)	302 miles (486km)

BuAer estimates	
Maximum speed	457mph (735km/h) at sea level, 487mph (784km/h) at 15,000ft (4,572m)
Sea level rate of climb	6,600ft/min (2,012m/min)
Combat radius (overload fuel)	180 miles (290km)

ABOVE Ryan FR-1 Fireball serial 39660 is seen at Patuxent River on 11 September 1945. *NARA II via Ryan Crierie*

FR-1 data	
Span	40ft 0in (12.19m)
Length	32ft 4in (9.85m)
Wing area	275sq ft (25.58sq m)
Gross weight	9,958lb (4,517kg)
Maximum take-off weight	11,652lb (5,285kg)
Powerplant	one 1,425hp (1,063kW) Wright R1820-72W piston and one 1,610lb (7.2kN) thrust General Electric J31-GE-3 jet
Armament	four 0.50in (12.7mm) machine guns plus rocket projectiles or 1,000lb (454kg) bombs
Maximum speed (both engines running)	399mph (642km/h) at sea level, 404mph (650km/h) at 17,800ft (5,425m)
Sea level rate of climb	4,650ft/min (1,417m/min)
Service ceiling	43,100ft (13,137m)
Maximum range	1,620 miles (2,607km)

production order stopped at sixty-six machines, but the type flew with the Navy until March 1947, providing the Service with valuable experience in operating jet-powered aircraft. The Fireball was followed by Ryan's XF2R-1 Dark Shark prototype, first flown in November 1946, which had a mixed turboprop/jet powerplant.

US Navy Fighter Designs in Perspective

The progress made in the advancement of Navy fighters during the war fully matched the impressive strides made by the USAAF. Planes such as the F8F Bearcat and the F4U Corsair were as outstanding in their respective ways as the Air Force's P-47 Thunderbolt and P-51 Mustang. Together these were not only the best fighters in their class, they were also among the most capable piston-engine fighters ever produced anywhere, and they would go on to have long operational careers. Even

today, seven decades later, slightly modified versions of these aircraft (together with their contemporary, the British Sea Fury) still dominate air races, achieving record times for piston-driven aeroplanes.

Aside from the successful naval fighters, a number of other promising designs were considered but not pursued. Ultimately, it was the use of the piston engine driving a propeller that would set an upper limit on what could be achieved. In an effort to overcome this constraint mixed powerplants were tried, but this really led nowhere, only one type (briefly) reaching service. It would take the introduction of the jet engine – and even then only on the second generation of jet fighters – before the performance of the ultimate piston fighters could be surpassed. The following chapter looks at the parallel development of the second important category of carrier-borne aircraft – those designed to attack ships or land targets.

Chapter Seven
US Navy Attack Aircraft

ABOVE One of the Douglas XBT2D-1 prototypes, a type that eventually became the AD Skyraider. Although making its mark after the war had ended, this type brought together the Navy's wartime experience in using different dive and torpedo bombers to produce the first generation of attack aircraft.
NARA II via Ryan Crierie

Naval attack aircraft were to play an increasingly important role as the war in the Pacific unfolded – arguably a decisive role in many battles. Not surprisingly, despite starting out with two quite capable aircraft – the Douglas TBD Devastator torpedo bomber and the Chance Vought SB2U Vindicator dive bomber (which had first flown in 1935 and 1936 respectively) – a great deal of effort went into the development of a greatly enhanced carrier-borne strike capability.

The resulting picture is quite complex. Not only did it bring forth a plethora of competing designs, many of which got as far as flight-testing, but the Navy also chose to categorise its attack-type aircraft in different groups: the BT Bomber-Torpedo (between 1942 and 1945), SB Scout-Bomber, actually a dive bomber (from 1934 to 1946), TB Torpedo-Bomber (1935 to 1946) and TS Torpedo-Scout (1943 to 1946). There was even a TSB (Torpedo-Scout-Bomber). Many of the proposed designs could, of course, span more than one of these categories, a fact eventually acknowledged in 1946 when they were all incorporated into a single new 'A' for Attack category.

Scout Bombers

In 1936 Brewster had flown the prototype XSBA-1 scout bomber, which went on to be built in small numbers by the Naval Aircraft Factory as the SBN. Brewster followed it with the SB2A Buccaneer, which was submitted to a VSB (carrier scout bomber) competition of August 1938 that required a 1,000lb (454kg) bomb load to be delivered over a range of 1,000 miles (1,609km). This also spawned the Curtiss SB2C Helldiver, both types being ordered because their speed performance with the Wright R-2600 engine was superior to proposals from other manufacturers that had chosen either the Pratt & Whitney R-1830 or the Wright R-1820. However, before this there was a very successful one-off design, Douglas's SBD Dauntless, which had a protracted development history of its own; in fact, the object of the Buccaneer/Helldiver competition was to find a replacement for the Dauntless.

Douglas SBD Dauntless

The Douglas SBD Dauntless was developed from the Northrop BT-1, which had first flown on 19 August 1935. In 1937 the Northrop Corporation in its then form was taken over by Douglas to become the latter's El Segundo Division, but work on the BT-1 continued and in due course Ed Heinemann and his design team produced a revision fitted with a Wright Cyclone engine. As the XBT-2, this first flew on 1 May 1940, and by early 1941 the type had entered service with both the US Marine Corps and the Navy as the SBD Dauntless. In production until 1944 and with near 6,000 built, the Dauntless was arguably the world's best dive bomber of its time (the Air Corps also acquired examples as the A-24). With a good bomb load and long range, as well as good handling, manoeuvrability and diving characteristics, it served extensively in the Pacific as well as other theatres.

ABOVE Serial JS997 was a Douglas SBD Dauntless that had been passed to British hands.

SBD-1 data

Span	41ft 6in (12.65m)
Length	32ft 2in (9.81m)
Wing area	325sq ft (30.225sq m)
Gross weight	8,138lb (3,691kg)
Maximum weight	9,790lb (4,441kg)
Powerplant	one 1,000hp (746kW) Wright XR-1820-32
Armament	three 0.30in (7.62mm) machine guns, c1,000lb (454kg) bombs
Maximum speed	231mph (372km/h) at sea level, 253mph (407km/h) at 16,000ft (4,877m)
Rate of climb	1,730ft/min (527m/min)
Service ceiling	29,600ft (9,022m)
Range (as scout)	965 miles (1,553km)

RIGHT A Brewster SB2A Buccaneer of V-S-5 Vero Beach Scout Bomber Training Unit. *Tommy Thomason*

XSB2A-1 data	
Span	47ft 0in (14.33m); folded 20ft 9in (6.32m)
Length	38ft 0in (11.58m)
Wing area	379sq ft (35.25sq m)
Gross weight	10,168lb (4,612kg)
Maximum take-off weight	10,982lb (4,981kg)
Powerplant	one 1,700hp (1,268kW) Wright R-2600-8
Armament (planned)	three 0.50in (12.70mm) and two 0.30in (7.62mm) machine guns, 1,200lb (544kg) bombs
Maximum speed	313mph (504km/h) at 18,000ft (5,486m)
Rate of climb	2,310ft/min (704m/min)
Service ceiling	27,000ft (8,230m)
Range with 1,000lb (454kg) bombs	979 miles (2,526km)

Brewster SB2A Buccaneer

A development of the SBN, Brewster's two-seat SB2A included a more powerful engine. A prototype was ordered in April 1939, and flew on 17 June 1941. The production run stretched to 770 aircraft, with most ordered by Britain (as the Bermuda) and Holland. It was a poor design and was not operated in its original role, being used mostly for training.

Chance Vought V-169

The V-169 project was Vought's offering to the scout bomber competition. In fact, there were two versions, the V-169A and B, which used the same airframe but had different engines. The design featured a gull wing similar to the manufacturer's F4U Corsair fighter, and a long rear cockpit canopy.

RIGHT The Chance Vought V-169A, redrawn from originals supplied by the Vought Archives (8.38).
Alan Griffith copyright

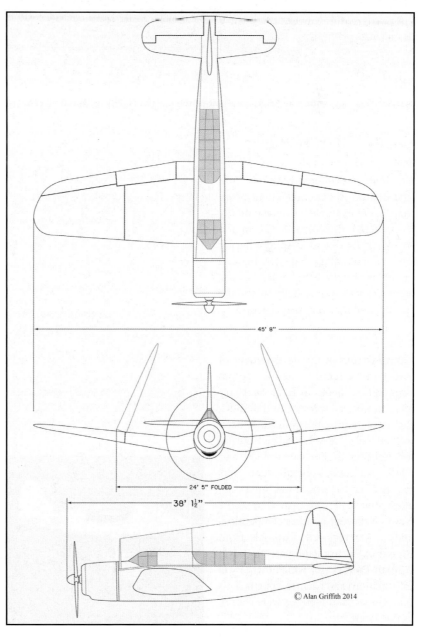

V-169 data	
Span	45ft 8in (13.92m); folded 24ft 5in (7.44m)
Length	38ft 1.5in (11.62m) (V-169A); 38ft 8.5in (11.80m) (V-169B)

ABOVE This view shows an SB2C-3 variant of the Curtiss Helldiver, serial 18774.

Curtiss SB2C Helldiver

The prototype Curtiss XSB2C-1 Helldiver was ordered May 1939 and first flew on 18 December 1940. More than 7,000 examples were eventually constructed, including A-25s for the Army Air Force and, despite suffering from poor handling characteristics and other problems, the type served throughout the war (particularly in the Pacific) and for some years beyond.

*

The next step in the development of VSB-type aircraft was a design competition held in early February 1941 to find a successor to the SB2C, the new requirements having been influenced by lessons learned during the fighting in Europe in 1939 and 1940. A heavier bomb load was requested and a torpedo was listed as an alternative load. This proved to be the Navy's last scout bomber competition, and BuAer received proposals from Brewster, Curtiss, Douglas, the Naval Aircraft Factory (for which there is no information) and Chance Vought. This time Curtiss and Douglas were chosen as the winners.

XSB2C-1 data	
Span	49ft 9in (15.16m); folded 22ft 6.5in (6.87m)
Length	35ft 4in (10.77m)
Wing area	422sq ft (39.25sq m)
Gross weight	10,261lb (4,654kg)
Maximum take-off weight	10,859lb (4,926kg)
Powerplant	one 1,700hp (1,268kW) Wright R-2600-8
Armament	one 0.50in (12.70mm) and two 0.30in (7.62mm) machine guns, two 20mm cannon, 1,200lb (544kg) bombs
Maximum speed	322mph (518km/h) at 14,600ft (4,450m)
Rate of climb	2,380ft/min (725m/min)
Service ceiling	30,000ft (9,144m)
Range with 1,000lb (454kg) bombs	996 miles (1,603km)

Brewster Model 37B

Brewster's high-wing Model 37B proposal of April 1941 was a rather advanced-looking project, having its engine buried in the centre of the fuselage and driving counter-rotating six-blade propellers. The pilot had a large canopy that should have provided him with excellent vision, while the gunner (beneath a heavily glazed rear canopy) operated two streamlined remote-controlled turrets in the rear, each with a single gun. There was a bomb bay in the middle fuselage, and two forward-firing guns appear to have been installed in the outer wings,

BELOW Manufacturer's model of the Brewster Model 37B project of April 1941. *Cradle of Aviation Museum*

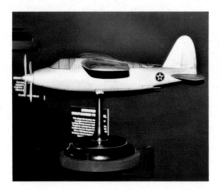

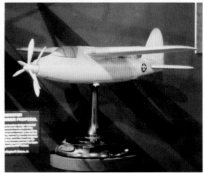

seemingly outside the wing fold. No data is available for this project, which was first designed by Dayton T. Brown before he left Brewster for Grumman (where he went on to work with the team that produced the F6F Hellcat, described in Chapter Six). The accompanying artwork shows the Model 37B, which suggests that there was also at least a Model 37A variant or alternative, about which nothing is known. In the sketch the aircraft's fin is marked 'XSB3A-1'.

Chance Vought (Vought-Sikorsky) VS-319

Vought's VS-319 proposal of 11 February 1941 showed a tapered mid-position wing and a combined cockpit canopy for the two crew members. Its four-blade propeller had a diameter of 12ft 6in (3.81m), split flap dive brakes were on the inner wing trailing edge with spoilers in the outer wing, and the drawing showed a 125-gallon (473-litre) tank in the forward part of each inner wing, with another of 67.5 gallons (256 litres) behind. A single gun (probably a 0.50in/12.70mm machine gun) was housed in each of two defensive turrets, in the upper and lower rear fuselage positions respectively, while two more guns (probably machine guns) went in the wing just outboard of the wing fold. One bomb was shown under each wing inside the main gears of the tricycle undercarriage, and a fuselage bomb bay was provided for larger stores.

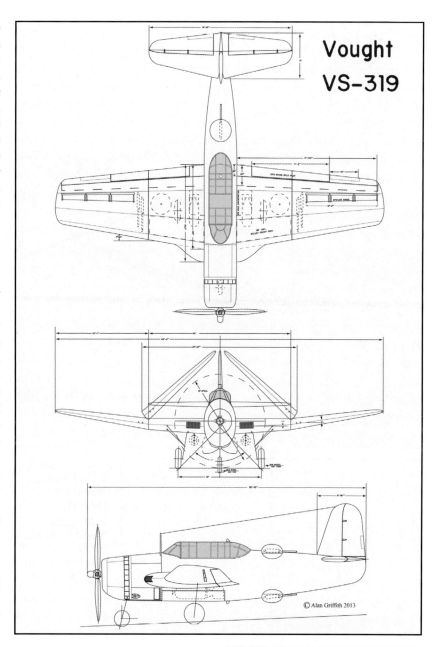

ABOVE The Vought VS-319 redrawn from the Vought original drawing dated 21.4.41. *Alan Griffith copyright*

VS-319 data (at 22 April 1941)	
Span	46ft 2in (14.07m); folded 21ft 10in (6.65m)
Length	38ft 10in (11.84m)
Wing area	402.5sq ft (37.43sq m)
Gross weight	14,511lb (6,582kg)
Powerplant	one 2,000hp (1,491kW) P&W R-2800
Armament	see text
Maximum speed	299mph (481km/h) at sea level
Service ceiling	29,000ft (8,839m)
Range as normal scout	1,545 miles (2,486km)

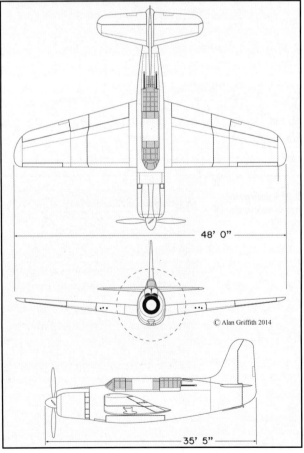

ABOVE Artwork for the Brewster Model 37B (30.4.41).

LEFT Curtiss Model 93/XSB3C-1 (c2.41).
Alan Griffith copyright

Curtiss Model 93/XSB3C-1

The Curtiss Model 93 response to the Navy's request for proposals was an enlarged SB2C with a revised wing, a bigger tailplane and a tricycle landing gear. It would have two crew – pilot and gunner/observer – and the internal bay could take two bombs up to 1,600lb (726kg) in size or two torpedoes, the latter semi-submerged, with, it is understood, two further 500lb (227kg) bombs going under the wings. There was a defensive turret with twin 0.50in (12.70mm) machine guns, while four 20mm cannon or six 0.50in (12.70mm) machine guns were to fit in the wings (one source lists just two forward-firing machine guns). BuAer inspected a mock-up of this design between 8 and 11 December 1941 and an order was placed for two XSB3C-1 prototypes, but during the following year it became clear that this aircraft would be inferior to the rival Douglas XSB2D-1 (see below). Other problems (for example extra weight, which gave a marginal take-off performance) contributed to the programme not moving forward at a suitable pace (Curtiss was also having to sort out difficulties with the Helldiver), so the XSB3C-1 project was cancelled in December 1942 before either prototype had been completed.

XSB3C-1 data	
Span	48ft 0in (14.63m); folded not available
Length	35ft 5in (10.80m)
Wing area	378sq ft (35.15sq m)
Gross weight	14,990lb (6,799kg)
Maximum take-off weight	16,800lb (7,620kg)
Powerplant	one 2,300hp (1,715kW) Wright R-3350-8
Armament	see text
Maximum speed	349mph (561km/h) at 16,000ft (4,877m)
Rate of climb	2,820ft/min (860m/min)
Service ceiling	29,800ft (9,083m)
Range with two 1,000lb (454kg) bombs	1,400 miles (2,253km)

Douglas XSB2D-1/BTD-1 Destroyer

In June 1941 prototypes of the two-seat Douglas entry were ordered as the XSB2D-1 Destroyer and, after some delays, particularly with the engine, the first of these began its flight-test programme on 8 April 1943. By then production orders had been placed, but the aircraft proved to be overweight and exhibited other unsatisfactory features. However, the fact that the Navy had by now switched to a policy of single-seat dive bombers without defensive turrets

meant that there was no need to work closely on the XS2B-1's deficiencies. Instead Douglas removed the SB2D-1's turrets and the gunner to produce a new version called the BTD-1, which flew on 5 March 1944. The original SB2D-1 orders were amended to cover BTD-1s, but the new type's flying characteristics were still far from satisfactory. Since all-new single-seat designs from Douglas and other manufacturers were now on the way (see below), the Destroyer production run was to be closed in 1945 after just twenty-eight machines had left the line.

HERE AND OVERLEAF TOP Photographs showing the Douglas XSB2D-1 Destroyer prototypes. Note the wing- and turret-mounted guns. *Mark Nankivil*

ABOVE A side view of the Douglas BTD-1 Destroyer after the rear turrets had been removed and the fin fairing extended. The picture was taken on 25 July 1944 while the aircraft was undergoing Navy evaluation. *NARA II via Ryan Crierie*

ABOVE Further pictures of the BDT-1, this time taken during a sortie on 4 September 1944. *NARA II via Ryan Crierie*

XSB2D-1 data	
Span	44ft 7.5in (13.60m); folded 20ft 4in (6.20m)
Length	38ft 7in (11.76m)
Wing area	375sq ft (34.875sq m)
Gross weight	16,273lb (7,381kg)
Maximum take-off weight	19,140lb (8,682kg)
Powerplant	one 2,200hp (1,641kW) Wright R-3350-14
Armament	six 0.50in (12.70mm) machine guns, two bombs up to 1,600lb (726kg) or two torpedoes in fuselage bay, two 325lb (147kg) bombs under wings
Maximum speed	357mph (574km/h) at 14,000ft (4,267m)
Maximum rate of climb	2,445ft/min (745m/min)
Service ceiling	27,400ft (8,352m)
Range with 1,000lb (454kg) bombs	1,105 miles (1,778km)

BTD-1 data	
Span	45ft 0in (13.72m); folded 20ft 4in (6.20m)
Length	38ft 7in (11.76m)
Wing area	373sq ft (34.69sq m)
Gross weight	18,140lb (8,228kg)
Maximum take-off weight	19,000lb (8,618kg)
Powerplant	one 2,200hp (1,641kW) Wright R-3350-14
Armament	two 20mm cannon, two bombs up to 1,600lb (726kg) or two torpedoes in fuselage bay
Maximum speed	344mph (553km/h) at 16,100ft (4,907m)
Sea level rate of climb	1,650ft/min (503m/min)
Service ceiling	23,600ft (7,193m)
Range with one torpedo	1,480 miles (2,381km)

Interviews with George Spangenberg, formerly of BuAer, reveal that the original requirements leading to the Destroyer 'were overdone', particularly in including for example the R-3350, two remote-control turrets, a bomb bay and tricycle landing gear. The XSB2D-1 was described as 'far from successful' and did not meet its performance goals, but both the Navy and the Douglas design organisation learned much from the project. In addition, as noted, in 1943 the Navy introduced a big change in its development of new carrier-based attack types – from now on dive bombers would be single-seat aircraft to increase their performance, thereby removing the scouting mission from the type's requirements. That role was transferred to the 'horizontal' torpedo bomber class, a step that in due course led to the Curtiss BTC and Douglas TB2D below.

ABOVE Revised artwork for the Curtiss VSB, showing how the design looked at 9.11.44. *NARA II via Tommy Thomason*

Curtiss VSB

In August 1944 the Curtiss design office produced a proposal for a VSB Class aircraft, submitted on or around the 21st of that month; the project was revised three months later. As proposed, the project was an effort to improve the Model SB2C Helldiver and was substantially the same as the SB2C-5 but for alterations that included the following:

1. A Wright R-3350-BD engine with engine-driven cooling fan and four-blade 13ft 8in (4.17m)-diameter propeller

2. An additional 20in (50.8cm) added to the tail

3. An internal fuel load of 420 gallons (1,590 litres)

4. Re-faired bomb bay doors and a lower forward section to enclose completely a 2,000lb (907kg) bomb

5. A semi 'all-glass' pilot's enclosure

6. Outer wing panels the same as the SB2C-5 except for clipped wingtips

7. Metal-covered ailerons and tail control surfaces and rudder

VSB data (at 16 August 1944)

Span	47ft 7in (14.51m); folded unknown
Length	c38ft 4in (11.68m)
Wing area	415sq ft (38.595sq m)
Gross weight	17,672lb (8,016kg)
Powerplant	one 2,900hp (2,163kW) Wright R-3350-BD
Armament	one flexible 0.50in (12.70mm) machine gun, two fixed 20mm cannon, one 1,000lb (454kg) or 2,000lb (907kg) bomb
Maximum speed	304.5mph (490km/h) at sea level, 320.5mph (516km/h) at critical altitude 16,800ft (5,121m); BuAer estimated maximum 323.5mph (521km/h) at 16,800ft (5,121m)
Sea level rate of climb	2,560ft/min (780m/min)
Service ceiling	25,700ft (7,833m)
Maximum range	1,402 miles (2,256km)
Combat radius	270 miles (434km)

**VSB data
(at 6 November 1944
with 1,000lb/454kg bomb)**

Gross weight	17,430lb (7,906kg)
Armament	two 0.30in (7.62mm) machine guns, two 20mm cannon; could carry up to 2,000lb (907kg) of bombs
Maximum speed	308mph (496km/h) at sea level, 325mph (523km/h) at 16,800ft (5,121m)
Sea level rate of climb	2,640ft/min (805m/min)
Service ceiling	26,250ft (8,001m)
Maximum range	1,390 miles (2,237km)
Combat radius	262 miles (422km)

**VSB data
(at 6 November 1944 with Mk 13 torpedo)**

Gross weight	18,576lb (8,426kg)
Maximum speed	305mph (491km/h) at sea level, 319mph (513km/h) at 16,800ft (5,121m)
Sea level rate of climb	2,360ft/min (719m/min)
Service ceiling	24,750ft (7,544m)
Maximum range	1,300 miles (2,092km)
Combat radius	247 miles (397km)

8. Two T-31 20mm cannon in the wings

This aircraft would carry the same bomb load as the SB2C-5, there would be provision to carry rocket projectiles, and its performance figures were based on a 1,000lb (454kg) load. Curtiss declared that the new design represented 'a substantial advance over the current SB2C models', but after close consideration BuAer reported that no further action was needed on this proposal, having concluded that it would not be available in production numbers before the arrival of other promising types already under development.

The November 1944 revision brought more changes since the aircraft (still with the same engine) was now able to carry a torpedo as an alternative to the previously specified bomb load. The bomb bay area had been altered again with the bay doors now extended to fully enclose the torpedo, the flexible armament in the rear cockpit was now two 0.30in (7.62mm) machine guns, and the internal fuel had been reduced slightly to 410 gallons (1,552 litres). Once again, BuAer did not order this VSB project.

Torpedo Bombers

The second key front-line category in the Navy inventory at the start of the war was the torpedo bomber, and besides the main players and programmes below in the spring of 1942 BuAer evaluated the TBV-1 Georgia, a US Navy version of the Vultee Vengeance described in Chapter Five.

The first competition for new aircraft took place under Specification SD-114-6 of March 1939, which sought a new three-seat VTB Class aircraft to replace the near obsolete Douglas TBD Devastator. The crew would be pilot, co-pilot/bombardier and radio operator/gunner, the aircraft was to have a range of 1,000 miles (1,609km) with 1,500lb (681kg) of bombs or one torpedo aboard, it would have a ceiling of at least 30,000ft (9,144m), and a loaded weight of 12,500lb (5,670kg). Submissions were made by 24 August and the competition generated proposals from the three manufacturers listed below and also from Brewster (three designs with one at least using the R-2600 engine), Hall Aluminium (one) and Vultee (two under its V-57 designation, a variant of what would become the A-31 Vengeance in Chapter Five). The competition resulted in the Grumman Avenger and Vought Sea Wolf.

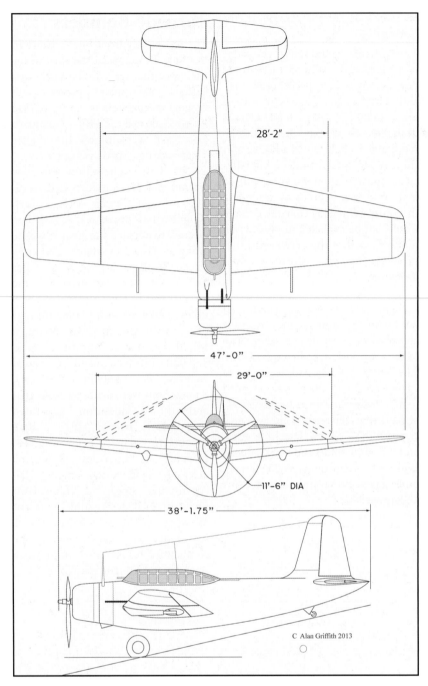

VTB data	
Span	47ft 0in (14.33m); folded 29ft 0in (8.84m)
Length	38ft 1.75in (11.63m)
Wing area	unknown
Weights	unknown
Powerplant	one 1,600hp (1,193kW) Wright R-2600
Armament	two 20mm cannon, two machine guns, bomb load unknown

ABOVE The Douglas VTB torpedo bomber proposal to SD-114-6 (c8.39).
Alan Griffith copyright

Grumman Model 40/TBF Avenger

Two versions of Grumman's Model 40 were submitted, both with the R-2600 engine, one having a two-speed supercharger, the other a two-stage supercharger. Two prototype XTBF-1s were ordered in April 1940 and the first flew on 7 August 1941, the new type entering service in 1942. More than 9,800 examples of this outstanding aircraft were built, both for the US Navy and a number of overseas air arms. It was involved in the destruction of many enemy warships and land installations and remained in service well beyond the end of the war.

TBF-1 data	
Span	54ft 2in (16.51m); folded 19ft 0in (5.79m)
Length	40ft 0in (12.19m)
Wing area	490sq ft (45.57sq m)
Gross weight	13,667lb (6,199kg)
Maximum take-off weight	15,905lb (7,215kg)
Powerplant	one 1,700hp (1,268kW) Wright R-2600-8
Armament	two 0.30in (7.62mm) and one 0.50in (12.70mm) machine guns, 2,000lb (907kg) bombs or one torpedo
Maximum speed	271mph (436km/h) at 12,000ft (3,658m)
Sea level rate of climb	1,430ft/min (436m/min)
Service ceiling	22,400ft (6,828m)
Range with torpedo	1,215 miles (1,955km)

Douglas VTB proposal

The Douglas proposal to SD-114-6, the company identity of which is unknown, showed some similarities to the Devastator but, unlike its competitors, it used a tricycle undercarriage that was then still a very novel idea. A single large canopy covered the crew and the Wright R-2600 drove an 11ft 6in

(3.51m) three-blade propeller. A 20mm cannon was housed in each wing, two machine guns sat on top of the nose fuselage just behind the engine cowling and, as required, the bombs were stowed in the fuselage. The drawing shows no sign of the aircraft having defensive turrets.

ABOVE A lovely close-up view of a Grumman TBF Avenger.

Chance Vought V-174 XTBU-1 Sea Wolf/ Convair TBY-1

Chance Vought was the other contender to receive a contract, an order for one prototype XTBU-1 also being placed in April 1940 with the name Sea Wolf. The original proposals had embraced four different variants of the basic layout – the V-174A, B, C and D – with at least one powered by a Pratt & Whitney R-2800. The first Sea Wolf flew on 22 December 1941 and promised a higher speed than Grumman's Avenger, but the production

TBU-1 data	
Span	57ft 2in (17.43m); folded 27ft 7in (8.41m)
Length	39ft 0in (11.89m)
Wing area	439.5sq ft (40.87sq m)
Gross weight with one torpedo	16,247lb (7,370kg)
Powerplant	one 2,000hp (1,485kW) P&W XR-2800-20
Armament	one 0.30in (7.62mm) and two 0.50in (12.70mm) machine guns, 3,200lb (1,452kg) bombs or one torpedo
Maximum speed	295mph (475km/h) at sea level, 311mph (500km/h) at 14,700ft (4,481m)
Maximum rate of climb	1,820ft/min (555m/min)
Service ceiling (clean)	30,200ft (9,205m)
Range with torpedo	1,480 miles (2,381km)

run was subsequently transferred to Vultee to permit Vought to concentrate on series manufacture of its F4U Corsair fighter (Vultee was shortly to become part of Convair through its merger with Consolidated). In Convair's hands the Sea Wolf was designated TBY, but the programme moved forward quite slowly and the aircraft itself was found in some respects to be inferior to the Avenger. In the end only 180 examples of the Sea Wolf were manufactured.

Torpedo-scout-bombers

This next section looks at the Navy's search for a VTSB, a carrier-based torpedo-scout-bomber covered by some requirements issued in February 1942, which subsequently resulted in two large twin-engine designs from Grumman and an equivalent single-engine type from Douglas. BuAer's original desire had been for a twin-engine aeroplane, and the Lockheed Vega V-141 twin-engine design, also produced in 1942, was also considered by the Bureau up until 23 July, at which point the manufacturer explained that it could not proceed with the project since its staff were required to handle contracts already received for patrol aircraft. Prior to this effort Vought had produced a private VSTB design.

BELOW The Chance Vought XTBU-1 prototype, photographed in 1941.
Tommy Thomason

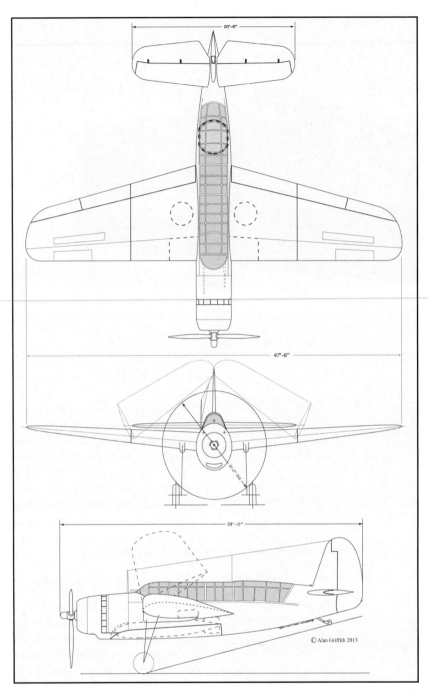

**ABOVE Chance Vought VS-307A
(14.9.39).** *Alan Griffith copyright*

VS-307A data	
Span	47ft 6in (14.48m); folded 24ft 8in (7.52m)
Length	39ft 0in (11.89m)
Wing area	426sq ft (39.62sq m)

Chance Vought VS-307A

In September 1939 Vought produced a VSTB combined scout-torpedo-bomber design study under its VS-307 number, which featured a tapered wing with a straight leading edge, a crew of three under a long glass canopy, a tailwheel undercarriage, a fuselage torpedo bay, and a three-blade propeller with a diameter of 13ft 9in (4.19m). Two fixed guns were mounted in the upper nose and there was a defensive gun in the rear of the cockpit. The project was not taken up.

Douglas D-544/XTB2D-1 Skypirate

Work on the Douglas XTB2D-1 began in March 1942 and the initial studies apparently embraced eight different designs (although an illustration has been found for a further study). Three of these were to have two 1,350hp (1,007kW) Pratt & Whitney R-1820s (turbocharged or two-speed) in conventional nacelles with three-blade props. The variations went on to include two designs having one turbocharged 2,600hp (1,939kW) Allison V-3420 unit housed in the fuselage to the rear of the pilot, the first with a four-blade prop connected to the engine by a long shaft, and the second with a three-blader placed ahead of each wing leading edge and connected by angled extension shafts. Finally there were three more single-engine layouts, each with a 3,000hp (2,237kW) Pratt & Whitney R-4360 two-speed unit and a four-blade prop, but differing in the tail region in that two had twin fins and rudders and the other a conventional tail. The weight range for these offerings was between 21,100lb (9,571kg) and 23,500lb (10,660kg).

In the end BuAer opted to choose the single-tail single-R-4360, and in November 1942 issued a Letter of Intent for two prototypes for what Douglas now called the D-544 (it was originally named Devastator II), but which was officially designated XTB2D-1 and named Skypirate (the orders were not actually placed for another eleven months). The mock-up of this three-seat design was inspected in March and May 1943, but the first example did not get airborne until 13 March 1945. In fact, the Skypirate received only limited support from the Navy and, since it was designed to fly from large Midway and Essex Class carriers only, a recommendation for cancellation came on 20 May 1944. All plans for production, including twenty-three pre-production airframes, were dropped, and the two prototypes were scrapped in 1948. In November 1944 a proposal by Douglas to fit an auxiliary jet engine instead of the dorsal turret was turned down.

RIGHT One of the eight layouts considered by Douglas on the lead up to the selection of the XTB2D-1 Skypirate configuration. A torpedo is housed in the bomb bay and there are dorsal and lower rear fuselage gun turrets. The original drawing is thought to show an alternative wing centre section chord. *Alan Griffith copyright*

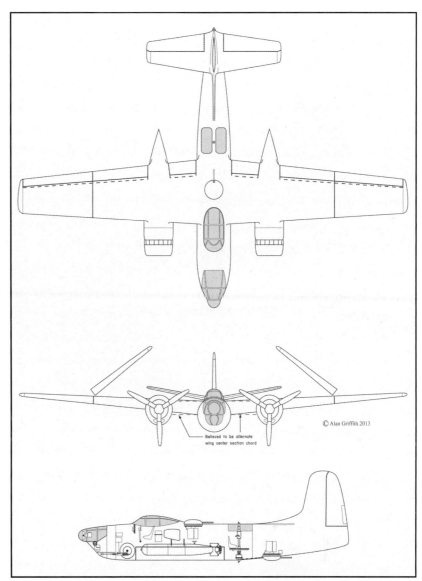

XTB2D-1 data	
Span	70ft 0in (21.34m); folded 36ft 0in (10.97m)
Length	46ft 0in (14.02m)
Wing area	605sq ft (56.265sq m)
Gross weight with torpedoes	28,545lb (12,948kg)
Maximum take off weight	34,760lb (15,767kg)
Powerplant	one 3,000hp (2,237kW) P&W XR-4360-8
Armament (not fitted)	seven 0.50in (12.70mm) machine guns, up to 8,000lb (3,629kg) bombs or four torpedoes
Maximum speed	310mph (499km/h) at sea level, 340mph (547km/h) at 15,600ft (4,754m)
Sea level rate of climb	1,835ft/min (559m/min)
Service ceiling	27,900ft (8,504m)
Range with torpedoes	1,250 miles (2,011km)

BELOW & OVERLEAF A selection of pictures that show nicely just how large the Douglas XTB2D-1 Skypirate prototypes were. *Mark Nankivil*

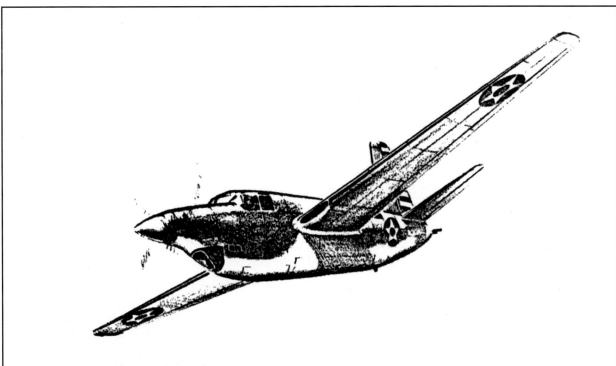

ABOVE Each of these copies of original artworks was labelled 'TB2D Design Study 1942', but they do not both match up with the descriptions of known layouts. The tractor design appears to have contra-rotating propellers. *René Francillon*

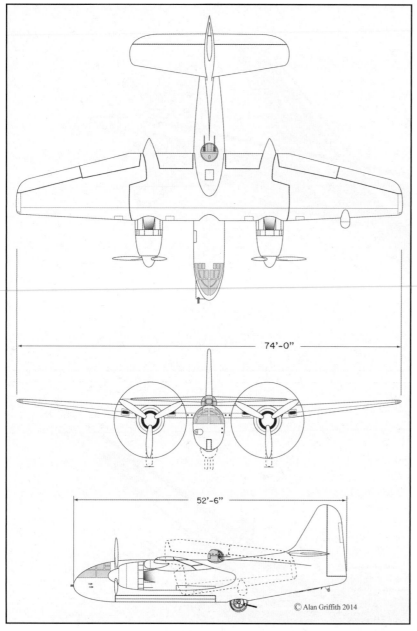

Grumman Model 55/XTB2F

Grumman's eventual response was the twin-engine four-seat Model 55 torpedo-scout-bomber project produced as a preliminary design study in December 1942. This was another big aeroplane and indeed a most ambitious project, both for Grumman and for the Navy, which had never attempted to build an aircraft of such a large size before. In essence this represented an outgrowth of the experience gained from the TBF, with an effort to increase the range, the bomb load and the effectiveness of the armament carried. The project appears to have begun after the single-engine Douglas XTB2D-1 had been selected, since BuAer at that stage still wanted to acquire a twin-engine torpedo bomber.

The Model 55 was designed to operate as a torpedo plane, glide or skip bomber, or as a scout aircraft both aboard an aircraft carrier and ashore. With a conventional high wing, it was somewhat similar to the Martin B-26 (see Chapter Three) except that the requirement that the G-55 be carrier-based had resulted in short, thick wings. The hydraulically operated flaps were of the fixed-hinge slotted type and the wing would fold back and outboard. The crew was made up of

LEFT Grumman Model 55/XTB2F-1, as at 17.943. *Alan Griffith copyright*
BELOW A full-size mock-up of the Grumman XTB2F-1.
Northrop Grumman History Center

74'-0"

52'-6"

© Alan Griffith 2014

the pilot, radio and radar operator and top turret and bottom turret operators, and there was to be a passageway over the bomb bay to connect the fore and aft decks, the aft deck containing the top and bottom turrets only. A tricycle-type landing gear with dual nose wheels was selected, and the three-blade propellers were 14ft 0in (4.27m) in diameter. The powerplant itself was a pair of Pratt & Whitney R-2800-22 single-stage two-speed engines that had no provision for War Emergency Power. A total of 960 gallons (3,634 litres) of fuel would go in the wings, and another 600 gallons (2,271 litres) in two auxiliary wing drop tanks.

For armament the Model 55 had six fixed forward-firing 0.50in (12.70mm) machine guns (two located in the left side of the fuselage under the pilot's compartment and four in the wings, two to each side of the fuselage) together with two turrets (an upper turret over the aft end of the bomb bay and a retractable lower turret behind the bomb bay), both housing two 0.50in (12.70mm) machine guns. Alternatives could be fixed 0.60in (15.24mm) machine guns or 20mm cannon on the same mountings, while provision was also to be made for a 75mm cannon on the right side of the pilot's deck. The bomb load could be one 4,000lb (1,815kg) bomb, four 2,000lb (907kg), 1,600lb (726kg) or 1,000lb (454kg) bombs, ten 500lb (227kg) or thirty-six 100lb (45kg) bombs, four 650lb (295kg) or ten 325lb (147kg) depth bombs (depth charges), two 2,000lb (907kg) or four 1,000lb (454kg) mines, ten 500lb (227kg) incendiary bomb clusters or twenty-four 100lb (45kg) fragmentation bomb clusters, or two 2,084lb (945kg) torpedoes. It was expected that another 2,000lb (907kg) bomb could go in place of each of the two external wing tanks.

Two prototypes were ordered in August 1943 as the XTB2F-1, but the official mock-up inspection did not take place until 22 May 1944, where it was concluded that the aircraft's performance fell short of the minimum now desired by the Army Air Forces. In fact, since the type was not expected to

ABOVE The defensive turret arrangement designed for the XTB2F-1. *Northrop Grumman History Center*

see combat for about another two years, it was realised that aircraft currently under development for the AAF and in production by then would far outperform Grumman's G-55 in all of its functions. However, it was recommended that the project should continue and that flight-test performance data be obtained for comparison with AAF aircraft. Production was expected to start during the summer of 1945, but in truth the G-55 would be a tight squeeze on the elevators and hangar decks of the new large Midway Class of carrier. It would not be possible to reduce the aircraft's size and weight by an appreciable amount unless one torpedo was eliminated, and even then, if it was to remain a twin-engine type, the overall dimensions could not be brought down sufficiently to effect the

deck spotting requirements.

In fact, after the mock-up inspection BuAer's Military Requirements Department recommended that the XTB2F-1 project be cancelled since, because of its weight and size, it could only ever be used from a Midway type of carrier, and its weight and clearances made even this use appear impractical and limited the number of airframes that could be carried on each ship. In comparison with other types, the XTB2F-1 was also only slightly faster than, for example, the TBY, and it would not be as fast as new upcoming designs of attack aircraft. In addition, no useful purpose could be gained by building the XTB2F-1 as a Navy land-based type. In the end only the mock-up was constructed, the prototypes were not built, and the XTB2F-1 programme was finally cancelled on 14 June 1944.

Model 55 XTB2F-1 data (at 22 May 1944)	
Span	74ft 0in (22.56m); folded 36ft 0in (10.97m)
Length	51ft 10in (15.80m)
Wing area	777sq ft (72.26sq m)
Gross weight	c38,000lb (17,237kg)
Powerplant	two 2,100hp (1,566kW) P&W R-2800-22 Double Wasp
Armament	see text
Maximum speed	309mph (497km/h) at sea level, 331mph (533km/h) at critical altitude
Sea level rate of climb	2,230ft/min (680m/min)
Service ceiling	27,380ft (8,345m)
Range	2,020 miles (3,250km)

Grumman Model 66/XTSF-1

In June 1944 Grumman proposed its two-seat twin-engine mid-wing G-66 design to the Navy to serve in the torpedo/scout aircraft category, in some respects as a replacement for the XTB2F described above. This was essentially a variation of the F7F-2 night fighter Tigercat (see Chapter Six) with a fuselage bay to carry a torpedo or a gasoline tank. In fact, the 66 would be identical to the Tigercat with the exception of the new aluminium alloy monocoque fuselage, which also included a larger cockpit. A tricycle undercarriage would be used and the aircraft was designed to operate both aboard carriers and ashore.

After BuAer had reviewed the project, a revised design (Model 66A dated 12 July) was submitted, using the same engines. At this stage all bar the fuselage, longer span outer wing panels and longer span tail surfaces were interchangeable with the F7F-2. This version was accepted and it is understood that the existing contract for the XTB2F-1 was modified to cover two XTSF-1 airframes; it was planned that the first example should be a converted F7F airframe. The bomb bay could hold a Mk 13 torpedo, one 2,000lb (907kg) bomb, two 1,600lb (726kg) armour-piercing bombs, two 1,000lb (454kg) bombs, four 500lb (227kg) bombs, or twelve 100lb (45kg) bombs, two 1,000lb (454kg) mines or 650lb (295kg) depth bombs, or a droppable 270-gallon (1,022-litre) fuel tank. An underwing hardpoint on each wing could each take a 1,000lb (454kg) or 500lb (227kg) bomb. Behind the cockpit were two fuel tanks carrying 185 gallons (700 litres) and 215 gallons (814 litres) respectively, and for overload fuel two 150-gallon (568-litre) external drop tanks could be carried. Two 0.50in (12.70mm) machine guns were housed in each wing root, and the two engines had four-blade propellers with a diameter of 13ft 2in (4.01m). The second crewman would operate an AN/APS-3 or -4 radar. A cockpit, centre fuselage and wing centre section mock-up was built, and during October this received an official BuAer inspection.

However, Grumman's considerable war workload was a problem and this new project began to be regarded with some doubt. A conference was held in December 1944 specifically to make a decision on the XTSF-1, and the resulting report from Cdr W. W. Hollister stated that 'a stop-work order had been sent to Grumman on the XTSF-1 … which automatically ends in a contract termination after 30 days.' His report added that 'Grumman does not want to proceed on the XTSF-1 at any priority, Grumman does not have sufficient engineering on the XTSF-1 for transfer to any other contractor,' and 'Grumman desires complete cancellation of the contract.' In fact, due to weight and installation changes, the original idea of similarity between the F7F and XTSF-1 had rapidly disappeared and practically a complete redesign of the landing gear and centre section could be expected. Therefore it was decided at the conference to terminate the XTSF-1 contract immediately, to drop all thoughts for

RIGHT Grumman Model 66A/XTSF-1 (7.44). *Tommy Thomason copyright*

BELOW A wooden cockpit mock-up built for the Grumman XTSF-1.

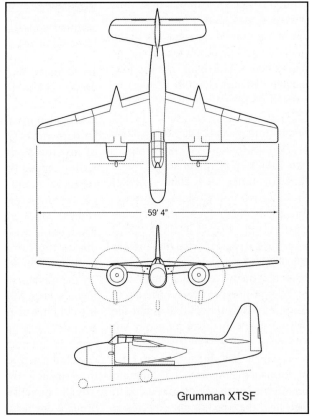

59' 4"

Grumman XTSF

turning the new type over to another contractor, and to seek a new proposal for a scout-attack-torpedo-bomber from another contractor to compete with Grumman's XTB3F (below). Douglas was recommended and this new design could be either a single, twin or composite engine (it seems likely that the DS-557 – see below – came out of this move). It was also agreed that the XTB3F-1 should continue with the highest priority. Grumman's XTSF-1 was the only project ever to receive a designation within the Navy's TS (Torpedo-Scout) classification.

Final Generation – the Bomber-torpedo

In a move referred to already, in early 1943 Navy policy was changed by a decision to replace over time the various scout and torpedo bombers in service with a new type of single-seat multi-role strike aeroplane. This was given the new title or category of Bomber-Torpedo (BT), and part of the theory was that with better quality and stronger fighter protection the new attack aircraft would not require defensive guns of its own, so the weight

saved could go towards increasing the fuel and warload. In September 1943 BuAer asked for proposals for new BT types and some submissions had been received by early 1944. In June of that year Douglas made a proposition to abandon its current BTD programme (see above) and move on to another new design, and this was ordered in prototype form. Prototypes would also be forthcoming from Curtiss, Kaiser-Fleetwings and Martin. In fact, back in 1942 Curtiss had begun a design that would become the first BT type, and separate from its 1944 proposals.

Curtiss VBT, Model 96 and XBTC

On 16 June 1942 Curtiss-Wright produced a revised brochure for a new VBT bomber-torpedo project, the artwork showing XBTC-1 on the aircraft's fin. The date of the original proposal is uncertain, but it had been submitted in response to BuAer requirements made in February 1942 that had asked for an R-3350-powered single-seater capable of carrying a 1,000lb (454kg) load over 1,000 miles (1,609km), or a torpedo. The June brochure stated that the aircraft was to be capable of being

Model 66 data (June 1944)

Span	52ft 2in (15.90m); folded 32ft 0in (9.75m)
Length	46ft 0in (14.02m)
Gross weight	23,275lb (10,558kg)
Powerplant	two 2,100hp (1,566kW) P&W R-2800-22 (2,400hp/1,790kW in War Emergency Power)

Model 66A data (July 1944)

Span	59ft 4in (18.08m); folded 32ft 0in (9.75m)
Length	46ft 4in (14.12m)
Wing area	500sq ft (46.50sq m)
Gross weight	23,955lb (10,866kg) with one torpedo, 26,171lb (11,871kg) with torpedo and two external tanks
Maximum speed	374mph (602km/h) at sea level, 414mph (666km/h) at 18,600ft (5,669m)
Sea level rate of climb	3,920ft/min (1,195m/min)
Service ceiling	36,500ft (11,125m)
Range with external tanks	1,455 miles (2,341km)

RIGHT Curtiss Wright Model 96 VBT artwork, dated 16 June 1942. 'XBTC-1' is marked on the fin. *NARA II via Tommy Thomason*

BELOW The Wright R-3350-8-powered Curtiss XBTC-1 prototype. *NARA II via Ryan Crierie*

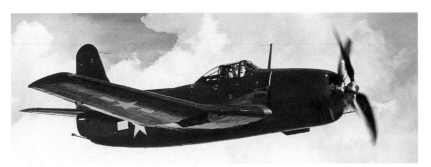

LEFT One of the Pratt & Whitney XR-4360-3-powered XBTC-2 prototypes pictured in 1946.
NARA II via Ryan Crierie

used primarily as a dive bomber, and secondly as a torpedo bomber or smoke screen layer (with smoke tanks replacing the normal stores). Curtiss declared that the use of a single-stage two-speed supercharged R-3350 powerplant would result in a performance that would permit this aircraft 'to enter into combat at medium altitudes with any present developed high-altitude fighter'. It was to have a single 20mm cannon in each side of the centre wing with provision for two more 20mm (the BuAer review declared that four 20mm must be the minimum carried), while three 0.50in (12.70mm) machine guns could be added in the wings just outboard of the fold line.

The wing would be constructed in five parts – two outer panels extending from the fold line outboard, two centre sections extending from the fold line to the fuselage, and one centre section integral with the fuselage – and the wing structure would be similar to that used on the SB2C-1 and XSB3C-1. The wing section was of the laminar flow type in order to give the maximum possible speed. Full-span flaps were incorporated to maintain the required stalling speed and improve the take-off distance, wingtip slats would ensure lateral control at low speeds for satisfactory carrier operation, and special emphasis was to be placed on the slat and flap fitting to ensure boundary layer control for the laminar flow. Actual flight-testing had shown that the 'hidden balance' type of aileron had proved satisfactory and offered a minimum of drag, while the dive brake flaps were to be so arranged that longitudinal trim changes during their operation would be eliminated. The landing gear would be housed in the wing in a similar way to the SB2C-1, such that when the gear was extended the slats

would be positively opened and when the gear was retracted the slats would be positively closed. There were two wing tanks with overload fuel to go in a bomb bay tank and on external tanks loaded on the wing bomb racks. The fuselage was of semi-monocoque construction, again similar to the SB2C-1 and XSB3C-1, while the bomb bay would be smaller than but similar to the SB2C-1.

As noted, the powerplant was to be the Wright R-3350-8 (called version A, and driving a four-blade 13ft 2in/4.01m-diameter propeller), but there was the possibility of installing later a Pratt & Whitney XR-4360-3 engine with a variable-speed supercharger (version B with a six-blade co-axial/counter-rotating 14ft 2in/4.32m propeller). This would be achieved by changing the powerplant group forward of the firewall, making minor changes to the equipment layout, and increasing the span of the outer panel by 1ft (0.305m) – no major structural redesign would be necessary.

Having reviewed the revised design, Capt Walter S. Diehl of the Bureau of Aeronautics (who undertook the direction of the Navy's work in aerodynamics and hydrodynamics for the period 1918 to 1951) reported on 19 June 1942 that 'considered as a whole the general impression of this design is entirely favourable. It is believed that there is an excellent chance of getting a good airplane by going ahead as it now stands.' Prototypes were therefore ordered for both versions, the Wright-powered type being known as the XBTC-1 and the Pratt & Whitney the XBTC-2; however, due to problems with the Wright engine it was the latter that flew first, on 20 January 1945. The XBTC-2 itself appeared in two forms – again using 'Model A', which had a

standard wing and Fowler flaps, while the 'Model B' received a full-span Duplex flap wing with a swept-back leading edge to form a taper on the outer wing with the straight trailing edge, the Fowler flaps being placed under longer ailerons. With its contra-rotating propeller, it was known as the 'Eggbeater'. Despite the XBTC-2's engine power and performance, it was not ordered into production, and during 1947 both machines were lost in accidents. A de-navalised version discussed in Chapter Five became the XA-40.

VBT proposal data with R-3350-8 engine	
Span	48ft 0in (14.63m); folded unknown
Length	unknown
Wing area	377.3sq ft (35.09sq m)
Gross weight	13,228lb (6,000kg)
Maximum take-off weight	13,765lb (6,244kg)
Fuel	200 gallons (757 litres)
Powerplant	one 2,300hp (1,715kW) Wright R-3350-8
Armament	guns see text, one (or two?) 500lb (227kg) or 1,000lb (454kg) bombs, one 1,600lb (726kg) armour-piercing bomb or one Mk 13 torpedo in fuselage bay, one 500lb (227kg) bomb under each wing
Maximum speed	350mph (563km/h) at sea level, 388mph (624km/h) at 16,500ft (5,029m)
Rate of climb (BuAer figure)	2,740ft/min (835m/min)
Service ceiling	31,250ft (9,525m)
Range	1,001 miles (1,611km)

Proposal with XR-4360-3 engine	
Span	50ft 0in (15.24m)
Wing area	387.8sq ft (36.06sq m)
Gross weight	15,601lb (7,077kg)
Maximum take-off weight	16,161lb (7,330kg)
Fuel	230 gallons (871 litres)
Powerplant	one 3,000hp (2,237kW) P&W XR-4360-3
Maximum speed	373mph (600km/h) at sea level, 409mph (658km/h) at 16,500ft (5,029m)
Service ceiling	31,850ft (9,708m)
Range	1,002 miles (1,612km)

XBTC-2 data	
Span	50ft 0in (15.24m)
Length	38ft 7in (11.77m)
Wing area	406sq ft (37.76sq m)
Gross weight	17,910lb (8,124kg) with normal load, 21,660lb (9,825kg) with torpedo
Powerplant	one 3,000hp (2,237kW) P&W R-4360-8A
Armament	four 20mm cannon, one bomb up to 1,600lb (726kg) in bay, two bombs up to 1,000lb (454kg) under wings or one torpedo beneath bomb bay
Maximum speed	374mph (602km/h) at 16,900ft (5,151m)
Rate of climb	2,250ft/min (686m/min)
Service ceiling	26,200ft (7,986m)
Maximum range with torpedo	1,245 miles (2,003km)

Curtiss Model 98/XBT2C-1

The XBT2C-1 project by Curtiss at Columbus, dated 7 August 1944, was proposed to the Bureau of Aeronautics as 'an orderly design improvement of the SB2C series'. This single-seater powered by an R-3350 engine (with a four-blade 13ft 8in/4.17m-diameter prop) had the tail lengthened by 20in (50.8cm) to improve the stability characteristics. It was a rework of the SB2C into a single-place VBT Class aeroplane, and had resulted from informal discussions between BuAer and Curtiss, the former declaring that such a step was desirable. The resulting brochure noted that as many of the features as practical of the present SB2C models would be retained, but other changes included revised and re-faired fuselage lines aft of the cockpit. Its wing was identical to that of the SB2C-5 and -6 variants except that the slat had been eliminated from the outer wing, and the ailerons, rudder and elevators were to be metal-covered. There was provision to carry 300 gallons (1,136 litres) in auxiliary droppable tanks on top of the 420 gallons (1,590 litres) of internal fuel. Curtiss concluded that 'the performance improvement and design features of the proposed airplane represent substantial progress and warrant further development.'

BELOW Ground and air-to-air views of the Curtiss XBT2C-1 prototype.
NARA II via Ryan Crierie

BuAer's review of this design reported that 'the directional stability of the XBT2C-1 airplane is expected to be about equal to or slightly better than that of the SB2C series. The higher vertical tail aspect ratio and longer vertical tail length of the XBT2C-1 is offset by increased propeller solidity and diameter. The SB2C-1 had experienced rudder lock in left and right sideslips in the clean condition with power on, and the XBT2C-1 may rudder lock also, unless the dorsal fin is enlarged by starting it at a point closer to the cockpit enclosure.' Despite having its design rejected, Curtiss persevered with the idea and followed up with a revised proposal on 10 February 1945, this time introducing a radar operator's position in the aft fuselage. During March ten examples, designated XBT2C-1, were authorised, and the prototype was able to move forward quickly since around 50% of the parts used in the airframe were common to the SB2C-5 Helldiver. First flight was achieved on 7 August 1945, but the aircraft showed weaknesses against the Douglas and Martin projects to be described shortly, and the programme was abandoned after only nine XBT2C-1s had been completed.

XBT2C-1 Project data

Span	47ft 7in (14.50m); folded 22ft 6.5in (6.87m)
Length	38ft 11in (11.86m)
Wing area	415sq ft (38.595sq m)
Gross weight	17,596lb (7,982kg) with 1,000lb (454kg) bomb and 100 gallons (379 litres) external fuel
Powerplant	one 2,500hp (1,864kW) Wright R-3350-24
Armament	two 20mm cannon, various bombs including one 2,000lb (907kg) or one Mk 13 torpedo
Maximum speed	324mph (521km/h) at sea level, 343mph (552km/h) at critical altitude 16,800ft (5,121m)
Service ceiling	26,800ft (8,169m)
Combat radius at 17,596lb (7,982kg) weight	329 miles (529km)

XBT2C-1 data

Span	47ft 7in (14.50m)
Length	38ft 8in (11.79m)
Wing area	416sq ft (38.69sq m)
Gross weight	15,975lb (7,246kg)
Maximum weight	19,022lb (8,628kg)
Powerplant	as Project
Armament	two 20mm cannon, up to 4,000lb (1,814kg) bombs or one torpedo
Maximum speed	349mph (562km/h) at 17,000ft (5,182m)
Sea level rate of climb	2,590ft/min (789m/min)
Service ceiling	28,100ft (8,565m)
Maximum range with torpedo	1,434 miles (2,307km)

Douglas D-556/BT2D/ AD-1 Skyraider

Destined to be the most successful of the studies undertaken at this time, prototypes of the Douglas BT proposal were ordered in July 1944 as the XBT2D-1, and the first flew on 18 March 1945. This design was the result of a new series of in-house studies at Douglas, which, among relatively conventional single-engine layouts, had also considered an auxiliary turbojet fitted in or beneath the rear fuselage; the project also benefited from designer Edward H. Heinemann's determination to keep down weight. Originally named Dauntless II, the BT2D was renamed Skyraider in February 1946 and a total of 3,180 were built. The type stayed in production well into the 1950s and, although having no involvement in the Second World War, it was very active in both the Korea and Vietnam conflicts (by which time it had an attack designation). It served in US hands until the 1970s and even longer in some overseas air arms.

BELOW A lovely colour shot showing a Douglas XBT2D-1 (Skyraider) prototype during an early test flight. *NARA II via Ryan Crierie*

XBT2D-1 data

Span	50ft 0.33in (15.25m); folded 24ft 0in (7.32m)
Length overall	39ft 3.25in (11.97m)
Wing area	400sq ft (37.20sq m)
Gross weight	13,500lb (6,124kg)
Maximum weight	17,500lb (7,938kg)
Powerplant	one 2,500hp (1,864kW) Wright R-3350-24W
Armament	two 20mm cannon, up to 6,000lb (2,722kg) bombs or three torpedoes
Maximum speed	357mph (574km/h) at sea level, 375mph (603km/h) at 13,600ft (4,145m)
Rate of climb	3,680ft/min (1,122m/min)
Service ceiling	33,200ft (10,119m)
Range with one torpedo	1,428 miles (2,298km)

ABOVE The Kaiser-Fleetwings XBTK-1 prototype serial 44313 is seen at Patuxent River on 13 September 1945.
Tommy Thomason

Kaiser-Fleetwings XBK-1/XBTK-1

Some of the designs under consideration at this time looked likely to be too heavy for carrier operations, so BuAer also initiated a search for a lighter dive bomber alternative. In December 1943 Kaiser-Fleetwings responded with a design that was awarded a two-prototype contract in February 1944. These were designated XBK since carriage of a torpedo was in the first instance not planned, and all of the warload was to be carried externally in order to keep size to a minimum. The mock-up was inspected in April and the first prototype flew (behind schedule) on 12 April 1945, but back in December 1944 BuAer had requested that the aircraft should now also be capable of carrying a torpedo on the centreline, and as such the type was redesignated XBTK-1. Plans were made to build twenty-two aeroplanes, but this figure had by the end of the war been cut to just five, and only four of those were completed. BuAer eventually decided that the Curtiss XBTC-1 described above and the XBTK-1 did not possess the operational potential offered by the Martin project, described next.

XBTK-1 data	
Span	48ft 8in (14.83m); folded 21ft 0in (6.40m)
Length	38ft 11in (11.86m)
Wing area	380sq ft (35.34sq m)
Gross weight	12,728lb (5,773kg)
Maximum take-off weight	15,782lb (7,159kg)
Powerplant	one 2,100hp (1,566kW) P&W R-2800-34W
Armament	two 20mm cannon, up to 4,000lb (1,814kg) bombs or one torpedo
Maximum speed	341mph (549km/h) at sea level, 373mph (600km/h) at 18,000ft (5,486m)
Sea level rate of climb	3,550ft/min (1,082m/min)
Service ceiling	33,400ft (10,180m)
Range with torpedo	1,250 miles (2,011km)

LEFT A Kaiser-Fleetwings BTK-1 makes a pass over the official photographer.
Tommy Thomason

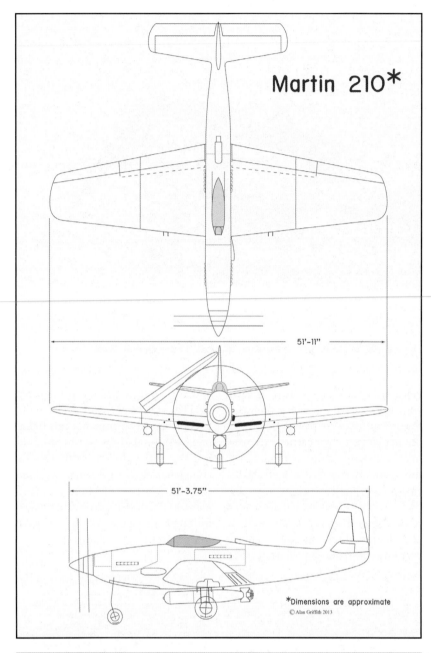

Martin 210*

51'-11"

51'-3.75"

*Dimensions are approximate
© Alan Griffith 2013

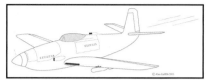

ABOVE Manufacturer's sketch for the Model 210-1. *Alan Griffith copyright*

LEFT Martin Model 210-1 (c8.43). *Alan Griffith copyright*

Martin Model 210/BTM-1/AM-1 Mauler

The studies leading to Martin's Mauler attack aircraft all came under the Model 210 designation, the first, Model 210-1, apparently appearing around August 1943. This sleek design was to be powered by an Allison V-1710, and in due course a version called Model 210-1A was also drawn, which showed the same aircraft with a jet engine in the lower rear fuselage. The 210-1 carried a 2,000lb (454kg) Mk 13 torpedo beneath the centre fuselage and had a tricycle undercarriage. A radial engine version, the Model 210-2A, came next with a Pratt & Whitney R-4360-13 Wasp Major; this was revised (the Model 210-8 appears to be November 1943) and two prototypes were ordered as the XBTM-1 Mauler. A mock-up inspection took place in February 1944, the first example flew on 26 August, and

XBTM-1 data	
Span	50ft 0in (15.24m); folded 24ft 0in (7.32m)
Length	41ft 2.5in (12.56m)
Wing area	496sq ft (46.13sq m)
Gross weight	19,000lb (8,618kg)
Maximum take-off weight	23,000lb (10,433kg)
Powerplant	one 3,000hp (2,237kW) P&W XR-4360-4
Armament	four 20mm cannon, up to 6,000lb (2,722kg) bombs or three torpedoes
Maximum speed	341mph (549km/h) at sea level, 367mph (591km/h) at 16,000ft (4,877m)
Sea level rate of climb	2,480ft/min (756m/min)
Service ceiling	26,800ft (8,169m)
Range with one torpedo	1,198 miles (1,928km)

LEFT A Martin AM-1 Mauler takes off during the type's carrier trials aboard USS *Kearsage* **in December 1948.**
NARA II via Ryan Crierie

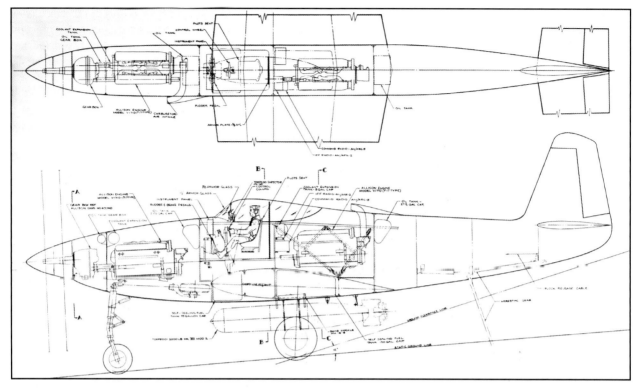

ABOVE Interior detail for the Martin Model 210-1 project, with the in-line Allison V-1710 engine. *Stan Piet, GLMMAM*

production orders saw the manufacture of 149 more, with deliveries beginning in 1947. However, another 651 were cancelled as the Navy's priority and preference passed to the Douglas Skyraider, which was a simpler and lighter aeroplane. The Mauler served in the front line until 1950 (and with reserve units until 1953) and, like the Skyraider, acquired a post-war attack designation.

*

BELOW A Martin AM-1 serving with the Navy Test Centre.

When considering the reviews and appraisals that BuAer had to undertake on the above designs, and indeed on any new design proposals made for future Navy aeroplanes, the George Spangenberg website notes that the Bureau had, for example, 'a substantial advantage over any single contractor in making weight estimates, since we had the records of all the aircraft already built. Each manufacturer was lucky if it had any records other than those of its

own designs.' Consequently the Bureau could bring all of that knowledge and experience to bear when making detailed estimates for a new design's weights and its resulting performance, thereby producing (hopefully) more accurate figures. (Note: for consistency, however, the data given for almost all of the unflown projects detailed in this book are the manufacturer's estimates.)

Miscellaneous Programmes and Mixed Powerplants

The war effort also produced the following projects. Although two became post-war programmes, they had been started well before the conflict was nearing its end, and of course they were influenced by war experience and by advances in technology. And, taking a similar route as it did for its carrier-based fighters, the US Navy also looked at composite piston/turbojet powerplants for attack aircraft, Kaiser-Fleetwings producing the rather advanced-looking Model 47.

Douglas DS-557/D-557/ BT3D/XA2D-1 Skyshark

This series of Douglas turboprop-powered proposals would eventually lead to the XA2D-1 Skyshark prototypes, which did not progress into production. The documentation does not make the story absolutely clear, but it appears that the original 25 January 1945 BT3D-1 proposal for a twin-engine carrier dive bomber, rocket attack and torpedo aircraft eventually turned into studies embracing three different designs, some Douglas paperwork stating how the project was an investigation into 'three of the most logical airplane arrangements of future attack-type airplanes'.

In its original form the two-seat (pilot and radar operator) DS-557's powerplant would comprise two General Electric TG-100 engines located side by side in the bottom of the fuselage below the pilot. Six-blade coaxial 14ft 1in (4.29m)-diameter propellers were to be located in the nose approximately 10in (25.40cm) above the centreline of the engines, and each propeller would be connected by specially designed reduction gearing. The props were to be capable of being feathered separately from one another, which meant that cruising could be accomplished on one engine. Ed Heinemann reported that the principal reasons for choosing the dual TG-100 powerplant was that Douglas believed it was necessary to depart from reciprocating engines in order to obtain an adequate performance for a new aircraft of this type, particularly at lower altitudes. Also, two TG-100 units were considered more desirable than one

since that it was only by cruising on one engine that a satisfactory radius of action could be obtained with a 2,000lb (907kg) bomb load in an aircraft whose size was limited by carrier dimensions. Pure jets had been considered, which would result in higher speeds than 'gasoline turbines', but again the latter (TG-100s) were believed necessary to obtain the satisfactory combat radius. Internal fuel totalled 600 gallons (2,271 litres), while the external fuel doubled this with two 300-gallon (1,136-litre) tanks.

The DS-557's structure was conventional with high-strength aluminium alloy used whenever possible to save weight. The wings were of single spar construction with chordwise hat-section stiffeners, and all of the control surfaces were metal-covered. The airframe was designed for a maximum

BELOW Douglas DS-557 (25.1.45). *Alan Griffith copyright*

BELOW Douglas D-557A (mid-to-late 1945). *NARA II via Tommy Thomason*

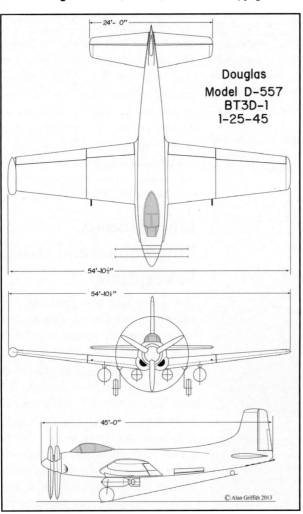

Douglas
Model D-557
BT3D-1
1-25-45

© Alan Griffith 2013

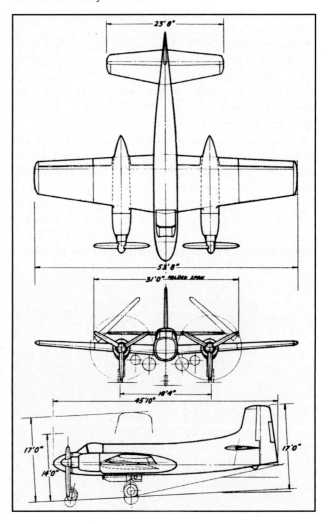

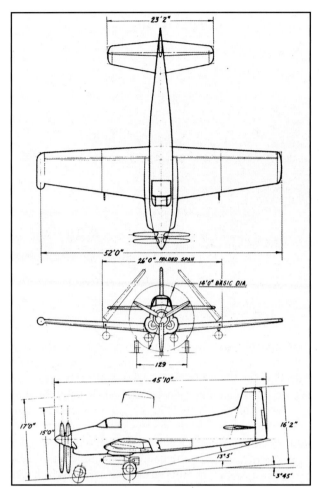

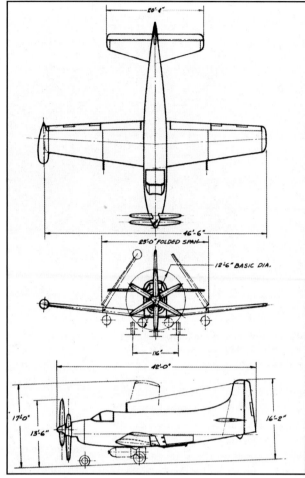

ABOVE Douglas D-557B (mid-to-late 1945).
NARA II via Tommy Thomason

ABOVE Douglas D-557C (mid-to-late 1945).
NARA II via Tommy Thomason

BELOW Artist's concept for the Douglas XA2D-1 Skyshark fitted with an Allison XT-40 engine. *NARA II via Ryan Crierie*

ABOVE The second prototype XA2D-1 Skyshark 122989 is prepared for a flight in 1952.

speed in a dive of 550mph (885km/h) at 7,500ft (2,286m). All bombs were to be carried externally on two racks under the fuselage, each designed for a 2,000lb (907kg) bomb or a torpedo, and there would be provision for further racks to take 1,200lb (544kg) rockets or twelve 5in (12.70cm) rocket projectiles, six on the inboard wing and six on the outboard panel. A 20mm cannon was fitted in the mid position of each wing.

The subsequent D-557 series of designs were described as follows (each having a radar):

1. Model D-557A had two TG-100 turboprops (or 'turbine engines' as they were known at the time) in conventional nacelles. It had a tapered wing, tricycle undercarriage and 13ft 0in (3.96m)-diameter three-blade propellers on each nacelle. The guns were in the nose and four bomb racks under the inner wings could each take 1,000lb (454kg) or 2,000lb (907kg) general-purpose bombs, a 1,600lb (726kg) armour-piercing bomb, a 1,000lb (454kg) 12in (30.48cm)-diameter Tiny Tim, or 2,000lb (907kg) 14in (35.56cm) Big Dick rockets, 1,000lb (454kg) or 2,000lb (907kg) mines, or a Mk 13 torpedo.

2. Model D-557B had two TG-100s in the fuselage driving dual counter-rotating six-blade propellers 14ft 0in (4.27m) in diameter, together with a tricycle undercarriage. The two bomb racks beneath the wing roots each had a 2,000lb (907kg) capacity, each rack in the mid-wing position inside the wing fold was limited to 1,000lb (454kg), and a 20mm cannon was housed just inside each wing fold.

3. The Model D-557C received a single Westinghouse X25D2 turbine engine in the fuselage driving dual counter-rotating six-blade propellers 12ft 6in (3.81m) in diameter. The tricycle undercarriage was retained and the gun and bomb rack arrangement and capacity were the same as the D-557B.

The contract awarded to Douglas for this new work would cover preliminary layouts, stress analysis, wind tunnel models and mock-ups, and the normal military load for every type was given as two 20mm cannon and a 2,000lb (907kg) bomb. Mock-ups for all three forms received official evaluation between 15 and 17 April 1946 and each was described as 'satisfactory'. These projects were abandoned because of engine development difficulties, but the work undertaken by Douglas to date was brought together into a 1947 project that the firm submitted against a new

BuAer requirement. After the mock-up had been approved in September 1947, two XA2D-1 Skyshark prototypes were ordered, but the first did not fly until 26 May 1950. Engine problems brought delays on a regular basis and, despite the placing of production orders for A2D-1s, the entire programme was finally abandoned in September 1954 with four of the ten production machines built not having flown.

DS-557 data	
Span (with radar pod on starboard wingtip)	54ft 10.5in (16.73m); folded 25ft 0in (7.62m)
Length	45ft 0in (13.72m)
Wing area	500sq ft (46.50sq m)
Take-off weight	21,350lb (9,684kg) with one 2,000lb (907kg) bomb and 600 gallons (2,271 litres) fuel; 25,367lb (11,506kg) with one 2,000lb (907kg) bomb and 1,200 gallons (4,542 litres) fuel; 19,350lb (8,777kg) as scout with no armament
Powerplant	two 2,750hp (2,051kW) + 630lb (2.80kN) General Electric TG-100
Armament	two 20mm cannon; for bombs see text
Maximum speed (no bombs)	430mph (692km/h) at sea level, 447mph (719km/h) at 20,000ft (6,096m)
Rate of climb (no bombs)	5,885ft/min (1,794m/min)
Service ceiling	41,600ft (12,680m) with 2,000lb (907kg) bomb
Combat radius	270 miles (434km)
Maximum range	1,110 miles (1,786km)

D-557A data	
Span	53ft 8in (16.36m); folded 31ft 0in (9.45m)
Length	45ft 10in (13.97m)
Wing area	unknown
Gross weight	23,100lb (10,478kg) with one 2,000lb (907kg) bomb and 600 gallons (2,271 litres) fuel; 27,166lb (12,322kg) with bomb and 1,200 gallons (4,542 litres) fuel; 23,290lb (10,564kg) with torpedo and 600 gallons (2,271 litres) fuel
Powerplant	two 2,750hp (2,051kW) + 630lb (2.80kN) General Electric TG-100
Armament	two 20mm cannon; for bombs see text
Maximum speed at 23,100lb (10,478kg)	401mph (645km/h) at sea level, 415mph (668km/h) at 20,000ft (6,096m)
Rate of climb	4,940ft/min (1,506m/min)
Service ceiling	41,300ft (12,588m)
Radius of action	167 miles (269km)

D-557B data	
Span	52ft 0in (15.85m); folded 26ft 0in (7.92m)
Length	45ft 10in (13.97m)
Wing area	unknown
Gross weight	21,825lb (9,900kg) with one 2,000lb (907kg) bomb and 600 gallons (2,271 litres) fuel; 25,854lb (11,727kg) with bomb and 1,200 gallons (4,542 litres) fuel; 22,016lb (9,986kg) with torpedo and 600 gallons (2,271 litres) fuel
Powerplant	two 2,750hp (2,051kW) + 630lb (2.80kN) General Electric TG-100
Armament	two 20mm cannon; for bombs see text
Maximum speed at 21,825lb (9,900kg)	407mph (655km/h) at sea level, 419mph (674km/h) at 20,000ft (6,096m)
Rate of climb	4,950ft/min (1,509m/min)
Service ceiling	41,500ft (12,649m)
Radius of action	243 miles (391km)

D-557C data	
Span	46ft 6in (14.17m); folded 23ft 0in (7.01m)
Length	41ft 8.5in (12.765m)
Wing area	unknown
Gross weight	17,400lb (7,893kg) with one 2,000lb (907kg) bomb and 600 gallons (2,271 litres) fuel; 21,429lb (9,720kg) with bomb and 1,200 gallons (4,542 litres) fuel; 17,591lb (7,979kg) with torpedo and 600 gallons (2,271 litres) fuel
Powerplant	one Westinghouse X25D2
Armament	two 20mm cannon; for bombs see text
Maximum speed at 17,400lb (7,893kg)	389mph (626km/h) at sea level, 394mph (634km/h) at 20,000ft (6,096m)
Rate of climb	4,650ft/min (1,417m/min)
Service ceiling	not given
Radius of action	236 miles (380km)

XA2D-1 data	
Span	50ft 0.25in (15.25m); folded 25ft 6in (7.77m)
Length	41ft 2.4in (12.55m)
Wing area	401sq ft (37.29sq m)
Maximum take-off weight	22,966lb (10,417kg)
Powerplant	one 5,100hp (3,803kW) Allison XT40-A-2
Armament	four 20mm cannon, up to 5,500lb (2,495kg) stores
Maximum speed	501mph (806km/h) at 25,000ft (7,620m)
Rate of climb	7,290ft/min (2,222m/min)
Service ceiling	48,100ft (14,661m)
Maximum range	2,200 miles (3,540km)

XTB3F-1 data	
Span	60ft 0in (18.29m); folded 24ft 0in (7.32m)
Length	42ft 1in (12.83m)
Wing area	549sq ft (51.06sq m)
Gross weight	19,065lb (8,648kg)
Maximum take-off weight	21,465lb (9,737kg)
Powerplant	one 2,100hp (1,566kW) P&W R-2800-34W and one 1,600lb (7.1kN) Westinghouse 19XB (J30)
Armament (not fitted)	two 20mm cannon, up to 4,000lb (1,814kg) bombs or two torpedoes
Maximum speed	393mph (632km/h) at sea level with jet, 341mph (549km/h) on piston only
Rate of climb	2,433ft/min (742m/min)
Service ceiling	35,200ft (10,729m)
Range with torpedo	1,278miles (2,056km)

Grumman Model 70/XTB3F-1 Guardian

Grumman's torpedo bomber effort continued with its two-seat Model 70, work on which had been started in mid-1944 as a mixed-powerplant aeroplane, having a nose-mounted piston engine coupled with an auxiliary jet in the rear, several versions being proposed with different combinations. In October the G-70F with an R-3350 and Westinghouse 24C was selected, and three XTB3F-1 prototypes were ordered, although delays with the propeller and the jet unit prompted BuAer to put the Pratt & Whitney R-2800 and Westinghouse J30 in the first two airframes, the third machine with the 'original' powerplant becoming the XTB3F-2. The first prototype made its first flight on 23 December 1946 (the jet was not operative) but, with the war over, on the very next day a Stop Work Order was placed on the Navy's last torpedo bomber programme. Subsequently the Navy altered the aircraft's role to anti-submarine duties, not a straightforward move since the equipment needed to perform such missions was too large to be accommodated within a single airframe. Consequently, two versions of the type had to be produced, one to operate as a 'hunter' aircraft and the other following up as the 'killer'. In this form the Guardian was redesignated AF-2 and served through the first half of the 1950s. In all, 389 examples were built.

Kaiser-Fleetwings Model 47

The attractive Model 47 project from the Fleetwings Division of Kaiser Cargo Inc was known as the Squirt. It was a mixed-powerplant (four-engine) dive bomber and was proposed in February 1944. The design (which at this stage was preliminary only and not a complete design study) had been conceived primarily with a view to having a dive bomber with two engines and their attendant advantages, but in a configuration similar to the Grumman F7F fighter (see Chapter Six) with jet motors also housed in the nacelles. To permit carriage of the maximum quantity of bombs, it was also intended that long range be provided without any external fuel. The chosen power units were the Packard Merlin with contra-rotating propellers and Westinghouse jets, and these fitted nicely into long narrow nacelles. The 47 had a tricycle undercarriage, 940 gallons (3,558 litres) of fuel would be carried, and the wings

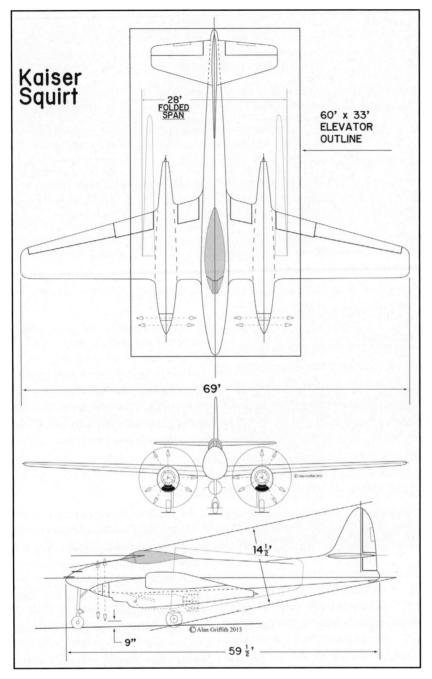

LEFT Kaiser-Fleetwings Model 47 (2.44).
Alan Griffith copyright

Model 47 data	
Span	69ft 0in (21.03m); folded 28ft 0in (8.53m)
Length	59ft 5in (18.11m)
Wing area	not available
Gross weight	in excess of 30,000lb (13,608kg)
Powerplant	two 1,600hp (1,193kW) Packard Merlin and two 2,200lb (9.8kN) Westinghouse jets
Armament	four 0.50in (12.70mm) machine guns or four 20mm cannon, up to 4,000lb (1,814kg) bombs
Maximum speed (jets operating)	slightly above 400mph (644km/h)
No other performance data	
Range	c2,600 miles (4,183km)

US Navy Bomber and Attack Aircraft Designs in Perspective

The wartime development of Navy attack aircraft is a complex story, involving not only a wide range of competing designs but also changes in their operational roles from those originally conceived. The ability of the best of these aircraft to undertake multiple tasks eventually rendered the Navy's narrow categorisation system obsolete. This effort resulted in some outstanding operational aircraft – machines that would not only alter the course of the war but would also serve for many years thereafter. Indeed, in the case of one such aircraft, the Douglas Skyraider, it would go on to serve in two more conflicts.

At the same time as these developments were being pursued, the Navy's offensive capability was also being extended by an entirely different and much larger category of aeroplane, the Patrol Aircraft. This forms the subject of the next chapter.

were tapered with a straight leading edge and folded rearwards. Machine guns and cannon were interchangeable, and the 4,000lb (1,814kg) warload would comprise either one centrally located store or combinations on wing racks. The fuel provided a 600-mile (965km) combat radius, the jets running on take-off and for 15 minutes. Kaiser's

Model 47 brochure noted that the 'ship is so large as to prevent use on any but the largest carriers using a 60ft x 33ft (18.29m x 10.06m) elevator. Since relatively few can be stored, the 47 is designed to have maximum hitting power, range, armour protection, high speed and assurance of returning.'

Chapter Eight
Maritime Patrol Aircraft and Flying Boats

As the Second World War progressed, both the fierce contest for naval supremacy in the Pacific and the battle to protect convoys against the German U-boats in the Atlantic emphasised the importance of long-range aerial capability. This chapter looks at the resulting efforts to develop maritime patrol, Navy bombers and anti-submarine (AS) aircraft. At first these efforts concentrated on flying boats, which were considered to hold the key to the future for such roles, but the arrival of the Lockheed Neptune and the Martin Mercator towards the end of the war marked a shift to land-based aeroplanes.

Despite the research carried out for this book, as far as unsuccessful designs in this area are concerned much remains to be uncovered. Nonetheless, all the known important projects are included here, and the text provides a good overview of maritime patrol aircraft development.

Early Types

Ironically, the story starts not just with an Army Air Corps programme but with an aircraft produced primarily for a foreign air force.

ABOVE The Martin Mariner was, together with the Consolidated Catalina, one of the most successful American flying boats of the Second World War. This view shows a PBM-5 variant.

A-28 data	
Span	65ft 6in (19.96m)
Length	44ft 4in (13.51m)
Wing area	551sq ft (51.24sq m)
Gross weight	17,500lb (7,938kg)
Powerplant	two 1,100hp (820kW) Wright R-1820-G102A
Armament (RAF Hudson Mk I)	four 0.303in (7.70mm) machine guns, 750lb (340kg) bombs or depth charges
Maximum speed	246mph (396km/h) at 6,500ft (1,981m)
Sea level rate of climb	2,180ft/min (664m/min)
Service ceiling	25,000ft (7,620m)
Maximum range	1,960 miles (3,154km)

Lockheed Model 14, A-28 Hudson

Lockheed's Hudson was a design produced for the UK before America had joined the war. Based on the company's Twin Electric civilian airliner, this was a six-seat light bomber and coastal patrol aircraft that remained primarily a Royal Air Force type throughout the conflict. First flown on 10 December 1938, a total of 2,941 were built, and when in American hands the type was known as the A-28 and A-29.

Lockheed-Vega Model 18, PV-1 Ventura

The Ventura had much in common with, and in fact was quite similar in appearance to, the Hudson in that it was another Lockheed patrol bomber type to be developed from an airliner, in this case the Lodestar. The first example flew on 31 July 1940 and the basic type was produced for the Navy both as the PV-1 Ventura and the redesigned PV-2 Harpoon, and for the Air Corps as the B-34 Lexington and the B-37. Again the type was ordered for the RAF, which to begin with used it on raids over enemy-held territory in Europe, but later made the switch to maritime work. The US Navy's contingent began their war career in 1943 in the Pacific.

ABOVE The Lockheed PV-1 Ventura in flight. *Alan Griffith*

PV-1 data	
Span	65ft 6in (19.96m)
Length	51ft 8in (15.75m)
Wing area	551sq ft (51.24sq m)
Gross weight	31,000lb (14,062kg)
Powerplant	two 2,000hp (1,491kW) P&W R-2800-31
Armament	six 0.50in (12.70mm) machine guns, up to 3,500lb (1,588kg) bombs or depth charges or one torpedo
Maximum speed	313mph (504km/h) at 15,200ft (4,633m)
Service ceiling	25,500ft (7,772m)
Patrol range	1,575 miles (2,534km)

Navy Patrol – Land-based

Consolidated Model 100/PB4Y-2 Privateer

The Consolidated PB4Y-2 Privateer was externally fairly similar to the same manufacturer's B-24 Liberator (see Chapter Four), an aircraft that also flew with the Navy as the PB4Y-1. However, it did introduce a tall single vertical fin rather than the B-24's twin-tail

ABOVE Views of the prototype Consolidated XPB4Y-2 Privateer flying in early July 1944. *Tommy Thomason*

PB4Y-2 data

Span	110ft 0in (33.53m)
Length	74ft 7in (22.73m)
Wing area	1,048sq ft (97.46sq m)
Gross weight	64,000lb (29,030kg)
Maximum weight	70,231lb (31,857kg)
Powerplant	four 1,350hp (1,007kW) P&W R-1830-94
Armament	twelve 0.50in (12.70mm) machine guns, up to 8,000lb (3,629kg) bombs, mines
Maximum speed	238mph (383km/h) at sea level, 248mph (399km/h) at 14,000ft (4,267m)
Maximum climb rate	1,090ft/min (332m/min)
Service ceiling	19,500ft (5,944m)
Patrol range	2,900 miles (4,666km)

ABOVE The name 'Truculent Turtle' was given to the third production Lockheed P2V-1 Neptune when it was used for record-breaking long-distance flights. In September 1946 this machine flew 11,236.6 miles (18,083.6km) non-stop in 55hr 18min between points in Australia and America, a record that lasted until 1962. ABOVE TOP Artwork for the original Vega V-146 proposal (1.1.43).

arrangement, and its fuselage had been stretched to make room for additional crew; in fact, the changes introduced in the PB4Y-2 reflected the need to make the B-24/PB4Y-1 more suited to patrol bomber duties. A twin-engine B-24 (Model 38) long-range patrol aircraft had been proposed to the Navy as the XP5Y-1 in October 1942, but it was the PB4Y-2 Privateer that was built, making its first flight on 20 September 1943. Production was held back to 736 machines by the close of the war, but the Privateer remained in service deep into the 1950s.

Vega V-146 and Lockheed P2V Neptune

The Model V-146 was based on an earlier preliminary design proposal from Vega chief engineer John B. Wassall and his team, called the V-135D,

and the aircraft was earmarked to replace the Hudson and Ventura. After relatively slow progress had been achieved on the V-135 series during 1942, the Navy took the revised V-146 on board and on 19 February 1943 issued a letter of intent for two XP2V-1 prototypes based on this later design study. Compared to the V-135 it showed a lower wing setting, a modified tailplane and a new position for the dorsal turret. The V-146 brochure, dated 1 January 1943, declared that the aircraft was a response to BuAer requirements for long-range AS patrol, photo reconnaissance, mine-laying, night torpedo attack and horizontal bombing missions; the prototypes were ordered

on 4 April 1944 and fifteen production P2V-1s were requested ten days later. The V-146 carried 2,200 gallons (8,328 litres) of internal fuel and had four-blade 15ft 0in (4.57m) propellers, and before being flown the design had to undergo some refinement.

Given the name Neptune, the Lockheed P2V-1 was to be the first land-based aircraft specifically designed for operation in the long-range maritime patrol and reconnaissance role, and the first prototype flew on 17 May 1945. It went on to have a very successful post-war career with nearly 1,100 examples manufactured in the US. Many Neptunes also served in foreign air arms.

V-146 data

Span	100ft 0in (30.48m)
Length	76ft 4in (23.26m)
Wing area	1,000sq ft (93.00sq m)
Design gross weight	45,000lb (20,412kg)
Overload weight	56,458lb (25,609kg)
Powerplant	two 2,300hp (1,715kW) Wright R-3350
Armament	six 0.50in (12.70mm) machine guns (two each in bow, mid top and tail turrets), up to 6,000lb (2,722kg) bombs, mines or depth charges, or two 2,000lb (907kg) torpedoes
Maximum speed	292mph (470km/h) at sea level, 315mph (507km/h) at 15,000ft (4,572m)
Service ceiling	30,000ft (9,144m)
Maximum range	4,150 miles (6,677km)

Neptune P2V-I data

Span	100ft 0in (30.48m)
Length	75ft 4in (22.96m)
Wing area	1,000sq ft (93.00sq m)
Maximum take-off weight	58,000lb (26,309kg)
Powerplant	two 2,300hp (1,715kW) Wright R-3350-8
Armament	six machine guns and up to 8,000lb (3,629kg) stores
Maximum speed	289mph (465km/h) at sea level, 318mph (512km/h) at 17,700ft (5,395m)

BELOW Production Martin P4M Mercator serial 121451 pictured before its conversion to P4M-1Q configuration.

Martin Model 219/P4M Mercator

Altogether larger and heavier than the Neptune, and which as a programme appeared a little later than Lockheed's aircraft, the Martin Model 219 Mercator was first designed as a replacement for the Consolidated Privateer described above. In appearance this handsome aircraft and the Neptune were quite alike, and its primary role was also to be maritime patrol. Again work was well advanced before the end of the war (two prototypes were ordered in July 1944) and the first XP4M-1 made its maiden flight on 20 September 1946. However, the production run would stretch only to nineteen machines, the first reaching service in 1950. After a short period on maritime work Mercators were turned into P4M-1Q electronic countermeasures aeroplanes, in which form they were used until 1960.

Convair Flying Wings

During 1943 and 1944 Consolidated, which at the time was in the process of merging with Vultee to form Convair, undertook a prolonged study into patrol bombers of tailless design. Several forms of the same basic layout were produced, together with a conventional layout to provide comparative data.

P4M-1 data

Span	114ft 1in (34.77m)
Length	84ft 0in (25.60m)
Wing area	1,311sq ft (121.92sq m)
Maximum take-off weight	88,375lb (40,087kg)
Powerplant	two 2,500hp (1,864kW) P&W R-4630-20 and two 4,600lb (20.4kN) Allison J33-A-23 jets
Armament	four 20mm cannon and four 0.50in (12.70mm) machine guns, up to 12,000lb (5,443kg) bombs, mines or depth charges, or two torpedoes
Maximum speed	379mph (610km/h) at sea level, 415mph (668km/h) at 20,100ft (6,126m)
Service ceiling	34,600ft (10,546m)
Range	2,840 miles (4,560km)

Consolidated/ Convair P5Y-1

In August 1943 Consolidated/Convair began work on a new ten-seat flying wing (tailless) patrol aircraft, and author Robert E. Bradley (in his book *Convair Advanced Designs 1923-1962*) has indicated that this effort may have been done against the same requirements for a PV Ventura replacement as had Lockheed's work that had led to the Neptune. The dates for the two design lines certainly match up, although the Convair flying wing's weight falls closer to that of the Mercator. Convair wrote a preliminary detail specification around

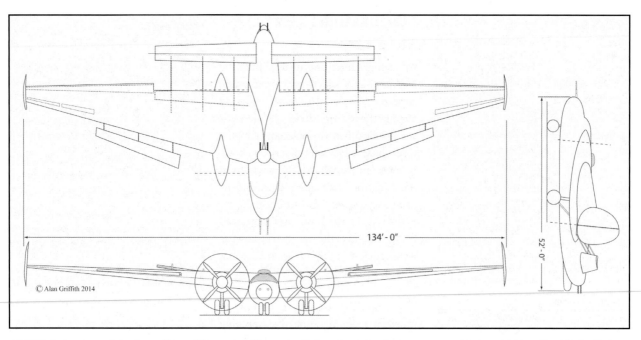

© Alan Griffith 2014

134' - 0"

52' - 0"

ABOVE A drawing of the Consolidated/Convair tailless patrol aircraft as the design appeared in late 1943, still with the high wing position and showing its forward and aft auxiliary surfaces all deployed. At this stage the span was 134ft 0in (40.84m) and the length 52ft 0in (15.85m). *Alan Griffith copyright*

BELOW Three-quarter starboard and underside views of a wind tunnel model of the Convair tailless project, both with and without the tailplane and elevators extended. The pictures are dated 2 December 1943. *NARA II*

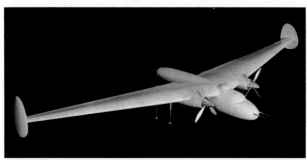

LEFT & BELOW LEFT A wind tunnel model for the Convair tailless project. *NARA II*

the project and gave it the designation P5Y-1, the second time that number had been offered against a new design.

In its original form the aircraft had a high-position wing with rounded wingtips, no vertical surfaces, a tricycle undercarriage all with twin-wheels, 14ft 0in (4.27m) contra-rotating propellers, and there was an extending horizontal tailplane and elevators to help with the expected problems of stability and control at low speeds. When extended (at low speeds only), these large surfaces on each side of the fuselage were supported out along the wings by substantial retractable struts, while at the fuselage ends they moved along tracks in the fuselage sides (for high-speed flight the surfaces would be retracted to

2 ENG. TAILLESS

ABOVE Artwork for the Convair tailless bomber, now in the form as at 1 April 1944 with a mid-position wing and the engines in nacelles ahead of the wing. *NARA II*

become integral with the wing). The wing had a two-spar metal-covered cantilever structure, its centre section was continuous through the fuselage and would include the engine nacelles, and the leading edge adjacent to the nacelles would house air intakes for the oil coolers. A set of spoilers was provided on each wing for lateral control, there were ailerons for trimming, and power-operated full-span ventilated split flaps. The fuselage was of metal construction with longitudinal members, transverse bulkheads and belt frames, and all sheet and drawn material (except for tubing and extrusions) was to be of clad aluminium alloy. This relatively small fuselage was smothered in gun turrets – five in all – with the nose and after top turrets housing twin-20mm cannon, while three more had 0.50in (12.70mm) machine guns, four in a tail turret and two each in forward and lower turrets. The standard offensive load was four 650lb (295kg) depth charges ('depth

bombs') and two 700lb (318kg) mines carried internally, but bombs could also be taken, including two 2,000lb (907kg) carried externally.

A revision was completed at the end of November 1943 that saw the weight increased and the wing area reduced, the various changes (which included the addition of wingtip fins and rudders) increasing the maximum speed and the range. The design was at this stage offered with six-blade contra-rotating propellers of 15ft 0in (4.57m) diameter, or an eight-blade arrangement of 14ft 0in (4.27m) diameter. A variant of this configuration was also considered for the Army Air Force, which had double the payload at 8,000lb (3,629kg).

Further revisions were made in April 1944, but most of the changes here centred on the wing and the extending tail surfaces; for example, the wing thickness was reduced to 17% at the root and 14% at the tip. The wing was swept 14° at its leading edge and a further

change to the extensible rear control surfaces saw them now provided with greater extension. The wing had been reset at the mid-fuselage position and, where previously they had been totally immersed within the wing, the engines were now housed in nacelles in a position ahead of the main wing spar. The contraprops were 15ft 0in (4.57m) in diameter and the turret and bomb loads were unchanged. The bomb bay could also take additional self-sealing fuel tanks, but the normal quantity of fuel to be carried internally in the wings was 4,400 gallons (16,656 litres).

By now, however, Lockheed had won its contract for what became the P2V Neptune, and the April 1944 study brought a close to Convair's research into this tailless type of patrol aeroplane. The last wind tunnel testing on the project appears to have been completed on 2 May 1944.

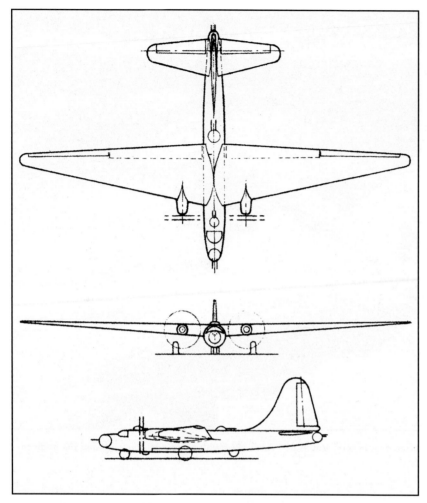

Longitudinal stability in either the conventional or tailless designs was obtained by locating the centre of gravity ahead of the centre of lift (aerodynamic centre) of the complete aeroplane. In the case of the conventional aircraft, the centre of the resultant lift of wing and tail was located further aft than that for the tailless aircraft. Therefore the range of the centre of gravity within which the aircraft was stable and controllable was much greater for the conventional than for the tailless. However, the absence of

LEFT This is the Convair conventional design prepared solely as a comparison to the firm's concurrent tailless patrol aircraft studies. *NARA II*

Consolidated/Convair flying wing patrol aircraft data (at August 1943)

Span	138ft 0in (42.06m)
Length	52ft 3in (15.93m)
Wing area	1,900sq ft (176.70sq m)
Maximum take-off weight	85,000lb (38,556kg)
Powerplant	two 3,250hp (2,424kW) P&W R-4360
Armament	for guns see text; up to 4,000lb (1,814kg) stores
Range	4,000 miles (6,436km)

Same aircraft at December 1943

Wing area	1,800sq ft (167.40sq m)
Maximum take-off weight	90,000lb (40,824kg)
Maximum speed	288mph (463km/h) at sea level
Range	5,000 miles (8,045km)

Same aircraft at 31 March 1944

Span	147ft 0in (44.81m)
Length	49ft 7in (15.11m)
Wing area	1,800sq ft (167.40sq m)
Maximum take-off weight	90,000lb (40,824kg)
Powerplant	two 3,250hp (2,424kW) P&W R-4360 (War Emergency Power 3,630hp/2,707kW)
Armament	as before
Maximum speed	304mph (489km/h) at sea level (War Emergency Power), 291mph (468km/h) at sea level (military rating), 294mph (473km/h) at 13,000ft (3,962m)
Sea level rate of climb (half fuel at 76,800lb/ 34,836kg)	1,330ft/min (405m/min)
Service ceiling (half fuel)	25,500ft (7,772m)
Maximum range	5,400 miles (8,689km)

Consolidated Conventional Wing Patrol Aircraft

An alternative design with a high-position long-span conventional wing, a long fuselage, a horizontal tail and a vertical fin was drawn to provide Convair with a comparison against its flying wing studies; the vertical fin looked particularly large. This design was produced in October 1943, it used 14ft 2in (4.32m) diameter contraprops, and would carry the same defensive and offensive weaponry as the tailless aircraft.

A separate report written by Consolidated on 16 October 1943 compared the conventional with the tailless design in its original August 1943 form, and declared that for the same mission requirements the tailless arrangement would be both lighter and smaller. The essential difference between the conventional and the tailless arose from the manner in which each design obtained control and stability. In order to secure the highest aerodynamic efficiency, the conventional aircraft employed a wing section designed mainly for high maximum lift, and for low drag in the high speed and cruising ranges of flight; however, this type of wing section was unstable, so a tail was necessary to provide satisfactory stability to the aircraft.

Consolidated conventional wing patrol aircraft data (at October 1943)

Span	152ft 0in (46.33m)
Length	87ft 4in (26.62m)
Wing area	2,100sq ft (195.30sq m)
Maximum take-off weight	89,500lb (40,597kg)
Powerplant	two 3,250hp (2,424kW) P&W R-4360
Armament	as flying wing
Maximum speed	252mph (405km/h) at sea level
Range without bombs	4,770 miles (7,695km)

the long fuselage in the tailless design reduced the ranges of centre of gravity for various loading conditions, so that the inherent limitations of the CofG range in the tailless design were actually of no practical consequence.

In the conventional design, longitudinal control was obtained through the additional moment produced by the elevators, but in the tailless form it required a change in the pitching moment of the wing itself; this was produced by deflection of portions of the trailing edge. Control in roll was of course obtained with ailerons and was substantially the same for both the conventional and tailless designs, while control in yaw for the conventional design was obtained using the rudder. The tailless design (at this stage) had no rudders, so drag-producing devices near the wingtips were to be used to provide the desired yawing moments. Finally, the use of high-lift wing flaps to reduce the landing speed required the use of devices to trim out the nose-down pitching moment caused by the flaps. On the conventional design this moment was of course readily balanced by the horizontal tail surface, but for the tailless aircraft

some auxiliary trim surfaces had to be developed that allowed trim at a maximum lift coefficient equal to that of conventional aeroplanes. These trim surfaces had an area approximately equal to that of the conventional design's horizontal tail surface, but were to be completely retracted in all flight conditions except when the high-lift flaps were extended during take-off, the landing approach and landing.

The overall flight characteristics of the tailless design compared favourably with those of a conventional aeroplane, but its performance had been improved considerably by the decrease in drag brought about by the elimination of the tail and a large fuselage. The tailless design utilised a high wing loading to provide greater range and higher speed while retaining a landing speed equal to that of a conventional aircraft. These theoretical studies had shown that the tailless design was dynamically stable, both longitudinally and laterally. Sadly, it appears that the tailless aircraft, even in its later forms, was never close to being ordered.

Navy Patrol – Water-based

In the context of this book the story of the US Navy's wartime flying boats is put a little out of balance because the type that was built in by far the greatest numbers, the Consolidated Model 28 PBY Catalina, with 3,305 produced worldwide, made its maiden flight on 28 March 1935, which takes it outside this book's date parameters. In fact, the PBY served extensively in several versions throughout the war and it was also used in large numbers by other countries and in several different roles – in truth it was one of the greats! The other types flown during the war years come next, and both Consolidated and Martin were quite prolific in their creation of new flying boat designs.

We begin with a 1935 competition to find a replacement for the PBY Catalina (which in prototype form was known as the XP3Y-1), and this resulted in orders for designs submitted by Sikorsky and Consolidated, the latter subsequently being selected for production. The requested payload for the new aircraft was 12,000lb (5,443kg).

BELOW This example of the Consolidated PBY Catalina is serial W8406, a Mk I serving with the RAF.

Sikorsky XPBS-1

The first to appear was Sikorsky's four-engine XPBS-1 prototype, which was first flown on 13 August 1937. With Consolidated winning the production order, only the single XPBS-1 patrol aircraft was ever built, but after evaluation by NACA it was used by the

Navy on patrol and then transport duties before being lost in an accident on 30 June 1942 (it sank after hitting a log). Three examples of a civilian version based on the XPBS-1 and called the VS-44 were also produced.

Consolidated Model 29/PB2Y Coronado

Consolidated's four-engine prototype, the single XPB2Y-1, had a single fin for its maiden flight on 17 December 1937. It then had finlets added to the horizontal tailplane before a new twin-

XPBS-1 data	
Span	124ft 0in (37.80m)
Length	70ft 2in (21.39m)
Wing area	1,670sq ft (155.31sq m)
Gross weight	46,617lb (21,145kg)
Maximum weight	48,541lb (22,018kg)
Powerplant	four 1,050hp (783kW) P&W R-1830-68
Armament	two 0.30in (7.62mm) and two 0.50in (12.70mm) machine guns, up to 12,000lb (5,443kg) bombs
Maximum speed	203mph (327km/h) at sea level, 227mph (365km/h) at 12,000ft (3,658m)
Sea level rate of climb	640ft/min (195m/min)
Service ceiling	23,100ft (7,041m)
Maximum range	4,545 miles (7,313km)

BELOW Views of the Sikorsky XPBS-1.
Gerald Balzer

ABOVE Consolidated's XPB2Y-1 is seen as built with a single fin. *Gerald Balzer*

fin tail was finally introduced, all of these steps being taken in attempts to cure directional problems in the air. In due course the type was put into production as the PB2Y-1 Coronado, and altogether 217 were manufactured in several increasingly upgraded versions, all having the twin fins as well

as a redesigned nose and hull. Those in the Pacific were used for anti-submarine, bombing and transport duties, but a batch of ten supplied to the RAF operated purely as transatlantic transports. Out of date at the end of the war, the surviving Coronados were quickly scrapped.

✴

Consolidated Model30/ Model 34/ XPB3Y-1

In many respects the four-engine Consolidated Model 30/34 remains something of a mystery. Work started on the Model 30 in 1937 under the XPB3Y-1

BELOW The XPB2Y-1 after receiving additional finlets. *Gerald Balzer*

XPB2Y-1 data (twin tail)	
Span	115ft 0in (35.05m)
Length	79ft 3in (24.16m)
Wing area	1,780sq ft (165.54sq m)
Gross weight	49,754lb (22,568kg)
Maximum take-off weight	52,994lb (24,038kg)
Powerplant	four 1,050hp (783kW) P&W R-1830-72
Armament	three 0.30in (7.62mm) and two 0.50in (12.70mm) machine guns, 12,000lb (5,443kg) bombs
Maximum speed	206mph (331km/h) at sea level, 230mph (370km/h) at 12,000ft (3,658m)
Sea level rate of climb	830ft/min (253m/min)
Service ceiling	22,000ft (6,706m)
Maximum range	4,950 miles (7,965km)

ABOVE Consolidated's XPB2Y-1 is now viewed with its later all-new twin-fin/tail arrangement. The picture was taken in July 1938. *Gerald Balzer*

LEFT A production Consolidated PB2Y-3 Coronado. *Gerald Balzer*

designation, and the layout was to change over the succeeding years, but prototypes were never started. A full-size partial mock-up had been completed by October 1942 and some sources indicate that the powerplant eventually became four R-3350-4 engines. At that later stage the span was 190ft (57.91m) and the wing area 3,200sq ft (297.60sq m), and 36,000lb (16,330kg) of bombs were to be carried; the potential range was as high as 8,200 miles (13,194km). However, in 1944 the project was finally cancelled by agreement between the manufacturer and the Navy, little or no progress having been made for some time. The full explanation as to why the programme dawdled along for so long is not clear, but other more urgent wartime commitments must have been a strong factor.

*

These next two designs are grouped together because they both made their appearance in 1939.

XPB3Y-1 data (at February 1942)	
Span	169ft 0in (51.51m)
Length (not including gun barrels)	104ft 8in (31.90m)
Wing area	2,600sq ft (241.80sq m)
Gross weight	121,500lb (55,112kg)
Powerplant	four 2,000hp (1,491kW) P&W R-2800
Armament	five defensive turrets, up to 20,000lb (9,072kg) bombs
Maximum speed	237mph (381km/h)
Range	5,000 miles (8,045km)

Martin Model 162/PBM Mariner

Alongside the Catalina, the Martin PBM Mariner was the other American military flying boat to become a major success story during the Second World War, with 1,285 built. Although the Mariner was a twin-engine type, some of the numerous designs and studies conducted under the Model 162 number looked at four-engine powerplants. The original design work had been started in 1937, with one prototype being ordered in June of that year, and this made its maiden flight on 18 February 1939. Service entry was achieved in September 1940 and the type served extensively both in the Atlantic and the Pacific, and also during the Korean War in the early years of the 1950s.

Consolidated Model 31/ XPB4Y-1 Corregidor

The twin-engine Model 31 from Consolidated was a private-venture project, the outcome of a series of designs started in about February 1938 to look into both two- and three-engine boats. The objective was to use the new Wright R-3350 Duplex Cyclone engine, and the Model 31 first became airborne on 5 May 1939. The prototype was subsequently acquired by the Navy in April 1942, where it was given the designation XPB4Y-1 and the name Corregidor. The designers had first proposed a militarised Model 31 to the Navy in February 1939, two versions were proposed against Specification 116-23 in November 1939 (see below), and other Navy variants were also considered, but in the end just the prototype flew with the Service. After receiving modifications such as defensive turrets, it become airborne again on 28 July 1943. Orders for a 200-strong production run were placed in July 1942, but were abandoned in December 1943.

XPBM-1 data	
Span	118ft 0in (35.97m)
Length	77ft 2in (23.52m)
Wing area	1,405sq ft (130.67sq m)
Gross weight	40,814lb (18,513kg)
Powerplant	two 1,600hp (1,193kW) Wright R-2600-6
Armament	one 0.30in (7.62mm) and five 0.50in (12.70mm) machine guns, up to c4,500lb (2,041kg) bombs or depth charges
Maximum speed	213mph (343km/h) at 12,000ft (3,658m)
Sea level rate of climb	840ft/min (256m/min)
Service ceiling	20,600ft (6,279m)
Range	3,450 miles (5,551km)

XBP4Y-1 data	
Span	110ft 0in (33.53m)
Length (not including gun barrels)	74ft 0.5in (22.57m)
Wing area	1,048sq ft (97.46sq m)
Maximum take-off weight	48,000lb (21,773kg)
Powerplant	two 2,300hp (1,715kW) Wright R-3350-8
Armament	one 37mm cannon and four 0.50in (12.70mm) machine guns, up to 4,000lb (1,814kg) bombs and two torpedoes or two 1,660lb (753kg) mines
Maximum speed at 46,620lb (21,147kg)	258mph (415km/h) at 16,600ft (5,060m)
Maximum rate of climb	1,230ft/min (375m/min)
Service ceiling	21,400ft (6,523m)
Maximum range	3,280 miles (5,278km)

BELOW This unidentified Martin PBM Mariner shows the type's angled tailplane and fins to good effect.

RIGHT The Consolidated Model 31 prototype in its original civilian form.
Gerald Balzer

ABOVE After being acquired by the US Navy, the Model 31 was designated the XPB4Y-1 Corregidor and given military fittings. *Gerald Balzer*

Flying Boat Competition

The designs that come next were tendered against a new specification SD-116-23 for a twin-engine long-range flying boat – a Martin project list indicates, for example, that the designs under Models 180, 181 and 183 were submitted on 8 November 1939. SD-116-23 outlined a flying boat to be powered by two R-3350 units, and another factor was that catapult and non-catapult versions of each design were requested. The idea was that the aeroplane could be launched from a barge at much higher gross weights, so providing it with far greater range.

Boeing Model 337

Boeing's submission to SD-116-23 was the Model 337, which employed a 'Davis' aerofoil for its straight wing. The design had an internal bomb bay and retracting underwing floats.

Model ... data	
'Normal' gross weight	52,500lb (23,814kg)
'Catapult' gross weight	82,... lb (37,286kg)
Maximum speed	237mph (38. km/h)

Consolidated BM-7 and BM-8

Consolidated's SD-116-23 proposals comprised two designs known in-house as the BM-7 and BM-8. The former was a slightly enlarged Model 31 (described above) with the same general layout and a choice of powerplant including the Pratt & Whitney H-3130-AG2, Wright R-3350 or Pratt & Whitney R-2800, while the BM-8 held the original Model 31 size and could use either of the latter two engine types. Earlier the Consolidated Model 31 had itself used the new high-efficiency wing known as the Davis wing.

BM-7 data	
Span	125ft 0in (38.10m)
Length	84ft 7in (25.78m)
'Normal' gross weight	55,554lb (25,199kg)
'Catapult' gross weight	89,092lb (40,412kg)
'Normal' range	4,600 miles (7,401km)
'Catapult' range	10,710 miles (17,232km)

Chance Vought Model V-301

There are two known designs that fall under Vought's twin-engine V-301 banner, the V-301A and V-301C. Although quite alike in terms of their fuselages, the former had an elliptical wing and overall was a little larger. The more detailed V-301C drawing, dated 6 November 1939, shows a tapered wing but with the inner section having a straight trailing edge. There were three-blade propellers having a diameter of 16ft 0in (4.88m), four bombs were carried in each inner wing adjacent to the engines, two more would go inside each side of the centre fuselage, and a Mk XV torpedo

V-301A data	
Span	134ft 0in (40.84m)
Length	80ft 2.5in (24.45m)
Wing area	1,888sq ft (175.58sq m)

V-301C data	
Span	124ft 0in (37.80m)
Length	76ft 11.5in (23.46m)
Wing area	1,670sq ft (155.31sq m)

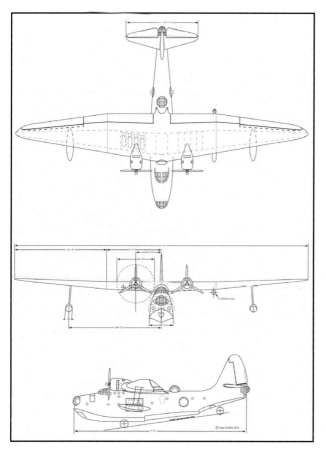

ABOVE Chance Vought V-301C (6.11.39).
Alan Griffith copyright

ABOVE Martin Model 180 (date appears to read 6.8.39).
Stan Piet, GLMMAM

went under each wing between the engine nacelles and the floats. The usual defensive guns were installed, although full details are not available.

Martin Model 180

Martin's Model 180 designation looked at designs for twin-engine long-range flying boat patrol bombers between at least August and October 1939. What seems to be the main study is reproduced here and featured a single fin, four-blade 15ft 0in (4.57m)-diameter propellers, and two 0.50in (12.70mm) machine guns in the nose, one in a tail turret and another in a universally rotatable ventral turret. The drawing indicates a variable incidence wing and nacelles; the latter would also act as floats, and each housed some bombs. Another Model 180 drawing

showed a gull wing layout, while one more design had twin booms.

Martin Model 181

Martin's Model 181 flying boat patrol bomber designs followed hard on the heels of the Model 180 (this series of drawings was dated November 1939). The main aircraft had a deep hull and long, slim, tapered wings, and the two power units were to drive 15ft 0in (4.57m) four-blade propellers. The drawing shows that one 1,000lb (454kg) and one 500lb (227kg) bomb could go in each wing nacelle, and another twelve 1,000lb (454kg) bombs would load into the centre fuselage bay. Nose, dorsal and tail turrets each appear to have received just a single 0.50in (12.70mm) machine gun, but there appear also to be gun points in

each side of the fuselage and in the lower rear fuselage.

BELOW Martin Model 181 (4.11.39).
Stan Piet, GLMMAM

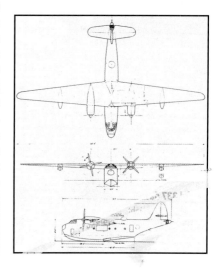

Model 180 data	
Span	132ft 0in (40.23m)
Length	83ft 4in (25.40m)

Model 181 data	
Span	129ft 0in (39.32m)
Length	76ft 9in (23.39m)

Martin Model 183

Another short set of designs for twin-engine VPB long-range flying boat patrol bombers came under Martin's Model 183. One drawing is dated April 1940, and another May, which indicates that the work continued after the design competition had been concluded. The design featured here had a gull-shaped inner wing section, near straight leading edges, twin fins and four-blade 14ft 0in (4.27m)-diameter propellers. Large fuel tanks stretched along much of the bottom of the fuselage, bombs were housed in a centre bay and in the wing nacelles, and each turret had 0.50in (12.70mm) machine guns, two in the nose and one each in dorsal, tail, lower rear fuselage and two side fuselage positions. On 13 May the Model 183D was drawn, which in appearance had much in common with the Mariner described above (although there was also a single-fin 183D variant).

Model 183 data	
Span	121ft 0in (36.89m)
Length	82ft 3in (25.07m)

Boeing Model 344/XPBB-1 Sea Ranger

Boeing's Model 337 was not chosen as the winner of this competition (in fact, the design fell within the lower half of the results table), and it was the Vought-Sikorsky proposal that came out on top. However, Vought already had a large workload and that might prevent the company from bringing its new type to fruition. In addition, the Navy wished to expand its flying boat industry base by adding Boeing to its military boat business set-up (in addition to Consolidated, Martin and Vought-Sikorsky). Therefore on 24 February 1940 Boeing was asked if it would take on this programme, and in the process the firm was given the Vought data as a starting point to revise the 337. Although this may sound a little underhand, George Spangenberg explains that this move 'was decided that on "industrial statesmanship" grounds', and was done honestly by the Navy, which wrote to Vought to explain that the company had 'won the competition, but we are going

LEFT Martin Model 183 (22.4.40). *Stan Piet, GLMMAM*

XPBB-1 data	
Span	139ft 8.5in (42.58m)
Length (including barrels)	94ft 11.5in (28.84m) gun
Wing area	1,826sq ft (169.82sq m)
Gross weight	62,006lb (28,126kg)
Maximum weight	64,034lb (29,046kg)
'Catapult' take-off weight	101,129lb (45,872kg)
Powerplant	two 2,300hp (1,715kW) Wright R-3350-8
Armament	eight 0.50in (12.70mm) machine guns, up to 20,000lb (9,072kg) bombs, four torpedoes
Maximum speed	219mph (352km/h) at 4,500ft (1,372m)
Maximum rate of climb	980ft/min (299m/min)
Service ceiling	18,900ft (5,761m)
Range	4,245 miles (6,830km

to give the award to Boeing'. Vought did receive payment for its design effort.

Within a month Boeing had produced a larger and heavier development of the Model 337, which was called the Model 344 (it was not a copy of the Vought project), and in June this proved successful in winning an order for one XPBB-1 prototype. Another fifty-seven production machines were ordered fifteen months later, and the new type was named Sea Ranger. The prototype began its flight-test programme on 9 July 1942, but the capabilities of other new land-based patrol aeroplanes, and the need for Boeing to get on with assembling B-29 bombers, meant that the XPBB-1 remained the sole example built. An excellent aircraft and a success as a flying machine, it was used on trials work until 1947.

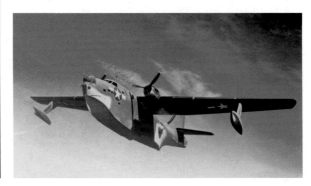

ABOVE & OPPOSITE BOTTOM RIGHT Photographs of the Boeing XPBB-1 Sea Ranger prototype. *Gerald Balzer*

XPB2M-1 data	
Span	200ft 0in (60.96m)
Length	117ft 3in (35.74m)
Wing area	3,683sq ft (342.52sq m)
Gross weight	144,000lb (65,318kg)
Powerplant	two 2,200hp (1,641kW) Wright R-3350-8
Armament	five 0.30in (7.62mm) machine guns, up to 10,000lb (4,536kg) bombs or combinations of depth charges or torpedoes
Maximum speed	221mph (356km/h) at 4,500ft (1,372m)
Maximum rate of climb	440ft/min (134m/min)
Service ceiling	14,600ft (4,450m)
Range with 4,000lb (1,814kg) load	6,200 miles (9,976km)

ABOVE Martin XPB2M-1 Mars prototype. *Gerald Balzer*

Martin Model 170/XPB2M-1 Mars

One more military flying boat prototype was put into the air by the US Navy during the Second World War, the giant Martin Model 170 XPB2M-1 Mars, covered by Specification SD-116-19. Work on what appears to have been a private venture was started in 1938 and one prototype XPB2M-1 was ordered early in the following year. Delays (such as an engine fire during water runs) held back the first flight until 23 June 1942, then in October the prototype was grounded to allow it to be converted into a pure transport type. Flying again in May 1943, it was to be followed by twenty JRM-1 production transports.

Patrol aircraft Designs in Perspective

Maritime patrol activities were not only to prove increasingly important as the Second World War progressed, they would also lay the foundations for a capability that would remain crucial for national security in the decades to come. Although the war saw the extensive use of the outstandingly effective Consolidated Catalina (and the British Short Sunderland), this era was to prove the heyday of the long-range flying boat. Despite some impressive post-war projects, the future lay with land-based aircraft, as heralded by the Mercator and the Neptune.

The following final chapter looks at two categories of aircraft that strictly speaking fall outside the subject of American Second World War fighter and bomber development. However, they are part of the history of design during that era. These are the Zimmerman concept and the jet fighter. The first would prove a dead end, whereas the second would open up a whole new future in terms of aircraft performance.

Chapter Nine
Miscellaneous Programmes

ABOVE Arguably the biggest step forward (of many) in aviation during the years of the Second World War was the introduction of the jet engine. This picture shows the first Lockheed XP-80A jet fighter prototype.

The preceding chapters have concentrated on what might be considered to be the main lines of development of American military aircraft during the Second World War. However, the story would not be complete without looking at two areas of development that were to have little or no influence on any aircraft involved in the conflict, but which instead explored the potential for much more radical design advances. One was an attempt to change the whole aerodynamic configuration of the aeroplane; the other was to utilise a new form of propulsion. The former was bold, resulting in several imaginative designs but eventually leading nowhere; the latter was to transform the future of aircraft design.

Zimmerman Flapjack

Aeronautical engineer Dr Charles Horton Zimmerman (1908-96) was especially well known for designing aircraft that had unusual configurations. He was always interested in short take-off and landing aeroplanes, and in the 1930s while working for NACA he came to the idea of designs that had no wings but instead made use of flat disc-shaped bodies to provide their lift. The aircraft resulting from this theory were called 'discoidal' aircraft by Zimmerman himself, although others nicknamed them 'Zimmer's Skimmers' or 'Flying Flapjacks'. The George Spangenberg website summarises the theory behind his idea: Zimmerman…

'…put propellers on the wing tips and rotated them opposite to the vortex that naturally exists at the wing tip, going from the high pressure to the lower pressure side of the wing. By running the propeller the other way you unwind the vortex and get the equivalent of a high aspect ratio. With the huge propellers you would get extremely good landing and take-off performance.'

A conventional very low-aspect ratio wing would experience poor performance from the amount of induced drag created at its wingtips by the vortices produced when the high-pressure air underneath the wing spilt over the tip into the lower-pressure region above. However, the alternative of having a long and narrow high-aspect ratio wing would bring structural problems through the need to have sufficient built-in stiffness, and it would also reduce the aircraft's manoeuvrability and rate of roll. Therefore the Zimmerman idea was to have the propellers rotate in the opposite direction to the vortices and thereby cancel them out. As a result of keeping the higher-pressure air below the wing, the induced drag would be eliminated and the aircraft would require much less wing area, and that offered considerably enhanced manoeuvrability.

At the start Zimmerman tried to sell his ideas as an individual, and that included making approaches to the Navy, but the Service would not deal with an individual and advised him to become associated with an established manufacturer. The company that took on his ideas in 1937 was Chance Vought, and Zimmerman's subsequent proposals were made through that firm – a trials aircraft was flown, a fighter prototype was built and there were other projects. The Navy looked at the original idea in terms of a fighter because at the time the Service was not permitted to fund research programmes, which of course was what this really was.

Vought V-173

The wood and canvas structure Vought V-173 'Flying Pancake' was produced as a 'proof-of-concept' research prototype and was funded in 1939. The sole example first flew on 23 November 1942 powered by two Continental A-80 engines with propellers taken from an F4U Corsair fighter, although these were later replaced by three-blade 16ft 6in (5.03m)-diameter units. Severe vibration experienced during ground runs from the V-173's complex gearbox had held back the first flight by several months, and wind tunnel work showed that the trailing edge elevons needed to

ABOVE The Vought V-173 research aircraft. The air-to-air picture was taken during the aircraft's maiden flight in November 1942.

be supplemented with additional ailevator surfaces, and these were fitted to the outer rear surfaces. Nevertheless, this machine went on to complete around 200 flights until 31 March 1947, in the process proving Zimmerman's theory that a fighter produced to his ideas could be capable of near-vertical take-offs and landings. The V-173 was in fact flown in sustained flight at a nose-up attitude of 45° and it would not go into a full stall or a spin. The unbuilt V-173C fighter development had a tricycle undercarriage rather than the research machine's original tall fixed

main undercarriage with small tailwheel that had given a nose-high angle of 22.3°, and which had been needed to ensure that the V-173's propellers would clear the ground.

V-173 data	
Maximum span	23ft 4in (7.11m)
Length	26ft 8in (8.13m)
Wing area	427sq ft (39.71sq m)
Loaded weight	3,050lb (1,383kg)
Powerplant	two 80hp (60kW)
	Continental A-80
Armament	none
Maximum speed	120mph (193km/h) level,
	138mph (222km/h) in dive

Vought V-315/XF5U-1

In September 1942 the Navy followed up with the go-ahead for a prototype of an experimental all-metal Zimmerman single-seat fighter that Vought called the V-315 and the Navy the XF5U-1. Powered by two Pratt & Whitney R-2000s, this offered some promise (and here the undercarriage could be retracted). But the time and cost taken to develop the XF5U-1 counted against it, and by 1946 (when the Navy was moving on to jet fighters) it had fallen well behind schedule due to development

problems and was still to fly; it had in fact been completed in August 1945. It was required by the Navy eventually to do 500mph (805km/h), but only ever achieved some taxi runs (with a possible short hop in March 1947), and it never made a proper flight. After the project was cancelled on 17 March 1947 the airframe was scrapped, although it was found to be so solid structurally that a wrecking ball was required to break it up. It is such a shame that this aeroplane was never flown.

XF5U-1 data

Maximum span (including elevon tips but not propellers)	32ft 6in (9.91m)
Length	28ft 7in (8.72m)
Wing area	475sq ft (44.175sq m)
Loaded weight	16,802lb (7,621kg)
Maximum take-off weight	18,917lb (8,581kg)
Initial powerplant	two 1,350hp (1,007kW) P&W R-2000-7 Twin Wasp
Armament	six 0.50in (12.70mm) machine guns or four 20mm cannon, two 1,000lb (454kg) bombs (prototype to be unarmed)

XR-2000 later planned performance

Maximum speed	504mph (811km/h) at 28,900ft (8,809m)
Sea level rate of climb	3,950ft/min (1,204m/min)
Service ceiling	32,000ft (9,754m)
Range	910 miles (1,464km)

LEFT A view of the incomplete XF5U-1 prototype taken in 1943, with F4U Corsair fighter propellers in place. *Alan Griffith*

BELOW The full-size mock-up of the Vought XF5U-1. *Alan Griffith*

RIGHT A rear angle view of the XF5U-1 after the correct propellers had been fitted. The picture is dated 'circa 1948', and the aircraft was never to fly. *Alan Griffith*

Vought V-162, V-172 and V-303

Despite the concept failing to provide a new combat aircraft, the Vought project list shows that a fairly wide range of aircraft types had been drawn using Zimmerman's ideas, three of which are highlighted here. The V-162 was a naval attack bomber proposal from August 1937 with an offset single-seat canopy and three-blade propellers for its twin engines (the Vought project list actually calls the V-162 a pursuit type). The V-172 two-seat attack aircraft of December 1938 was prepared for the Army Air Corps and featured 20ft 0in (6.10m) three-blade propellers; it carried two bombs in the centre body, and had four defensive machine guns.

BELOW Vought V-162B attack bomber (8.37). *Alan Griffith copyright*

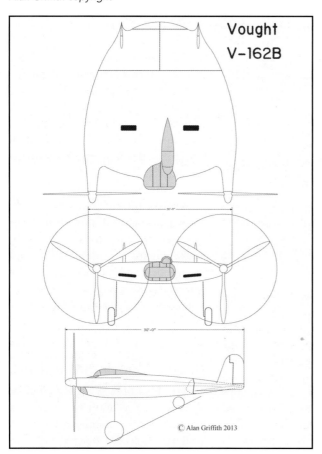

BELOW Vought V-172 attack aircraft (12.38). *Alan Griffith copyright*

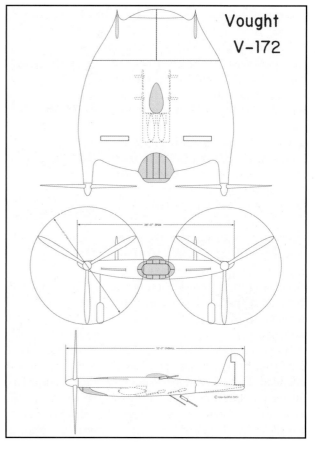

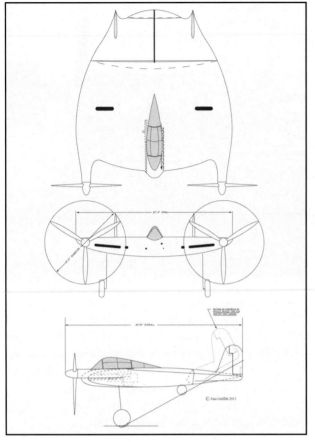

ABOVE Vought V-303 fighter (drawing dated 16.6.39).
Alan Griffith copyright

ABOVE Boeing Model 390 (early 1943).
Alan Griffith copyright

Looking at the surviving drawings, more work appears to have been done on the V-303 Air Corps high-speed single-seat fighter of May 1939 that preceded the V-315/XF5U-1. An interesting feature here was how the tail section could be moved upwards to set the controls to provide proper trim for take-off and landing. Three-blade propellers 12ft 0in (3.66m) in diameter were fitted, two 92-gallon (348-litre) fuel tanks were placed in the leading edge either side of the cockpit, with another 184-gallon (697-litre) tank behind the cockpit, three guns (seemingly two cannon and a machine gun) were installed at each side of the cockpit, and, like many of the Zimmerman drawings, the V-303 had twin fins.

There were other studies: the V-318 from December 1940, for example, was intended to be a Zimmerman-type fighter for the Navy, but in this case either with a single or twin-engine powerplant.

V-162 data	
Span	26ft 0in (7.92m)
Length	30ft 0in (9.14m)
V-172 data	
Span	28ft 0in (8.53m)
Length	32ft 0in (9.75m)
V-303 data	
Span	23ft 4in (7.11m)
Length	26ft 10in (8.18m)
Wing area	427sq ft (39.71sq m)
Loaded weight	10,500lb (4,763kg)
Powerplant	two 2,500hp (1,864kW)
	Continental O-1430-7
Armament	three guns

The Spangenberg website described the Zimmerman proposals as 'very interesting' and highlighted the main problem that prevented the programme from being a success. The XF5U-1's two R-2000 engines with their propellers at the wingtips required a cross-shafting system and the project failed principally because it proved impossible to build a mechanical-drive transmission system that was capable of transmitting to the propellers the substantial power produced by the fighter's engines. A considerable amount of trouble was also experienced during wind tunnel tests in establishing good low-speed characteristics, but in the end the project 'died its own death' because the powerplant transmission system was never able to pass its tests. Overall, the Navy showed considerable interest in Zimmerman's projects and Spangenberg added that, because of the potential performance, had the fighter worked 'we really had a world beater'.

*

Boeing Models 390 and 391

In early 1943 Boeing began to look at some low aspect ratio all-wing ideas that matched the Zimmerman work at Vought. Indeed, Boeing's design philosophy was similar to Zimmerman's, but it is not known just how much the Boeing engineers might have been influenced by the man himself. Three designs in all were apparently completed and proposed, the Models 390 and 391 pursuit fighters accompanied by the Model 396 test aircraft. The big difference between the Boeing fighters and the XF5U-1 lay in their powerplants, the former having a more straightforward single radial engine and a counter-rotating propeller rather than the Vought's twin units.

The single-seat compact Model 390 was to have a simple lightweight structure and use just three separate control surfaces: the elevators, two wing flaps that would also serve as ailerons, and the rudder. The one-piece aluminium semi-monocoque wing had two main spars together with an auxiliary spar, and the control surfaces were to be fabric-covered. Fed by an intake beneath the leading edge, the single-stage Wasp Major sat in the middle of the wing to the pilot's rear and drove a six-blade 13ft 6in (4.11m)-diameter counter-rotating propeller. Underwing drop tanks were available, and the 390 had a tailwheel undercarriage (with dual rear wheels)

Model 390 data

Span	33ft 4in (10.16m)
Length	34ft 4in (10.46m)
Wing area	not given
Gross weight	14,000lb (6,350kg)
Powerplant	one P&W R-4360-3 Wasp Major
Armament	four 20mm cannon, provision for two 500lb (227kg) bombs
Maximum speed	379mph (610km/h) at sea level, 414mph (666km/h) at 13,500ft (4,115m)
Sea level rate of climb	4,250ft/min (1,295m/min)
Maximum range	1,000 miles (1,609km)

Model 391 data

Gross weight	14,500lb (6,577kg)
Powerplant	one P&W XR-4360 Wasp Major
Armament	four 20mm cannon, provision for two 500lb (227kg) bombs
Maximum speed	375mph (603km/h) at sea level, 425mph (684km/h) at 25,000ft (7,620m)

and four cannon in the outer sections of the wing. On the ground the aircraft would sit at an angle of 20°.

Apart from an extra pair of air ducts on either side of the ventral scoop, the Model 391's airframe was identical to that of the 390; the key difference came with the engine, a two-stage XR-4360 Wasp Major that estimates indicated would give a higher top speed.

Boeing Model 396

The Model 396 was to be a relatively cheap flying scale model for Boeing's 390 and 391 fighters and would have only a low-power engine to enable it to explore the configuration's low-speed characteristics and handling. It was expected that the unconventional wing planform selected for these fighters could well provide some unusual characteristics, so testing beyond the normal wind tunnel research would almost certainly prove beneficial. The 396 was to have a primarily wooden structure but with aluminium control surfaces (and fabric covering) together with a steel tube frame around the cockpit. A Lycoming engine with a fixed-pitch propeller was used, and the fuel load was 15 gallons (57 litres). A Navy report stated that the 396 was 'excellent' in the way that it matched overall the shape of the full-size machines, but unfortunately no orders were to be placed for any of these designs.

Jet Propulsion

The story of the establishment of the jet engine in America is well known and need not be duplicated here; suffice to say that the greater part of the initial engine design effort centred on General Electric, which was given direct access to the work

Model 396 data

Span	25ft 0in (7.62m)
Wing area	319sq ft (29.67sq m)
Gross weight	1,400lb (635kg)
Powerplant	one 125hp (kW) Lycoming O-290

undertaken in this field by the British. Once America's engine manufacturers had the nation's first jets up and running, designs for jet fighters automatically appeared in the pipeline. Indeed, before the end of the war (before the end of 1944 in fact) both the Army Air Corps and the Navy had programmes and design competitions under way for new fighter types powered by jet engines, and these are covered in Tony Buttler's book *Early US Jet Fighters* published by Hikoki in 2013. What follows covers what is thought to be the only jet fighter work undertaken by US manufacturers prior to the start of 1944.

Bell P-59A Airacomet

It will always be on record that the Bell XP-59A was America's first jet aircraft to fly, but the project was not to provide an operational jet fighter. The P-59 designation was reused from the twin-boom piston fighter described in Chapter One, and three XP-59A prototypes were ordered, the first making its flight debut on 2 October 1942. Named Airacomet, this initial design was a modest affair that employed an airframe of pure piston technology, a point reflected by the type's maximum speed of 404mph (650km/h). Another thirteen YP-59As with higher-thrust engines followed, and there were fifty production machines, but it was clear that the Airacomet could never make a combat aircraft. In fact, relatively little attention had been given to developing the airframe's aerodynamics – this was essentially a proof-of-concept programme. Nevertheless, experience is everything and these aeroplanes were used to train pilots and ground crew in the techniques and methods of operating this vital new propulsion system.

XP-59A data

Span	45ft 6in (13.87m)
Length	38ft 2in (11.63m)
Wing area	386sq ft (35.90sq m)
Maximum take-off weight	12,562lb (5,698kg)
Powerplant	two 1,250lb (5.6kN) thrust General Electric I-A
Armament	two 37mm cannon
Maximum speed	404mph (650km/h) at 25,000ft (7,620m)
Absolute ceiling	45,756ft (13,946m)

ABOVE Serial 42-108778, pictured at Patuxent River, was a YP-59A Airacomet that had been passed to the US Navy.
Gerald Balzer

BELOW Old and new fly together (though in this case the piston aircraft might possibly have had the slightly better performance). In fact, this is YP-59A Airacomet 42-108778 again, this time flying in formation with a Vought F4U Corsair.
Gerald Balzer

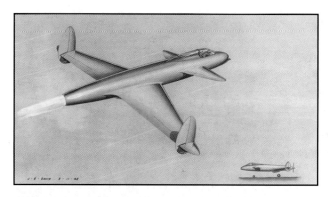

ABOVE Artwork for one of the jet fighter designs considered by Lockheed under its L-133 number, but which was rejected. It is dated 11 March 1942. Note the two guns under the nose.

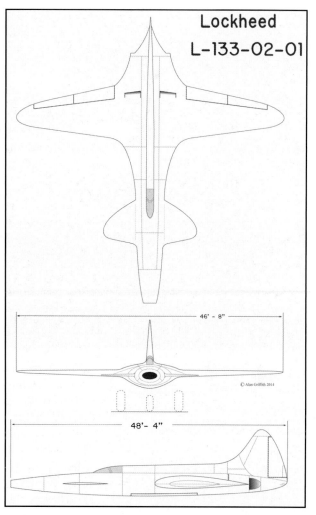

Lockheed L-133

Lockheed's very first study into jet fighter aircraft was opened during early 1942 with designs that came under the company's L-133 banner. In fact, the resulting single-seat L-133-2, the final proposal, looks extremely advanced when set against almost every other early jet fighter design from the mid-1940s. In addition, the L-133 was to be powered by one of Lockheed's own engines, the L-1000 created by Nathan C. Price, the design of which was complete before British jet units had been supplied to America. The L-133-2 fighter was especially distinguished in having a foreplane rather than a tailplane, in part to offset having the

RIGHT The foreplane layout was retained by the L-133-2, which was eventually submitted to the Air Corps as a proposal (3.42). *Alan Griffith copyright*

BELOW & OVERLEAF The original manufacturer's model of the L-133-2. *John Aldaz*

L-133-2 data

Span	46ft 8in (14.225m)
Length	48ft 4in (14.73m)
Wing area	325sq ft (30.225sq m)
Maximum take-off weight	19,500lb (8,845kg)
Overload weight	18,000lb (8,165kg)
Powerplant	two 5,100lb (22.7kN) Lockheed L-1000
Armament	four 20mm cannon
Maximum speed	615mph (990km/h) at sea level, 620mph (998km/h) at 20,000ft (6,096m)
Sea level rate of climb	3,740ft/min (1,140m/min)
Rate of climb at 40,000ft (12,192m)	6,350ft/min (1,935m/min)
Normal range at 40,000ft (12,192m)	390 miles (628km)

engines towards the rear of the aircraft rather than near the front as on most piston types. It was considered that this final configuration (from several examined) offered the best solution for accommodating jet engines while at the same time keeping the design simple. The straight main wing was set mid-position and the two power units, fed by a nose air intake, were placed to the rear of the pilot in the wing root fairings. Four cannon were mounted in the nose and would fire from the intake, the fuel load was 500 gallons (1,893 litres), and the aeroplane had a tricycle undercarriage.

On 30 March 1942 Lockheed made a formal submission of its L-133-02 project to the Army Air Corps, but despite having been a thorough preliminary study it was rejected. In addition, the L-1000 turbojet, officially called the XJ37, was tested on the bench but never entered production. Nevertheless, this effort had given the Lockheed design team, formed by Clarence 'Kelly' Johnson and Hall J. Hibbard, plenty of knowledge and experience in readiness for the P-80 described below.

Lockheed L-140/XP-80 Shooting Star

Lockheed's next jet fighter would, as the P-80 Shooting Star, become the Army Air Corps's first operational jet, but that was a little way ahead when the original L-140 project got going in May 1943. The L-140 was designed around the British de Havilland H.1B turbojet (to be built under licence as the J36), and a single prototype was ordered in October 1943 as the XP-80. It made its maiden flight on 8 January 1944 and the effort by Lockheed to produce this prototype in such an incredibly fast time has become legendary. However, the Air Corps also ordered two further, very

slightly larger prototypes that were to be powered by the 4,000lb (17.8kN) General Electric J33 (I-40) jet, and the first of these L-141/XP-80As flew on 10 June 1944. It was this second version that went into production as the Shooting Star, and the fighter entered service before the end of the war, although it did not see any combat. More than 1,700 were produced (together with many more T-33 trainers based on the fighter), and the type completed a long career, in the process making a major contribution to the Korean War. The jet fighter in American hands was on its way.

XP-80 data

Span	37ft 0in (11.28m)
Length	32ft 10in (10.01m)
Wing area	240sq ft (22.32sq m)
Maximum take-off weight	9,916lb (4,498kg)
Overload weight	8,620lb (3,910kg)
Powerplant	one 2,460lb (10.9kN) de Havilland H.1B Goblin
Armament	six 0.50in (12.70mm) machine guns
Maximum speed	502mph (808km/h) at 20,480ft (6,242m)
Sea level rate of climb	3,000ft/min (914m/min)
Service ceiling	41,000ft (12,497m)

Second World War Aircraft Design in Perspective

Behind the successful aircraft of the Second World War – planes such as the P-47 Thunderbolt, P-51 Mustang, F8F Bearcat and B-29 Superfortress – there were dozens of other preceding or competing designs. This book has attempted to describe those designs and their place in history. Together they illustrate the ingenuity and efforts of an industry under immense pressure to respond to the urgent needs of its armed forces.

It is interesting to note that most of the operationally successful warplanes were progressive developments of earlier designs. At the end of the war aircraft did not look very different from those of the immediate pre-war period. That is not to belittle the work or imagination of the designers; they were up against the fundamental constraint of the operating limits of the only available means of propulsion, namely a piston engine driving an airscrew. This was not a problem in terms of available power but one of the maximum speed and altitude at which this means of propulsion could operate effectively. Moreover, the use of such a powerplant largely dictated the configuration of the aeroplane: either a forward-mounted single engine, driving a propeller at the front, or multiple engines mounted on the leading edge of the wing. Within these constraints the designers developed the propeller-driven, piston-engine aeroplane to its ultimate limits. It would take the advent of the jet engine to push aircraft performance to a new level and, in doing so, bring about new concepts in wing shape and aerodynamic layout. This final chapter has shown how, before the war had ended, engineers were already looking to such horizons.

The jet engine would transform aircraft performance. During the war aircraft maximum speeds increased by around 40%; during the following decade they would increase by 300%. The wartime development of the jet engine in Germany and Great Britain, and the German exploration of transonic aerodynamics, would lay the foundation for this dramatic advance in capability. As a result the US aircraft industry would go on to produce an amazing variety of high-performance fighters and bombers, as described in earlier volumes in this series. Meanwhile one can only marvel at the work of designers facing huge demands to exploit available technology to serve the needs of a nation at war. Their job was to produce aircraft that not only could out-perform the enemy but also had to be robust, reliable, suitable for mass production, easily maintained and able to be flown by the average service pilot. The outcome speaks for itself – and helped to change history.

Appendix One

American Second World War Fighter and Bomber Project Summary

This list embraces all known American fighter and bomber projects and model numbers produced between 1937 and 1945, together with research aircraft specifically intended to help and advance the art of the designer working in these categories of aircraft. Some basic details of the backgrounds and specialities of the manufacturers are given.

BEECH

The Beech Aircraft Company at Wichita in Kansas was set up in 1932 and was a specialist in light aircraft and trainers for the military and general aviation. During the war it made a rare foray into the combat aircraft scene with the XA-38 attack aircraft.

Model 28   Project for 'Destroyer' twin-engine attack aircraft, which became XA-38, first flown 7.5.44. No production orders.

BELL

A relatively new company, having been established only in 1935, Bell Aircraft, based at Buffalo in New York, was responsible for two very successful fighter designs and several other types, before moving on to a series of research aircraft and helicopters in the years following the war. It also produced the first American jet fighter design to reach the flight-test stage.

Model 1   Twin-engine fighter and attack aircraft. Became prototype XFM-1 Airacuda, first flown 1.9.37.

Model 3   Single-engine interceptor prototype submitted against Specification X-609, 3.37.

Model 4   Single-engine interceptor prototype submitted against Specification X-609, 3.37. First flown as XP-39 Airacobra 6.4.38.

BELOW Bell D-6 (1.4.42). *NARA II*

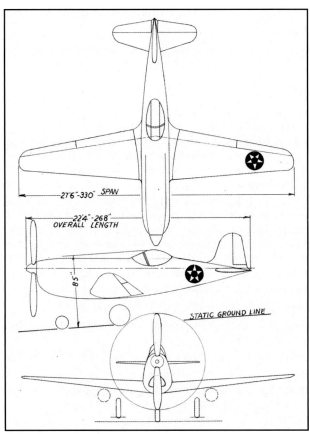

BELOW The Bell Model 11 (c1938/39). At the time of writing no data is available for this design except that its span was 30ft 0in (9.14m) and its length 28ft 10in (8.79m).
Alan Griffith copyright

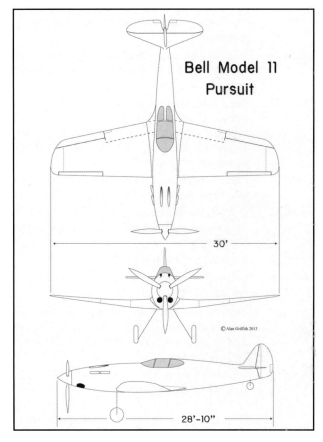

Model 5	Single-engine fighter for carrier operations based on XP-39. First flown as XFL-1 Airabonita prototype 13.5.40. No production.
Model 7	Twin-engine pre-production YFM-1 Airacuda fighters.
Model 8	YFM-1A fitted with tricycle undercarriage.
Model 9	Attack bomber proposal with liquid-cooled in-line Allison engines submitted to USAAF competition, 1938. Thought to be derivative of YFM-1 Airacuda.
Model 10	Attack bomber proposal, c1938.
Model 11	Interceptor and pursuit aircraft proposal, c1938/39.
Model 12	Single-engine interceptor. YF-39 Airacobra first flown 13.9.40.
Model 13	Single-engine interceptor proposal to Specification XC-622 (R40-C), 3.40. Four versions submitted. Model 13 also allocated to P-39C production aeroplanes, which were initially designated P-45.
Model 14	Version of Airacobra for Great Britain and France (P-400).
Model 15	P-39D Airacobra.
Model 16	Single-engine interceptor with tail booms and pusher engine, 1940. Prototype ordered as XP-52. Cancelled 11.41 before flown.
Model 17	Attack bomber proposal, 1939/40. Not built.
Model 19	Single-engine interceptor with tail booms and pusher engine, 1940. Version of XP-52 offered to Navy.
Model 20	Similar project to Model 19, which became two-seat XP-59 proposal. Prototype ordered but abandoned c9.41 and replaced by XP-59A jet fighter programme.
Model 21	Single-engine naval fighter of P-39 type fitted with arrester hook. Study begun 10.39 but not submitted until 2.41. Not ordered.
Model 22	Bell project index gives Model 22 as twin-turbojet fighter (to become XP-59A), but other original company drawing and papers indicate a piston fighter, its brochure submitted to SD-112-18 (Grumman F7F) competition, 1.41.
Model 23	XP-39E Airacobra first flown 26.2.42. To have entered production as P-76 but order cancelled.
Model 24	Single-engine interceptor that became XP-63 Kingcobra prototype, first flown 7.12.42. Developed out of XP-39E.
Model 25	P-63A version of Kingcobra.
Model 26	Model 26A onwards covered several further versions of P-39.
Model 27	Twin-turbojet fighter. Project index indicates that number covered the XP-59A, XP-59, YP-59A and P-59B fighter and trainer versions of Airacomet. XP-59A first flew 2.10.42.
Model 28	Allocated to production version of XP-39E.
Model 29	Turbojet fighter, XP-59B.

Model 32	Single-engine lightweight interceptor that became XP-77, first flown 1.4.44.
Model 33	Covered several further versions of P-63.
Model 34	XP-63B Kingcobra.
D-6	'Model XFL' single-seat lightweight Class VF fighter for Navy; dated 1.4.42 (pencil note on document corrects as XF2L). Single Ranger SVG-770-D4 engine. Span 27ft 6in (8.38m), length 22ft 4in (6.81m), wing area 100sq ft (9.30sq m), maximum weight 4,036lb (1,831kg), one 20mm cannon, two 0.50in (12.70mm) machine guns, maximum 345mph (555km/h) at sea level, 433mph (697km/h) at 30,000ft (9,144m), service ceiling 41,000ft (12,497m), sea level rate of climb 3,610ft/min (1,100m/min).
Model 35	Single-engine lightweight interceptor proposal similar to Model 32, c1942/43.
Model 36	Twin-engine 'offensive' fighter proposal with Chrysler engine, c1943. Not built.
Model 37	P-63D-1 Kingcobra.

BELLANCA

A light aircraft manufacturer based at New Castle (Wilmington) in Delaware. During the lead-up to the war it offered several designs for front-line military types.

Model 17-110	Fighter interceptor to Air Corps Circular Proposal 39-770, 6.39.
Model 20-115	Fighter interceptor to Air Corps Circular Proposal 39-770, 3.8.39.
Model 26-100B	Single-seat land-based fighter-bomber, c1939.
Model 27-86	Two-seat fighter, c1939.
Model 33-220	Response to Air Corps Circular Proposal 39-775, 6.39.

BOEING

During the period covered by this book the Boeing Airplane Corporation, founded in Seattle in 1916, was very much a large aircraft, bomber and transport manufacturer, although there were a good number of fighter studies as well. Where a project number was allocated, in some cases it would embrace a number of different layouts in the search for the ideal configuration. The famous Model 299 B-17 Flying Fortress actually appeared before the period covered by this book, having made its first flight in July 1935. It preceded the manufacturer's one-off Model 294 XB-15 prototype, which first made it into the air on 15 October 1937, having been started way back in January 1934 (in the middle of the war the 294 was converted into a transport with the new designation XC-105). Many of the missing numbers relate to civil projects.

Model 321	Twin-engine VPB flying boat, early 1937.
Model 322	Four-engine USAAF bomber with pressurised cabin, 6.38.
Model 324	Four-engine VPB flying boat, 1937. Conversion of civil Model 314.
Model 329	Twin-engine attack bomber to Specification 98-102, mid-1938.

ABOVE Examples of the Boeing B-17 Flying Fortress were test-flown by the Aeroplane & Armament Experimental Establishment at Boscombe Down, UK. This view shows Fortress Mk III HB796. *Phil Butler*

Model 330   Six-engine bomber, c5.38.

Model 331   Twin-engine high-speed attack aircraft with Allison V-1710s, 1938.

Model 332   Twin-engine high-speed attack aircraft with Allison V-3420s, 1938.

Model 333   Four-engine six-seat USAAF bomber with two pusher and two tractor Allison V-1710 engines, 26.1.39. Model 333A (27.1.39) had four buried V-1710 tractor engines. Model 333B (21.2.39) had four buried tractor P&W '1800' 'flat' engines.

Model 334   Four-engine high-altitude USAAF heavy bomber with buried P&W X-1800 flat engines, 4.3.39. Model 334A (7.39) had four R-3350 engines and tricycle landing gear.

Model 337   Patrol flying boat submission to SD-116-23, mid-1939. Developed into Model 344.

Model 338   Single-engine pursuit aircraft, 1939.

Model 339   Twin-engine pursuit aircraft, 1939.

Model 340   Three-engine pursuit aircraft, 1939.

Model 341   Four-engine high-altitude bomber project to XC-218 and R40-B, 8.39 to 3.40.

Model 344   Navy project of 3.40, which became XPBB-1 Sea Ranger patrol flying-boat, first flown 9.7.42. One prototype only.

Model 345   Project of 5.40 that became B-29 Superfortress long-range bomber, first flown 21.9.42. One YB-29 airframe fitted with Allison V-3420-11 engines as XB-39. Model 345-2 became post-war B-50, first flown 25.6.47.

Model 346   Four-engine high-altitude bomber, 1940.

Model 348   Single-engine high-wing pursuit aircraft, 1940.

Model 349   Dive bomber project, 1940.

Model 350   XPBB-1 boat variant with four single-stage two-speed R-2800s, 1940/41.

Model 351   XPBB-1 development with four two-stage two-speed R-2800s, 1940/41.

Model 352   Twin-engine Navy fighter to SD-112-18 competition, 1.41.

Model 353   XPBB-1 flying boat development with four single-stage two-speed R-2600s, two centre fuel tanks and armour, 1940/41.

Model 354   XPBB-1 development with four two-stage two-speed R-2600s, 1940/41.

Model 355   Twin-engine XPBB-1 development with centre tanks and armour, 1940/41.

Model 356   Twin-engine pursuit aircraft for Air Corps, 1940/41.

Model 357   Twin-engine XPBB-1 development with four tanks, 1940/41.

Model 358   XPBB-1 development of Model 353 without armour, 1940/41.

Model 359   XPBB-1 development of Model 353 with four tanks, 1940/41.

Model 360   Four-engine flying wing high-altitude heavy bomber with pusher engines, c1941/42. 8,000-mile (12,872km) range.

Model 361   Four-engine high-altitude heavy bomber with buried ('submerged') P&W X-Wasp (R-4430) tractor engines, c1941/42.

Model 362   Eight-engine flying wing high-altitude heavy bomber with pusher engines. 10,000-mile (16,090km) range.

Model 363   Six-engine twin-boom high-altitude heavy bomber with pusher engines, c1941/42. Possibly transcontinental bomber project, 4.41 onwards, as rival to Consolidated B-36, but not confirmed.

Model 364   XPBB-1 development with twin P&W X-Wasp engines, 1941/42.

Model 365   Four-engine high-altitude long-range heavy bomber with pusher X-Wasp engines, c1941/42.

Model 368   Series of advanced shipboard piston fighter designs with unconventional wings, c1942. Included variations of twin-boom pusher layouts.

Model 369   B-17 fitted with pressurisation, c1942.

Model 370   Four-engine long-range heavy bomber powered by P&W X-Wasp engines with counter-rotating propellers, c1942. Essentially same as Model 365 but with tractor engines.

Model 372   XPBB-1 development with twin P&W X-Wasp engines, c1942.

Model 373   Six-engine long-range heavy bomber powered by P&W X-Wasp R-4360 engines with counter-rotating propellers, c1942. Based on Model 370.

Model 374   Twin-engine naval fighter aircraft proposal similar to Grumman F7F, 1942. Two Wright R-1820 engines.

Model 375   Single-Lycoming tractor engine Navy fighter, 1942.

Model 376   Preliminary study for single-engine naval fighter aircraft, 5.12.42.

Model 378   Navy twin-engine coastal patrol bomber, 1942. Conversion of AT-15 bomber crew trainer. Boeing Wichita design. R-1340 engines. XAT-15 first flew 1942 but only two built.

Model 379   Twin-engine pilotless radio-controlled torpedo bomber study, c1942.

Model 380   Air Corps twin-engine patrol bomber similar to AT-15, c1942. Boeing Wichita design. R-1830 engines.

Model 383   Navy single-engine carrier-based fighter, 1942. Counter-rotating propellers.

Model 384   Four-engine intercontinental bomber project derived from B-29, 1942. Not ordered.

Model 385   Six-engine intercontinental bomber project, 29.8.42. Not ordered.

Model 386   Preliminary study for single-engine naval fighter aircraft, 7.12.42.

Model 387   Preliminary study for single-engine naval fighter aircraft, 8.12.42.

Model 388   Navy twin-engine carrier-based fighter, 1942/43. Revision of Model 352.

Model 389   Air Corps twin-engine bomber or fighter study, c1942/43.

Model 390   Unconventional configuration Navy fighter project, contemporary to Vought XF5U, early 1943. Described as research project. One P&W R-4360-3 power unit.

Model 391   Fighter project, early 1943. Same airframe as Model 390 but more powerful XR-4360 engine.

Model 394   Preliminary study for single-engine naval fighter aircraft, 5.3.43.

Model 396   Scale model test aircraft for Models 390 and 391, early 1943. Single Lycoming O-290 power unit.

Model 397   Single-engine low-altitude carrier-based fighter, 1943.

Model 398   Single-engine high-altitude carrier-based fighter, 1943.

Model 398   Preliminary study for single-engine naval fighter aircraft, 5.3.43.

Model 399   Long-range heavy bomber study for Air Corps with four liquid-cooled engines, 1943.

Model 400   Project of 1.4.43 that became prototype XF8B-1 naval fighter first flown 27.11.44.

Model 404   Six-engine pusher flying wing bomber, c1944.

BREWSTER

One of the less well known of American aircraft manufacturers, after its formation in 1932 it built several fighter and bomber aircraft types and produced a number of other proposals. It also built under licence the Vought F4U Corsair as the F3A-1. A badly run company, the Brewster Aeronautical Corporation had its final contracts cancelled in July 1944 and was subsequently dissolved by its shareholders on 5 April 1946. Its headquarters were in the Brewster Building in Long Island City, New York.

Model 39/139/239   Design that became the XF2A-1 fighter prototype, first flown 2.12.37. Entered service as Buffalo but not a success.

Fighter   Possible twin-engine design to SD-112-14, c3.38.

VTB   Three torpedo-bomber proposals to SD-114-6, c8.39. Lost competition to Grumman Avenger and Vought Sea Wolf.

Model 37   Proposal for scout-dive-bomber with powerplant in fuselage and remote-control defensive turrets, 1941. Model 37B (30.4.41) submitted against design competition won by Curtiss XSB3C-1 and Douglas XSB2D-1.

Model 33   Navy fighter proposals (Models A to E) to SD-112-18 competition, 1.41.

Model 40/140/340   Scout bomber project that became prototype XSB2A Buccaneer, first flown 17.6.41. Known as Bermuda in British service. Planned orders for USAAF as A-34 not fulfilled.

XA-32   Prototype single-seat attack aircraft first flown 22.5.43. No production. Thought to be Brewster Model 41/341.

BURNELLI

Vincent Justus Burnelli specialised in working with flying wing designs and lifting bodies, producing, for example, the UB-14 transport of 1934. He promoted his airfoil-shaped fuselage transport planes over many years and the work included proposals for bomber types.

BX-AB-3   Attack bomber project, 1939.

Model XBA-1   Medium bomber project designed to Specification C-213 and Circular Proposal CP 39-640, 1.7.39. Full-size mock-up built, or at least mock-up sections.

B-2000B   Very large Burnelli bomber project from Canadian Car & Foundry, 1942. Possibly part of competition leading to Convair B-36. Large, twin-boom, lifting fuselage design powered by eight Allison V-3420 driving contra-rotating propellers. Span 222ft (67.67m), gross weight 220,000lb (99,792kg).

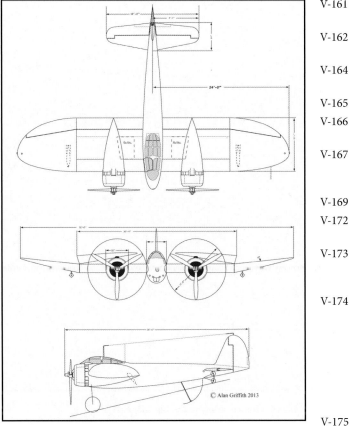

ABOVE Chance Vought V-155B, as at 5.37.
Alan Griffith copyright

CHANCE VOUGHT

Chance Vought at East Hartford, Connecticut, was very much a naval aircraft specialist, for both fighters and attack aircraft, and continued to be so deep into the jet age. The F4U was its major aircraft type of the Second World War, while the SB2U Vindicator, which served during the war, began its flying programme on 4 January 1936. First established in 1917, the company had since 1928 been part of the United Aircraft Corporation, then in the spring of 1939 it became the Vought-Sikorsky Aircraft Division following a merger with the latter manufacturer (which is the reason why some projects have VS project numbers in the text). In 1949 Vought moved to Dallas in Texas.

V-155   Twin-engine fighter proposal for Navy, 22.3.37. Straight wing with parallel leading and trailing edges for inner wings, dihedral on heavily curved outer wings. Four machine guns in lower nose and small bomb under each outer wing. Three-blade propellers. V-155A: span 52ft 0in (15.85m), length 36ft 0in (10.97m), gross wing area 475.6sq ft (44.23sq m), prop diameter 11ft 6in (3.51m), fuel tank capacity 120 gallons (454 litres) in each inner wing. Smaller V-155B: span 48ft 6in (14.78m), length 34ft 8.5in (10.58m), gross wing area 414.5sq ft (38.55sq m), prop diameter 10ft 0in (3.05m), inner wing tanks 108 gallons (409 litres) each.

V-161   Pursuit aircraft proposal for Navy with P&W R-3130 engine, 7.6.37.

V-162   Zimmerman attack bomber proposal for Navy, 9.8.37.

V-164   Designation given to what became SB2U-3 version of Vindicator, 19.11.37.

V-165   SB2U-1 fitted with P&W R-1830 engine, 1.12.37.

V-166   Naval fighter (VF) proposal, 24.2.38. Became XF4U-1 Corsair prototype first flown 29.5.40.

V-167   V-156 was SB2U-1 used as company demonstrator, and when fitted with more powerful P&W R-1830 engine was redesignated V-167. One example only.

V-169   Proposal for Navy Scout Bomber (VSB), 8.8.38.

V-172   Zimmerman-type attack aircraft proposal for USAAF, 15.12.38.

V-173   Zimmerman-type scale model research aircraft, 16.2.39 onwards, and (V 173C) Navy fighter. Research machine first flown 23.11.42.

V-174   Designs for torpedo bomber submitted against Navy requirement SD-114-6, begun 28.3.39. Won competition with Grumman TBF Avenger and selected design became XTBU-1 Sea Wolf prototype, first flown 22.12.41. With Vought's commitment to F4U fighter programme, TBU-1 production switched to Convair, which produced type as TBY. First example flown 20.8.44.

V-175   Scout Bomber VSB project for export, 26.4.39 onwards. Several versions. V-175B: span 45ft 6in (13.87m), length 37ft 8in (11.48m), four-blade 10ft 6in (3.20m) propeller. V-175D: span 45ft 8in (13.92m), length 39ft 3in (11.96m), wing area 410sq ft (38.13sq m), four-blade 12ft 6in (3.81m) propeller. Both carried two nose guns.

V-301   Twin-engine patrol bomber project for Navy, 17.5.39 onwards, to SD-116-23.

V-302   Twin-engine high-speed bomber for USAAF to Circular Proposal 39-640, 24.5.39.

V-303   Zimmerman-type high-speed pursuit aircraft project for USAAF, 31.5.39.

V-306   Pusher-type pursuit aircraft project for Army, 19.7.39.

V-307   Scout torpedo bomber VSTB project for Navy, 14.9.39.

V-315   Zimmerman Navy fighter that became XF5U-1, 30.6.40. Prototype completed but not flown.

V-317   XF4U-1 Corsair fighter, 4.9.40.

V-318   Zimmerman-type single- or twin-engine fighter proposal for Navy, 27.12.40.

V-319   Single-engine scout bomber dive bomber VSB project for Navy, 11.2.41. Drawing dated 21.4.41. Unsuccessful in competition against Curtiss XSB3C-1 and Douglas XSB2D-1.

V-321   F4U-1 variant for Army, 22.4.41.

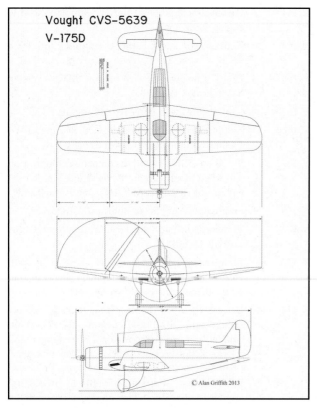

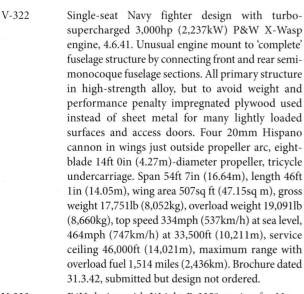

Vought CVS-5639
V-175D

ABOVE Chance Vought V-175D (4.39).
Alan Griffith copyright

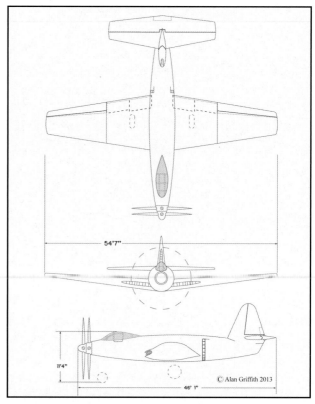

ABOVE Chance Vought VS-322 (31.3.42).
Alan Griffith copyright

V-322	Single-seat Navy fighter design with turbo-supercharged 3,000hp (2,237kW) P&W X-Wasp engine, 4.6.41. Unusual engine mount to 'complete' fuselage structure by connecting front and rear semi-monocoque fuselage sections. All primary structure in high-strength alloy, but to avoid weight and performance penalty impregnated plywood used instead of sheet metal for many lightly loaded surfaces and access doors. Four 20mm Hispano cannon in wings just outside propeller arc, eight-blade 14ft 0in (4.27m)-diameter propeller, tricycle undercarriage. Span 54ft 7in (16.64m), length 46ft 1in (14.05m), wing area 507sq ft (47.15sq m), gross weight 17,751lb (8,052kg), overload weight 19,091lb (8,660kg), top speed 334mph (537km/h) at sea level, 464mph (747km/h) at 33,500ft (10,211m), service ceiling 46,000ft (14,021m), maximum range with overload fuel 1,514 miles (2,436km). Brochure dated 31.3.42, submitted but design not ordered.
V-323	F4U design with Wright R-3350 engine for Navy, 4.6.41.
V-324	Proposals for major changes to F4U-1 for Navy, 4.6.41.
V-325	Additional proposals for major changes to F4U-1, 4.6.41.
V-326	Example of F4U-1 with X-Wasp engine, 4.6.41.
V-328	XTBU production study, 10.11.41.

V-329	XTBU production study with two-stage engine, 10.11.41.
V-330	Study for composite VSB-VTB (scout/dive and torpedo bomber) design for Navy, 10.11.41.
V-331	F4U-1 with turbo-supercharged engine, 1.12.41. Became XF4U-3.
V-332	Six-engine flying boat proposal for Sikorsky, 5.5.42.
V-334	Navy fighter design with Wasp Major engine, 24.12.42. Revised drawing dated 5.43.
V-335	Land-based Army fighter based on XF5U-1, 25.9.43.
V-336	F4U-1 with Wasp Major engine, 19.10.43.
V-337	Land-based fighter with 'special' engine, 14.10.43. Research project that became V-345.
V-338	Single-seat twin-engine carrier-based fighter project for Navy, 30.3.44.
V-339	Single-seat twin-engine land-based fighter for Navy, 30.3.44.
V-340	Jet fighter project that became XF6U-1 Pirate, 12.9.44.
V-341	XF5U-1 fitted with 'special powerplant', 3.10.44. Listed as research project.
V-342	Carrier-based 'Corsair' with single-stage 'E' engine, 23.5.45. Marked as research project.
Fighter	Version of F4U proposed with V-tail, 3.10.45. No V-number allocated.
V-347	High-speed interceptor for Navy, 28.9.45.

CONSOLIDATED

Most of Consolidated's military work was done for the Air Force. In 1943 the Consolidated Vultee Aircraft Corporation (Convair) was formed by a merger with Vultee. One important Consolidated aircraft was the PBY Catalina flying boat, which served extensively during the war but had made its maiden flight on 28 March 1935. In the lead-up to the war there was a series of 'Land Bomber' designs with LB-numbers that appear to have been produced between 26 August 1938 and 7 March 1940. Consolidated's headquarters was in San Diego in California, although when founded in 1923 its first home had been at Buffalo in New York.

Flying wings   General series of flying wing bombers and large aircraft types made in 1937.

Model 28   Designs for a more advanced PBY, 1937.

Model 29   Design for a heavy four-engine flying boat that became PB2Y Coronado, first flown 17.12.37. Prototype had single fin. Twin-engine version offered 1.40.

Model 30   Designs for very large maritime flying boat, 5.37 onwards. Designated XPB3Y-1 and became Model 34 but not ordered and abandoned in 1944.

Model 31   Designs for two- and three-engine flying boats from 2.38 onwards resulting in twin-engine private-venture Model 31 prototype, first flown 5.5.39. Prototype bought by USN as XPB4Y-1 Corregidor but follow-on production order cancelled. Three-engine patrol bomber flying boat design drawn as 'Modified Model 31', 9.38, with three XV-3420s, one in nose, one in each wing. Maximum weight 50,000lb (22,680kg), maximum speed 338mph (544km/h). BM-7 and BM-8 variants proposed against SD-116-23, 11.39.

LB-4   Two- and three-engine medium bomber designs of 50,000lb (22,680kg) gross weight, 8.38. Wing-mounted Allison XV-3420 units with three-engine format having additional propeller on nose. Span 110ft 0in (30.5m), length 66ft 10in (20.37m).

LB-5   Two- and three-engine medium bomber design, 9.38. Allison XV-3420 engines.

LB-6   Single-engine attack aircraft of 15,000lb (6,804kg) gross weight, 22.9.38.

LB-8   Twin-engine attack bomber to Specification C-103, 31.10.38.

LB-9   Three-engine attack bomber to Specification C-103, c1.11.38.

LB-12   Attack bomber with Rolls-Royce Merlin engines, possibly to C-103, 1.11.38.

LB-13   Single-engine scout bomber of gross weight 10,250lb (4,649kg), 2.12.38. To Specification SD-110-25. Allison V-1710, span 48ft (14.63m), length 35ft (10.67m).

LB-14   Twin-engine attack bomber to Specification C-104, 1.39.

LB-15   Twin-engine attack bomber to C-104, 1.39.

LB-16   Four-engine heavy bomber, 1.39. Evolved into Model 32.

LB-17   Twin-engine medium bomber design, 20.1.39. Wright R-3350 turbo engines, gross weight 41,629lb (18,883kg), four 600lb (272kg) bombs, five machine guns, nine crew. Design prepared as comparison to four-engine LB-16 with very similar body and same offensive and defensive loads and crew.

LB-19   Twin-engine attack bomber to Specification C-103A, 3.39.

LB-20   Twin-engine attack bomber with twin-booms to C-103A, 4.39.

LB-22   Twin-engine bomber to Specification C-213, 7.5.39. Variant of Model 32/XB-24 fitted with two engines.

LB-24   Twin-engine attack bomber apparently submitted to Air Corps requirements, 8.2.39 and 6.39. Believed to be C-213 competition resulting in Martin B-26 and North American B-25.

LB-25   Four-engine heavy bomber to XC-218 and R40-B, 6.5.40. Evolved into Model 33.

LB-26   Lighter version of LB-24, drawing dated 1.2.40.

LB-27   Export version of LB-19, 9.2.40.

LB-28   Very similar to LB-27 but longer and with different nose arrangement, 2.40. Two Wright R-3350 engines, gross weight 24,443lb (11,087kg).

LB-29   Twin-engine version of XB-24 Liberator produced for export, 7.3.40. Two Wright R-3350 engines but rest of airframe same as XB-24. Estimated top speed 361mph (581km/h), gross weight 35,353lb (16,036kg).

Model 32   Four-engine bomber that became B-24 and PB4Y-1 Liberator, first flown 29.12.39. Addition of extra guns to one B-24D airframe as 'escort bomber' in 1943 resulted in designation XB-41.

Model 33   Became B-32 Dominator, first flown 7.9.42. Version with twin engines proposed 11.9.42, turboprop version studied 10.44, neither built.

Model 35   Several designs for intercontinental heavy bomber, 1940 onwards.

Model 36   Winner of 1941 competition against Douglas and Boeing, became B-36 Peacemaker, first flown 8.8.46.

Model 100   Four-engine maritime patrol bomber based on B-24 that became PB4Y-2 Privateer, first flown 20.9.43. Development of B-24 with longer fuselage and single fin. Model 100 designation also covered PB4Y-1 version of B-24.

Model 38   Twin-engine B-24 long-range patrol aircraft offered to USN as XP5Y-1, 10.42.

Large flying wing bomber   Very large bomber design study prepared as comparison to B-36 and Northrop B-35, early 1942. Six P&W R-4360 Wasp Major engines, 10,000lb (4,536kg) bomb load, top speed 394mph (634km/h).

TBY   Vought Sea Wolf torpedo bomber design as produced by Convair at new facility in Allentown, Pennsylvania.

Flying boats   General series of studies for two- and four-engine seaplanes and flying boats, 1943.

Flying wing patrol bomber Series of twin-engine studies for Navy as P5Y-1, begun 8.43 and revised up until 4.44. Conventional twin-engine tailed design also produced for comparison 10.43.

Flying wing bomber Scaled-up four-engine development of twin-engine type produced for Army, 8.43.

Attack aircraft Twin-engine four-seat light attack design, 6.4.43 onwards. Two 3,250hp (2,424kW) P&W R-4360, span 72ft 0in (21.95m), length 66ft 6in (20.27m), wing area 650sq ft (60.45sq m), gross weight 35,000lb (15,876kg), dorsal and tail turrets each with two 0.50in (12.70mm) machine guns, one flexible gun under rear fuselage, four fixed in wing and option for six more in nose (alternative nose weapons, one 75mm or three 37mm cannon). Bomb load 4,000lb (1,814kg), top speed 397mph (639km/h). Brochure dated 7.43 but not ordered.

Model 102 Project to USAAF requirements for escort fighter, 1943. Design selected and flown as XP-81 prototype 11.2.45. No production.

Flying boats/ seaplanes Series of three general studies of seaplanes and flying boats made 12.44 onwards. Introduced mixed jet/piston powerplants (compound propulsion – two R-4360 piston and TG-180 jets) and covered flying boat configuration, twin-float seaplane and single-float with crew and equipment inside float; all 85,000lb (38,556kg) weight. None built.

Heavy bomber design Four turboprop engines, 17.3.45. Gross weight 175,000lb (79,380kg).

Jet flying boat All-jet powerplant seaplane study, 5.45. Weight 90,000lb (40,824kg).

Model 117 Four-engine patrol bomber flying boat, 1.45, weight c105,000lb (47,628kg). Versions with all-piston and all-turboprop powerplants drawn. Led to P5Y programme.

CURTISS-WRIGHT

This was one of the most famous of piston fighter aircraft designers and manufacturers with a string of designs produced in the lead-up to and during the war. Separate branches of the company also produced engines (Wright) and propellers, the aircraft themselves usually being labelled Curtiss products. First made public in 1916, during the 1940s the company failed to move much beyond the basic P-40 airframe and became rather left behind by competing designs. The Curtiss-Wright Aviation Division was closed in 1951 having principally been unable to prepare itself for modern developments in aircraft design, and after the failure of the F-87 jet fighter programme the entire Aeroplane Division was shut down and its assets sold to North American Aviation. The main airframe manufacturing facility was at Buffalo in New York, but there were other major manufacturing factories at Columbus, Ohio, St Louis, Missouri, and Louisville, Kentucky. In 1937 the principal Curtiss fighter was the Model 75/P-36 Hawk, first flown on 15 May 1935. A version of the P-36 fitted with an in-line engine was flown as the XP-37 on 20 April 1937, while another with a P&W R-1830 engine flew as the XP-42 in 1939. A new separate series of '20s' Curtiss model or design numbers was introduced in about 1939.

Model 77 SB2C Helldiver, first flown 18.12.40. USAAF version known as A-25.

Model 78 Single-seat midwing pursuit proposal, c1936/37.

Model 80 Interceptor fighter proposal with extension shaft, c1937.

Model 80A Interceptor fighter proposal, c1937.

Model 81 XP-40 Tomahawk for USAAF, first flown 14.10.38.

Model 83 Army attack bomber proposals to CP 38-385, 1938. Model 83A dated 25.10.38.

Model 84 Helldiver SB2C production.

Model 21 CW-21 prototype interceptor, first flown 22.8.38.

P-241 Light bomber project to C-104, 15.1.39.

P-244 Study to define ideal fighter, 1939. Model 244-01 approximately early 1940 had noseplanes, swept wings and tip fins – span 35ft 0in (10.67m), length 24ft 11in (7.60m).

P-247 Single-engine interceptor fighter based on CW-21, 4.40.

CP-40-1 & 2 Two designs submitted to Specification XC-622 (R40-C), 3.40.

P-248 Three designs submitted to Specification XC-622 (R40-C), 3.40. Development of CW-21.

P-249 Three designs submitted to Specification XC-622 (R40-C), 3.40. Evolution of P-244-01.

P-250 Single-engine interceptor fighter based on CW-21, 4.40. Similar to P-247 but different engine.

P-259 Twin-engine fighter, c1940/41.

P-264 Twin-engine fighter, c1941.

Model 86 XP-46A prototype first flown, 15.2.41.

Model 87 P-40D and later variants of Kittyhawk/Warhawk, first flown 22.5.41.

Model 88 Planned XP-53 prototype that led to Models 90 and 95 (XP-60 series), mid-1940.

Model 90 XP-60 fighter prototype, first flown 18.9.41. Sometimes called 'Hawk 90'. Several prototypes with different engines. Model 90B became XP-60D.

Model 24 (Became CW-24, originally P-249C) XP-55 Ascender prototype, first flown 13.7.43.

CW-24B Scale model test aircraft for XP-55 (below), first flown 2.12.41.

Model 26 (CW-26) Twin-engine heavy escort fighter project ordered 1941 as XP-71. Abandoned 1943. Described as 'outgrowth of P-259 and P-264' projects.

Model 91 XP-62 prototype, first flown 21.7.43.

Model 92 Originally XSB2C-2 Helldiver but reassigned to jet-powered XA-43 attack aircraft of 1944.

Model 93 Helldiver development scout bomber proposal with R-3350 to 2.41 design competition. Ordered as XSB3C-1 but contract terminated before prototypes complete.

Navy fighter Proposals for single-engine VF fighter with single Wasp Major powerplant, 3.43. Two known but possibly three in all.

Model 94A   XF14C Navy prototype fighter begun mid-1941. Not flown in original XF14C-1 form, but with different powerplant second prototype flown 7.44 as XF14C-2. No production.

P-276   Attack dive bomber, 26.10.42. Single-seat development of A-25 with changes including R-3350 engine replacing R-2600, removal of rear cockpit and gun turret, fixed guns increased to two 37mm and six 0.50in (12.70mm), provision in fuselage bomb bay for single 2,000lb (907kg) as alternative to one 1,000lb (454kg), two 500lb (227kg) or one torpedo, two 500lb (227kg) bombs in wing racks, tail length increased with proportional reduction in horizontal tail area. Span 49ft 8.6in (15.15m), length 42ft 3in (12.88m), wing area 422sq ft (39.25sq m), design gross weight 15,854lb (7,191kg). Possibly formed beginning of XA-40 programme.

P-279   Attack dive bomber, 18.1.43. Same as P-276 except R-2800 instead of A-25's R-2600, and four or six 0.50in (12.70mm) machine guns. One 37mm in each centre wing panel, two or three 0.50in (12.70mm) in each outer wing panel. Bombs, dimensions and tail modifications unchanged from P-276. Gross weight with guns only 17,533lb (7,953kg). Estimated 315mph (507km/h) at sea level, 335mph (539km/h) at 18,500ft (5,639m), service ceiling 29,500ft (8,992m), maximum range 1,310 miles (2,108km).

P-509 VSB   Navy bomber and torpedo bomber proposals, 16.8.44 and 6.11.44.

Model 95   Covered XP-60A/B/C/E variants.

Model 96   Revised proposals of 6.42 for torpedo bomber (date of original studies unknown but post-2.42) ordered as XBTC prototypes, first flight 20.1.45. No production.

XA-40   Dive bomber project that did not go beyond prototype stage, 1942/43.

Model 98   Experimental XBT2C torpedo bomber. Prototype first flown 7.8.45.

Model 99   XF15C mixed powerplant fighter prototype, first flown 27.2.45.

DOUGLAS

Formed in 1921, Douglas designed most categories of aircraft (although it seems to have forayed rarely into fighter design until after the war), and had two centres of design that used separate sets of project numbers (the company had no central system of allocation). The three-digit series listed here originated from its El Segundo, Long Beach, facility, while a '1,000' series was applied to products from its headquarters at Santa Monica (although none of the latter are available for the Second World War, and it is possible that this was not introduced until around 1945). At the end of the war the Douglas facilities embraced sites at Santa Monica, El Segundo and Torrence, all in California, Tulsa and Midwest City in Oklahoma, and Chicago in Illinois. The reason why there are overlapping 3xx, 4xx and 5xx numbers is unknown.

D-167   Design that became XB-19 prototype, first flown 27.6.41.

Model 7   Douglas Model 7A project of 1936 for light twin-engine bomber, not ordered. Revised Model 7B submitted to Air Corps requirement in competition with Martin 167F, North American NA-40 and Stearman X-100. First flew 26.10.38 and further developed into A-20.

DB-10   Attack bomber project to Specification 98-102, 11.8.38.

Model 9   Flying wing bomber proposal for Army Air Corps, 5.10.38.

VSB   SBD Dauntless scout dive bomber, first flown 1.5.40.

D-312   XP-48 fighter project. Prototype ordered 1939 but not flown. D-312A had pusher propeller.

D-320   Twin-engine bomber project that became B-23 Dragon, first flown 27.7.39.

D-332   Four-engine bomber project studies to XC-218 and R40-B, c3.40. Became XB-31.

VTB   Torpedo-bomber proposal to SD-114-6, c8.39. Lost competition to Grumman Avenger and Vought Sea Wolf.

D-403   Light bomber for USAAC, 10.2.41. Became A-20C Havoc, first flown 23.1.39.

D-409   Detailed specification for USAAC light bomber, 17.4.41. DB-7B/A-20C Havoc.

D-412   Long-range bomber modification of DC-4 airliner, 22.4.41.

D-413   General specification for design study of long-range supercharged bombardment aircraft, 12.5.41.

D-415   Detailed specification for long-range bomber and transport aircraft similar to DS-413, 11.6.41.

D-416   Long-range high-altitude heavy bomber design for USAAC, 27.6.41.

D-423   Long-range high-altitude bomber for USAAC, 31.10.41. Part of B-36 competition.

D-424   Pursuit aircraft variant of A-20 bomber, 27.10.41. Became P-70.

D-427   USAAC attack bomber, 22.1.42. A-20C Havoc.

D-459   Pusher attack bomber, 7.4.43. Also appears in list as Model 740 and became XB-42 Mixmaster prototype, first flown 6.5.44.

BELOW Only one example of the Douglas XB-19 was built.

D-460	A-20H Havoc, 15.4.43.
D-488	A-26D Invader attack bomber, 4.12.44.
SS-501	Attack bomber seaplane project, 8.12.38.
D-503	Two-engine attack bomber, 10.1.39.
D-507	Two-engine attack bomber (DB-7A above), 7.3.39.
D-508	Two-engine attack bomber (DB-7B), 7.3.39.
D-509	Two-engine attack bomber (DB-7C), 7.3.39.
D-513	Single-engine attack aircraft with Allison power unit, 3.1.39.
D-514	Single-engine attack aircraft with P&W R-1830 power unit, 3.1.39.
D-515	Single-engine attack aircraft with Wright R-1820 power unit, 3.1.39.
D-517	Proposal for two-seat scout bomber to 2.41 design competition. Ordered as XSB2D-1 Destroyer, first flown 8.4.43. Turned into single-seat XBTD-1, flown 5.3.44, but limited production run.
D-519	Single-engine attack aircraft, 10.2.39. Revised version of Northrop A-17-A.
TS-525	Attack bomber similar to 7-B, 20.1.39.
D-527	Revised version of TS-525 (DB-7), 1.3.39.
D-528	Two-engine attack bomber (DB-7D), 27.3.39.
D-529	Two-engine attack bomber (DB-7E), 27.3.39.
D-530	Two-engine attack bomber (DB-7F), 7.4.39.
D-531	Two-engine attack bomber (DB-7G), 7.4.39.
D-532	Two-engine attack bomber (DB-7H), 19.4.39.
TS-533	'Type Spec' attack bomber with P&W R-1830, 1939.
TS-534	'Type Spec' attack bomber with Wright R-1820F, 1939.
SS-536	DB-7 bomber variant, 22.6.39.
D-538	USAAF light bombardment aircraft, 26.12.40.
D-539	USAAF light bombardment aircraft, 16.6.41. Both D-538 and D-539 mark start of programme for XA-26 Invader, first flown 10.7.42.
Model 423(?)	Transcontinental bomber project in competition with Consolidated B-36, 4.41 onwards. B-36 endorsed 10.41 and Douglas project not ordered.
D-540	Navy dive bomber, 19.9.41. Became XSB2D-1 prototype after D-517.
D-541	XA-26A night fighter, 30.10.41. First flight of only example 27.1.43.
D-542	XA-26B modified light bomber, 1.12.41.
D-543	A-26B Invader production light bomber, 23.12.41.
D-544	Several designs for torpedo bomber, 30.3.42 onwards. One produced as XTB2D-1 Skypirate prototype (previously Devastator II), first flown 13.3.45. Only two examples built.
D-545	Also allocated to TB2D-1, 5.42.
D-546	Dive bomber. SBD-5 version of Dauntless, 1.6.42.
D-547	Dive bomber. SBD-4 version of Dauntless, 6.42.
D-548	TB2D-1, 19.8.42. Superseded D-545.
D-549	SB2D-1 version, 15.11.42.
D-550	TB2D-1, 12.42. Superseded D-548.
D-551	Dive bomber. SBD-5 version of Dauntless, 5.43.
D-552	A-24B 'Banshee' USAAF version of Dauntless, 15.5.43.
D-553	Dive bomber. SBD-6 version of Dauntless, 21.5.43.
D-554	Dive bomber. SBD-5 version of Dauntless, 27.5.43.
D-555	BTD-1 dive bomber-torpedo, 27.9.43.
D-556	XBT2D-1 project ordered 7.44. Prototype first flew 18.3.45 and became AD-1 Skyraider attack aircraft.
DS-557/D-557	BT3D-1 dive and torpedo bomber projects, 24.1.45 onwards. DS-557 eventually gave way to Model D-557A with twin nacelles, D-557B with twin fuselage engines and D-557C with Westinghouse engine. Resulted in XA2D-1 Skyshark prototypes, first flown 26.5.50. No production.
D-559	BT2D-1 production, 3.5.45. Covered twenty-sixth and subsequent airframes.

FAIRCHILD

The Fairchild Aviation Corporation at Hagerstown in Maryland was established in 1924 at Farmingdale and East Farmingdale in New York as a manufacturer of civil aircraft, but by the Second World War the company was also building trainers for the Army Air Force. On occasion it offered proposals for combat aircraft, although none were ever ordered or built.

M-85	Twin-engine fighter project preliminary design, 16.5.44.

GENERAL MOTORS/FISHER

The Fisher Body Division of the General Motors Corporation was responsible for a quite unique fighter design that was ordered in prototype form. General Motors also manufactured large numbers of aircraft developed by other companies.

XP-75 Eagle	Fighter design utilising components used by other types (e.g. P-51 outer wings). Prototype first flew 17.11.43. Prototype for much-modified XP-75A first flew 15.9.44. Small number of P-75As also built.

GOODYEAR

The Goodyear Aircraft Corporation was created by Goodyear in 1939 at Akron in Ohio to handle US military contracts, and during the Second World War the company built a large number of Vought F4U Corsairs under the designation FG-1. Another manufacturing facility was established at Phoenix in Arizona. The company also produced a modified version of the Corsair with a P&W R-4360 engine; called the F2G-1 'Super Corsair', it first flew on 15 July 1945. Some jet fighter designs were produced by the company after the war, but it is currently unknown if brand new designs for military types were produced during the conflict itself.

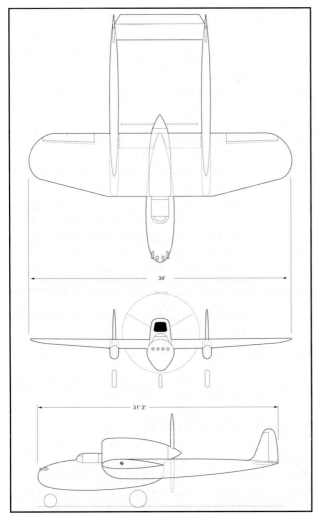

ABOVE Grumman Model 29 (17.12.37). *Tommy Thomason*

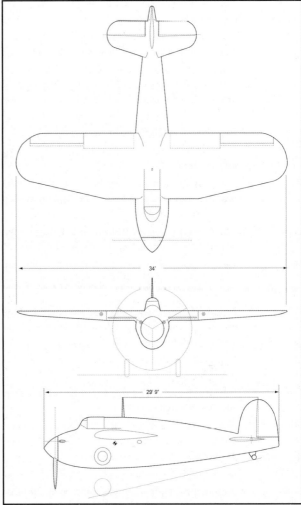

ABOVE Grumman Model 30 (16.12.37). *Tommy Thomason*

GRUMMAN

Founded in 1929 by Leroy Grumman, this company was a major aircraft manufacturer and was always heavily involved in naval aircraft, both with fighters and attack aircraft. It was based at Bethpage on Long Island, New York. The design of its F4F fighter began before the period embraced by this book.

G-18   XF4F-2 Wildcat fighter, first flown 2.9.37.

G-25   High-altitude single-seat Navy fighter with twin Allison engines, 5.37. Not built.

G-29   Twin-boom pusher monoplane two-seat fighter for Navy with Allison V-1710 engine, 17.12.37. Span 34ft 0in (10.36m), length 31ft 3in (9.525m), wing area 237sq ft (22.04sq m), gross weight 5,854lb (2,655kg), fuel capacity 110 gallons (416 litres).

G-30   Tractor monoplane two-seat fighter for Navy with Allison V-1710 engine, 16.12.37. Span 34ft 0in (10.36m), length 29ft 9in (9.07m).

G-33   Proposed XF4F-2 modified with R-2600 engine, 2.38.

G-34   Twin-engine fighter design of 3.38 that became XF5F-1 Skyrocket prototype, first flown 1.4.40. Another project called SP-1 may have been part of research.

G-35   Single-engine fighter with Wright R-2600 power unit, 3.38. Appears to have been early study to put bigger engine, R-2600, into F4F Wildcat; ultimately resulted in F6F.

G-36   XF4F with two-stage R-1830 engine, 5.38.

G-40   XTBF-1 Avenger prototype torpedo bomber, first flown 7.8.41. Originally designed to SD-114-6, c5.39.

G-41   XF5F-1 modified for USAAF with conventional undercarriage, 6.39.

G-43   XF4F-2 for USAAF, 7.39.

G-45   Series of designs showing modified forms of XF5F-1 for USAAF, 9.39.

G-46   XP-50 development of XF5F-1 with tricycle landing gear, 10.39. First flown 18.2.41.

G-49	Proposal for export fighter powered by two R-2600 engines, 2.40.
G-50	Single-seat single-engine naval fighter, 9.40. Became XF6F-1 Hellcat prototype, first flown 26.6.42.
G-51	Twin-engine naval fighter submitted to SD-112-18, 1.41. Won competition and became XF7F-1 Tigercat prototype first flown 2.11.43. Parallel XP-65 version for USAAF abandoned 1.42.
G-53	F4F fitted with full-span Duplex flaps, 1943.
G-54	Proposal to fit F6F with laminar flow wing having greater area, 2.42.
G-55	Twin-engine torpedo bomber for Navy, 6.42 onwards. Ordered as XTB2F-1 but only mock-up built. Abandoned 6.44.
G-56	TBF Avenger proposal fitted with R-2800 engine and Martin CE-250 dorsal turret, 2.43. Not built.
G-57	Design study for Navy fighter with combined powerplant of single R-2800 piston and one jet engine, 7.43.
G-58	Lightweight single-seat Navy fighter study, 8.43. First brochure dated 20.9.43 and design ordered as XF8F-1 Bearcat. Prototype first flew 31.8.44.
G-59	Proposed modified F6F with two-speed R-4360 power unit, 8.43.
G-60	Proposed modified F6F with two-stage supercharger and R-4360 engine, 8.43.
G-61	Proposed F6F development with auxiliary General Electric jet engine supplementing normal piston power unit, 8.43.
G-62	Design study for small jet fighter, 8.43.
G-66	Proposed twin-engine single-seat torpedo bomber development of F7F called XTSF-1, 12.6.44. Revised Model 66A variant of 11.7.44 accepted for prototype construction, but abandoned 12.44.
G-67	F7F-2 modification with I-20 turbojet in rear of each engine nacelle, 8.6.44.
G-68	Navy fighter proposal powered by TG-100 propeller turbine (turboprop), 6.44.
G-69	Proposed single-seat attack aircraft derivative of F6F powered by one R-2800-22, 7.44.
G-70	Torpedo bomber project of 8.44 that became XTB3F-1 prototype, first flown 23.12.46. Entered service as AF Guardian.
G-71	Jet fighter project, 11.44.

HALL ALUMINIUM

During the 1930s the Hall Aluminium Aircraft Corporation, with facilities at Bristol, Pennsylvania, and Buffalo, New York, produced several aircraft designs. The XPTBH-2 flying boat torpedo bomber prototype was built at Bristol and flown in 1937, but did not progress further. Hall Aluminium had in earlier years flown biplane designs in several categories.

VTB	Unknown torpedo bomber proposal to SD-114-6, c8.39. Lost competition to Grumman Avenger and Vought Sea Wolf.

HUGHES

Founded at Glendale in California in 1932 by Howard Hughes, during the Second World War the Hughes Aircraft Company would build several prototype aeroplanes that flew from Hughes Airport near Westchester and Los Angeles. The team also proposed other designs, but the factory was mostly occupied with building other companies' aircraft. Post-war Hughes moved on to helicopters, missiles and electronics.

Fighter	Single-engine fighter possibly proposed against X-609, 1937. Possibly designated H-1.
Fighter	Twin-engine fighter proposed against X-608, 1937. Possibly designated H-2.
D-2	Twin-engine fighter-bomber, early 1939 onwards. First flight 20.6.43. Very briefly designated XP-73 or XP-74 (references refer to both) but changed to XA-37.
D-3	Project for airframe that could be adapted as required into bomber convoy-protector, fighter, interceptor or bomber convoy-destroyer, 1941.
D-4	Light interceptor project, 1941/42. Response to idea first proposed by Air Corps Material Division, 11.41, and believed to be in Bell XP-77 class.
D-5	Twin-engine bomber and bomber escort project development of D-2, 1942.
XF-11	High-speed reconnaissance aircraft developed from D-2, first flown 7.7.46. No production.

KAISER-FLEETWINGS

Fleetwings at Bristol, Pennsylvania, became Kaiser-Fleetwings in 1943 after its acquisition by industrialist Henry J. Kaiser. It was responsible for a small number of attack aircraft designs.

H-60	Attack aircraft design of 1942 that became XA-39, but did not proceed beyond mock-up stage.
XBTK-1	Dive and torpedo bomber prototype, first flown 12.4.45.
Model 46	Navy dive bomber proposals, c1.44. Models 46, 46A and 46B variants with mixed piston/jet powerplant. None built. Model 46 used one P&W R-1830 and 1,700lb (7.55kN) jet unit, span 43ft 0in (13.11m), wing area 320sq ft (29.76sq m), 320 gallons (1,211 litres) fuel for piston, 100 gallons (379 litres) for jet, gross weight 12,800lb (5,806kg), maximum speed 393mph (632km/h) at sea level, rate of climb 4,460ft/min (1,359m/min) at sea level, range 1,930 miles (3,105km). Forward section of fuselage in Alclad and aft conical section in stainless steel. Model 46A had one R-2800 piston and Westinghouse jet, wing area 400sq ft (37.20sq m), 440 gallons (1,666 litres) fuel and two 55-gallon (208-litre) auxiliary tanks, two 0.60in (15.24mm) machine guns, with 1,000lb (454kg) bomb, gross weight 16,410lb (7,444kg), maximum speed at full load using jet 381mph (613km/h). Model 46B appears same as 46A except wing area 580sq ft (53.94sq m), fuel 530 gallons (2,006 litres), gross weight with two 1,000lb (454kg) bombs 21,968lb (9,965kg).
Model 47	Navy multi-engine dive bomber proposal, 2.44. Twin-piston engines in wing nacelles with turbojets in rear of each nacelle. Not built.

LOCKHEED

Formed in 1912, and relocating to Burbank in California in 1928, Lockheed diversified into fighters and reconnaissance aircraft, civil and military airliners, transports and patrol aircraft. The series below covers the Temporary Design Designations allocated by Lockheed to the preliminary design effort made towards a new requirement or idea, and each number could embrace a number of layouts. If a project was committed to detail drawings or funding for hardware it would receive a Basic Model number (highlighted where applicable in the text with a couple of additions at the end).

Model 14	Twin-engine attack aircraft of 1937 that became the Hudson, first flown 10.12.38. Entered USAAF service as A-28 and A-29.
Model 22	Twin-engine fighter to Specification X-608, 1937. Became P-38 Lightning, first flown 27.1.39.
L-100	Derivative of Hudson I, 1939.
L-101	Version of Hudson proposed for export, 1939.
L-102	P-38 Lightning I for the UK, 1939. Not built.
L-103	Project that subsequently became **Model 32**. After being terminated, project was resurrected as L-108, then assigned **Model 32**. Then as Vega **Model 37** Ventura patrol bomber it first flew 31.7.40. Developed into B-34 Lexington, B-37, PV-1 Ventura and PV-2 Harpoon.
L-106	Pursuit aircraft that eventually became **Model 23** XP-49, first flown 14.11.42.
L-107	Hudson derivative for British Air Ministry.
L-108	Update of L-103 above.
Model 29A	Proposed twin-engine attack bomber, c1939/40.
Model 30	Proposed twin-engine attack bomber with forward canard trimmers and swept wing, 1939. Two turbo-supercharged Allison XV-3420s with pusher propellers, rear turret. Estimated top speed 430mph (692km/h) at height.
L-109	Five-seat long-range bomber derivative of Hudson referred to as Model EB-14, 1940. Aircraft not designed.
L-111	P-38 derivative for France, 1940.
L-114	Derivative of Hudson I, 1940.
L-116	Developed into Ventura I.
L-117	Four-engine bomber project to XC-218 and R40-B, c3.40. Labelled **Model 51** and designated XB-30 by Air Corps but not built, Boeing B-29 being produced instead.
L-118	Later assigned **Model 52** designation, this single-seat fighter pursuit project was studied in some depth but not built, c1940. No other information appears to have survived.
L-121	Fighter project eventually built as **Model 20** XP-58 Chain Lightning prototype, first flown 6.6.44.
L-124	High-altitude XP-38A.
L-129	Series of design studies for long-range bombers, mid-1941.
L-130	Five versions of design for long-range bomber, 1941.
L-131	Two-seat single-Tornado engine-powered fighter, 1941. Not built.
L-133	Lockheed's initial studies into producing jet fighter, early 1942. None built.
L-134	Redesign of XP-58, 1942. Alternative designs also considered.
L-137	Twin-engine bomber design produced against Army Air Corps request, approximately late 1942.
L-140	Jet fighter project that eventually became XP-80 Shooting Star prototype, first flown 8.1.44.
L-141	Refined jet fighter that entered production as P-80A.

MARTIN

The Glenn L. Martin Company was founded in 1912 at Santa Ana in California. A second incarnation appeared at Cleveland Ohio in 1917 and this time it survived, moving to Middle River near Baltimore in Maryland in 1929. In general Martin was a producer of large and medium-size bomber and patrol aircraft, including flying boats, for the USAAF and the Navy. However, several studies for light bombers/attack aircraft and fighters also appear in the list.

Model 160	Long-range flying boat patrol aircraft for Navy, 1936/early 1937.
Model 161	Twin-engine high-speed and long-range bombers for Army, several designs 1936 to 7.37.
Model 162	Twin-engine flying boat that became PBM Mariner, first flown 18.2.39.
Model 164	Four-engine bomber, 10.37. Three designs produced: conventional tractor type with 825hp (615kW) P&W R-1535s, version with 1,200hp (895kW) Allison V-1710 with two wing nacelles and two engines in each (one driving tractor, the other pusher propellers), and twin-boom type with V-1710s in wing driving four pusher propellers.
Model 167	Twin-engine experimental attack bomber that became XA-22 Maryland, first flown 13.3.39. Also submitted to CP 38-385 and Specification 98-102. Model 167A submitted to CP 39-460 and Specification C-103A.
Model 168	High-speed single-seat fighter project for Navy, 1938.
Model 169	Twin-engine heavy attack bomber, 18.4.38. Weight 18,000lb (8,165kg).
Model 170	Four-engine long-range flying boat bomber (ex-Model 160B) covered by Specification. SD-116-19. Became XPB2M-1 Mars, first flown 23.6.42. Production aeroplanes built as JRM Mars transports.
Model 171	High-speed long-range patrol flying boat bomber, 5/38. Very large span wing, six engines with four tractors in nacelles in wing leading edges and two pushers in trailing edge nacelles, twin fins, nose, dorsal and tail turrets.
Model 172	Export bomber based on XA-22, 9.38.
Model 174	Attack bomber for USAAF based on Maryland, 10.38. Submitted 25.10.38 to C-104.

Model 175   Attack bomber for USAAF based on Maryland, 10.38. Submitted 25.10.38 to C-103.

Model 176   Attack bomber for USAAF based on Maryland and shown with blended wing, 12.38. Designed against Specification C-104 but appears not to have been submitted.

Model 177   Light attack bomber for USAAF, 4.39. Submitted to CP 39-460 and Specification C-103A 17.4.39. Model 179A of same date similar but smaller.

Model 178   Studies for twin-engine light bomber. Work submitted against CP 39-640, 5.7.39.

Model 179   Twin-engine high-speed medium bomber for USAAF, 1.7.39. Became B-26 Marauder, first flown 25.11.40.

Model 180   Series of designs for twin-engine long-range flying boat patrol bomber to SD-116-23, 9.39 onwards.

Model 181   Twin-engine long-range flying boat patrol bomber, part of SD-116-23 studies, 11.39.

Model 182   Twin-engine high-altitude medium bomber ordered as XB-27 under XC-21 but not built, 1939.

Model 183   Series of designs for twin-engine long-range flying boat patrol bomber, also to SD-116-23, 11.39 onwards.

Model 187   Reconnaissance bomber development of Maryland for Britain and France that became XA-23 Baltimore, first flown 14.6.41. Production machines designated A-30 to permit supply under Lend-Lease Act.

Model 189   Twin-engine high-altitude bomber, 10.40 onwards. Believed ordered as XB-33 but not built. Canard version also drawn.

Model 190   Four-engine high-altitude bomber, 4.41 onwards. Two prototypes ordered with XB-33 designation reassigned (possibly as XB-33A) but not completed. Planned production abandoned.

Model 191   Twin-engine medium bomber development of B-26, 1941. Very similar to B-26 but tapered wings had greater span. Span 87ft 6in (26.67m), overall length 63ft 8.5in (19.42m).

Model 192   Studies for twin-engine torpedo bomber, 1942. Several different designs including flying-wing Model 192-5.

Model 194   Four-engine 'Long Ranger' heavy bomber, 12.42. Swept and straight-winged version. Weight 160,000lb (72,576kg). Not built.

Model 195   Twin 3,000hp (2,237kW) Wasp Major high-performance medium bomber, late 1942/early 1943. One version carried one 75mm cannon in nose, another two 37mm, and there were two 0.50in (12.70mm) machine guns in each wing root. Bomb load 4,000lb (1,814kg).

Model 196   Twin-engine (Wasp) multi-role medium bomber, 16.12.42.

Model 197   Twin-engine (Wasp Major) medium bomber, 1943. Gross weight 43,500lb (19,732kg), nose, deck and tail turrets.

Model 198   Twin-engine (Wasp Major) high-speed patrol bomber, 1943.

Model 201   Twin-engine high-speed attack aircraft, 5.43 onwards.

Model 204   High-performance low-altitude bomber, 1943. Gross weight 34,500lb (15,649kg).

Model 205   Designation given to production of Northrop B-35 flying wing intercontinental bomber. Four Allison V-3420s, gross weight 200,000lb (90,720kg).

Model 206   Twin-engine patrol bomber landplane for Navy, c1943. Two Wasp Major engines, 79,000lb (35,834kg) weight.

Model 207   Twin-engine 'Convoy Fighter' project with both units in fuselage. Several versions, 8.43.

Model 208   Allocated to Boeing PBB-1 Sea Ranger twin-engine patrol bomber, 1943.

Model 209   Four-engine (Allison V-3420) long-range bomber, c1943.

Model 210   Carrier-based attack aircraft and dive bomber studies of mid-1943 onwards that became BTM-1/AM-1 Mauler, first flown 26.8.44.

Model 211   Land-based patrol bomber for Navy, 11.43. Included flying wing design.

Model 212   Twin-engine (Wasp Major) long-range patrol boat bomber, 1943. Gross weight 80,000lb (36,288kg).

Model 217   Flying wing pursuit fighter project, 1944. One 19BJP unit, gross weight 3,500lb (1,588kg). Inactive 8.8.44.

Model 219   Land-based long-range patrol aircraft that became P4M Mercator. Prototype XP4M-1 first flew 20.9.46.

McDONNELL

McDonnell was a new company established at St Louis in June 1939 by James Smith McDonnell, and it was to become a specialist in fighter design, both for the Air Force and Navy. However, its strong reputation really only came together after the conflict was over.

Model 1   Twin-engine pusher fighter for USAAF, 11.39. Four variants submitted to Specification XC-622 (R40-C), 3.40.

Model 2   Twin Rolls-Royce attack aircraft, 1939/40. As Model 2A developed into XP-67 'Moonbat' pursuit aircraft, first flown 6.1.44. No production. Mixed-powerplant XP-67E also drawn.

Model 3   Twin-engine interceptor pusher fighter, c1940. Model 3A turbo-supercharged to permit altitudes of 25,000ft (7,620m), Model 3B turbo-supercharged to go to 33,000ft (10,058m).

Model 4   Single-engine turbo-supercharged fighter, 1940.

Model 5   Single-engine interceptor pusher, 1940.

Model 6   Single Allison-engine pusher fighter for Navy, 2.41. Entered in SD-112-18 competition (F7F).

Model 7   Fighter for Navy with P&W R-2800 tractor engine, 2.41. SD-112-18 competition.

Model 8   Single engine P&W R-2800 pusher engine fighter for Navy, 2.41. SD-112-18 competition.

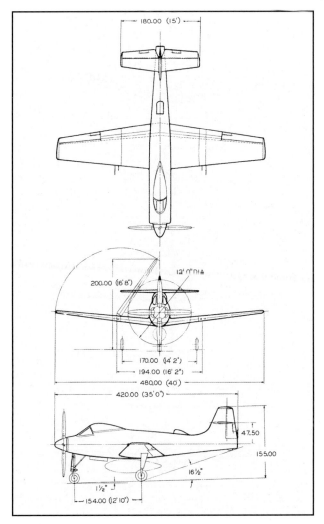

ABOVE McDonnell Model 17A (2.9.44). *Tommy Thomason*

Model 10   Single-engine single-seat Class VF fighter for Navy, 1.11.42. One Wright R-2000 engine, four-blade 12ft 2in (3.71m)-diameter prop. Span 39ft 6in (12.04m), wing area 260sq ft (24.18sq m). Model 10B-1 version with two-stage turbo: gross weight 8,320lb (3,774kg), overload 9,382lb (4,256kg), normal fuel 125 gallons (473 litres), overload 245 gallons (927 litres), maximum speed 418mph (673km/h) at 30,000ft (9,144m), service ceiling 39,800ft (12,131m), sea level rate of climb 3,470ft/min (1,058m/min). Model 10C-1 variant had two-stage two-speed engine, Model 10D-1 had single-stage two-speed, both slightly lighter.

Model 11   Jet fighter design that eventually became FH-1 Phantom, first flown 26.1.45.

Model 12   Long-range twin-engine pursuit fighter designs, 1942/43. Long series of designs under this number.

Model 16   Proposed P-67D version of Moonbat, c1944. P-67E proposal called Model 16A.

Model 17   Navy fighter with single 2,430hp (1,812kW) TG-100 turboprop engine and tapered straight wing, 2.9.44. Model 17A had extension shaft, Model 17B did not. Exhaust at rear of fuselage. Model 17A: four-blade propeller of 12ft 0in (3.66m) diameter, span 40ft 0in (12.19m), folded span 16ft 2in (4.93m), length 35ft 0in (10.67m), wing area 250sq ft (23.25sq m), normal gross weight 10,253lb (4,651kg), internal fuel 250 gallons (946 litres), external fuel 200 gallons (757 litres), top speed 455mph (732km/h) at sea level, 505mph (813km/h) at 25,000ft (7,620m), sea level rate of climb 4,800ft/min (1,463m/min), service ceiling c44,000ft (13,411m).

Model 18   Various designs for Army fighter with different combined powerplants, 1944. Model 18J with R-2800-C piston and I-40 jet proposed to Navy 13.9.44.

Model 19   Fighter for Army with Allison compound and Westinghouse 18XB powerplant, c1944.

Model 20   Army fighter with two TG-100 engines and I-40 jet, c1945.

Model 21   Army fighter with two TG-100 engines with fuel injection, c1945.

Model 22   Navy fighter with R2800-C and Westinghouse 24C jet, c1945.

NAVAL AIRCRAFT FACTORY

Established at Philadelphia in 1918, the Naval Aircraft Factory provided the US Navy with its own manufacturing and test organisation, but it also built other companies' aeroplanes for evaluation purposes. Aircraft production came to a close in early 1945 and its testing role was passed to the new Naval Air Test Center at Patuxent River. As part of its wartime work the NAF submitted two designs to the F7F Navy fighter competition.

Model A   Fighter design submitted to SD-112-18, c1.41.

Model B   Fighter design submitted to SD-112-18, c1.41.

Scout Bomber Proposal for scout bomber to 2.41 design competition.

NORTH AMERICAN

North American was formed in 1928 and later moved to Inglewood in southern California after having decided to concentrate on training aircraft. However, the P-51 Mustang would establish North American as a world leader in fighter design, by which time the company had also made its mark in the field of light bombers. During the war it would open manufacturing facilities at Columbus (Ohio), Dallas (Texas) and Kansas City (Kansas). North American project numbers headed by the 'NA-' designation generally related only to real aircraft, and consequently those covering just prototypes are listed here – many production aircraft designations are omitted, but some NA- allocations were also given to projects. The NA- programme numbers were part of a cost accounting system covering the allocation of resources and payments from the Government. Very recently, a separate 'D' series of North American project numbers has been uncovered, which appears to have been started towards the end of the war and does include projects, as did the earlier 'P' series. Prior to the entries listed below, North American's twin-engine XB-21 bomber prototype had achieved a first flight on 22 December 1936.

'P-500'   Lightweight fighter proposed to Anglo-French Commission. Covered by SC-49, 19.12.39. Possibly powered by Ranger engine.

NA-40   Twin-engine bomber demonstrator prototype, first flown 28.1.39.

NA-52   Single-seat fighter design, c9.38. Not proceeded with.

NA-62   Medium bomber developed from NA-40. Studies made first under P-439 number but proposal selected from series of designs under P-442. P-442 proposal brochure dated 5.6.39. Became B-25 Mitchell, first flown 19.8.40.

'P-509'   Single-engine fighter covered by North American specification 1592. Allison engine. Transferred to NA-73, 14.4.40.

NA-63   Twin-engine high-altitude bomber prototype that became XB-28, first flown 26.4.42. No production.

NA-67   One-off XB-28A prototype.

NA-68   Fighter version of NA-16 trainer, first flown as P-64 1.9.40.

NA-73X   Single-seat single-engine fighter that became P-51 Mustang, first flown 26.10.40. NA-73 was allocated to early production machines.

NA-97   A-36 Apache ground attack variant of P-51, first flown 9.42.

NA-101   Allocated to Mustang fitted with Rolls-Royce Merlin installation as XP-51B and first flown 30.11.42. Designated XP-78 for short period.

NA-116   Intercontinental twin-boom bomber proposal submitted to Air Corps, 8.43.

NA-120   Prototype XP-82 twin-Mustang very-long-range escort fighter, first flown 16.6.45.

NA-133   Naval version of P-51H made in response to informal BuAer request for fighter with liquid-cooled engine, 10.44. Proposal also requested from Chance Vought. Similar to P-51H, fitted with 2,270hp (1,693kW) Packard Merlin V-1650-11, folding wing, six 0.50in (12.70mm) machine guns, 11ft 0in (3.35m)-diameter four-blade prop. Span 37ft 0.25in (11.28m), folded span 24ft 7in (7.49m), length 34ft 0in (10.36m), wing area 246sq ft (22.88sq m), gross weight 8,680lb (3,937kg), 150 gallons (568 litres) fuel, top speed 417mph (671km/h) at sea level, 484mph (779km/h) (NAA estimate) or 460mph (740km/h) (BuAer figure) at 25,200ft (7,681m), sea level rate of climb 5,720ft/min (1,743m/min). Compared with Grumman F8F, most serious disadvantages were increased vulnerability inherent in any liquid-cooled arrangement over air-cooled types, increased maintenance through addition of radiators and aftercoolers, and as presented NA-133 would have poor ditching characteristics of P-51 series. One Navy report described liquid-cooled design type as having 'no outstanding advantages'.

D-1   Twin-engine heavy fighter, c1944/45.

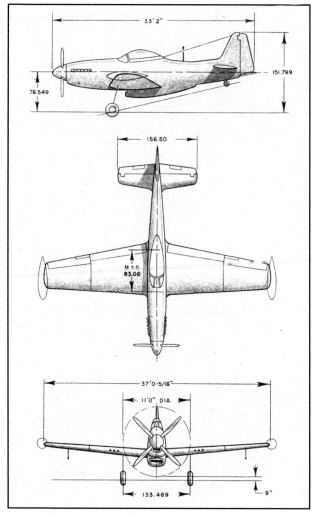

ABOVE North American NA-133 (10.44). *NARA II*

D-4   P-82 fitted with TG-100 engines, c1945. Entry indicates NA-123 allocated.

D-17   P-51 with swept forward wing, c1945/46.

NORTHROP

Having formed two separate 'Northrop' companies up until 1937 (one of which was taken over by Douglas in 1937), Jack Northrop established the Northrop Corporation at Hawthorne in California in 1939. Much of the company's wartime effort seems to have been dominated by flying wings, but in fact its most successful product was the P-61 night fighter.

N-1   Proposal for twin-engine flying wing medium bomber, 9.39 onwards. In part intended to be flying laboratory/research aircraft. N-1M scale model first flown 3.7.40.

N-2   Fighter to Specification XC-622 (R40-C), 3.40. Five variants offered. Became XP-56 Black Bullet, first flown (short hop) 6.9.43.

N-3   Single-engine float-equipped patrol bomber (N-3PB) for Norway, first flown 22.12.40.

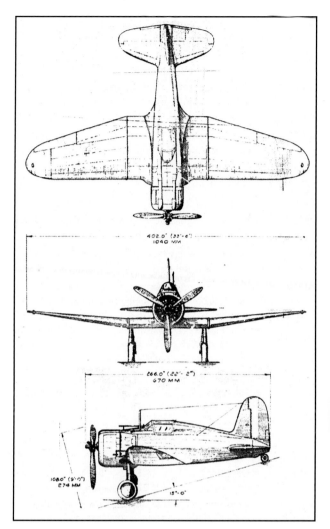

ABOVE Northrop N-4 (7.3.40). *Gerald Balzer*

ABOVE Northrop N-6 (5.40). *Gerald Balzer*

BELOW A wind tunnel model of the Northrop N-6.
Gerald Balzer

N-4	Small all-metal interceptor pursuit fighter project, 7.3.40. One 700hp (522kW) P&W R-1535 Twin Wasp Junior, two 0.30in (7.62mm) machine guns in nose with provision for two 0.50in (12.70mm). Span 33ft 6in (10.22m), length 22ft 2in (6.76m), gross weight 4,300lb (1,950kg), 112 gallons (424 litres) fuel, top speed 280mph (451km/h) at 9,500ft (2,896m), service ceiling 30,000ft (9,144m), sea level rate of climb 2,700ft/min (823m/min).
N-5	Interceptor pursuit fighter project, c1940.
N-6	Single pusher-engine fighter for Navy, 5.40. Engine in body behind pilot. Drawing shows high-wing design, span 47ft 0in (14.33m), length 33ft 6in (10.21m), wing area 315sq ft (29.295sq m), five nose guns, 7ft 3in (2.21m)-diameter propeller. Version with mid-wing position also tested in wind tunnel.
N-8	Twin-engine night interceptor pursuit fighter that became P-61 Black Widow. Prototype XP-61 first flew 26.5.42. XP-61 long-range day fighter prototype flown 3.1.45.
N-9	Covered B-35 flying wing bomber programme. XB-35 first flown 25.6.46 and scale model N-9M first flew 27.12.42, but B-35 production programme abandoned.
N-12	Rocket-propelled flying wing research aircraft serving as testbed for XP-79 jet fighter. Also unpowered glider used to test aerodynamic feasibility of XP-79, which first flew 5.7.44.
N-14	Rocket-powered flying wing interceptor pursuit aircraft that became XP-79. One flight only, 12.9.45.
N-21	Night intruder XP-61F version of Black Widow.

RYAN

The Ryan Aeronautical Company was founded in 1934 at San Diego in California and built up its business producing trainers. During the war it moved into the field of naval combat aircraft.

Model 26	Gull-winged dive bomber/attack aircraft proposal, 15.2.42.
Model 27	Preliminary specifications for interceptor fighters, c1942. Models 27B and 27C proposed to USAAF.
Model 28	Mixed jet/piston fighter that became FR-1 Fireball, first flown 25.6.44. Small production run only.

SEVERSKY/REPUBLIC

Originally known as the Seversky Aircraft Company and founded in 1931, the Republic Aviation Corporation at Farmingdale on Long Island, New York, was so named in 1939 and during the Second World War was responsible for the design and production of heavy piston fighters, in particular the P-47 Thunderbolt. This list provides all known projects, but there are gaps that most likely will include further still unknown fighter and bomber projects. 'AP' stood for Army (USAAF) Project, while designs for the Navy would receive an 'NP' number. The P-35 fighter on which were based several succeeding designs first flew on 15 August 1935.

AP-1	Seversky P-35 fighter modified for trials, 1937.
AP-2	Losing competitor in 1939 pursuit fighter design competition. Featured flush retracting gear. Prototype flown as XP-41 3.39.

AP-3	Fighter proposal with liquid-cooled Allison V-1710 engine. Abandoned in favour of AP-4.
AP-4	Adaptation of P-35. Thirteen examples ordered as YP-43 Lancer. First flown 3.40.
AP-4J	Development of P-43 with 1,400hp (1,044kW) P&W R-2180-1. 80 ordered 13.9.39 as P-44 Rocket but cancelled.
AP-4L	Proposal with 2,000hp (1,491kW) R-2800-7, also not constructed. Some sources use name 'Warrior' instead of 'Rocket'.
AP-5	Single-seat fighter, c1939.
AP-6	Single-seat fighter, c1939.
AP-8	Single-seat fighter development of P-35 series, 1939. Never completed. Formed basis for AP-9.
AP-9	Entrant in 1939 Air Corps fighter competition. Used improved airfoil. Rejected in favour of Bell XP-39.
AP-10	Response to Air Corps circular proposal 39-770. Design submitted 8.39 for lightweight fighter powered by Allison V-1710. Army placed order as XP-47. Additional XP-47A was stripped version of XP-47, but in 9.40 all work on XP-47 and XP-47A was stopped. In same month contract placed for XP-47B, which became Thunderbolt, first flown 6.5.41.
AP-12	Submission to XC-622 (R40-C), 3.40. Highly streamlined design with engine behind cockpit driving tractor contraprop in nose via long shaft. Illustrations label design 'Republic Rocket'.
AP-16B	P-47N version of Thunderbolt.
AP-18	Development of AP-12 'Rocket'. Intended powerplant Wright R-2160 and design ordered 7.41 as XP-69. Scale mock-up, 6.42. Final configuration had long bubble cockpit. Cancelled 1943.
AP-19	Fighter design that eventually became XP-72 prototype, first flown 2.2.44.
AP-23	Jet fighter project, 19.9.44. Became XF-84 Thunderjet.

SIKORSKY

Founded in 1925, the Sikorsky Manufacturing Company at Stratford, Connecticut, specialised in the development of multi-engine landplanes and also amphibious aircraft, before in 1939 being merged with Vought to form Vought-Sikorsky. Sikorsky later became a key name in the field of rotary wing aircraft/helicopters.

XPBS-1	Four-engine flying boat prototype, first flown 13.8.37.

STEARMAN

The Stearman Aircraft Corporation was established at Wichita in Kansas in 1927 and built a reputation for manufacturing training aeroplanes. The odd foray into designing larger types did produce one attack prototype.

X-100	Twin-engine attack design to 7.38 competition for which prototype ordered. First flew 3.39 and became XA-21, but no production.

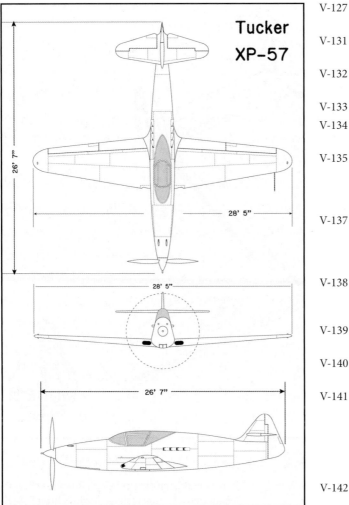

ABOVE Tucker XP-57 (7.40). *Alan Griffith copyright*

TUCKER

Tucker Aviation was incorporated in Detroit in 1940 with the objective of building a very lightweight fighter.

AL-5   Concept design that evolved into XP-57 lightweight fighter prototype ordered 7.40. Plan was to build large numbers cheaply and quickly, but company went bankrupt 2.41 before prototype drawings had been completed.

VEGA

The Vega Aircraft Company was a subsidiary of Lockheed and undertook much of its parent firm's production during the Second World War, having in 1940 switched its focus from light aircraft to military aeroplanes. By the end of 1943 Vega had merged back within Lockheed.

V-107   Export bomber project with maximum gross take-off weight between 8,000 and 12,000lb (3,629 and 5,443kg), c1940. Not built.

V-108   Attack bomber study, c1940. Gross take-off weight 16,000lb (7,258kg).

V-127   Initial design effort for Lockheed Model 21 B-34 Ventura bomber.

V-131   Study to install 2,200hp (1,641kW) Wright R-3250 engines in Boeing B-17.

V-132   Reconnaissance bomber study based on Lockheed Model 37 Ventura, c1940/41.

V-133   Lockheed Model 23/B-34 production.

V-134   Assigned to cover conversion of one Boeing B-17E bomber into XB-38.

V-135   Reconnaissance bomber project, gross take-off weight 25,000 to 35,000lb (11,340 to 15,876kg), 9.41 onwards. Two 2,000hp (1,491kW) Wright R-3550s. Replaced by V-146, based on V-135D variant.

V-137   Further reconnaissance bomber study based on Lockheed 37 Ventura, c1941. Noted in Vega master log as 'cancelled due to similarity with Lockheed-California's own Model L-137 project'.

V-138   Further reconnaissance bomber study based on Lockheed 37 Ventura, c1941. Gross take-off weight 32,000lb (14,515kg) and 2,100hp (1,566kW) engines.

V-139   Assigned to cover conversion of Boeing B-17F bombers into XB-40 'Flying Escorts'.

V-140   Several two- and four-engine studies for heavily armed bomber escort project, c1941/42.

V-141   Twin-engine torpedo-scout bomber study, VSTB Class for Navy, mid-1942. Little work completed due to shortage of staff, who were allocated to more urgent work. Douglas XTB2D-1 and Grumman XTB2F-1 prototypes apparently ordered to same requirements.

V-142   Ground attack bomber study based on Lockheed 37 Ventura, c1942.

V-143   Lockheed Model 15 PV-2 Harpoon.

V-144   Study to fit P&W Wasp Major engines in B-17F, c1942.

V-145   'Standardised' USAAF and USN bomber covering PV-1-1/2 and B-34A.

V-146   ASW patrol aircraft based on V-135D. Brochure dated 1.1.43 and became Lockheed Model 26 P2V Neptune, first flown 17.5.45.

V-147   Proposed XB-34D bomber for USAAF, c1943.

V-149   Study of armament installation to create night fighter version of PV-1 Ventura, c1943.

V-150   Study for 30,000lb (13,608kg) gross weight fighter bomber, c1943. No further information.

V-153   PV-1 Ventura fitted with PV-2 Harpoon tail (PV-1 1/2).

V-154   Upgraded PV-2 as PV-4, c1943.

V-155   High-performance bomber study based on Lockheed Model 44 Excalibur, c1943.

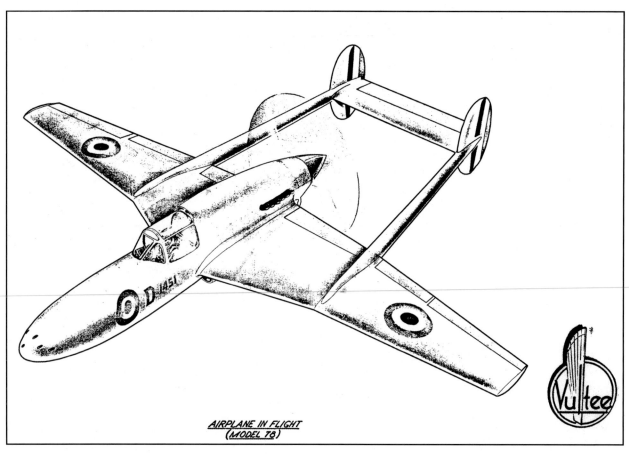

AIRPLANE IN FLIGHT
(MODEL 78)

ABOVE Artist's concept for the Vultee Model 78 (2.1.41). *Alan Griffith*

VULTEE

Vultee started life in 1932 as the Airplane Development Corporation. In 1939 it became an independent company as the Vultee Aircraft Corporation, and in 1943 the company, based at Downey, California, merged with Consolidated Aircraft to form the Consolidated Vultee Aircraft Corporation, or Convair. The AB-2/V-12 attack bomber flown in September 1938 was an upgrade of the V-11 of 1934 and was sold to China.

P-1015	Pursuit fighter project to X-608, c2.37. Lost competition to Lockheed P-38.
XP-35	Pursuit fighter project, 8.37. Based on P-1015, having same configuration but smaller overall and with different nose. Apparently designed for export. Span 48ft 0in (14.63m), length 41ft 0in (12.50m), two Hispano-Suiza 12Y-21 engines, four nose guns. British magazine *Flight* reported on XP-35 on 14.3.40, stating that armament was to be four shell guns (cannon).
V-38	Attack bomber project, c1937.
V-39	Mid-wing observation-bomber project, c1937.
V-40	Pursuit fighter project, c1937.
V-42	Pursuit fighter project, c1937.
V-44	Pursuit fighter project, c1937/38.
V-45	Pursuit fighter project, c1937/38.

XP-46-2	Pursuit fighter project, c1937/38. Rounded nose, V-tail, five nose-mounted guns, single Allison V-3420 in body driving twin wing-mounted shaft-driven 11ft 6in (3.51m) three-blade propellers. Span 52ft 0in (15.85m), length 38ft 8in (11.79m).
V-47	Attack bomber project, c1938.
V-48	Single-seat fighter project, 1938. Redesignated V-61 and became Vanguard company demonstrator.
V-49	Projected development of V-48 powered by Wright engine, 1938.
V-50	Scout bomber project, c1938.
V-55	Bomber project, c1939.
V-56	Proposals for single-seat fighter and/or possibly bomber project, together with two-place pursuit proposal, 1939.
V-57	VTB torpedo-bomber submission, 1939. Not built.
V-61	P-66 Vanguard fighter, first flown 8.9.39.
AB-69	Single-engined dive-bomber project that eventually led to privately funded Vengeance, 1939.
V-70	Twin-boom single-pusher-engine single-seat pursuit to Specification XC-622 (R40-C), 3.40. Three variants. As XP-54 Swoose Goose, first flew 15.1.43.
V-72	A-31 Vengeance dive bomber, first flown 30.3.41.

V-78 Twin-boom 'Shrike' pusher pursuit variant of XP-54, 2.1.41. Span 46ft 0in (14.02m), length 48ft 0in (14.63m).

V-79 Two versions of Navy fighter (Models 79A and 79C) to SD-112-18 design competition, won by Grumman F7F, 1.41.

V-83 Projected development of Model 48 Vanguard with supercharger, c1942.

V-84 Version of XP-54 with P&W X-1800 to Specification 24-C, c1942. V-84E had 2,200hp (1,641kW) Lycoming XH-2470. V-84 number also covered modification of XP-54 with Wright R-2160 radial, sometimes called 'Tornado' after engine's name. Became XP-68, but not built.

V-85 Covered further versions of Vengeance dive bomber, c1942/43.

V-86 Projected single-seat pursuit fighter version of Vengeance, c1942/43.

V-88 A-35 version of Vengeance, produced 9.42. Version of Vengeance evaluated by US Navy in 1942 known as TBV-1 Georgia.

V-89 Covered example of Vengeance used to test four-blade propellers in B-29 development programme and as testbed for 2,200hp (1,641kW) Wright R-3350 engine.

V-90 Project that became XA-41 attack aircraft prototype, first flown 11.2.44. V-90 first proposed 9.9.42.

VP-43-3 'Strato' lightweight fighter proposal made after company became part of Convair, 1943. Single Allison V-1710-75, span 39ft 5in (12.01m), length 28ft 4.5in (8.65m), wing area 225sq ft (20.925sq m), gross weight 7,850lb (3,561kg), four 0.50in (12.70mm) machine guns, maximum speed 450mph (724km/h).

WALLACE-MARTIN

The little-known Wallace-Martin Aircraft Corporation of New York submitted a design to the Grumman F7F Navy fighter competition.

Model A Fighter design submitted to SD-112-18, c1.41.

Appendix Two
Specifications

The sets of Specifications that cover the fighters and bombers in this book are quite complex. In the late 1930s the US Army Air Corps had a system that would see the introduction of a CP or Circular Proposal to solicit proposals from industry against an official Air Corps Type Specification. By 1940 the CP appears to have been replaced by a 'Request for Data'. The known specifications are listed below, with the C-100-series covering attack types, the 200 series bombers, and the 600 series fighters.

98-102 – Attack Aircraft covered by CP 38-385, 1938.

C-103 – Attack Aircraft, July 1938. C-103A covered by CP 39-460, early 1939.

C-104 – Light Bomber/Attack Aircraft, September 1938.

C-212 – Four-engine Bomber, 1938/39. Resulted in Consolidated B-24.

C-213 – Twin-engine Bomber involving CP 39-640, 1.39. Resulted in North American B-25 and Martin B-26.

XC-214 – Twin-engine Bomber, 1939. Covered Martin XB-27.

XC-218 – Four-engine Bomber covered by R40-B, January 1940. Resulted in Boeing B-29, Lockheed XB-30, Douglas XB-31 and Consolidated B-32 programmes.

XC-219 – Twin/four-engine Bomber, 1941/42. Covered Martin XB-33.

X-608 – Specification for High-altitude Interceptor, February 1937. Won by Lockheed P-38.

X-609 – Experimental Interceptor, March 1937. Won by Bell P-39.

XC-615 – Twin-engine Escort Fighter resulting from CP 39-775, March 1939. Won by Lockheed XP-49 and Grumman XP-50.

XC-616 – Lightweight Fighter resulting from CP 39-13 and CP 39-770, 1939. Several designs built.

XC-619 – Replacement for XC-616.

XC-618 – Multi-place Fighter covered by CP 39-780, 1939. No details. Abandoned.

XC-622 – High-performance Fighter covered by R40-C, 1939/40. Resulted in Vultee XP-54,Curtiss XP-55 and Northrop XP-56.

In early 1941 the 'MX' series of code numbers was introduced, embracing research and development in pretty well every area of fighter and bomber design and equipment, including engines and weaponry and other topics related to military aviation. The series was established by the Experimental Engineering Section of the US Army Air Corps's Material Division (soon to become USAAF Air Material Command, or AMC) and an MX designation was usually assigned to a project very soon in its development life. Consequently many were cancelled early in the study phase before any hardware had been produced, but this list does show the MX allocations that are known to have covered specific Second World War fighter and bomber requirements and studies.

MX-2 – Lockheed XP-58.

MX-3 – Bell XP-52.

MX-4 – Curtiss XP-53.

MX-7 – Dive Bomber design studies.

MX-12 – Vultee XP-54.

MX-13 – Curtiss XP-55.

MX-14 – Northrop XP-56.

MX-16 – McDonnell Model 2.

MX-17 – Boeing XB-29.

MX-18 – Lockheed XB-30.

MX-20 – Tucker XP-57.

MX-21 – Consolidated XB-32.

MX-34 – Martin XB-33.

MX-43 – Curtiss Convoy Escort Fighter

MX-45 – Bell XP-59.

MX-54 – Night Fighter studies.

MX-69 – Curtiss XP-60.

MX-73 – Douglas XA-26.

MX-85 – Torpedo Bomber.

MX-88 – Curtiss XP-62.

MX-90 – Bell XP-63

MX-97 – Single-engine Pursuit Interceptor studies, 1941-44.

MX115 – Medium Bombardment Aircraft preliminary designs, 1942-43.

MX-127 – McDonnell XP-67.

MX-134 – Douglas Long-range Heavy Bomber, 6,000-mile (9,650km) range, 1941.

MX-136 – Brewster XA-32.

MX-137 – Long-range four-engine Bomber, 1941.

MX-138 – Grumman XP-65.

MX-139 – Design studies for Dive Bomber, 1941.

MX-140 – Northrop XB-35.

MX-147 – Curtiss XP-71.

MX-149 – Consolidated XB-36.

MX-159 – Long-range Bomber design study, 1941-1943.

MX-162 – Republic XP-69.

MX-176 – Preliminary work for new Pursuit designs.

MX-189 – Republic XP-72.

MX-203 – Boeing (Vega) YB-40.

MX-217 – Development studies for Dive Bombers.

MX-230 – Boeing (Fisher body) XB-39.

MX-234 – Boeing (Vega) XB-38.

MX-260 – Republic XP-47H.

MX-261 – Night Fighter studies.

MX-272 – Bell XP-77.

MX-278 – North American XP-78/XP-51B.

MX-280 – Curtiss XP-60D.

MX-297 – Beech XA-38.

MX-299 – Studies for 'Destroyer' aircraft.

MX-300 – Fleetwings XA-39.

MX-305 – Vultee XA-41.

MX-317 – General Motors/Fisher XP-75.

MX-320 – Consolidated XB-41.

MX-327 – General studies for Bomber Escort aircraft.

MX-392 – Douglas XB-42.

MX-397 – Bell twin-jet XP-59A.

MX-398 – Bell single-jet XP-59B.

The Navy used an 'SD' series of specifications and the following are those known to relate to programmes within this book. It is thought that many more still wait to be discovered.

SD-110-25 – VSB Class Bomber, 1938.

SD-112-13 – Single-engine Fighter, 1.38. Resulted in Chance Vought F4U.

SD-112-14 – Twin-engine Fighter, 1938. Resulted in Grumman XF5F-1.

SD-112-18 – Twin-engine Fighter, 1941. Resulted in Grumman F7F.

SD-114-6 – VTB Class Bomber, 1939. Resulted in Grumman TBF Avenger and Chance Vought TBU Sea Wolf.

SD-116-19 – VPB Flying Boat, 1.38. Resulted in Martin XPB2M-1 Mars.

SD-116-23 – Patrol Flying Boat, 1939. Resulted in Boeing XPBB-1 Sea Ranger.

SD-260 – Twin-engine Fighter, 5.38. Covered Grumman XF5F-1 Skyrocket.

SD-284A – Single-engine Fighter, 5.42. Covered Curtiss XF14C-1.

SD-349 – Single-engine Fighter, 4.43. Covered Boeing XF8B-1.

SD-368 – Single-engine Attack, 1944. Covered Martin BTM-1 Mauler.

SD-381 – Patrol Aircraft, 1944. Covered Martin P4M-1 Mercator.

Bibliography and Source Notes

A huge amount of primary source material has been consulted during the preparation of this work, namely original documents and project brochures held by the various museums and groups listed in the Acknowledgements. Drawings and photographs are credited individually unless from the authors' collections. A great deal of important supplementary information was forthcoming from many secondary (published) sources to fill in gaps and to link elements of the story together. The most important of these were as follows:

Aldridge, Major John F. Jnr 'Final Report on the XP-67 Airplane' (Official Army Air Forces Air Material Command Report, 31 January 1946)

Angelucci, Enzo with Bowers, Peter *The American Fighter* (Haynes, 1987)

Balzer, Gerald H. *American Secret Pusher Fighters of World War II* (Specialty Press, 2008)

Bradley. Robert E. *Convair Advanced Designs II: Secret Fighters, Attack Aircraft and Unique Concepts 1929- 1973* (Crécy Publishing, 2013)

Convair Advanced Designs: Secret Projects from San Diego 1923-1962 (Specialty Press, 2010)

Breihan, John R., Piet, Stan and Mason, Roger S. *Martin Aircraft 1909-1960* (Narkiewicz/Thompson, 1995)

Buttler, Tony *American Secret Projects: Fighters & Interceptors 1945-1978* (Midland Publishing, 2007)

Carter, Dusty *Vultee 'P-38'* (*American Aviation Historical Society Journal*, Spring 1988)

Dean, Francis H. and Hagedorn, Dan *Curtiss Fighter Aircraft: A Photographic History 1917-1948* (Schiffer Publishing, 2006)

Francillon, René J. *From Torpedo and Scout Bombers to Attack Aircraft* (Parts 1, 2 & 3) (*Air International*, August, September and October 1995)

McDonnell Douglas Aircraft since 1920, Vol II (Putnam, 1990)

Hendrix, Lin *Hughes' Twin Boomer* (*Aeroplane*, October 1984)

Jenkins, Dennis R. *Magnesium Overcast: The Story of the Convair B-36* (Specialty Press, 2001)

Johnson, E. R. *American Attack Aircraft since 1926* (McFarland, 2008)

Tactical Turnabout: Development of the Last US Propeller-Driven Attack Aircraft (*American Aviation Historical Society Journal*, Winter 2009)

Jones, Lloyd S. *US Bombers, B-1 1928 to B-1 1980s* (Aero Publishers, 1974)

Knaack, Marcelle S. *Post-World War II Bombers 1945-1973* (Office of Air Force History, 1988)

Post-World War II Fighters 1945-1973 (Office of Air Force History, 1986)

Lucabaugh, David and Martin, Bob *Skyrocket* (*Aeroplane Monthly*, June and July 1994)

Norton, Bill *American Bomber Aircraft Development in World War 2* (Midland Publishing, 2012)

US Experimental & Prototype Aircraft Projects: Fighters 1939-1945 (Specialty Press, 2008)

Ostrowski, Dave *Burnelli's Bombers* (*Skyways*, Issue 34, April 1995)

Pape, Garry R. with Campbell, John M. *Northrop Flying Wings: A History of Jack Northrop's Visionary Aircraft* (Schiffer Publishing, 1995)

The Airplane Designs of Hughes Aircraft Company (*American Aviation Historical Society Journal*, Fall 2010)

Pelletier, Alain *Une Doublure Oubliée: Vought XTBU-1/Convair TBY-2 Sea Wolf* (Fana de l'Aviation 512, July 2012)

Slayton, Bill *Lockheed Model L-133* (*Aerospace Projects Review*, July-Aug 1999)

The Lockheeds That Never Were (*American Aviation Historical Society Journal*, Summer, Winter 1999 & Spring 2000)

Stern, David *Snake: Genesis of the Bell P-39 Airacobra* (*American Aviation Historical Society Journal*, Summer 2013)

Taylor, John W. R. *Superfortress Development: The Genealogy of a Notable Long Range Heavy Bomber* (*Flight*, 7 February 1946)

Thomason, Tommy H. *Strike from the Sea: US Navy Attack Aircraft from Skyraider to Super Hornet 1948-Present* (Specialty Press, 2009)

Wagner, Ray *American Combat Planes* (Hanover House, 1960)

Zichek, Jared *Boeing's Flying Flapjacks* (Airpower, July 2002)

Several websites were also consulted. The George A. Spangenberg site is an oral history put together by a man who was involved in naval aviation for the whole of his professional career, particularly in regard to the procurement of new types. As Evaluation Division Director, Spangenberg was responsible for the Design Requirements for many new naval aircraft from the 1940s to the 1970s. His memoirs can be found on http://www.georgespangenberg.com/indexhtm and they give good accounts for several design competitions as well as general background information for new naval aircraft from the early years of the war until many years afterwards.

Andreas Parsch (with George Cully) has produced a most valuable site that serves as a reference directory for the American weapon system numbers. This can be found on www.designationsystem.net. Ryan Crierie has posted a good selection of Standard Aircraft Characteristics Sheets on www.alternatewars.com. Finally Paul Martel-Mead has created a splendid web-based 'Secret Projects' forum that can be found on http://www.secretprojects.co.uk, and contains material that has filled numerous important gaps in this book.

Index

INDEX OF HARDWARE

INDEX OF PEOPLE

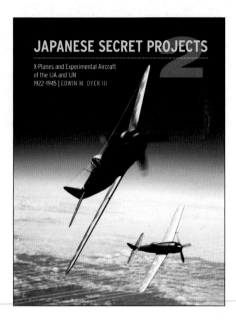

Japanese Secret Projects Volume 1

During the final years of World War II, Japan was desperate to combat the threat from America's high-altitude B-29 bombers and the planned invasion of their homeland. As cities were flattened and antiquated aircraft (such as the infamous Zero fighter) fought on only to be shot out of the skies by superior Allied aircraft the Japanese military, like their German counterparts, sought innovative aircraft designs to turn the tide of the war. Japanese Secret Projects volume 1 looks in detail at many of the aeronautical designs and concepts that Japan developed to counter the Allied onslaught.

Beautifully illustrated by the world's leading aviation artists, this book features stunning colour renditions of the projected aircraft in combat, including profiles based on genuine markings and camouflage schemes. Notable emphasis is placed upon the transonic rammer aircraft, strategic long-range bombers, high altitude fighters, Kamikaze aircraft and how the Japanese military adapted German technology such as the Messerschmitt 262 jet fighter and 163 Komet rocket interceptor.

Volume 1
Experimental Aircraft of the IJA and IJN 1939-1945
Edwin M. Dyer III
Hardback, 160 pages
ISBN 9 781857 803173
£24.95 US $42.95

Japanese Secret Projects Volume 2

After five years of dedicated research, the next volume in the series continues the story of the secret projects of the Japanese aviation industry, focussing in particular on designs that actually progressed beyond the drawing board (whether or not they flew). The aircraft described in Japanese Secret Projects Volume 2 include significant pre-war types such as the Mitsubishi 1MT1N Torpedo Carrier and the record-breaking Gasuden Koken-Ki, as well as projects for long range bombers and advanced fighters to replace the increasingly antiquated designs in service as the war progressed. Later, as Japan's situation became increasingly desperate, the concept of suicide missions came to the fore and existing aircraft designs were modified to deliver the maximum destruction by 'special attack' units. Later still, when invasion looked inevitable, purpose-built suicide aircraft, capable of being assembled by semi-skilled labour and f own by novice pilots, were developed as part of the anti-invasion plan Operation Ketsugo.

Japanese Secret Projects Volume 2 also examines the influence of German wartime aircraft, such as the proposed Hitachi He-Type Heavy Bomber, based on the Heinkel He-177 and looking beyond just aircraft designs, the Ku-Go directed energy weapon project and Japan's nuclear weapons programs are also described.

Volume 2
X-Planes and Experimental Aircraft of the IJA and IJN 1922-1945
Edwin M. Dyer III
Hardback, 164 pages
ISBN 9 781906 537418
£25.00 US $42.95

Both titles are illustrated throughout with rare photographs, drawings, 3-view illustrations and colour profiles, and form an essential reference for any serious aviation and military enthusiast, modeller or historian.

Available in the UK from Crécy Publishing Ltd,
1a Ringway Trading Est, Shadowmoss Rd,
Manchester M22 5LH
Tel 0161 499 0024
www.crecy.co.uk

Distributed in the USA by Specialty Press,
838 Lake Street S.
Forest Lake, MN 55025
Tel (651) 277-1400 / (800), 895-4585
www.specialtypress.com